EXPLORING *the* RELIGIONS *of* OUR WORLD

EXPLORING *the* RELIGIONS *of* OUR WORLD

Third Edition

Ave Maria Press AVE Notre Dame, Indiana

Nihil Obstat: Reverend Monsignor Michael Heintz, PhD
Censor Librorum

Imprimatur: Most Reverend Kevin C. Rhoades
Bishop of Fort Wayne-South Bend

Given at: Fort Wayne, Indiana, on May 28, 2021

The *Nihil Obstat* and *Imprimatur* are official declarations that a book or pamphlet is free of doctrinal or moral error. No implication is contained therein that those who have granted the *Nihil Obstat* or *Imprimatur* agree with its contents, opinions, or statements expressed. The *Nihil Obstat* applies specifically to those parts of the text that are concerned with a presentation on Christianity and Catholicism.

Textbook Writer
Nancy Clemmons, S.N.J.M.

Founded in 1865, Ave Maria Press is a ministry of the United States Province of Holy Cross.

www.avemariapress.com

Paperback: ISBN-13 978-1-64680-096-4

E-book: ISBN-13 978-1-64680-097-1

Cover images © Getty Images and Unsplash.

Cover and text design by Andy Wagoner.

Printed and bound in the United States of America.

CONTENTS

1

BEGINNING THE JOURNEY

SETTING THE STAGE FOR THE STUDY OF THE WORLD'S RELIGIONS

We live in a global village. All around us are people with racial, ethnic, cultural, and religious backgrounds different from our own. We see different clothing and accessories in our shopping malls, along our city streets, on the internet, in our schools, and perhaps even in our homes. We hear various accents, languages, and music on the streets, on the bus, at the gym, and on social media. The aromas of various ethnic cuisines enrich our neighborhoods. The great diversity of the world's cultures is more apparent than ever.

As a high school student, you live in a somewhat protected environment with adult guardians to help you navigate our complex world. Once you leave high school, however, you will be on your own to encounter the world as an adult. One of the foremost roles of high school is to prepare students to live as responsible, thinking, loving, productive, active adults in a very diverse global village.

Religious diversity abounds in our world. It is most prevalent in large cities. Just look at London, Sydney, Montreal, Rome, Paris, Frankfurt, Johannesburg, Mumbai, Singapore, New York, Los Angeles, San Francisco, and Chicago. In many of these cities, one may find not just Buddhists but Buddhists from such diverse places as Japan, India, and Vietnam. Not only do Christians live in all these places but there may be Roman Catholics, Chaldean

Catholics, Russian Orthodox, Anglicans, German Lutherans, and Southern Baptists.

This is a different kind of religion textbook; it is about religion itself. In other religion courses, you learned about one particular religious tradition—Christianity, and specifically Catholicism. You have most likely taken courses on such topics as Jesus of Nazareth, the Bible, sacraments, morality, justice and peace, and Church history. A class on the world's religions is different. Rather than an in-depth study of one religious tradition, this class is an overview of many religious traditions, including Catholicism. This book challenges Catholic students to dialogue with and learn from other religious traditions through the inspiration of the Holy Spirit while proclaiming in word and deed Jesus Christ as "the way and the truth and the life" (Jn 14:6, NABRE).

You are probably familiar with the term *world religions*. It refers to religious traditions that are worldwide, such as Buddhism, Christianity, and Islam. Adherents of these worldwide religions are found on most continents. In this class, you will study both *worldwide religious traditions* and others of our *world's religious traditions* that have great significance but are not as widespread. For example, Chapter 5 is about Hinduism. The vast majority of Hindus (80 percent) live on the subcontinent of India. Hinduism's significance is found, among other things, in its great number of adherents (one billion) and its foundational influence on Buddhism, which is very widespread.

What Is Religion?

As we begin our study, it's important to try to define the word *religion*. Though we glibly refer to religion, the vast majority of scriptures used by the various religious traditions, including the Bible, do not contain the word. Until modern times, religion was not separated from the rest of life. In birth and death, work and play, relationships with people, and connections with nature, what we now call *religion* was once—and for many cultures still is—all wrapped up in the fabric of life.

Even now, a definition of *religion* is elusive. The word is derived from the Latin word *religare*, meaning "to bind." Under the name of religion, a person or community "bound" itself to something that was worthy of reverence and respect. Generally, certain obligations came with these strong ties with an entity that was over and beyond them. When we ask people to define *religion*, we hear phrases like "worshipping God," "living a moral life," or "one's belief system." Religion is not just one of those things. The spectrum of religious expression among the world's religious traditions is vast.

Why Study the World's Religions?

You may wonder, "If religion cannot be clearly defined and if the spectrum of religious expression is so vast, why study the various religious traditions?" This is a fair question. At first glance, it may seem impossible to get a handle on what we have described as elusive. However, there are some elements or patterns that can be included in a systematic study of religious traditions. These elements—sacred stories and sacred scriptures, beliefs and practices, sacred time, and sacred places and sacred spaces—will be introduced later in this chapter.

Reasons to study the world's religious traditions include the following:

- to gain a clearer understanding of your own religious tradition, which in turn allows more commitment to and thus growth in your own religious tradition
- to become more open to and accepting of people who on the surface seem very different
- to dispel fears and misunderstandings relating to persons of other religious traditions
- to gain better insight into human beings through understanding their religious activities
- to gain a better understanding of the history of humankind's various civilizations, since religion is almost always an important factor
- to gain a better understanding of the various cultures around the globe today
- to learn from some of the world's great sources of wisdom

Until very recently, the study of religious traditions was a peculiarly Western discipline. Nowadays, the study of religious traditions is universal.

A Different Kind of Religion Class

As you have no doubt already experienced, religion courses are different from any other course in school because they engage both the head and the heart. More than any other class, religion courses call on you to deal with both facts and experiences. They do address the rational, but also integral to religion courses are topics such as life and death, good and evil, love and hate, and joy and sorrow, along with questions about where we came from, why we are here, and where we are going. In studying the full array of the world's religions, you learn that each tradition addresses and interprets these and other topics and questions differently.

Studying with a New Attitude

As students of the world's religions, we are not to pass judgment upon the various religious traditions. In 1965, the Catholic Church officially updated its perspective on how Catholics are to understand other religious traditions at the Second Vatican Council:

> The Catholic Church rejects nothing that is true and holy in these religions. She regards with sincere reverence those ways of conduct and of life, those precepts and teachings which, though differing in many aspects from the ones she holds and sets forth, nonetheless often reflect a ray of that Truth which enlightens all men. (*Nostra Aetate*, 2)

The Church asks us to suspend judgment as to the truth claims of a religious tradition and accept the tradition on its own terms. Catholicism has something to teach other religious traditions, but all of the religious traditions that we will study have something to teach us. We are asked to cultivate an attitude of empathy. The word *empathy* means identifying and understanding the situation of another. In other words, as we study some of the world's religious traditions, we are asked—to paraphrase a Native American proverb—to "walk a mile in the moccasins of another."

At the same time, we are not asked to accept what others believe and practice. Instead, we are asked to be humble, open, and respectful. As Pope Benedict XVI once wrote, "*Equality*, which is a presupposition of inter-religious dialogue, refers to the equal personal dignity of the parties in dialogue" (*Dominus Iesus*, 22). Pope John Paul II also emphasized this attitude in his encyclical *Redemptoris Missio*:

> Those engaged in this dialogue must be consistent with their own religious traditions and convictions, and be open to understanding

> those of the other party without pretense or close-mindedness, but with truth, humility, and frankness, knowing that dialogue can enrich each side. There must be no abandonment of principles nor false irenicism, but instead a witness given and received for mutual advancement on the road of religious inquiry and experience, and at the same time for the elimination of prejudice, intolerance and misunderstandings. Dialogue leads to inner purification and conversion which, if pursued with docility to the Holy Spirit, will be spiritually fruitful. (56)

We return from our journey of studying the other religious traditions with more insight into our own faith—particularly the Catholic faith—which "proclaims and must ever proclaim Christ 'the way, the truth, and the life' (John 14:6, NABRE), in whom men may find the fullness of religious life, in whom God has reconciled all things to Himself (cf. 2 Cor 5:18–19)" (*Nostra Aetate*, 2).

SECTION *Assessment*

Reading Comprehension

1. Briefly describe religious diversity in the world today.
2. From which language does the word *religion* derive?
3. What attitude should Catholics have in studying the world's religious traditions?
4. What makes a course about the world's religious traditions different from other religion courses?
5. Name some reasons for studying the world's religious traditions.

For Reflection

6. Why do you think *religion* is such a difficult term to define?
7. What religious diversity are you aware of in your region?
8. What is one reason you are studying this subject?

Flash Search

9. Cite a recent news story from your local area that mentions a religious tradition other than your own.

SETTING THE CONTEXT OF CATHOLICS IN DIALOGUE

Before becoming Pope John XXIII in 1958, Angelo Roncalli during the 1930s and 1940s was a Vatican diplomat to Turkey and Greece, where he was in contact with Greek Orthodox Christians and Muslims. During World War II, Roncalli helped thousands of Jewish people escape death under the Nazis. As Pope John XXIII, he worked toward Christian unity. In his first encyclical, *Ad Petri Cathedram* (*To the Chair of Peter*), the pope referred to Protestants as "separated brethren" rather than as "heretics," as they had been called before. After centuries of strained relations between Catholics and Anglicans and between Catholics and Eastern Orthodox, the pope received the archbishop of Canterbury, Geoffrey Fisher, at the Vatican and sent a delegation to greet the patriarch of Constantinople, Athenagoras I.

Pope John XXIII was not only interested in improving relations between Catholics and other Christians. Because of his deep affection and respect for the Jewish people, the pope had the egregiously offensive language of praying for the "perfidious Jews" removed from the Good Friday **liturgy**. The Second Vatican Council later soundly denounced the rejection of the Jewish people (see *Nostra Aetate*, 4; cf. *CCC*, 839).

These gestures of respect for persons of other religious traditions may seem minor today, but they were tremendously significant in the early 1960s. Before the pontificate of Pope John XXIII, Catholics were not allowed to set foot in

---

liturgy A definite set of forms for public religious worship; the official public worship of the Church. The Seven Sacraments, especially the Eucharist, are the primary forms of Catholic liturgical celebrations.

a Protestant church except to attend a funeral. As late as 1960, one could still hear and read Catholic leaders calling Protestants "heretics," Eastern Orthodox Christians "schismatics," Muslims "infidels," and Jews "Christ killers."

Pope John XXIII's vision was that the Catholic Church not set itself *against* the world but engage in dialogue *with* others, including people of other religious traditions. He wanted the Second Vatican Council, which he opened in October 1962, to be a truly ecumenical council. To that end, not only did more than 2,200 Catholic bishops from across the world attend the opening session but also a number of leaders from other religious traditions were invited as observers of the Council. Protestant, Anglican, Eastern Orthodox, and Jewish leaders were all present. Pope John XXIII died after the convening of the first of the four sessions of the Second Vatican Council. His successor, Pope Paul VI, and the bishops of the Council continued in the direction of Pope John XXIII's vision.

Second Vatican Council: Impetus for Dialogue

Three of the sixteen documents that came out of the Second Vatican Council (1962–1965) set an expectation for Catholics to dialogue with other Christians and non-Christians alike. *Dignitatis Humanae* (*Declaration on Religious Freedom*) addressed the right of the individual to social and civil freedom with regard to religious matters. *Unitatis Redintegratio* (*Decree on Ecumenism*) spoke to the Catholic Church's relationship with other Christians, while *Nostra*

Among the non-Catholic observers of the Second Vatican Council (1962–1965) were delegates from the Russian Orthodox Church, the Anglican Communion, the Lutheran World Federation, the World Methodist Council, and the Syrian Orthodox Church.

Aetate (*Declaration on the Relation of the Church to Non-Christian Religions*) addressed the Church's relations with non-Christian religious traditions.

These documents are essential for showing Catholics the path to respect and dialogue with persons not of their religious persuasion. Popes Paul VI and John Paul II put the words and spirit of these documents into action by following and expanding on the example of Pope John XXIII. Pope Paul VI was very interested in **ecumenism** and religious freedom. Not only did he meet with Ecumenical Patriarch Athenagoras I, but at the end of the Second Vatican Council in December 1965, they issued a joint resolution regretting the mutual excommunication of 1054 that has kept Catholics and Eastern Orthodox separate ever since. Pope Paul VI also met with two successive archbishops of Canterbury, Michael Ramsey and Donald Coggan, issuing with the latter a joint declaration to seek unity.

Pope John Paul II was the most traveled pope in history. On his international visits, he typically made it a point to sit down and talk with the religious leaders of each region. In 1986 and again in 2002, he invited religious leaders from all over the world to Assisi, Italy, for a World Day of Prayer for Peace. As far as history can tell us, Pope John Paul II was the first pope since St. Peter to visit a synagogue. In 2001 in Damascus, Syria, he became the first pope to visit a mosque. He supported meaningful theological dialogue with Lutherans that produced a 1999 document called the *Joint Declaration on the Doctrine of Justification*. Serious about healing the wounds between Catholicism and Eastern Orthodox churches, Pope John Paul II worked mightily for that cause. The success of Pope John Paul II's outreach to members of religious communities all over the world was seen in the number and diversity of religious leaders who attended his funeral at the Vatican in April 2005.

Pope Francis continued the fifty years of ecumenical and interreligious dialogue of his predecessors. Pope Francis emphasized that, in Baptism, all Christians are grafted onto Christ and are from the same stock. He advocated for Catholics to accompany members of other Christian traditions in mutual projects and prayer services. On October 31, 2016, 499 years after the start of the Protestant Reformation, Pope Francis traveled to Lund, Sweden, to attend festivities to mark the beginning of a yearlong celebration of that historical

---

ecumenism The movement, inspired and led by the Holy Spirit, that seeks the union of all Christian faiths and eventually the unity of all peoples throughout the world.

event. As part of the commemoration, Pope Francis and Lutheran bishop Munib Younan signed a joint declaration for greater reconciliation between Catholics and Lutherans.

When he was archbishop of Buenos Aires, Pope Francis worked on a joint television program with a Jewish rabbi. Regarding Catholic-Islamic relations, Pope Francis and the grand imam of Al-Azhar, Ahmed el-Tayeb, formulated together the *Document on Human Fraternity for World Peace and Living Together* in Abu Dhabi, United Arab Emirates, on February 4, 2019.

Ecumenical and Interreligious Dialogue Is a Duty of All Catholics

All baptized Catholics are called to share the Gospel of Jesus Christ with the world (see *CCC*, 849). This is known as **evangelization**, which is traditionally understood as desiring to convert others to Catholic Christianity. However, today we live in a world of great religious diversity, full of people with their own strong religious convictions. How can Catholics engage in dialogue with persons of other religious traditions without the expectation that they must try to convert them? The Catholic Church is very clear that there is no conflict between dialogue and proclamation. In dialogue, Catholics are evangelizing by **witnessing** to their faith without trying to get people to change their religious allegiance. God, who is the Father of all, offers the gift of salvation to all the

Pope Francis shakes hands with Israeli Sephardi Chief Rabbi Yitzhak Yosef during a visit to the Heichal Shlomo Center in Jerusalem, Israel.

---

evangelization From the Greek root word translated into English as "Gospel"; the "sharing of the Good News."

witnessing Giving testimony of one's religious faith to another.

nations. Through the grace of the Holy Spirit, who is also at work outside the visible limits of the Church, people in every part of the world seek to adore God in an authentic way.

The scriptures of other religious traditions point to a future of communion with God, of purification and salvation, and they encourage people to seek the truth and to defend the values of life, holiness, justice, peace, and freedom. When Christians engage in interreligious dialogue, they bring with them their faith in Jesus Christ, the Savior of the world. This same faith teaches them to recognize the authentic religious experiences of others and to listen to others in a spirit of humility in order to discover and appreciate every ray of truth from wherever it comes (see Pope John Paul II, General Audience, para. 4, November 29, 2000). There are many avenues of interreligious dialogue, but one must never forget that the Holy Spirit is present with us no matter how we take on this task.

Dialogue can be carried out through words, actions, or both. For example, youth groups from various religious traditions getting together to care for people who have been displaced because of man-made or natural disasters is a type of dialogue. Meeting socially and sharing experiences from the different religious traditions is a dialogue. Classroom sharing on experiences such as prayer, God, how families celebrate a religious festival, or what symbols in their religious tradition are most meaningful to them is also a dialogue. You are not asked to be a specialist in every religious tradition in order to participate in interreligious dialogue. You only have to share your faith experiences and listen intently while others share theirs.

Of course, participating in this class is a form of dialogue with other religious traditions.

SECTION *Assessment*

Reading Comprehension

1. Relate some of the ways in which Popes John XXIII, Paul VI, John Paul II, and Francis have broken new ground in the Church's relationship with other religions.

2. What is one avenue of interreligious dialogue that teenagers can participate in today?

Vocabulary

3. How is the practice of *evangelization* different today from how it was prior to the Second Vatican Council?

For Reflection

4. Which of your personal behaviors witness to your religious beliefs?

Flash Search

5. Summarize a time when a recent pope met with a leader of another Christian or non-Christian religious tradition.

SOME COMMON ELEMENTS OR PATTERNS OF RELIGIOUS TRADITIONS

Since we have found a definition of the term *religion* elusive, we will study some of the world's religious traditions from a slightly different angle. We will look at "what a religion is" rather than "what is religion." We can then see that there are some common elements or patterns that can be broadly categorized as aspects of religious traditions. These aspects, covered in the following subsections, overlap.

Sacred Stories and Sacred Scriptures

Most religious traditions have stories that tell how the world came to be; how humans, plants, and animals were created; why; and where we are going. Some of these sacred stories, particularly creation stories, are commonly called **myths**. They are not *true* stories but *truth* stories that aim to convey sacred truths. For some religious traditions, these sacred stories are part of *sacred history*. Certain core historical events—for example, the birth of Muhammad, the Exodus of the Jewish people, or the death of Jesus—have become part of that religious tradition's sacred history. These events are known as *empirical*

---

myths Traditional or ancient stories that help explain a people's creation, customs, and/or ideals.

history—that is, history verifiable or provable from other sources. Generally, these stories were first passed on orally. Later, some sacred stories became part of the collective memory of the adherents of a religious tradition and often defined them as a community.

Modern Jewish schools teach their students to study the Torah. See Chapter 2, Judaism.

The history of a particular religious community often includes myths, sacred history, and empirical history. For example, the story of the Jewish people includes creation stories; the sacred history of the patriarchs, prophets, and a nomadic tribe; and centuries of empirical history up to the establishment of the State of Israel in the twentieth century.

We know many sacred stories because they move from oral telling through the ages to the writing down of the sacred stories into some form that readers deem sacred scripture. The Upanishads, the *Bhagavad Gita*, the Holy Bible, and the Qur'an are all considered not just writings but sacred writings. Some religious traditions consider their sacred scriptures to be inspired by God or the gods, while others consider their sacred scriptures as the exact word of God or the gods.

Other sacred stories may not have the authority of sacred scripture. For Muslims, stories about Muhammad are collected into the Hadith. Christians treasure the many lives of the saints. Jews revere the many stories told by Eastern European spiritual leaders known as *rebbes*. Whether sacred stories are codified into sacred scripture or not, they help unite, preserve, and perpetuate a community of people who have similar beliefs and values. One major way sacred stories are passed on is through ritual.

Beliefs and Practices

Though not all religious traditions have a formal set of beliefs, each holds certain truths that separate it from other religious traditions. Buddhism and Christianity have well-formulated doctrines. The Four Noble Truths and the

The Ka'bah is considered by Muslims to be the house of God. *See Chapter 4, Islam.*

Noble Eightfold Path are clearly delineated Buddhist doctrines. The Apostles' Creed is a formal statement of Christian beliefs. Though the Sh'ma is the one formal doctrine of Judaism and the Shahadah is the one formal doctrine of Islam, this does not mean that Judaism and Islam have nothing to say about human nature, sin or how to relate to widows and orphans. Often, individuals or groups communicate their beliefs through how they act or how they explain their actions when faced with such issues rather than through formal doctrinal statements. The faithful of the various religious traditions act out their beliefs in the vertical and the horizontal. The vertical is how adherents relate to the divine, while the horizontal is how they relate to both other believers and nonbelievers.

Practices are part of every religious tradition. They may be as simple as a child's bedtime prayers or as formal as the Eastern Orthodox Divine Liturgy. Practices can be personal or communal. Prayer, meditation, and ritual washing may be personal practices, while the sacrifice of animals, going on pilgrimage, or participating in a sacred meal may be communal practices. The more formal the ritual is, the more likely it is based on at least one sacred story. For example, in the Book of Exodus, God exhorts the Israelites to remember and recount his saving power in the Exodus of their spiritual ancestors from the slavery of Egypt to the freedom of the Promised Land. Thus arose the annual Jewish celebration of *Pesach*, or Passover, held every spring.

A person's behavior tells us about his or her beliefs. For example, observing our Muslim neighbors praying several times a day tells us that prayer is very important to Muslims. Noticing that a pulpit is front and center in many Protestant churches tells us that preaching is important to Protestant Christians.

Each religious tradition has some sort of moral code—written or unwritten—that lays out expected conduct for adherents. Proper beliefs and behaviors make a person a good Buddhist or a good Hindu. However, some religious traditions place more emphasis on behaviors than on beliefs, while other religious traditions place more emphasis on beliefs than on behaviors. For many religious traditions, behaviors also determine how one will spend the next life or eternal life. The moral code of a number of religious traditions is found in, or at least based on, their sacred stories and sacred scriptures.

Sacred Time

Though most religious traditions consider all time sacred, they mark particular times when certain actions or attitudes give greater focus to the sacred. In one sense, participating in a sacred ritual seems to transport an individual or community from ordinary time to sacred time. In another sense, participating in a sacred ritual reminds participants that all time is sacred. In still another sense, sacred time is timeless. It draws the past and the future into the present so that adherents can live in and celebrate the now. Whether these times occur daily, weekly, monthly, yearly, or even every seven years, observers are able to document that time is sacred to them.

Though times for personal devotions are often at the discretion of the individual, communal observances are more formal. Muslims have Friday, Jews have Saturday, and Christians have Sunday as their day for weekly communal observances. Muslims have Ramadan, Jews have Yom Kippur, and most Christians have Lent as annual times of fasting for spiritual renewal and growth. Festivals mark times of celebration for the different religious

The Obon Festival, an annual event for remembering ancestors, is based in Japanese Buddhist traditions. See Chapter 8, Japanese Religious Traditions.

traditions. Buddhists celebrate Bodhi Day, Sikhs celebrate Gobind Singh's birthday, and Hindus celebrate Diwali. Festivals and religious observances give members of a religious tradition a sense of belonging and are opportunities for personal recommitment and renewal.

Rites of passage are also sacred times. In particular, rites of birth, coming-of-age, marriage, and death are observed as sacred times in many religious traditions.

During the Kumbh Mela Festival, Hindu devotees bathe at a pilgrimage site to wash away their sins. *See Chapter 5, Hinduism.*

Sacred Places and Sacred Spaces

Generally, sacred time can be observed and celebrated anywhere. However, sacred time is often experienced at a sacred place or in a sacred space. Places where the religious tradition began or where the founder traveled often become sacred places. Hence, Mecca and Medina are sacred places for Muslims. Christians call the region of Palestine the Holy Land. Some religious traditions call places in nature, such as mountains and rivers, sacred places. The Jordan River for Christians and the Ganges River for Hindus come to mind. Mount Sinai is a sacred place to Jews, while Mount Fuji is a sacred place for practitioners of **Shinto**. Shrines, temples, churches, mosques, and synagogues are all sacred

---

Shinto The indigenous religious tradition of Japan. It was the state religion of Japan until the end of World War II.

spaces. Other places can be temporary sacred spaces; for instance, a gym or a large tent can be converted temporarily into a sacred space.

Other Elements or Patterns

As you study some of the world's religious traditions with this book, each chapter covers the above common elements or patterns found in the various religious traditions. This book is like inviting a panel of people from various religious traditions to speak about their religious tradition. Each speaker is given the same allotted time, and each is asked to confine remarks about their respective religious traditions to the following topics: a brief historical overview, sacred stories and sacred scripture, basic beliefs and practices, sacred time, and sacred places and sacred spaces. Expanding the dialogue, a final section in each chapter explores topics about which Catholics and adherents of the particular religious tradition can have a meaningful dialogue.

Religious traditions have other aspects in common. In particular, adherents of religious traditions have sacred symbols and objects they use in their various rituals. Some sacred symbols and objects are considered by people both in and out of the religious tradition to be beautiful works of art, such as the icons of Orthodox Christianity, the architecture of Islam, and the statuary of Hinduism.

Other aspects common to many religious traditions are implicit in the descriptions of the various religious traditions. Some religious traditions have laws that adherents are to follow; for example, Muslims have *shari'ah* and Jews have *halakhah.* Some religious traditions have more institutional structure than others; for example, Roman Catholicism has much more institutional structure than Reconstructionist Judaism. The various religious traditions have holy people, or faithful adherents—be they saints, gurus, shamans, or mystics—whose lives embody the ideal or point to the divine in their respective religious traditions. Sacred symbols and objects, laws, institutional structure, and holy people are important in any study of the world's religious traditions, whether or not they are addressed separately. Each chapter of this book includes sections on a key image, a faithful adherent, and a prayer from the religious tradition it covers.

Finally, although we will begin our study of the world's religions with Judaism in Chapter 2, followed by Christianity in Chapter 3, this order is not meant to suggest that these are the two oldest of the world's religious traditions. They are not. The purpose of beginning with these religious traditions is that the Judeo-Christian religious tradition is the one most familiar to a majority of Western high school students. By the time you study the other religious traditions, you will be versed in the structure of each chapter through surveying traditions that are more familiar to you.

SECTION *Assessment*

Reading Comprehension

1. What are some of the common elements or patterns you will investigate in your study of some of the world's religious traditions?

For Reflection

2. What times are sacred to you? What do you do to mark those times as sacred?
3. What places and/or spaces are sacred to you? What makes these places/spaces sacred?

Flash Search

4. Research and record the date when your church or religious space was built. Include a photo of the building's cornerstone or dedication plaque, if possible.

Chapter Summary

Religious diversity abounds in our world. One of the major tasks for a Catholic is to determine how to grow as a Catholic amid such diversity. There is a difference between the terms *world religions* and *world's religions*. Empathy is the attitude to cultivate in studying the world's religious traditions. Though difficult to define, the term *religion* comes from a root word meaning "to bind." Interreligious dialogue is the duty of all Catholics, for it is part of the Catholic Church's mission of evangelization. In describing a religious tradition, some common elements or patterns to consider include sacred stories and sacred scriptures, beliefs and practices, sacred time, and sacred places and sacred spaces.

Chapter Projects

Complete one of these projects by the conclusion of your study of this chapter.

1. Digital Presentation of Sacred Places, Sacred Spaces, and Religious Festivals

   Recalling the common elements or patterns found in religious traditions, create a digital presentation with photos and captions of sacred places, sacred spaces, and holidays or festivals representing at least four of the religious traditions mentioned in this chapter.

2. Pope Francis on Interreligious Dialogue

   Research and write a one- to two-page essay on statements from Pope Francis (written prior to or during his pontificate) that support the Catholic call to dialogue with other religious traditions.

Prayer

This "Peace Prayer" attributed to St. Francis is one that adherents of most religious traditions would be comfortable praying.

> Lord, make me an instrument of your peace:
> where there is hatred, let me sow love;
> where there is injury, pardon;
> where there is doubt, faith;
> where there is despair, hope;
> where there is darkness, light;
> and where there is sadness, joy.
>
> Lord, grant that I may not so much seek
> to be consoled as to console;
> to be understood as to understand;
> to be loved as to love.
> For it is in giving that we receive;
> it is in pardoning that we are pardoned;
> and it is in dying that we are born to eternal life.
> Amen.

2

JUDAISM

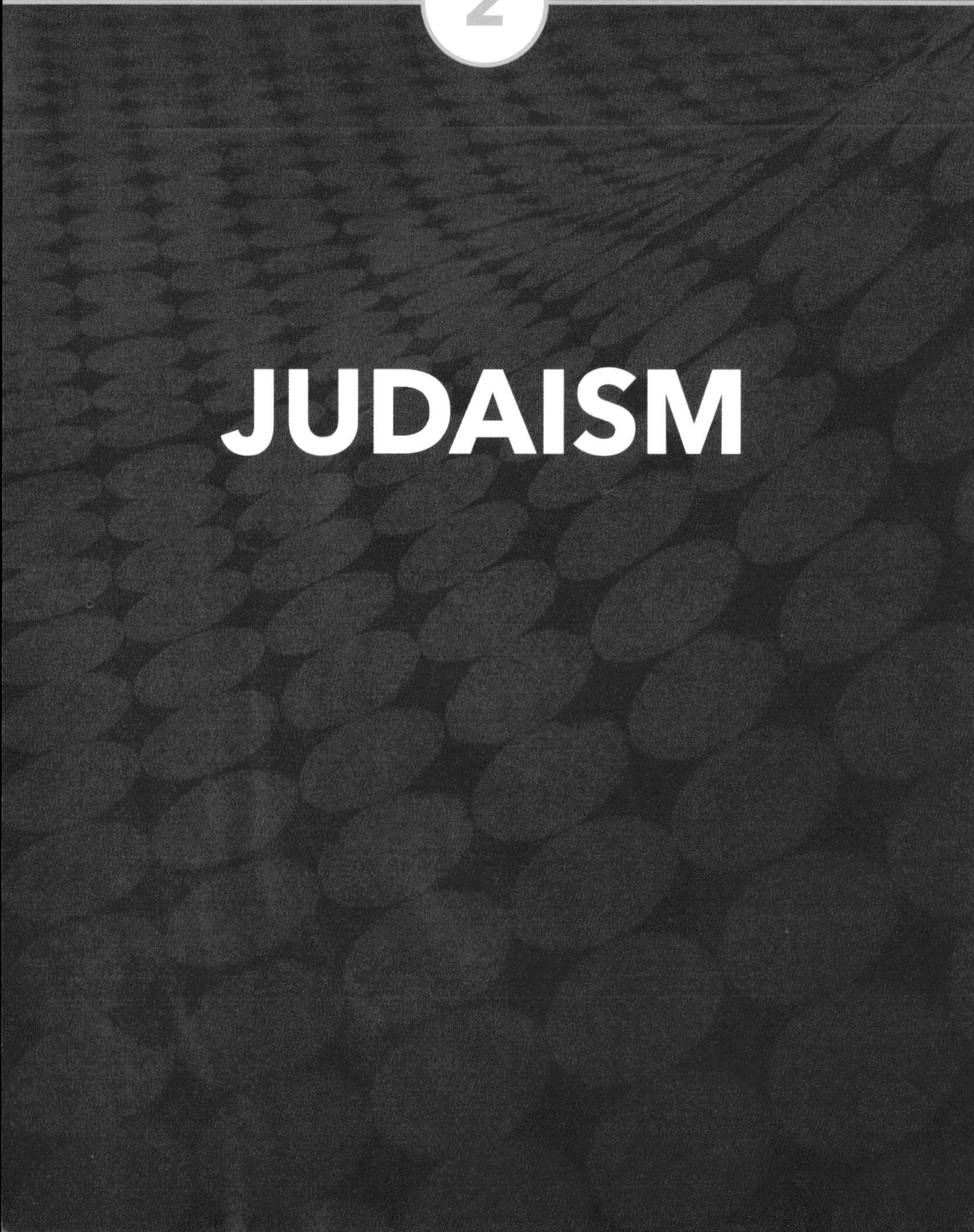

ISRAEL

Introduction

A LIVING RELIGION

Many Christians think of Judaism as the religious tradition described in the Old Testament. Christians also understand Judaism as the religion practiced by Jesus when he was living on earth. Alternatively, they may think of Jews as people who do not accept Jesus as Messiah and who are still anticipating their own Messiah, or "anointed one." (Unfortunately, some Christians wrongly have held Jews or Jewish leaders responsible for the Crucifixion of Jesus.) Christians are correct in defining Judaism as the religious tradition of the Hebrew Bible, the religious tradition of Jesus, and a religious tradition still longing for God's anointed one. However, definitions do not describe the essence of Judaism.

This chapter points out further elements that define Judaism as a living religious tradition not based on a set of abstract doctrines. Ideally, the actions of a Jewish person reveal what it means to be part of this historical religious tradition and what the core values are in a Jewish person's life. The proclamation of the one God, the reverence and study of the Torah, the recognition of Israel as both a nation and a people, and the setting aside of sacred spaces and times all combine to reveal the religious expression of Judaism.

Before attempting to define the religious tradition of Judaism, it is important to first look at what it means to be a Jewish person. To say that Judaism is the religion of Jews is not to say that all Jews practice Judaism. Being a Jewish person has both an ethnic and a religious connotation. Just who is a Jew is rather difficult for non-Jewish persons to understand. Whereas a Christian is a follower of Christ and a Muslim is an adherent of Islam, a Jewish person may or may not practice Judaism. Therein lies the confusion. There are *ethnic* Jews and *religious* Jews. A religious Jew practices Judaism. An ethnic Jew may or may not practice Judaism. A religious Jewish person may also be an ethnic Jew, but it is possible for a religious Jew to be from another ethnic group. Both

Israeli women celebrate Sigd, an Ethiopian Jewish holiday that includes fasting, scripture study, and prayer. The fast ends mid day with a feast and dancing.

ethnic Jews and religious Jews are found on every settled continent. The rest of this chapter will focus on an understanding of Judaism, the religion of religious Jewish people.

SECTION *Assessment*

Reading Comprehension

1. How do Christians typically think of Judaism?
2. Name four things that reveal the religious expression of Judaism.

For Reflection

3. Briefly describe your understanding of Judaism.

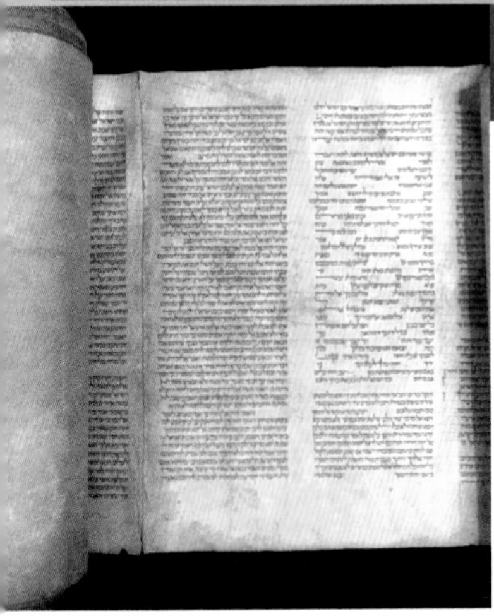

Section 1
A BRIEF HISTORY OF JUDAISM

Judaism is the religion of the Jews, the religious expression of a people whose history spans thousands of years. Judaism can be dated to the time of Moses, although the seeds of Judaism can be traced to the time of Abraham. From its formation in the Sinai desert, triumphs and tragedies, ambiguities and misunderstandings, laughter and tears have written the history of Judaism and of the Jewish people. Though a minority group throughout much of their history, Jews have contributed substantially to the history of the world, particularly the Western world.

Biblical Period

The history of Judaism finds the Jewish people on the move or controlled by foreign governments much of the time. The *Biblical Period* of Judaism is typically dated from Abraham (ca. 1800 BCE) to the death of the Greek ruler Alexander the Great (323 BCE). Jews believe God called Abraham to leave his country and travel to a foreign land. Abraham left not only his country of birth but also his former religious practices to sojourn to a land and relationship with the one God. With great faith and obedience to God's will, Abraham and his wife, Sarah, left Ur in Mesopotamia and moved to the land of Canaan along the Fertile Crescent. There, despite many obstacles, God's promise that Abraham and Sarah would have a son and that Abraham would be the "father of a multitude of nations" (Gn 17:5, Tanakh) was fulfilled. In Canaan, the *Habiru*, or Hebrews, formed nomadic tribes that gradually settled into an agricultural system.

Generations later, many Hebrew people moved to prosperous Egypt to avoid a major drought in Canaan. Though at first welcomed, they soon found themselves slaves under the powerful Egyptian government. As slaves, the Hebrew people made up a small part of an immense army of people that helped build the majestic cities of Egypt. In approximately 1260 BCE, Moses freed the Hebrew people from Egyptian bondage and led them back to Canaan, known to the Hebrew people as the "Promised Land." In the forty years they took to return to Canaan, the Hebrew people became a covenantal community, meaning they were in relationship with and owed their allegiance to the one God only. Moses died on the outskirts of Canaan, leaving Joshua to lead the Hebrew people back into the land "flowing with milk and honey."

However, after having lived for four centuries in Egypt, the Hebrews found it necessary to conquer the inhabitants of Canaan before they could resettle. Mission accomplished, the Hebrew people became a confederation of twelve tribes and established a powerful kingdom called Israel beginning around 1030 BCE under the leadership of Kings Saul, David, and Solomon. A temple was built in Jerusalem under the patronage of David's son Solomon. Thus, Jerusalem became both the political and religious center of the Hebrew people and remained so for more than one thousand years. As the people became more

The Israel Museum holds a model of Second Temple–era Jerusalem built to reflect the Jerusalem of 66 CE. The model covers 10,764 square feet and was designed and built in the 1960s by an Israeli historian and geographer named Dr. Michael Ave-Yonah.

JUDAISM: TIMELINE OF KEY EVENTS

BCE

ca. 1800 .... Abraham migrates from Ur to Canaan

ca. 1260 .... Moses leads Hebrew people out of Egyptian enslavement

ca. 1030–930 .... Kingdom of Israel with Kings Saul, David, and Solomon

ca. 1000 .... Rise of the Hebrew prophets

ca. 950 .... First Temple in Jerusalem built by Solomon

722 .... Fall of the kingdom of Israel to the Assyrians

587–586 .... Babylonian Exile and destruction of First Temple

538 .... Return from Babylonian Exile

ca. 500 .... Construction of Second Temple begins; Torah completed

332 .... Jerusalem conquered by Alexander the Great

323 .... Death of Alexander the Great

168 .... Antiochus IV demands Jews cease Temple rituals

167–160 .... Maccabean Revolt

ca. 150 .... Septuagint completed

63 .... Romans under Ptolemy conquer Jerusalem

CE

ca. 10 .... Schools of Hillel and Shammai

66 .... Start of Jewish Revolt against Romans in Jerusalem

70	Destruction of Second Temple
132	Start of Bar Kochba Revolt
ca. 200	*Mishnah* standardized
313	Constantine issues Edict of Milan declaring religious freedom for all
ca. 500	Completion of the Talmuds
638	Muslim conquest of Jerusalem
912	Golden Age of Jewish culture in Spain begins
1135	Birth of Moses Maimonides
1099	Western Christian crusaders destroy Jewish communities on way to Jerusalem
1492	Jews expelled by Isabella and Ferdinand of Spain
1543	Martin Luther publishes *On the Jews and Their Lies*
ca. 1750	Baal Shem Tov founds Hasidism
1907	Birth of Abraham Joshua Heschel
1933	Beginning of Shoah
1947	Discovery of the Dead Sea Scrolls
1948	Establishment of the State of Israel
1967	Six-Day War
1993	First Oslo Accord signed between Israel and the Palestinian Liberation Organization; Israel and Holy See sign fundamental agreement
2020	Israel and United Arab Emirates sign normalization agreement

powerful, they saw less need for the God who once freed them. Prophets such as Samuel and Nathan became more prominent, exhorting the Hebrew people to follow the ways of the one God rather than the ways of the local Canaanite gods. During this time, the oral tradition of the Hebrew people began to be transcribed into what became known as the **Torah**, a word meaning "law" or "instruction."

After the death of Solomon, the kingdom was divided into the kingdom of Israel in the north with ten tribes and the kingdom of Judah in the south with two tribes. The political, military, and economic strength of these kingdoms declined over the next few centuries. Hebrew prophets became more numerous and blamed the decline of Israel and Judah on **idolatry**. This decline made these two kingdoms more vulnerable to outside threats. Around 722 BCE, Israel fell to the Assyrians, who scattered its people in various directions. By 586 BCE, the Babylonians conquered Judah, ravaging their land, destroying their Temple, and sending the majority of the people to Babylon.

Exiled to a foreign land away from the center of their religious tradition where God was worshipped and sacrifices were offered, the captives found a way to strengthen their cultural and religious identity. As prophets had predicted the fall of Judah, so they predicted its rising again. Approximately fifty years after the destruction of Judah, the Persians conquered the Babylonians and allowed Judeans to return to their land. Some chose to stay in Babylon, while others returned to a country that, though destroyed by war, was nevertheless holy because God had given it to them. They would restore the land and rebuild the Temple.

Once back to living in the land of Judah, the Hebrew people became known as Jews. The compilation of the Torah was completed during this time. Prophets were becoming less numerous, but the writings of such prophets as Isaiah, Jeremiah, and Ezekiel kept their words alive for generations to come. In addition, wisdom literature was emerging. Writings such as Psalms, Proverbs, Job, Ruth, Esther, and Chronicles later came to be included in the Hebrew Scriptures.

Torah A term meaning "law" or "instruction"; the first five books (and the first of the three sections) of the Hebrew Bible. It also refers to the parchment scroll of these writings used in Jewish rituals. It can also refer to the body of Jewish Sacred Scripture.

idolatry Giving worship to something or someone other than the one, true God.

Rabbinic Period

Alexander the Great, Basileus of Macedon, Hegemon of the Hellenic League, Shahanshah of Persia, Pharaoh of Egypt, Lord of Asia, ruled over one of the largest empires of the ancient world, stretching from Greece to northwestern India.

The second major historical period of Jewish history is the *Rabbinic Period.* Also known as *Classical Judaism*, this historical period began in 323 BCE, the year Alexander the Great died. The closing of the period may be dated to 638 CE, the year Jerusalem fell to the Islamic army coming out of the Arabian Peninsula. By the end of this era, many Jews lived in a world that was both Christian and Muslim. Also, through foreign occupation and conquest over a number of centuries, Jewish people had been driven from their homeland. The growing number of Jews not living in Judea—as the area around southern Palestine came to be called—was known as the **Diaspora**, for they were dispersed from their land. The rise of the synagogue and the establishment of centers for Jewish learning were features of this period.

At his death, Alexander the Great ruled much of the known world, including Judea. About 150 years later, the Greek Seleucid ruler Antiochus IV prohibited the practice of Judaism in Judea and took over the Temple. The Jewish Hasmonean family, also known as the Maccabees (a name derived from the Hebrew word for "hammer"), initiated a revolt against the Greek Seleucid Empire in 167 BCE, regaining possession of the Temple in 165 BCE.

Alexander the Great's conquests had lasting repercussions and led to the **Hellenization** of much of his original empire. Judea was no exception. Jews accepted Hellenistic influences to varying degrees. For example, in Egypt, the

---

Diaspora A Greek word meaning "dispersion"; originally referring to the large community of Jews living outside of Palestine, today, the term refers to Jews who live outside of Israel.

Hellenization The adoption of Greek ways and speech, as happened with many Jews living in the Diaspora.

city of Alexandria became a thriving Jewish center. Philo of Alexandria was a very prominent Jewish philosopher living around the time of Jesus and was comfortable integrating Jewish theology and Greek philosophy. The Hebrew Bible was translated into Greek in the third century BCE. According to tradition, seventy translators, working independently of one another, came up with precisely the same Greek text from the Hebrew Scriptures. This Greek translation became known as the **Septuagint**, from the Latin word meaning "seventy." It is very likely that some of the New Testament authors were familiar with this Greek translation of the Hebrew Bible.

The Rabbinic Period saw tremendous Jewish sectarian development into a variety of competing groups or **sects**. The three largest sects were the Sadducees, the Pharisees, and the Essenes. The Sadducees were Jews who defined themselves as biological descendants of Zadok, the first high priest to serve in the First Temple. The Sadducees held a strict position on the interpretation

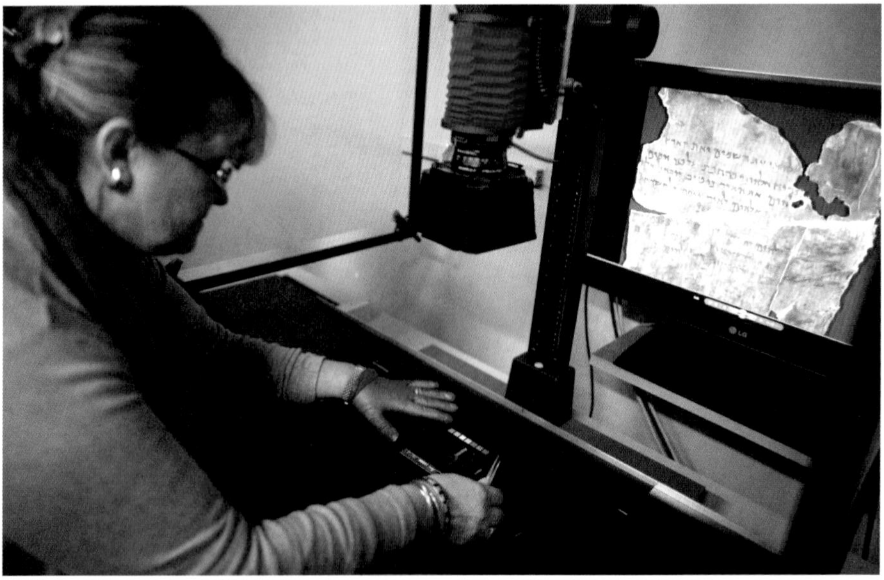

The Qumran Caves Scrolls, also called the Dead Sea Scrolls, were preserved in clay jars in caves in the Judean Desert by the Essenes. The Israel Antiquities Authority has digitized their entire collection of scrolls and put it online for the public.

Septuagint The earliest Greek version of the Hebrew Bible, completed around the second century BCE.

sects Religious groups that separate from or distinguish themselves within a larger religious denomination.

of Torah. The Pharisees, on the other hand, held a looser interpretation of Torah, incorporating oral tradition and popular customs in their interpretation of Mosaic Law. The Pharisees also accepted the doctrine of the resurrection of the dead; the Sadducees did not. While Sadducees and Pharisees are mentioned in the New Testament, the existence of the Essene community was unknown until 1947. In that year, in caves near Qumran near the Dead Sea (in the present State of Israel), a young boy found clay jars filled with writing fragments from the Essene community. These writings, which became known as the **Dead Sea Scrolls**, indicated the monastic nature of the Essenes and their scrupulosity in following the Mosaic Law.

Greek rule in Judea ended in 63 BCE when the Roman army conquered the region. Romans occupied Judea during much of the Rabbinic Period. More than one hundred years later, in 66 CE, Jews in Judea mounted a rebellion against Roman rule. In 70 CE, Roman soldiers stormed Jerusalem and destroyed the Temple. At that time, Jews had to choose between disappearing into history and reinterpreting their religious practice without the Temple. They chose the latter. The Sadducee and Pharisee sects disappeared, and the position of the **rabbi** gained new prominence. To this day, rabbis are the spiritual leaders in Judaism.

The rabbis began a process of systematically transforming the Temple rituals for practice outside the Temple in synagogues. Dozens of rabbinical schools sprang up, and with them, dozens of varying interpretations of how to live an authentic Jewish life. During the time of Jesus, the schools of Rabbis Shammai and Hillel were the most notable. A famous story is told about these two men:

> A heathen once came to Shammai and said, "I will become a proselyte on the condition that you teach me the entire Torah while I stand on one foot." Shammai chased him away with a builder's measuring stick. When he approached Hillel with the same request, Hillel said, "Whatever is hateful to you, do not do to your neighbor. That is the entire Torah. The rest is commentary; go and learn it." (*Mekhilta Bachodesh* 1)

Dead Sea Scrolls A series of mostly partial manuscripts containing both biblical and nonbiblical material discovered in 1947 by a Bedouin boy in caves near the Dead Sea.

rabbi A Hebrew word for "my master" or "my teacher"; someone who is authorized to teach and judge in matters of Jewish law.

This school for boys on the island of Djerba in Tunisia teaches both secular and Jewish religious education courses.

Over the next few centuries, Torah commentaries were compiled, codified, and recorded in two works called the Babylonian Talmud and the Jerusalem or Palestinian Talmud. Along with the Torah, the **Talmud** inspires and guides Jewish people in both their spiritual and their everyday lives.

Meanwhile, during the Roman occupation of Judea, an itinerant Jewish preacher, Jesus of Nazareth, spoke of the coming reign of God, told stories, and performed miracles. His death around 30 CE by crucifixion at the hands of the Romans was commonplace. It was only after Jesus' disciples testified that they had seen him, talked with him, and eaten with him after he died that the lives of Jewish people changed forever.

By the end of the first century CE, there was a growing tension between Jews who believed Jesus was the long-awaited Jewish Messiah and Jews who did not. Some Jews were looking for the Messiah to be a warrior-king like King David. This warrior Messiah would bring an army against their enemies and restore the land of Israel to justice under Jewish sovereignty, enabling the Jews of the Diaspora to return to their homeland. Jesus was not an earthly

Talmud Two long collections of Jewish religious literature that include and have commentaries on the Mishnah, the Hebrew code of laws that emerged about 200 CE.

king, nor did an age of justice return after his Resurrection. Both groups used the same Hebrew Scriptures, but their interpretations of them began to diverge radically.

A growing number of Gentiles were becoming followers of Jesus, and as the number of Gentiles increased, the Jewish identity of Christians eroded. A separation of traditional Jews from Jewish Christians was inevitable. How the separation occurred is ambiguous, but distinctions were relatively clear by the middle of the second century. However, Judaism made an indelible mark upon Christianity that remains with it to this day.

Well into the second century, the emperor Hadrian wanted to establish a new Roman city where Jerusalem had once thrived. His interest in constructing a shrine to the Roman god Jupiter on the site of the Temple Mount outraged a number of Jews, who viewed this as a defilement of their holiest of places. In 132 CE, a Jewish military leader, Simon bar Kociba, nicknamed "bar Kochba," or "son of the star," led a revolt against the Romans. Hadrian sent in whole legions of soldiers, swiftly putting down all Jewish revolt. He constructed his desired city, built the shrine to Jupiter, changed the name of the land from Judea to Palestine, and banned Jews from ever returning to Jerusalem.

Emperor Hadrian at first allowed the Jews to return to Jerusalem and granted permission for the rebuilding of their Holy Temple. However, he then requested that the site of the Temple be moved from its original location and began deporting Jews to North Africa. Led by Simon bar Kociba, the Jewish rebellion begun in 123 CE ended in 135. As punishment, Jews were sold into slavery, and many were transported to Egypt. Jerusalem was turned into a pagan city called Aelia Capitolina, and the Jews were forbidden to live there. Hadrian changed the country's name from Judea to Palestine.

The Jewish people of the Diaspora fared far better. They were part of the Roman Empire. After having been influenced by

Greek culture and civilization, they were now influenced by Roman culture and civilization. Although Jews were very different from most other groups of people in the Roman Empire, Romans allowed them to live their lives as they wished because of their moral standards and their belief in only one God. In fact, their beliefs and ethics attracted people scattered throughout the Roman Empire to convert to Judaism, to the displeasure of some despotic, decadent Roman rulers. The number of Christians continually grew as well.

Like all empires, Rome reached its glory and moved into a long, slow decline politically, economically, and militarily. At the end of the third century, the emperor Diocletian separated the empire into eastern and western portions, appointing a leader for each. Of course, powerful men do not like to share their control, and soon after Diocletian's death at the beginning of the fourth century, Constantine emerged as the victor of a power struggle between various aspiring rulers of the empire. On the eve of his victory, Constantine believed he had a vision of the Cross and that he was to conquer through the power of the Cross.

When Constantine became emperor, he desired a worldwide religion for his worldwide empire, and that religion was Christianity. One reason for Christianity's spread was that many Christian missionaries went to Jewish centers in the various cities of the Diaspora. Although many Jewish persons were Roman citizens and shared in the privileges of that citizenship, when Christianity became the official religion of the Roman Empire at the end of the fourth century, Judaism became less prominent, and its adherents were treated as inferior. However, by the beginning of the fifth century, the strength of the Roman Empire resided in the east with the Byzantine Empire, while the Western Roman Empire broke into smaller states such as that of the Franks. The leader of Christianity in the West, the pope, or bishop of Rome, once merely a spiritual leader, now also emerged as a temporal leader in the once great and now dispirited Rome.

Medieval Period

During the Medieval Period (638–1783), the Diaspora moved farther away from Palestine. Jewish people began to live in places they had never lived before: western, central, and eastern Europe; Asia; the Arabian Peninsula; and portions of North Africa. There was a resurgence of science, mathematics, philosophy, and commentaries on the Hebrew Bible and Talmud. Rabbi Shlomo ben Itzhak (1040–1105), a French Jew who became known as "Rashi,"

"Rashi" is an acronym for Rabbi Shlomo ben Itzhak, an outstanding biblical commentator of the Middle Ages. He worked to standardize the text of the Talmud.

wrote commentaries on the Hebrew Bible and Talmud that most Jewish men of the time learned at a very young age. Through the development of Jewish philosophy, there were attempts to harmonize reason with the Jewish religious tradition. The most famous Jewish philosopher was Moses Maimonides (1135–1204), born in Muslim-ruled Córdoba, Spain. He argued that there was no contradiction between the philosophy of Aristotle and the Jewish religious tradition.

The Medieval Period was also marked by persecution of the Jews. At the beginning of the seventh century, another **monotheistic** religion, Islam, came out of the Arabian Peninsula and was in competition with both Judaism and Christianity. Living under Muslim rule, Jews were a "protected people" as long as they paid the tax for that protection. They were able to worship as they wished as long as their synagogues were not taller than mosques, and they could conduct their own courts. However, Jewish people were clearly treated as second-class citizens, and there were times when the protection did not hold. Just four years after the death of Islam's founder, Muhammad, Muslims invaded Jerusalem, taking it away from the Byzantine Christians. This was a mixed blessing for Jews. The Muslims constructed a beautiful shrine called the Dome of the Rock on the spot where the **Holy of Holies** of the Second Temple once stood. Although Jews were outraged over the defilement of such a sacred place, they were not sorry to see the persecuting Byzantine Christians ousted.

While Jews in Jerusalem faced persecution, Jews of Babylon were able to flourish under Persian rule. They built great schools and synagogues. In the middle of the eighth century, the Muslims moved their capital from

---

monotheistic Subscribing to the doctrine or belief that there is only one God.

Holy of Holies The sanctuary inside the tabernacle in the Temple of Jerusalem where the Ark of the Covenant was kept.

Damascus to Baghdad, very near the Jewish center of Babylon. Muslims took on the daunting task of reintroducing ancient Greek writings to the medieval world. Jews helped translate the writings from Greek to Arabic for Muslims and from Arabic to Latin for Christians of the West.

From its center in Baghdad, Islamic culture flourished and Islamic civilization expanded, and Jews were very much a part of the expansion. Although Muslims and Christians were at odds with each other, trade between Christians and Muslims happened indirectly through the mediation of a large class of Jewish merchants, who opened up trade routes between east and west. As Muslim empires and trade routes expanded during the Medieval Period, groups of Jewish people moved beyond the borders of the Middle East. A remnant of Muslims moved early in the eighth century from Damascus to Córdoba, Spain, and Jews moved there as well.

Jews in Spain, known as *Sephardim*, thrived, developing their own combination of the Jewish and Spanish language now called *Ladino*. Along with the Muslims, Jews excelled in such fields as science, medicine, philosophy, metal crafts, and trade. In the twelfth century, however, a Muslim Berber dynasty came to power in Spain and ousted Jews from the country. Among those who had to flee was the family of philosopher Moses Maimonides.

Moses Maimonides is known by the acronym "Rambam," for Rabbi Moses ben Maimon.

The Medieval Period brought other persecutions to the Jewish people. French and German Christian crusaders, marching to Jerusalem to regain the Holy Land from the Muslims, burned and destroyed almost all the Jewish communities along the Rhine River, murdering thousands. Other Jews, along with Muslims and Christians, were killed when the battle reached Jerusalem in 1099.

During this time, Jews in some areas of Europe were forced to wear identifiable clothing and live in areas of a town that would distinguish them from non-Jews. Distinguishing Jews from other members of society was meant to humiliate them. The only way out of such degradation was to convert to Christianity.

The economic system of this period was moving from a barter system to a cash system, making the borrowing of money increasingly important. Charging interest on a loan was considered the sin of **usury** for Christians at the time, so some Jews, unable to own land, became moneylenders. This led to some abuses. For example, some who did not or could not pay back their loans accused the Jewish lenders of crimes, thus freeing themselves from their fiscal obligation. However, the economy could not have thrived without its moneylenders, so persecutions over this issue were rare.

Jews in the Middle Ages were forced to wear identifying badges.

In the second half of the thirteenth century, when riots directed against Jews (called **pogroms**) started in England, Polish duke Boleshaw the Pious invited Jews to come to his country. There they would be employed in various areas of finance and administration. Because of the protection of the monarchy, Jews were able to thrive in Poland until the seventeenth century, when persecutions began there as well. In Poland, and later in other parts of Europe, Jews became known as *Ashkenazim*, and they developed their own language, called Yiddish, a combination of Hebrew and German. (About 80 percent of Jews in the United States are of Ashkenazi

---

usury In the Middle Ages, the charging of interest on a loan. Later the definition became charging of an exorbitant, perhaps even illegal, amount of interest on a loan.

pogroms Organized massacres of communities, particularly of Jewish people.

descent.) In the fifteenth century, France, Germany, and Austria also expelled Jews. In addition, Jews were commonly blamed for the Black Plague, a devastation that killed around one-third of the population of Europe. Catholic Church leaders came to the aid of Jews in this incident.

Jews living in Spain did not receive the same support from the Catholic Church. In the fifteenth century, the reigning Catholic monarchs of Spain, King Ferdinand and Queen Isabella, had been fighting an uphill battle, against the Muslims especially, to reclaim Spain as a purely Christian country. This *Reconquista*, or "reconquering," required all inhabitants who were not Christian to convert to Christianity or leave the country. A number of Jews, known as *conversos*, did convert to Christianity. However, a number of these conversions were in name only, and some Jews continued their religious practices secretly. This was unacceptable to the Spanish monarchs.

In 1492, the Decree of the Alhambra, also known as the Edict of Expulsion, declared that the presence of a Jew in Spain was illegal. Its purpose was to ensure that new Catholic converts and their descendants did not revert to Judaism.

The infamous **Spanish Inquisition** was explicitly instituted to weed out conversos who continued Jewish practices; later, the Inquisition targeted all heretics living in Spain. Even if conversos came forward and admitted to continuing secretly in some Jewish practices, they were still put to death. In 1492, the year Ferdinand and Isabella were procuring funding for the first voyage of Christopher Columbus, most Jews were expelled from Spain.

Spanish Inquisition A bureau or commission that had branches in most of the larger dioceses of Spain that was empowered to call on civil authorities to help weed out heretics. Once the heretics were discovered, the Church authorities conducted a trial with those accused presumed guilty and required to prove their innocence.

Thirteen Fundamental Principles of MOSES MAIMONIDES

The twelfth-century Sephardic Jewish philosopher Moses Maimonides drew up these Thirteen Fundamental Principles of Jewish Faith that he gleaned from the Torah. For him, they were the fundamental truths of Judaism and foundational to the Jewish religious tradition.

1. God exists.
2. God is one.
3. God has no corporeal aspect.
4. God is eternal.
5. God alone (and no intermediaries) should be worshipped.
6. Prophecy is to be accepted.
7. Moses was the greatest of prophets.
8. All of the Torah in our possession is divine and was given through Moses.
9. The Torah will never be changed or superseded.
10. God knows the actions of man.
11. God rewards those who keep the Torah and punishes those who transgress it.
12. The Messiah will come.
13. There is a resurrection of the dead.

Writing Task

The Jews do not have a tradition of formulating doctrine or a belief system. It was not until the twelfth century when Moses Maimonides formulated his Thirteen Principles that there was any systematic articulation of what every Jew should believe. Drawing on what you know about Jewish history up to the time of the twelfth century CE, why do you think doctrine played such a small role in Jewish religious tradition? Write three to four paragraphs using examples to explain your answer.

In response to such widespread persecution and expulsions, the majority of European Jews went to Portugal, Italy, the Netherlands, and Turkey in the fifteenth and sixteenth centuries. Jews in Turkey fared the best, helping to expand the Islamic Ottoman Empire by numbers alone.

The Protestant Reformation of the sixteenth century was no kinder to Jews. Protestant reformer Martin Luther of Germany wrote *On the Jews and Their Lies*, which advocated the destruction of everything Jewish—including Jews' homes, synagogues, books, and property—and forbade Jews themselves from being anywhere near a Christian town.

The various persecutions of Jews in Europe during the Medieval Period left the majority of Jews in grim poverty. Many Jews were driven from cities into the countryside. Unable to own land, they were serfs and servants to mostly Christian landowners. Economic poverty and discrimination left Jews in religious poverty as well. It was a struggle for many to practice Judaism or even to muster the strength to pray to God. Into this religious vacuum of the late seventeenth century came Rabbi Israel ben Eliezer, nicknamed the Baal Shem Tov, or "Master of the Good Name." Born in what is now Ukraine and traveling throughout eastern Europe, the Baal Shem Tov emphasized the presence of God in all aspects of Jewish life. Into the darkness that befell so many Jewish people and communities, particularly in eastern Europe, the Baal Shem Tov brought the message of God, joy, and life itself in a new way. His message spread into a new movement within Judaism called **Hasidism**, from the Hebrew word for "pious." Forms of Hasidism, with each group leader called a **rebbe**, are found in Orthodox Judaism today.

Modern Period

The *Enlightenment*, a philosophical movement of the eighteenth century that emphasized the use of reason to analyze previously accepted doctrines and traditions, ushered in the Modern Period (1783–present). Closely associated with this western European movement was a movement of Jewish Enlightenment that was meant to emancipate Jews from their social and legal situation. No longer the chattel or property of prelates or feudal monarchs, Jews

---

Hasidism An Orthodox Jewish sect founded by the Baal Shem Tov in Poland in the eighteenth century that emphasizes religious experience.

rebbe A Hasidic rabbi.

were achieving equality before the law alongside their fellow Christian citizens of Germany, France, the Netherlands, and Britain.

Czarist Russia, however, was a different story. The nineteenth century was especially brutal, with hundreds of government-sponsored pogroms, expulsions, and deportations of Jews across the empire. In 1882, Czar Alexander III promulgated temporary laws and regulations against Jews in what became known as the May Laws. The next czar, Nicholas II, then produced a forged document called *The Protocols of the Elders of Zion*, purportedly written by Jewish leaders, that outlined a Jewish conspiracy to take over the world. The Russian government's purpose was to make Jewish people scapegoats for the corruption and economic failings of the government. Many Russian people went along with blaming the Jews.

Polish Jews in Jedwabne, Poland, were massacred by a group of their neighbors with the collaboration of German soldiers on July 10, 1941, during World War II. This memorial was erected to commemorate the murdered Jews in the spot where the pogrom took place.

In western Europe, there was an explosion of sectarian groups in the Jewish religious tradition. In Germany and later in the United States, *Reform Judaism* emerged, advocating full integration into the culture where one lived. In the United States, the rise of *Conservative Judaism* counteracted Reform Judaism, modifying Jewish tradition in a limited manner. *Orthodox Judaism* was another reactionary movement in response to Reform Judaism. Orthodox Judaism is the most traditional branch of Judaism, insisting that its members strictly follow the Torah. In the 1930s, *Reconstructionist Judaism* emerged from Conservative Judaism, advocating Judaism not only as a religious tradition but also as a culture. Reconstructionist Jews do not believe in an all-powerful God, nor do they accept the Torah as divinely inspired.

Rabbi Regina Jonas was ordained as the world's first female rabbi in 1935. A German Jew, she died in the gas chambers of Auschwitz in 1944.

The Jewish movement known as **Zionism** began in the nineteenth century. Zionism sought the return of Jews to the Jewish homeland, Palestine. The worldwide Jewish community was more responsive to the goals of Zionism after the murder of about six million Jews at the hands of the Nazi Germans in the **Shoah**, more commonly known as the Holocaust, of the 1930s and 1940s. In response to the Holocaust, the United Nations returned Palestine to the Jewish people in 1948. The new nation was named the State of Israel.

Several contentious issues were apparent from the start. Returning Palestine to the Jews caused a tremendous upset in much of the Middle East. The city of Jerusalem was still divided between the countries of Jordan and Israel. The holy places of Christians, Muslims, and Jews were under the jurisdiction of a Muslim country, Jordan. In 1967, the State of Israel recaptured all of Jerusalem in what became known as the Six-Day War. One of the results of the Six-Day War was that the ancient holy places in Jerusalem were opened to all visitors. However, the delicate balance required to bring peace to that part of the world has yet to be found.

The State of Israel was founded as a secular, democratic state, but Orthodox Judaism was given the privilege to set religious standards. Hence, there is no public transportation or shopping on the Sabbath, and weddings are celebrated in an Orthodox manner alone. This has caused tension with other branches of Judaism. Non-Orthodox Jews find Orthodox Judaism becoming

---

Zionism From Zion, the name for the historical land of Israel; the movement with origins in the nineteenth century that sought to restore a Jewish homeland in Palestine in response to anti-Semitism.

Shoah The Hebrew word for "calamity"; the mass murder of Jews by the Nazis during World War II.

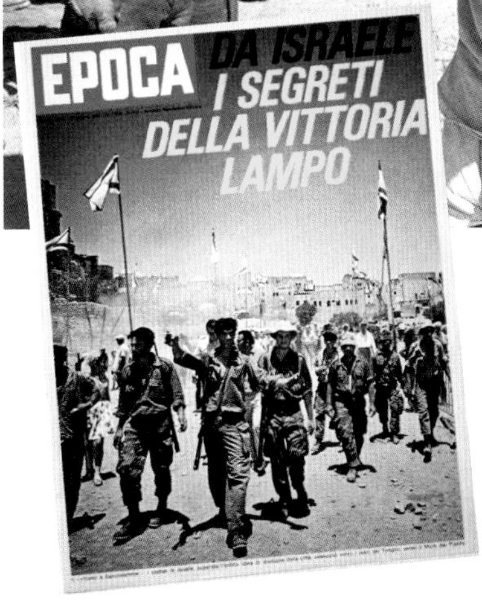

(Above) The Six-Day War (June 5–10, 1967) was the third of the Arab-Israeli wars. Israel's victory over the coalition of Egypt, Jordan, and Syria left them with possession of the Sinai Peninsula, Gaza Strip, West Bank, Old City of Jerusalem, and Golan Heights. (Left) The cover of the Italian news magazine Epoca. *The headline reads "From Israel: The secrets of lightning fast victory."*

more exclusive and more stringent and are working for equality among the various branches of Judaism existing in the State of Israel.

In the United States, there is a history of strong support for the State of Israel not only among Jewish people but also among certain Evangelical Christian groups. However, support is starting to wane among those who are critical of what they see as an imbalance between secular democracy and the sway of Orthodox Judaism. While the State of Israel is in a precarious geographic position surrounded by so many countries that deny its sovereignty, it remains crucial for all parties involved to find a solution that treats Palestinians, both Christian and Muslim, in an equitable manner.

The traditional definition of a Jewish person is one whose biological mother was Jewish, regardless of whether one is an observant Jew or not. Late in the twentieth century, Conservative, Reform, and Reconstructionist Judaism redefined a Jewish person as one with at least one Jewish parent. One who converts to Judaism is also a Jew, although some Orthodox Jewish groups do not accept this.

SECTION *Assessment*

Reading Comprehension

1. What did the Hebrew people become in the forty years they took to return to Canaan from Egypt?
2. After the death of Solomon, why did the Hebrew kingdom become more vulnerable to outside attacks?
3. According to Rabbi Hillel, what is the summation of the Torah?
4. Why did the synagogue gain importance during the Rabbinic Period?
5. Who was Moses Maimonides, and what did he argue?
6. Distinguish between Sephardim and Ashkenazim.
7. Name and briefly differentiate between the four branches of Judaism present in the Modern Period.

Vocabulary

8. What is the *Diaspora*? How did it arise?
9. What is *Hasidism*? What are its leaders called?

Critical Thinking

10. Why would Jews say the year 70 CE was one of the worst years in Jewish history?
11. Name and explain two issues of concern among Jews in the twenty-first century.

12. What character traits and values are needed to sustain a community through centuries of persecutions, expulsions, genocides, and foreign occupation?

For Reflection

13. Explain one way you can apply Hillel's teaching on the Torah to your own life.

Flash Search

14. What year did a Jewish community first establish itself in your country? What prompted them to immigrate?

Section 2
SACRED STORIES AND SACRED SCRIPTURES

In addition to the Hebrew Bible, there are several sources of sacred Jewish writings. Each centers around the Torah, which is the first five books of the Hebrew Bible. These sacred writings offer not only Jewish beliefs about God but also commentaries that delve further into the teachings of the Torah.

Tanakh

Central to all of Jewish life is the Hebrew Bible, which is what Christians call the Old Testament. Jews tend to call these Scriptures the *Tanakh*, an acronym for the names of its three sections. The first section of the Tanakh is the *Torah*, or Law, comprising the first five books—Genesis, Exodus, Leviticus, Numbers, and Deuteronomy. The second section is the *Nevi'im*, or Prophets. This includes the Former Prophets (Joshua, Judges, 1 and 2 Samuel, and 1 and 2 Kings) and the Latter Prophets (the Major Prophets [Isaiah, Jeremiah, and Ezekiel]) and the Twelve, or Minor, Prophets, such as Hosea and Amos. The third section, the *Ketuvim*, or Writings, includes Job, Psalms, and Proverbs.

Of the three sections of the Tanakh, Torah is the most important. Traditional Jews also call Torah the Five Books of Moses, for they believe Moses was the author. Torah is the source of the 613 commandments traditional Jews believe they must follow to be good Jews. These 613 laws are divided into two main types: 248 positive laws and 365 negative laws. However, fewer than half of these laws can be observed in the modern era. Laws pertaining to the Temple or to criminal proceedings can no longer be observed because neither the Temple nor the ancient style of government exist today.

As the holiest writing of Judaism, the Torah used in synagogue services is no mere printed book. Torah is produced as a scroll. The Five Books of Moses are handwritten in Hebrew on a series of parchments. The parchments are then hand sewn together and sewn onto two wooden rollers, dressed, and decorated. A portion of Torah is read in the synagogue every Sabbath so that the entire Torah is read in a one-year cycle, with the year beginning right after the Sukkot festival (see Section 4, "Sukkot").

Rabbi Yehuda Teichtal holds the Torah scroll in his right arm, because—according to some sources—Deuteronomy 33:2 says, "The LORD came from Sinai. . . . Lightning flashing at them from His right." (Tanakh).

Some Jews believe God gave Moses two Torahs at Mount Sinai that cannot be separated from each other—the Written Torah, described above, and the Oral Torah. The Oral Torah is the explanation and interpretation of the Written Torah. For example, the Written Torah mandates no work on the Sabbath but does not define what constitutes work. The Oral Torah was written down eventually, and codified and arranged by Judean rabbi Yehudah HaNasi (Judah the Prince) around 200 CE. Called the *Mishnah*, or "teaching," it is organized into six sections: agriculture and the land of Israel, the Sabbath and festivals, family life, relations with other people, sacrifices and dietary laws, and ritual purity.

Talmud

Two centers of rabbinic Judaism emerged in the centuries following the destruction of the Second Temple in 70 CE. One center, in the Roman province of Judea but outside Jerusalem, was made up largely of refugees from the Jerusalem area. The second major rabbinic center was in Babylonia, where the descendants of the Jews who had been taken into exile five centuries earlier formed a number of thriving Jewish communities. Rabbinic scholars from both of these centers studied the Torah and the Mishnah and wrote commentaries and discussions that later became two very different *Talmuds*, or "learnings." The earlier one was called the Palestinian, or Jerusalem, Talmud, while the other was called the Babylonian Talmud. The Babylonian Talmud incorporates the Mishnah and is generally what is meant when people refer to the Talmud. The Babylonian Talmud was and still is considered the more authoritative of the two.

One of the functions of midrash is to make the characters of the Bible more relateable. Some of the most famous midrashim are written about Abraham and Sarah depicted here in the Rodef Shalom Synagogue in Pittsburgh, Pennsylvania.

Midrash

Midrash is a way of interpreting the biblical text. Sometimes the interpretation includes the author's use of imagination or a story to describe the text. Midrash fills in the blanks of the biblical text; it is a lot like historical fiction. Midrash is not unique to the Jews—there is also Christian midrash. For example, the book *Ben Hur*, and later the movie, could be called Christian midrash. If someone wrote about St. Peter's wife (who is not mentioned in the Bible), that could be an example of Christian midrash.

The term *midrash* comes from the Hebrew for "to examine" or "to seek out." After the return of the exiled from Babylon, Jewish sages began to "seek out" the real meaning of biblical passages that might be missing some information,

---

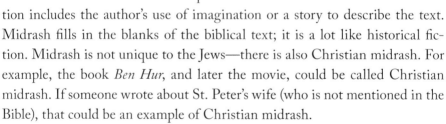

midrash A type of scriptural interpretation found in rabbinic literature, especially the Talmuds. Midrash assumes that the Scriptures provide answers for every situation and every question in life.

seem contradictory, or be in the form of metaphor. They wrote their interpretations in various literary genres, such as parables, homilies, or narratives. Midrash is not a particular book, but much of it can be found in the Talmud. Midrash has never really ceased. The contemporary book *Does God Have a Big Toe? Stories about Stories in the Bible* is midrashic in nature.

SECTION *Assessment*

Reading Comprehension

1. Why do Jews call the Hebrew Bible the Tanakh?
2. What is the significance of the Talmud?
3. Which Talmud is considered the more authoritative?
4. How does midrash relate to the Hebrew Bible?

Vocabulary

5. What is the origin of the term *midrash*?

Critical Thinking

6. Why do Jews not call the Hebrew Bible the Old Testament?
7. Explain the difference between the Written Torah and the Oral Torah.

For Reflection

8. Studying the Torah is a spiritual, sometimes even prayerful, exercise. How can your study of sacred writing be a prayerful exercise?

Flash Search

9. What is Kabbalah?

Section 3
BELIEFS AND PRACTICES

If Judaism could be summed up in three words, those words would be *God*, *Torah*, and *Israel*. God gave the Torah to Israel. In this sense, Israel is to be thought of not as the political State of Israel with national boundaries but as a people chosen by God with a specific purpose.

God

Who is this God who chose a small group of people to be a "light to the nations" (Is 49:6, Tanakh)? The opening words of the **Sh'ma**, a statement recited daily by devout Jews, offers an answer: "Hear, O Israel! The LORD is our God, the LORD alone" (Dt 6:4, Tanakh). For Jews, God exists, God is one, God is Creator, and God is good. Judaism is a monotheistic religious tradition, meaning that Jews believe in one supreme God.

Unlike Christians, Jews, except for the Reconstructionist branch of Judaism (see Section 1, "Modern Period"), do not have a set of formal doctrines that articulate their beliefs. Jewish belief is summarized by the assertion that not only does God exist but God is also the Creator of all things. The opening line of the Torah reads, "When God began to create . . ." (Gn 1:1, Tanakh). God created, and thus God is good. Because God is good, God desires goodness from all creation. Scripture is again helpful in clarifying Jewish understanding of the responsibility of humankind:

> And now, O Israel, what does the LORD your God demand of you? Only this: to revere the LORD your God, to walk only in His paths, to love Him, and to serve the LORD your God with all your heart

> and soul, keeping the Lord's commandments and laws, which I enjoin upon you today, for your good. (Dt 10:12–13, Tanakh)

Torah

The golden chamber shown here houses the Torah of the Norsa-Torrazzo synagogue in Mantua, Italy.

The central source for how to live a Jewish life is the Torah. The Torah is literally God's self-Revelation to the Jewish people. It is the most sacred of objects of faith. Yet there is at once a formality and an intimacy with regard to Torah; both reverence and familiarity are operational. When not in use, the Torah scrolls are kept in a specially made place within the synagogue that is called an **Ark**. There are special prayers to be prayed before and after reading from the holy book. When the scrolls are taken out of their place of honor, they are carried around the synagogue by the rabbi for people to reverence by a touch, a kiss, or even a dance. The presence of Torah is a joyous occasion, for Jews believe that where there is Torah, there is God, in an ordinary yet extraordinary way.

A Jew finds the study of Torah to penetrate every aspect of his or her life. Though Torah may mean "law" or "teaching," there is nothing sterile about

---

Sh'ma A Hebrew term meaning "hear"; the first word and the name of a prayer observant Jews pray every morning and evening.

Ark A repository traditionally in or against the wall of a synagogue for the scrolls of the Torah.

it. The study of Torah is more a spiritual exercise than an intellectual one. In Torah, one encounters God and God's will for one's life: "O how I love your teaching [Torah]! It is my study all day long" (Ps 119:97, Tanakh). Keeping Torah is keeping the Law, meaning the teaching or commandments of God. When Christians think of Jewish law, they imagine it as contained in the Ten Commandments. However, to Orthodox Jews, the Torah contains 613 commandments that are particular ways in which Torah is made real in the world. The Jewish sages explain that as there are 613 words in the Torah, there are 613 commandments implicit within the Ten Commandments, which are the first 10 of the 613.

The commandments are called **mitzvot**. God issues mitzvot not only to command his people but also to issue guidance for what will make people truly happy. Keeping Torah brings not bondage but freedom. What has taken place in the history of Judaism is the interpretation and application of these commandments through a variety of new situations that Moses and the ancient Israelites could not have anticipated. For example, in following the Third Commandment to keep **Shabbat** holy, Jews desist from thirty-nine categories of labor ("forty minus one"). Each category refers to one of the forty levels of God's work of creation, except for the highest level—creation from nothing, which is reserved to God alone. From such categories, rabbis interpret various bodies of knowledge in order to apply a specific commandment or injunction to a specific situation. This process of interpretation produces **halakhah**, the total body of Jewish law. For example, according to halakhah, kindling a fire is prohibited on Shabbat. A Jew may place tape over the light mechanism in a refrigerator on Shabbat, not because this is one of the 613 commandments, but because it is related to a Jewish law prohibiting the kindling of a fire on the Sabbath.

Israel

Jews are often described as God's Chosen People, or the People of Israel. (Many religious traditions have the belief that their members are chosen or

---

mitzvot Commandments of the Jewish law.

Shabbat The seventh day of the week; the Jewish Sabbath.

halakhah The legal part of the Talmud, an interpretation of the laws of Scripture.

"The LORD *said to Abram, 'Go forth from your native land and from your father's house to the land that I will show you. I will make of you a great nation, And I will bless you; I will make your name great, And you shall be a blessing. I will bless those who bless you And curse him that curses you; And all the families of the earth Shall bless themselves by you'" (Gn 12:1–3, Tanakh).*

elected.) "Chosen" is another meaning for the Hebrew word for "separation to be holy." When Jews talk about being God's Chosen People, they are really talking about being "holy" or "separate." Often the terms *Jew*, *Israelite*, and *Hebrew* are used interchangeably.

The call of the Jewish people to holiness originated with the call of Abram (later named Abraham) in Genesis 12:1–3. In that biblical passage, God calls Abram to leave Ur, the land of his father, and to follow God. In return for his breaking with idolatry and for his show of faith in the one God, God gifts Abraham with progeny and land. In addition, God blesses those who bless Abraham and his descendants and curses those who curse them.

Being chosen by God brings with it both privilege and responsibility. Being "chosen" is not passive but active. Jews are Jews only insofar as they respond to being chosen—that is, insofar as they are holy. The privilege of belonging to God's Chosen People is that God has made a special **covenant** with the Jewish people to be their God. The responsibility of belonging to the Chosen People is that Jews must "choose" to accept God's commandments and live lives that are holy and righteous, lives that are examples to the rest of humanity. This chosen nature of the Jews is passed from one generation to the next: "I created you, and appointed you a covenant people, a light of nations" (Is 42:6, Tanakh).

What are ways in which Jews act as a chosen people? A traditional Jew is an "observer of the commandments" and participates in the various halakhic obligations. For Jews, all life is holy. Setting aside sacred times at sacred places is just part of ongoing religious expression.

SECTION *Assessment*

Reading Comprehension

1. What is the Sh'ma?
2. What do Jews believe about God?
3. How are both reverence and familiarity operational with Torah?
4. When did the call of the Jews to be a Chosen People originate?
5. What does it mean to say that the Jews are God's Chosen People?
6. What are the two meanings of the term *Israel* to Jews?

Vocabulary

7. What is one obligation of *halakhah*?

---

covenant A binding and solemn agreement between human beings or between God and his people, holding each to a particular course of action.

Critical Thinking

8. What does it mean to say that Jews emphasize law and action over doctrine?
9. "Legal systems promote harmony within a community." Explain why you agree or disagree with that statement.
10. What freedoms might one exercise in keeping Torah?

For Reflection

11. What do you feel chosen or destined to do in your life?

Flash Search

12. Why does some Jewish literature spell God "G-d," without the letter *o*?

Section 4
SACRED TIME

Sacred time is cyclical for the Jews. From the earliest waking hours of the day through the long hours of the night, from infancy to old age, all life is holy. Hence, all life is to be devoted to God, including a person's very thoughts, actions, memory, and talents. To mark the sacredness of life, Jews take special moments annually to remember and to celebrate and record the dates on a calendar.

Most people operate under several different types of calendars. There is the academic calendar that starts in the fall and ends in late spring. There is the civil calendar that begins on January 1 and concludes on December 31. A personal income tax calendar follows the civil calendar, but many nonprofit organizations have a fiscal year that begins on July 1 and concludes on June 30. Christians use a liturgical calendar that begins with the first Sunday of Advent, occurring in late November or early December. The civil calendar currently used by most of the world is the Gregorian calendar, introduced by Pope Gregory XIII in the sixteenth century. To understand Jewish sacred time, one needs a better grasp of the Jewish calendar.

The Jewish Calendar

For Jews, God is the God of history. It therefore made sense to the Jewish sages to begin the Jewish calendar at the beginning of history—that is, at the creation of the world. Using only the Torah, the sages calculated when the world was created and began their annual twelve-month calendar in that year. The beginning of the second millennium on the Roman calendar, January 1, 2001, was Tevet 6, 5761, on the Jewish calendar, meaning 5,761 years since God created the earth.

While the Gregorian calendar is a solar calendar, the Jewish calendar is a lunisolar calendar in which months are based on the lunar cycle of 354 days

The two numbers on this building's facade, 5662 on the Jewish calendar and 1902 on the Gregorian calendar, are equivalent dates.

and years are based on the solar cycle of 365 days. Also, the Jewish calendar begins in the fall on Rosh Hashanah, the Jewish New Year. The Jews found it necessary to adjust for the eleven-day discrepancy between the lunar and solar cycles so that a holiday that is celebrated in the fall, as commanded in the Hebrew Bible, will not eventually end up in the spring. The eleven-day difference is reconciled in two ways. First, a month is added seven times every nineteen years. Second, one day is added or subtracted each year to two different months. One additional difference between the civil and Jewish calendars is that while our day begins and ends at midnight, a Jewish day begins and ends at sunset.

The major Jewish holy days and festivals are divided into two main cycles: the Tishri cycle in the fall and the Nisan cycle in the spring. Tishri is named for the first month of the cycle beginning in September or October and contains, besides Rosh Hashanah, the holy day of Yom Kippur and the festival of Sukkot. Nisan is the first month of the spring cycle. The name *Nisan* comes from the Sumerian word for "firstfruits." The Nisan cycle contains two festivals, Pesach (Passover) and Shavuot. Rosh Hashanah and Pesach are similar in that both are memorial celebrations. Rosh Hashanah memorializes the creation of the world, while Pesach memorializes the creation of the Jews as a people. Sukkot and Shavuot are both harvest festivals. In addition to these major feasts, two relatively minor festivals are celebrated during the Jewish year: Hanukkah and Purim are both festivals that commemorate freedom from the wrath of foreign rulers.

This section describes the two main cycles of the Jewish calendar and the festivals and holy days that occur in each. It also discusses the crown jewel of Jewish sacred time, Shabbat.

Rosh Hashanah and Yom Kippur

The period in the Tishri cycle beginning with Rosh Hashanah and ending with Yom Kippur—which means "Day of Atonement"—is known as the Days of Awe. This penitential period is the high holy time for the Jewish people.

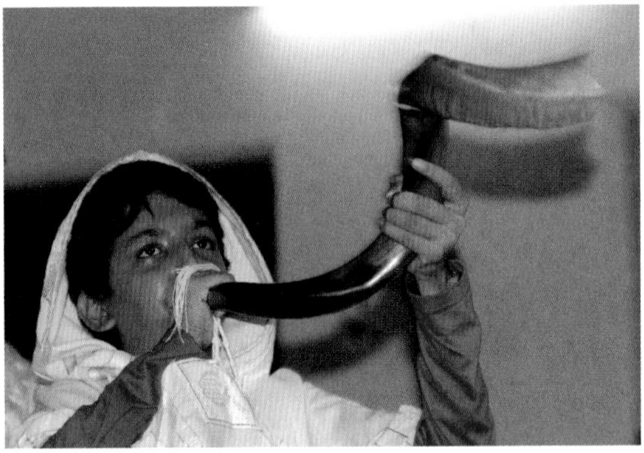

A Jewish Indian boy blows the shofar to gather devotees around the Torah in his synagogue on the Jewish New Year.

Rosh Hashanah is celebrated on the first day of the Jewish month of Tishri (September or October on the Gregorian calendar). Besides ritually commemorating the creation of the world and of all living things, Rosh Hashanah is the day when Jews believe God judges their actions of the previous year. Yom Kippur, generally accepted as the holiest day of the year, is a day of prayer, fasting, and repentance. Jews ask forgiveness for both communal and personal sins. In asking for forgiveness, Jews go directly to the person they offended, if possible.

During the Days of Awe, Jews strive for repentance, or more accurately, a turning back to the proper way of living. This is known as **teshuvah**, meaning "return." God's judgment on whether teshuvah took place is sealed in a symbolic Book of Life at the end of Yom Kippur.

---

teshuvah A Hebrew term meaning "return"; the act of repentance in Judaism.

shofar A ram's horn used as a musical instrument in Jewish religious rituals, especially on Rosh Hashanah and Yom Kippur.

A central ritual in the celebrations of Rosh Hashanah and Yom Kippur is the blowing of the **shofar**, or ram's horn. A ram's horn is used rather than a calf's horn because the latter conjures up the image of the idolatrous golden calf from the Israelites' time in the desert. Also, the bent shape of the ram's horn signifies that Jews must bend their hearts toward God.

Sukkot

Sukkot (Hebrew for "booths"), also known as the Feast of Tabernacles or the Feast of Booths, is another festival during the Tishri cycle. Beginning five days after Yom Kippur and lasting for eight days, Sukkot commemorates times during the Jews' forty years in the desert and later times in Israel when they had to protect themselves from the elements during harvest by building temporary huts or booths. With this protection from the weather, Jews came to understand that God alone was their great protector. Sukkot also marks the end of the fruit harvest season, especially the harvest for grapes used for making wine.

Today, Jews often build a hut in their homes where they gather during Sukkot for storytelling and the reading of Scripture. They also collect and bind

The sukkah, a temporary hut in which one sleeps, eats, and communes, during Sukkot, is symbolic of the time the Israelites spent in the wilderness after they were freed from slavery in Egypt.

together one palm branch, two willow branches, and three myrtle branches, which they wave in different directions during the Hallel prayer (a prayer of praise recited from Psalms 113–118) to symbolize that God is everywhere.

Pesach

Pesach, more commonly known as Passover, retells the story of the Exodus of the Hebrew people from Egypt. It is the first major feast of the spring Nisan cycle. Pesach celebrates the Hebrews' release from Egyptian slavery after the angel of death "passed over" the houses of the Hebrews that were marked with blood from a lamb. The Passover meal probably included unleavened bread, wine, some herbs, and an unblemished lamb. The ceremony—as it does today—would have consisted of a blessing of both the cup and the bread. The story of the first Passover is told in the Book of Exodus:

> Moses then summoned all the elders of Israel and said to them, "Go, pick out lambs for your families, and slaughter the passover offering. Take a bunch of hyssop, dip it in the blood that is in the basin, and apply some of the blood that is in the basin to the lintel and to the two doorposts. None of you shall go outside the door of his house until morning. For when the LORD goes through to

A family gathers for Passover seder in Moscow, Russia.

> smite the Egyptians, He will see the blood on the lintel and the two doorposts, and the LORD will pass over the door and not let the Destroyer enter and smite your home.
>
> "You shall observe this as an institution for all time, for you and for your descendants. And when you enter the land that the LORD will give you, as He has promised, you shall observe this rite. And when your children ask you, 'What do you mean by this rite?' you shall say, 'It is the passover sacrifice to the LORD, because He passed over the houses of the Israelites in Egypt when He smote the Egyptians, but saved our houses.'" The people then bowed low in homage. (Ex 12:24–27, Tanakh)

Today, each Jewish person celebrates being personally freed by God. Jews believe that if God had not freed them, they would still be slaves. They see themselves as enslaved in each generation and freed by God in each generation. This means that Jews from every generation symbolically go forth from Egypt toward the Promised Land.

Shavuot

Shavuot (Hebrew for "weeks") is celebrated seven weeks after the first day of Pesach, so some see Shavuot as the conclusion to Pesach. Shavuot was originally a harvest festival celebrating the firstfruits of the wheat harvest. Eventually, Jews began to associate Shavuot with the giving of the Torah by God to Moses on Mount Sinai.

These twins celebrated their Bat/Bar Mitzvah together.

Today, Jews also combine Shavuot's celebration of the reception of the Torah with the Jewish coming-of-age. In a coming-of-age ceremony, Conservative and Reformed Jewish teenagers publicly state their acceptance of Judaism as a way of life. These ceremonies are known as Bar Mitzvah for boys and Bat Mitzvah for girls (see in this section, "Life-Cycle Celebrations," for more information).

A Hanukkah celebration in the Kharkiv Choral Synagogue, in Kharkiv, Ukraine.

Hanukkah

Hanukkah celebrates one of the great military victories in Jewish history. Nevertheless, Hanukkah is not a major Jewish holiday, and it is not found in the Hebrew Bible. In fact, Hanukkah was not celebrated much at all until Jewish parents recognized it was essential to counteract the strong influence of Christmas on Jewish members of American society. Since Hanukkah, like Christmas, is a winter celebration with light as one of its symbols, placing a greater emphasis on the celebration made Hanukkah a natural Jewish counterpart to the Christmas season.

Hanukkah celebrates the victory of the Jews, led by Judas Maccabeus of the Hasmonean family, over the Seleucid Greeks, led by Antiochus IV. Besides mandating Hellenism in Judea, Antiochus denied Jews the freedom to practice their religion. Worst of all, Antiochus captured the Second Temple and converted it into a pagan temple. In December 165 BCE, the Jews recaptured the Second Temple, cleansed it of pagan impurities, and rededicated it to God.

Hanukkah is an eight-day celebration. Its main ritual is the lighting of one additional candle of a Hanukkah **menorah** each evening. This commemorates a tradition that after the Maccabees recaptured the Second Temple, they had enough oil to relight the Temple menorah for just one day. However, the candle miraculously stayed lit for eight days.

Purim

Purim (Hebrew for "lots"—objects used to decide a matter by chance) commemorates the victory of Jews living in Persia in the fifth century BCE over Haman, the prime minister of Persia. The story is recounted in the Book of Esther. This "feast of lots" refers to the lots Haman randomly cast to determine on which day he would slaughter the Jews. Queen Esther, who was Jewish, heard about the plot and was able to convince her husband, King Ahasuerus of Persia, to stop Haman's plan. Haman and his family were executed on the gallows prepared for the Jews.

Today, Jews exchange gifts and donate items to the poor on Purim. They also share in a celebratory meal called *se'udat*.

Challah and wine are prepared for the Shabbat meal.

Shabbat

While the festivals described in the previous sections occur annually, Shabbat, the Jewish Sabbath, is a weekly event. Shabbat is celebrated from sunset Friday until sunset Saturday. Keeping the Sabbath holy is the fourth commandment (according to Jewish count) given by God to Moses on Mount Sinai. It is a reminder to the Jews that God

---

menorah A candelabra found in both Jewish homes and synagogues, usually having nine branches, especially for Hanukkah, but sometimes seven.

rested from work on the seventh day, and so too must they. As the Scripture reads:

> Remember the sabbath day and keep it holy. Six days you shall labor and do all your work, but the seventh day is a sabbath of the LORD your God: you shall not do any work—you, your son or daughter, your male or female slave, or your cattle, or the stranger who is within your settlements. For in six days the LORD made heaven and earth and sea, and all that is in them and He rested on the seventh day; therefore the LORD blessed the sabbath day and hallowed it. (Ex 20:8–11, Tanakh)

On this holiest day of the week, observant Jews refrain from work, attend synagogue services, and study the Torah. A standard greeting for the Sabbath is "Shabbat Shalom," or "Sabbath peace."

Friday evening is the Shabbat dinner, a family ritual that ushers in the Sabbath. Shabbat begins eighteen minutes before sunset with the lighting of the Sabbath candles. A prayer of blessing over the candles is generally recited by the woman of the house: "Blessed are you, Lord our God, King of the Universe, who has blessed us with your commandments and commanded us to

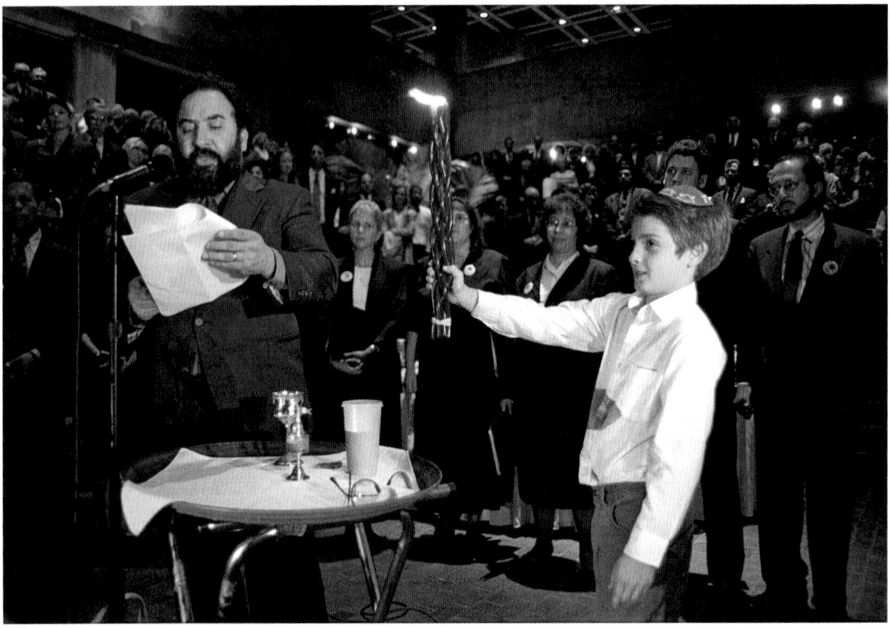

The Havdalah ceremony—here recited in Boston, Massachusetts—emphasizes the difference between the sacred and the ordinary.

light the Sabbath candles." Then a blessing over the wine and bread is shared: "Blessed are you, Lord our God, King of the Universe, who creates the fruit of the vine. Blessed are you, Lord our God, King of the Universe, who brings forth bread from the earth."

After these blessings, the meal begins. The Shabbat dinner table includes a white tablecloth, two candles, wine, and a braided loaf of bread called *challah*. The Sabbath candles are not extinguished but are allowed to burn themselves out.

Sabbath ends at sunset Saturday. A brief ceremony called **Havdalah** concludes this sacred time. A braided candle with several wicks is lit and held in the hand so one can see its reflection of light on the fingertips. Wine accompanies this closing ceremony as a symbol of thanksgiving and joy. A box of aromatic spices is also lit, signifying the carrying of the aroma of the Sabbath into the week.

Life-Cycle Celebrations

For Jews, life-cycle celebrations focus on transitional moments in their personal lives. Here are some of the ways Jews mark important times in life.

Birth

Circumcision, the cutting away of the foreskin of a male's penis, usually takes place at a ceremony eight days after birth. This practice dates from the time of Abraham when God commanded that Abraham and all his male descendants be circumcised as a sign of the covenant between God and God's people (see Genesis 17:10–11). Circumcision permanently marks male Jews as a way to differentiate them from non-Jews.

The rite of circumcision is called the brit milah.

Havdalah A religious ceremony that symbolically ends Shabbat. It is usually recited over kosher wine or kosher grape juice.

The ceremony for an infant girl involves the giving of her name. She is brought to the synagogue, where she is welcomed into the congregation and the rabbi reveals her full Hebrew name for the first time.

Coming-of-Age

When a Jewish child becomes a mature individual, he or she is responsible for keeping Torah. Religious majority is associated with the age of thirteen for boys and twelve for girls. When the individual is minimally competent in prayer and the Torah, he or she is called to read publicly from the Torah.

The first Bat Mitzvah was conducted in New York City in 1922.

Until recently, these ceremonies were male-oriented, with no female counterpart. Bar Mitzvah (literally "Son of the Commandment"), the coming-of-age ceremony for a thirteen-year-old boy, recognizes that the boy has become an adult and is responsible for his own religious and moral training. While the Bar Mitzvah was likely developed in the Medieval Period, the counterpart ceremony for girls, the Bat Mitzvah, was created late in the twentieth century.

Marriage

Most often a Jewish wedding is held in a synagogue, though it doesn't have to be. The three major elements of the Jewish marriage ritual are the **huppah**, the blessings, and the breaking of the glass. The huppah is a canopy held up by four poles representing the future home of the bride

In the Jewish wedding ceremony, the bride and groom stand beneath the huppah and recite seven blessings in the presence of a minyan, *a prayer quorum of ten adult Jewish men.*

and groom. There are usually vegetative symbols embroidered on the canopy to represent the notion that the bride and groom are in the Garden of Eden and are the first man and woman. The breaking of the glass is in recognition of the destruction of the Second Temple in Jerusalem in 70 CE. A rabbi is present to supervise a Jewish wedding.

Death

For Jews, funerals take place as soon as possible, often within twenty-four hours of the death. At the burial, blessings are made, prayers are said, and psalms are read aloud.

SECTION *Assessment*

Reading Comprehension

1. Name the feasts in the Tishri and Nisan cycles of the Jewish calendar.
2. How is the Jewish calendar different from the Gregorian or civil calendar?
3. What happens on Yom Kippur?
4. Cite the similarities between Rosh Hashanah and Pesach.
5. What are the Days of Awe, and what is their significance?
6. Why did the relatively minor feast of Hanukkah take on more significance, especially in the United States?
7. Describe what takes place on Shabbat.
8. How do Jews mark major times in the life cycle: birth, coming-of-age, marriage, and death?

Vocabulary

9. When is *Havdalah* held?

---

huppah A canopy under which the bride and groom stand during a Jewish wedding ceremony.

Critical Thinking

10. What is the value of setting aside one day a week for worship and rest?
11. The Jewish calendar is a unifying factor among the various branches of Judaism. Is this true for the liturgical calendar with Christianity as well? Why or why not?

For Reflection

12. What is something in your life to which you are metaphorically or literally a slave?
13. For you, what does it mean to keep a day "holy"?
14. What would be a first step if you were to seek repentance for the purpose of reordering your life?

Flash Search

15. What are the Four Questions asked at a Passover Seder?

16. Why do some Jewish men wear long sidelocks and dress in a hat and long coat?

17. Why do Jews put rocks on graves?

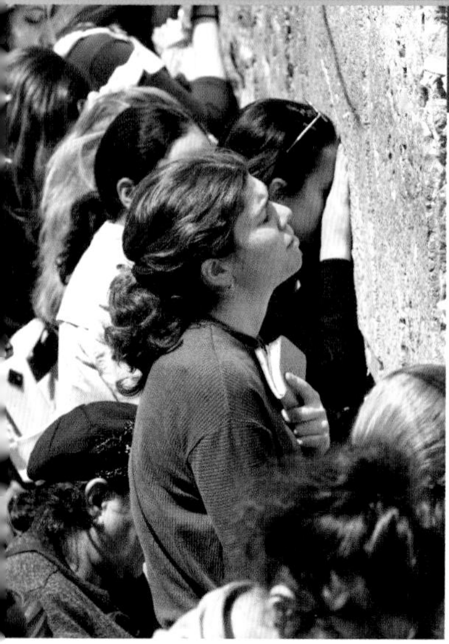

Section 5
SACRED PLACES AND SACRED SPACES

Judaism is unique in that most of its religious festivals and life-cycle rituals are performed in the synagogue with a corresponding ritual in the home. *Synagogue* comes from a Greek word meaning "place of assembly." This section features the sacredness of the synagogue and the home for Jews. Also, the very land of Israel—more than the political entity of Israel—along with its holy city Jerusalem and its Western Wall remain sacred and significant to the spiritual life of Jews worldwide.

Synagogue

The Temple in Jerusalem was the center of Jewish worship for centuries. The Temple was where the ritual sacrifice of animals, the primary expression of worshipping God, took place.

With the scattering of the Jews in the Diaspora and the eventual destruction of the Second Temple in 70 CE, a number of alternative rituals were established over the centuries to replace those that were held in the Temple. Some Jews maintained that the deeds of righteous people were equivalent to the sacrificial offerings of the Temple. Others equated personal prayer with Temple sacrifices; three daily periods of prayer therefore replaced the three daily animal sacrifices. While captives in Babylon, Jews initially met in private homes for worship; these were the forerunners of synagogues. After the destruction of the Second Temple, synagogues became the place where Jews could worship God communally.

Synagogues are now typically built to replicate Zion (Jerusalem) in the shape of a square with the ***bimah*** *in the center representing Mount Zion. There is a gathering space for men, women, and children; however, in most Orthodox synagogues, men and women are separated. A central chamber exists for the reading of the Torah and for prayer. The Torah is kept in an Ark on the wall facing Jerusalem. Thus, when the people face the Ark, they are also facing Jerusalem.*

Over the centuries, the functions of the synagogue and the number of synagogues multiplied. The synagogue became multidimensional. It became a House of Prayer where God was worshipped, a House of Study where Torah was studied, and a House of Assembly where Jews met socially. These three names suggest the three separate yet interrelated functions of the synagogue.

Home

Jewish homes are distinct because they are transformed into sacred space. In a traditional Jewish home, a **mezuzah** is attached to at least one outside doorpost. In some Jewish homes in the West, one wall is designated the

---

bimah The elevated platform in a Jewish synagogue where the person reading aloud from the Torah stands during the service.

mezuzah A Hebrew word meaning "doorpost"; a small parchment containing Hebrew Scripture, usually the Sh'ma, that is placed in a case on or near the right doorframe at the home of an observant Jew. This fulfills the commandment in Deuteronomy 6:9 to "inscribe [God's instructions] on the doorposts of your house and on your gates."

mizrakh, or eastern wall. This wall is sometimes marked with a special picture or embroidery showing the direction one must face for prayer. A **kosher** home is one that has special dishes for eating and cooking that separate meat from dairy products. Since a traditional Jewish table is not only a place for building familial relationships but also a place for ritual, food must be kosher, or "proper." Pork and shellfish are forbidden. Other meats must be slaughtered in a kosher manner. The combination of meat and dairy products is forbidden. On Shabbat, a reverent atmosphere prevails in the home. The house must be spotless, and a Shabbat cloth must be on the table along with the Shabbat candlesticks.

Land of Israel

The land of Israel, also known as Canaan, the Promised Land, Palestine, and the State of Israel, is of considerable significance to the Jewish people. The land promised by God to Abraham and his descendants is "flowing with milk and honey" (Ex 3:8, Tanakh). It is holy ground.

Over their more than three-millennia history, Jews have had to leave the land because of famine, exile, deportation, and the like. However, there were always a few who remained. Wherever Jews were in the world, they never forgot the Promised Land. Many of the mitzvot (commandments) are connected with the land of Israel. Hence, some Jews believe that they must live in Israel to fulfill God's will and that the many centuries Jews have had to live in the Diaspora have been an exile from the land. Some Jews even believe that Israel is so sacred that the presence of any groups there that are not Jewish defiles the land.

---

kosher From the Hebrew word *kaser*, meaning "proper"; commonly refers to food permitted by Jewish dietary laws. Jews observe kosher laws to remind themselves that they are to be a holy and separate people.

The Temple mount and the Western Wall in modern Jerusalem.

Jerusalem

Jerusalem is a holy city for each of the three religious traditions that trace their roots to Abraham: Judaism, Christianity, and Islam. For Jews, however, Jerusalem is the holiest city; there is no other. It is in Jerusalem where Mount Moriah, part of the Moriah mountain range, was believed to be located. Mount Moriah is where Abraham intended to sacrifice his son Isaac (see Genesis 22:2) and where Jacob had his dream about the ladder:

> Jacob awoke from his sleep and said, "Surely, the LORD is present in this place, and I did not know it!" Shaken, he said, "How awesome is this place! This is none other than the abode of God, and that is the gateway to heaven." (Gn 28:16–17, Tanakh)

King David captured the city of Jerusalem from the Jebusites and called it the City of David (see 2 Samuel 5:6–9). Solomon's Temple was also built on Mount Moriah (see 2 Chronicles 3:1), though centuries later it was destroyed by the Babylonians. After the Jews returned from the Babylonian Exile, the Second Temple was built on the same place, also known as the Temple Mount.

Jews Mourning in Babylonian Exile, *by Eduard Bendemann.*

Hence, for Jews, God is *most present* in Jerusalem. Jews face Jerusalem daily in prayer. At the end of Pesach, Jews pray, "Next year in Jerusalem!" Orthodox Jews believe a messiah will come and rebuild Jerusalem to its former glory and usher in a time when "they shall beat their swords into plowshares" (Is 2:4, Tanakh). At Jewish weddings, a glass is broken in commemoration of the destruction of the Second Temple. Jews have worked hard to keep the land of Israel and Jerusalem in their collective memory. The State of Israel fought hard to take back Jerusalem in the Six-Day War in June of 1967. Jerusalem has been remembered in prayer since the days of the Babylonian Exile:

> If I forget you, O Jerusalem, let my right hand wither;
> let my tongue stick to my palate if I cease to think of you,
> if I do not keep Jerusalem in memory even at my happiest hour. (Ps 137:5–6, Tanakh)

Western Wall

The Jewish king Herod the Great came to power in Jerusalem in 37 BCE. He undertook massive building projects, and expanding the Second Temple was one of them. The Western Wall, a retaining wall of the Second Temple, is all that remains from the disaster of the destruction of the Second Temple by the Romans in 70 CE. It has been a place of pilgrimage for Jews for centuries, whenever they had access to it. When the State of Israel was founded in 1948, the city of Jerusalem was divided between Israel in the western part of the city and Jordan in the eastern part. The eastern part included the Old City, where the Temple Mount stands. In the 1967 Six-Day War, the State of Israel defeated Jordan and reunited the city under Israeli rule.

With the Israeli government responsible for the entire city, members of the Orthodox Jewish community immediately set up a synagogue near the Western Wall. All are welcome to pray at the site, but there are rules to be observed. Men and women are separated. All are to dress very modestly, and men are to wear a head covering. Orthodox men wear their *tallit* (prayer shawl), pray out loud, and read from a Torah scroll provided at the site. Women may *not* wear a tallit, pray out loud, or read from a Torah scroll. While some see the permitted activities of men and women at the Western Wall as gender inequality that must be corrected, others see it as a well-tested tradition. Since the Western Wall is a public site, some have appealed to the secular Israeli government to make the rules the same for men and women, but the Orthodox community proves very powerful.

In 2016, Israel decided to allow women to join men in praying at the Western Wall, although the men's section is divided from the women's by a wall.

Rabbi Alina Treiger

The gender issue at the Western Wall highlights the fact that for centuries, public worship within Judaism was the prerogative of men. It still is in many Orthodox communities. The private sphere—especially the home—was the sanctuary of women. Women were not tied to the obligations of the Jewish liturgical calendar, especially with regard to the synagogue, for that could interfere with the care of children. This dynamic gradually changed with the rise of Reform, Conservative, and Reconstructionist Judaism. In these Jewish communities, men and women sit together, and women play a much larger role in leadership. Girls are educated in the Jewish faith along with boys. Women can wear a prayer shawl, study Torah, and become a rabbi in those Jewish communities.

SECTION *Assessment*

Reading Comprehension

1. What takes place in a synagogue?
2. How is a Jewish home made sacred?
3. What is the significance for the Jewish people of the land of Israel and the city of Jerusalem?

For Reflection

4. How would your religious tradition survive if its place of worship was taken away?
5. What outward signs designate your home as holy?

Flash Search

6. There is a practice of placing slips of paper into the Western Wall in Jerusalem. Why, and why there?
7. Who was Regina Jonas?

Section 6

CATHOLICS DIALOGUE WITH JEWS

The relationship between Catholics and Jews is unique. Catholicism is historically, scripturally, liturgically, and theologically rooted in Judaism. No two other religious traditions have so much in common. Catholics and Jews both believe in the one God (see *CCC*, 200–202). They share Abraham as a father in faith, the first to believe in the one God (see *CCC*, 59–60). They both believe God made multiple covenants with the Jewish people—with Noah, with Abraham, with Moses, and with David—and that God has broken no covenant (see *CCC*, 71). They both affirm God's Revelation on Mount Sinai first to Moses, then to the Jewish people, and then to all humankind (see *CCC*, 72). They both accept the Ten Commandments as a minimum guide for moral living (see *CCC*, 1962). They pray the same psalms. They both believe God has spoken to them through the prophets. They both accept the Hebrew Bible as the Word of God (it is contained in the Christian Old Testament). They both know that at the end of time, they will see that history has meaning, there will be a final judgment, and the world will be redeemed (see *CCC*, 1060).

Yet those things that are common to both religious traditions are also the sources of differences. The following sections discuss both the similarities and the differences.

Messiah

The most notable difference between Catholics and Jews is belief about Jesus. Both agree that Jesus was a historical figure who was born of a Jewish woman named Mary; was raised in a traditional Jewish home in the Jewish homeland; was a charismatic itinerant preacher and wonderworker; and died as a

A Jewish sign in Brooklyn, New York, announces that the Messiah is coming soon.

criminal, crucified by Romans around 30 CE. Here the commonalities end and the differences begin.

Most Jews still expect a messiah or messianic age to come. Some Jews believe the Messiah ("Anointed One") will be a wise person who will reestablish the House of David and will bring about the messianic era when "they shall beat their swords into plowshares" and "the wolf shall dwell with the lamb" (Is 2:4; 11:6, Tanakh). Other Jews await not a person but a messianic era. Catholics believe the Messiah has already come in the Divine Person of Jesus of Nazareth. While Jews at the time of Jesus were looking for a messiah who would be a warrior-king—a political figure—from the House of David, Jesus of Nazareth was a spiritual rather than a political figure. Catholics believe that the coming of Jesus the Messiah was the inauguration of God's reign on earth. It is a spiritual, moral reign rather than an earthly, political reign, for Christ's Kingdom is not of this world. The Gospel of Luke cites Jesus reading in the synagogue from the scroll of the prophet Isaiah:

> "The Spirit of the Lord is upon me,
> because he has anointed me
> to bring glad tidings to the poor.
> He has sent me to proclaim liberty to captives
> and recovery of sight to the blind,
> to let the oppressed go free,
> and to proclaim a year acceptable to the Lord."

> Rolling up the scroll, he handed it back to the attendant and sat down, and the eyes of all in the synagogue looked intently at him. He said to them, "Today this scripture passage is fulfilled in your hearing." (Lk 4:18–21, NABRE)

Catholics believe that at the end of time, it will be revealed that Jesus was indeed the long-awaited Jewish Messiah and Redeemer of the entire world. For Catholics, the end of time will be the Second Coming of the Messiah, while for Jews it will be the first coming.

Incarnation

Catholics believe that Jesus is something else in addition to the Messiah, the Anointed One of God (see *CCC*, 453): Jesus is God.

> And the Word became flesh
> and made his dwelling among us,
> and we saw his glory,
> the glory as of the Father's only Son,
> full of grace and truth. (Jn 1:14, NABRE)

This is the Catholic doctrine of the **Incarnation**. God became a human in Jesus. At conception, the Divine Person of the Son took upon himself a complete human nature (see *CCC*, 479). Jesus is not part human and part divine. Rather, Jesus is truly God and truly human (see *CCC*, 480). God became human to bring about our salvation, to reconcile us to God.

The creation of the world, from the Book of Genesis.

Some Jews expect the coming Messiah to be a human being, anointed by God but not divine. Jews see no reason for a mediator between them and God. For Jews, each person has the power within to reconcile, to make right, with God.

However, the doctrine of the Incarnation is not totally foreign to Jews. Both Jews and Catholics believe that the Word of God was present at creation, for God spoke, and what he spoke came to be. While for Catholics the Word became incarnate in the Divine Person of Jesus, for Jews the Word became incarnate in the Torah. They both say that God is present through something concrete, but these are not the same or even similar doctrines. For Catholics, the concrete is Jesus, who is truly God and truly human. For Jews, the concrete is the Torah, which has a divine and a human nature as well. The words of Torah make God present within the human reader.

Scripture

To Catholics, the Hebrew Bible isn't the only repository of God's inspired Word in Scripture. All Christians accept the New Testament as revealed Scripture. While Jews accept the New Testament as documents written, for the most part, by first-century Jews, they do not accept the New Testament as revealed by God. Catholics commonly

---

Incarnation A term meaning "enfleshment"; for Christians, the taking on of human nature and a human body by God's Son, Jesus.

believe that the Old Testament is the same as the Hebrew Bible, but that is not exactly true. The Catholic Church includes seven books (Tobit, Judith, 1 and 2 Maccabees, Wisdom, Sirach, and Baruch and parts of Esther and Daniel), mostly written in Greek after 300 BCE, that are not included in the Hebrew Bible. These seven books are referred to as **deuterocanonical**—"of the second canon"—to show that they are not accepted in the Jewish canon.

The word *testament* means "covenant." While Catholics could say that their Scriptures are made up of the Old Covenant and the New Covenant, as noted above, God made multiple covenants with the Jewish people, the most important of which was the covenant on Mount Sinai. God does not break covenants. God's covenants are eternal. Jesus did not enter human history to render the Old Covenant void (see Matthew 5:17).

Liturgy

There are striking similarities between the annual Passover meal of the Jews and the daily Eucharistic celebration of Catholics, also known as the Mass or the Lord's Supper. In each, there are readings from Scripture; the offering, blessing, and fracturing of unleavened bread; and the offering, blessing, and consumption of wine. Even the beginning of the blessings can be similar. Jews pray, "Blessed are you, Lord our God, King of the universe," and Catholics pray, "Blessed are you, Lord God of all creation."

Holy Thursday and Passover

There is also a connection between Holy Thursday and Passover. The Gospels of Matthew, Mark, and Luke report that the Last Supper was a Passover meal. The Passover commemorates the historical Jewish Exodus from Egypt under the leadership of Moses. After God sent many plagues to convince the pharaoh to release the Jewish slaves, it was the tenth plague, the death of firstborn sons, that caused the release. To avoid the death of their own firstborn sons, the Jews were to slaughter an unblemished lamb and mark the post and lintel of their door with its blood. The angel of death would "pass over" any dwelling that was marked with blood. The death of the firstborn sons (including his own) was too much for the pharaoh, and he let the Jews go free. Catholics

---

deuterocanonical A term meaning "of the second canon"; refers to seven books in a Catholic Bible that are not found in the Hebrew Bible or in most Protestant Bibles.

Jesus celebrated the Last Supper with his disciples as part of Passover.

see Jesus as the Lamb of God who was slain and whose blood released believers from the slavery of sin to freedom in Christ Jesus.

Pentecost and Shavuot

The Christian feast of Pentecost and the Jewish feast of Shavuot are related. In fact, Shavuot is also known as Pentecost. While Shavuot means "weeks," referring to seven weeks after Passover, the name "Pentecost" refers to the fiftieth day after Passover. Shavuot began as a spring harvest feast, but it is better known as a celebration of when God gave the Torah and the Law to the Jews through Moses. When the first followers of Jesus were celebrating the first Shavuot/Pentecost in Jerusalem after his Death and Resurrection, the Holy Spirit came upon them. They too became a people. Pentecost is sometimes called the "birthday of the Church." Christians believe that Jesus did not nullify the Mosaic Law but fulfilled it.

Topics for Dialogue

Catholics and Jews have had both a rich and a troubled history together. The difficulties between the two have left some Jews wary of Catholic intentions about being equal partners in dialogue. Jews have faced contempt, discrimination, violence, expulsions, deportations, and death at the hands of people claiming to be Catholic. This includes the burning of their synagogues and sacred texts. Sometimes Catholics have put Jews in situations in which it was difficult to maintain their human dignity. Catholics have called Jews "Christ killers" because of the role some Jewish leaders had in Christ's trial and Crucifixion. Jews have been told that their lot in life was poor because they did not accept Jesus and that if they did accept Jesus, all would be well. Some were

Pope John Paul II met with Chief Rabbi Elio Toaff in the 1980s.

forced into conversion. Some chose to convert but were accused of secretly practicing Judaism.

Many of these offenses were perpetrated by mob violence rather than by spiritual or temporal leaders of the Catholic Church. For example, there are stories that when the first crusaders plundered Jewish communities in the Rhineland, Jews went to the bishops of the region for help. Not only did the bishops help but some were killed for helping the Jews.

Rabbi Samuel Sirat and Cardinal Jean-Marie Lustiger both received the Nostra Aetate Award, named for the Second Vatican Council document.

In the Second Vatican Council document *Nostra Aetate* (1965), the Catholic Church set a course for righting these horrific wrongs toward the Jewish people. Even before the Second Vatican Council began, Pope John XXIII removed the Latin word *perfidis*, or "perfidious," from the Good Friday prayer for the Jews. Contempt for the Jewish people was to be no more. On the contrary, the Jewish people were, and remain, God's Chosen People. God never severed the covenant made on Mount Sinai. Jews share no collective guilt for the Death of Jesus (see *CCC*, 597); Roman soldiers crucified Jesus at the instigation of some, not all, Jewish leaders. Jews do not need to become Catholic to be saved. Jews who adhere to their covenant with God are in line with his plans for them (see *CCC*, 839–840). The Catholic Church no longer has an organized missionary program to convert Jews.

The long, shared history between Catholics and Jews requires that Catholics engage in dialogue with people who adhere to the Jewish religious tradition. With such a painful past, meaningful dialogue is not always easy. Jews find it difficult to hear about Jesus as the source of salvation. Many Jews are uncomfortable with the Christian symbol of the cross, for it evokes many painful memories. Catholics find it painful to hear that Jews cannot accept Jesus as the long-awaited Jewish Messiah. While Jews find the cross a sign of human hatred, Catholics find the cross a sign of God's unconditional love for humankind.

Because of the painful history of forced conversions, especially during the Medieval Period, Jews find it difficult to listen to Catholics talk about evangelization or missionary activity. Catholics must acknowledge the difficulty Jews have with evangelizing activity and assure Jews that converting others to Catholicism is not the sole purpose of the Church's missionary activity. Evangelization is part of Catholic religious identity. Giving witness to Jesus—sharing the Good News about him—is a consequence and requirement of Catholic faith. Witnessing and attempting to convert others are two very different things. And Jews and Catholics do have one missionary activity they can share. Catholics and Jews, as well as Muslims, can all call people to conversion from idolatry to faith in the one, true God.

Two significant areas of dialogue for Catholics and Jews to pursue at this time in their history together are the Shoah and the defense of human dignity. Jews prefer to use the word *Shoah* rather than *Holocaust*. *Shoah* means "catastrophe" or "devastation," and it evokes a better understanding of their experience under Nazism than *Holocaust*, which means "burnt offering." For Jews, the Shoah was an experience of the extermination of millions of their own people in "civilized" Europe at the hands of the Nazis. The Shoah can be a very emotionally charged topic, but meaningful sharing sometimes goes beyond being merely nice or polite. Just as the Passover and the Paschal Mystery are not just events that happened in the past but are at all times present, profound, and powerful, so too is the Shoah. As the Passover is part of the collective memory of Jews and the Paschal Mystery is part of the collective memory of Catholics, so too must the Shoah become part of the collective memories of both religious traditions. Neither Catholics nor Jews must ever forget, lest it happen again somewhere, sometime, to some other group of people. In their own ways, Catholics and Jews must pass on the memory of the Shoah to future generations. Though it is painful on both sides for very different reasons, people of goodwill must never lose courage in confronting historical truth, for therein lies a source for reconciliation and healing.

Finally, Catholics and Jews in Western countries live in a materialistic, consumeristic, secular, individualistic world. It is a world where the human person is treated as an object. Human worth is measured only in how useful a

Survivors of the Auschwitz concentration camp walk by the main gate at the former Auschwitz I site on January 27, 2020, in Oswiecim, Poland, to commemorate the seventy-fifth anniversary of the camp's liberation. The Nazis killed an estimated one million Jews, Slavs, Romani, Catholic clergy, homosexuals, and handicapped people at the camp during World War II.

Remembrances of the Shoah

"First They Came . . ."

The following words were spoken by a prominent German Lutheran pastor, Martin Niemöller (1892–1984). At first a Nazi sympathizer, Niemöller came to see Adolf Hitler as a brutal dictator. His words express his sentiment about what he saw as the complacency of the German people through their silence when the Third Reich systematically murdered their fellow Germans.

> First they came for the socialists, and I did not speak out—
> Because I was not a socialist.
> Then they came for the trade unionists, and I did not speak out—
> Because I was not a trade unionist.
> Then they came for the Jews, and I did not speak out—
> Because I was not a Jew.
> Then they came for me—
> And there was no one left to speak for me.

This is the most common version of Martin Niemöller's words. He spoke out freely after the war ended, so there are other variations. Other people and groups have also modified the terms to fit their particular issues.

Writing Task

Adapt Niemöller's words to fit issues of your particular interest. Write out your adaptation.

Anne Frank

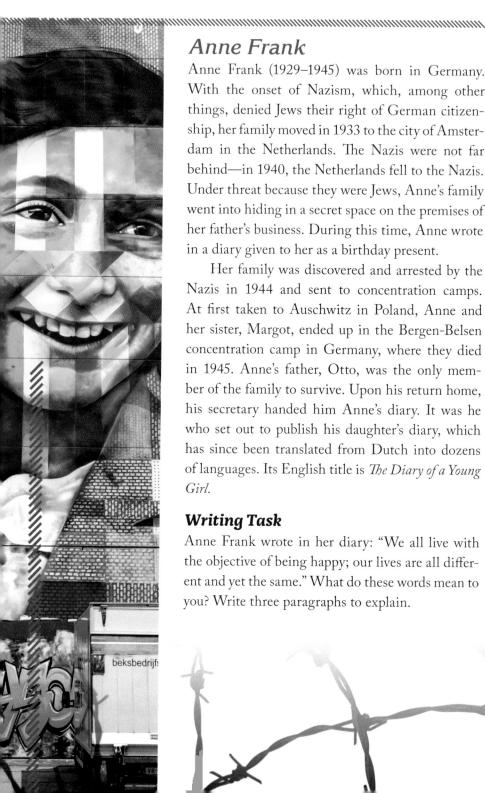

Anne Frank (1929–1945) was born in Germany. With the onset of Nazism, which, among other things, denied Jews their right of German citizenship, her family moved in 1933 to the city of Amsterdam in the Netherlands. The Nazis were not far behind—in 1940, the Netherlands fell to the Nazis. Under threat because they were Jews, Anne's family went into hiding in a secret space on the premises of her father's business. During this time, Anne wrote in a diary given to her as a birthday present.

Her family was discovered and arrested by the Nazis in 1944 and sent to concentration camps. At first taken to Auschwitz in Poland, Anne and her sister, Margot, ended up in the Bergen-Belsen concentration camp in Germany, where they died in 1945. Anne's father, Otto, was the only member of the family to survive. Upon his return home, his secretary handed him Anne's diary. It was he who set out to publish his daughter's diary, which has since been translated from Dutch into dozens of languages. Its English title is *The Diary of a Young Girl.*

Writing Task

Anne Frank wrote in her diary: "We all live with the objective of being happy; our lives are all different and yet the same." What do these words mean to you? Write three paragraphs to explain.

"Never Again! Never Forget!"

These words—"Never Again! Never Forget!"—are the collective cry of the Jewish community ever since its experience in Europe during World War II. Jews were condemned by the Nazis simply because they were Jewish, and precious few came to their aid. As philosopher George Santayana wrote more than a century ago, "Those who cannot remember the past are condemned to repeat it." Jews do not want to see such contempt poured upon them or any other group ever again. Of course, remembering has been in the bones of Jews for millennia. As the psalmist sang while Jews suffered exile in Babylonia,

> If I forget you, O Jerusalem, let my right hand wither;
> let my tongue stick to my palate if I cease to think of you. (Ps 137:5–6a, Tanakh)

Writing Task

While memory plays a significant role in peoples of many cultures, it seems to play a lesser role in Western societies. Why do you think this is so?

"Never Again," written in Hebrew, French, English, German, and Russian, at the site of the former Dachau Nazi concentration camp in Bavaria, Germany.

person is to another. Ours is a society in which greed is a virtue. Another good topic for dialogue between Jews and Catholics is how this dark side of human nature, the contempt for God's creation, can be dispelled, and light and hope can reign. Maintaining the beauty of the earth, building healthy families and communities, and promoting justice, peace, and equality are some of the many issues about which Catholics and Jews can agree and affirm their common faith in God.

SECTION *Assessment*

Reading Comprehension

1. Why are some Jewish people wary of dialogue with Catholics?
2. List four areas in which Jews and Catholics are in agreement.
3. What is the difference between what Catholics believe about Jesus and what Jews believe about Jesus?
4. What are some of the similarities between the Mass and Passover, Holy Thursday and Passover, and Shavuot and Pentecost?

For Reflection

5. If a Jewish person asked you, "Who is Jesus to you?" how would you answer?
6. How can the Shoah be a source of unity between Catholics and Jews? What are some other topics that can further Jewish-Catholic dialogue in a positive way? Explain why.

Flash Search

7. How do the list and order of the books in the Hebrew Bible differ from the list and order of the books in the Catholic Old Testament?

Section Summaries

Introduction: A Living Religion

Judaism is the religious tradition of the Jews and of Jesus. It is a vibrant religious tradition that is practiced differently today from how it was depicted in the Hebrew Bible. After the destruction of the Second Temple in 70 CE, rabbis established a whole new expression in being a covenantal people. The answer to the question "Who is a Jew?" is rather complicated, and even some Jews do not agree on it.

- The words *Hebrew*, *Jew*, and *Israelite* are commonly used interchangeably with regard to the Jewish people. Write three to four paragraphs explaining the difference between these terms.

Section 1: A Brief History of Judaism

The history of Judaism can be divided into four periods: Biblical, Rabbinic, Medieval, and Modern. In the early history of Judaism, the Jewish people found their homeland occupied by various foreign governments or were exiled to distant lands. After the destruction of the Second Temple, Jewish institutions and religious expression had to be reimagined and reconstructed. As Jewish communities expanded outside of the Middle East, Jews contributed much to the emerging Western culture. In the nineteenth century, after much internal and external exclusion, Jews in Europe became equal partners in citizenry, as long as they were willing to assimilate. The twentieth century was one of the most devastating *and* triumphant eras of Jewish history. After centuries of persecution culminating in the Shoah, Jews were able to return to and gain self-rule in the land God gave them.

- Research Hasidism and its presence in your country or a country of your choice. Write a three- to four-paragraph summary.

Section 2: Sacred Stories and Sacred Scriptures

The Tanakh is the sacred text of Judaism. *Tanakh* is the acronym for the three main sections of the Hebrew Bible: *Torah* (Law or Instruction), *Nevi'im*

(Prophets), and *Ketuvim* (Writings). The Written Torah is also known as the Five Books of Moses. The Oral Torah, or Mishnah, is best represented in the Talmud, sometimes called the second Torah. There are two main versions of the Talmud, the Babylonian Talmud being in much wider use than the Palestinian, or Jerusalem, Talmud. Midrash is written commentary on the Hebrew Scriptures using the interpretive mode and is still written to this day.

- Look through the Gospels and find examples of Jesus having discussions with the various Jewish leaders. List and explain three of the topics discussed.

Section 3: Beliefs and Practices

The essence of Judaism can be summed up in three words: God, Torah, and Israel. Judaism is a monotheistic religious tradition; worship is of one God alone. The Torah is God's self-Revelation to the Jewish people. It is the most sacred of all objects. The term *Israel* refers to both a people and a nation-state. For Jews, being God's Chosen People brings both privilege and responsibility.

- Watch or read a summary of the movie musical *Fiddler on the Roof.* Write a three- to four-paragraph summary of some of the Jewish traditions found or aspired to in this film. Be specific.

Section 4: Sacred Time

For Jews, all life is holy. Not just religious practices but a person's every thought, action, memory, and talent are to be devoted to God. That said, there are particular times in the Jewish calendar set aside for communal devotion. Two main festival cycles in the Jewish year are the Tishri cycle in the fall and the Nisan cycle in the spring. Yom Kippur is the most important feast in the fall, and Pesach is the most important feast in the spring. Sukkot and Shavuot were originally harvest festivals that gained more profound religious significance in the Jewish people's relationship with God. Shabbat, the Jewish Sabbath, is celebrated weekly from sunset Friday to sunset Saturday. Keeping the Sabbath holy is the fourth commandment God gave to Moses on Mount Sinai. The Jewish religious tradition also has ceremonies for birth, coming-of-age, marriage, and death.

- Research and compare in four to five paragraphs how Orthodox, Conservative, Reform, and Reconstructionist Jews celebrate one of the following: Rosh Hashanah, Yom Kippur, Sukkot, Hanukkah, Purim, Shavuot, Shabbat, birth, Bar/Bat Mitzvah, or marriage. Include both the synagogue and home observances when applicable. Note the similarities and differences between the practices of the different branches of Judaism.

Section 5: Sacred Places and Sacred Spaces

After the destruction of the Second Temple in Jerusalem in 70 CE, the synagogue replaced the Temple as the central place of worship for Jews. The synagogue has three main functions: House of Prayer, House of Study, and House of Assembly. The traditional Jewish home is also an important place for rituals. The land of Israel, its historic city Jerusalem, and the ancient Western Wall of the Second Temple are the holiest places for Jews.

- Research a current news story about the Western Wall. Write two to three paragraphs summarizing the event and its significance.

Section 6: Catholics Dialogue with Jews

There are striking similarities between Catholic and Jewish history, Scripture, liturgy, and theology, but in these same areas we can find the greatest differences between the two religious traditions. Some Jews are wary of any serious dialogue with Catholics because a long history of contempt, forced conversions, and persecutions is hard to forget. Two major areas of dialogue between Jews and Catholics are the Shoah and the defense of human dignity.

- Write three to four paragraphs explaining why Jews and Catholics need one another.

Chapter Projects

Complete one of these projects by the conclusion of your study of this chapter.

1. Reading and Reporting on *The Chosen*

    Read the novel *The Chosen* by Chaim Potok. Describe, in a two- to three-page essay with examples, how the novel addresses the following five aspects of Judaism: history, sacred stories and sacred scriptures, beliefs and practices, sacred time, and sacred places and sacred spaces. Note any differences in these aspects between the two main characters.

2. A Dialogue between a Rabbi and a Priest

   The God Squad was a television program hosted by Rabbi Marc Gellman and Monsignor Tom Hartman that aired in the 1990s and early 2000s. Gellman and Hartman discussed issues that touched both the Jewish and Catholic communities. Today a similar program might very well be a podcast. With a partner, create a recorded dialogue with one of you taking the role of a priest and the other taking the role of a rabbi as you address themes discussed in Section 6 of this chapter: Messiah, Incarnation, Scripture, Liturgy, Holy Thursday and Passover, Pentecost and Shavuot, the impact of the Second Vatican Council on Jewish-Catholic relations, the Shoah, and the defense of human dignity. If you wish to work on the assignment alone, you can play the roles of both the rabbi and the priest. Your recording should be between five and ten minutes long and shareable with your teacher.

3. Creating and Describing a Jewish Symbol

   The Key Image feature following these projects concerns the Jewish symbol known as the Star of David. The feature (1) gives a brief history of the symbol, (2) lays out a number of interpretations of the symbol, and (3) presents various ways in which it is used today. Do the same with one of the following Jewish symbols: menorah, Torah scroll, or Seder plate. Illustrate the symbol you chose and write caption-style summaries of the three aspects given above.

4. Preparing Jewish Food

   Look up a recipe and follow the instructions to bake challah, a bread that is part of the feast of the Passover. Basic ingredients are warm water, active dry yeast, honey, vegetable oil, eggs, salt, unbleached all-purpose flour, and poppy seeds. Write down the measurements of the ingredients and the instructions for the recipe you followed. Write three to four paragraphs explaining the symbolism and history of challah bread in Passover meals. Bring the challah to class for your classmates to sample.

5. Orthodox Jewish Life in Brooklyn

   Research and report on the Orthodox Jewish community in Brooklyn, New York. Tell about its origins, history, lifestyle, and religious practice in the context of news stories from recent times. Cite one book, one article, and one film in a three- to five-page report.

Key Image

Star of David

The hexagram, shown here, is used almost universally as a symbol of the Jewish religious tradition. Perhaps the modifier "modern" should be inserted because for centuries, the menorah was recognized as the predominant symbol of Judaism. The hexagram became a widely known symbol of Judaism relatively recently, though still several centuries ago. This is no mere geometric figure; the symbol is full of meaning. In English, it is known as the Star of David. In Hebrew, it is the *Magen David*, or "Shield of David." God is the "shield" or protector of David (see Psalm 18:31, 36, Tanakh) and, by extension, the protector of all. Though "shield" can be found in the Hebrew Bible as an *attribute* of God, this symbol is not named in either the Bible or the Talmud.

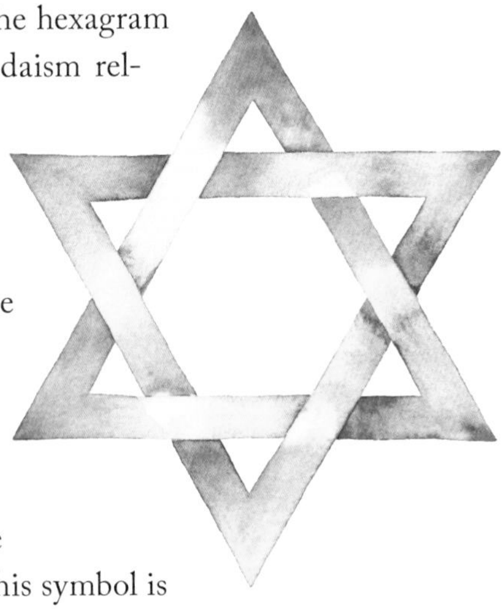

In ancient times, the hexagram was sometimes used as ornamentation or decoration. It was also used in combination with magic among many groups of peoples, not just the Hebrew people. The symbol is visible on a **frieze** of a second- or third-century CE synagogue in Capernaum, where Jesus once ministered, and it is also found in medieval Christian cathedrals such as the thirteenth-century cathedral in Valencia, Spain.

---

frieze A wide decorative band on a wall, often near a ceiling.

It was in seventeenth-century central Europe that the hexagram started to become prominent as a Jewish symbol. Historians point to Prague, Czechoslovakia, where the Jewish community was permitted to have their own flag bearing the Magan David. The Star of David marked the Jewish neighborhoods of Vienna, Austria, around the same time. Because Jews wanted a recognizable symbol as their Christian neighbors had, the nineteenth century saw widespread use of the Star of David on synagogues and other places and objects representing Jewish culture.

The Star of David has been used for political purposes as well. Seeking a symbol of the Zionist movement that encouraged Jewish immigration to Palestine, Theodor Herzl, the father of the Zionist movement, had a flag bearing the Star of David displayed at the First Zionist Congress in Basel, Switzerland, in 1897. During World War II, the Nazis compelled all Jewish people six years of age and older, under pain of punishment, to wear a prominent yellow Star of David. When the State of Israel was established in 1948, the new country's flag proudly bore the Star of David.

Two interlocking equilateral triangles create the Star of David. Because of the long and varied history of the acceptance of the Star of David as the main symbol of Judaism, the symbol has diverse meaning. Jews most commonly understand the Star of David as representing God as the "shield" that protects the entire six directions of the universe—north, south, east, west, up, and down. Another interpretation is that the upward-pointing triangle represents humankind's need for God as Protector and Redeemer, while the downward-pointing triangle serves as God reaching down to humanity. The upward- and downward-pointing triangles also represent the intertwined mutuality between God and his people. Franz Rosenzweig, a German Jewish theologian of the early twentieth century, suggested that the two triangles forming the Star of David represent triads of Jewish belief: creation/Revelation/redemption and God/World/Israel. These various interpretations are accepted as valid by most Jews; it is a matter of which aspects of the meaning of the Star of David are emphasized.

The Star of David can be found on synagogues, prayer shawls, Jewish community centers, jewelry, and the Israeli flag. There is a red one on Israeli ambulances. The Star of David is the premier symbol of Judaism today.

Faithful Adherent

Abraham Joshua Heschel: He Prayed with His Legs

Rabbi Abraham Joshua Heschel (1907–1972) was a Polish-born American Jewish leader, author, philosopher, theologian, social activist, and mystic. He came from a long line of Hasidic rabbis on both sides of his family. As a young man in Poland, he studied to become a rabbi. He then moved to Berlin, where he pursued doctoral work and rabbinical ordination and taught Talmud. In 1938, while teaching in Frankfurt, Germany, Heschel was arrested by the Nazi Gestapo and deported back to Poland.

In Warsaw, he continued his teaching, but six weeks before the Nazi invasion of Poland on September 1, 1939, he found his way to London. In 1940, he moved to New York. Although his father had died when Heschel was nine years old, his mother and three of his sisters died at the hands of the Nazis.

Rabbi Heschel (center, left) with Martin Luther King Jr. and Catholic, Protestant, and Jewish protesters in 1968.

Heschel taught at Jewish seminaries in America for the rest of his life. In the 1950s and 1960s, he wrote several books, including *The Sabbath*, *God in Search of Man*, and *The Prophets*. Two of Heschel's fundamental teachings were that God cares for all people and that through human suffering everyone makes the world a better place.

Heschel was a man not only of powerful words but also of great deeds. Like the Baptist leader Dr. Martin Luther King Jr., and sometimes along with him, Heschel was an activist in the civil rights and antiwar movements of the 1950s and 1960s in the United States. Both men were known as prophetic voices for their time. As Heschel would say, "When I marched in Selma, I felt my legs were praying."

Heschel was also involved in interreligious dialogue. This experience put him in an excellent position to participate in the Second Vatican Council as part of the American Jewish Committee. There, he played a key role along with Cardinal Augustin Bea, S.J., first president of the Secretariat for Promoting Christian Unity, in developing the Catholic Church's teaching on its relationship with Jewish people. Heschel wanted to make sure the Church formally said that the Jewish people were not responsible for the death of Jesus. Also, Heschel wanted Jews to be seen as a faithful people in their own right and not as subjects for conversion to the Catholic Church. The resulting 1965 document from the Second Vatican Council, *Nostra Aetate*, or *Declaration on the Relation of the Church to Non-Christian Religions*, included these components and officially condemned **anti-Semitism**.

Weeks before Heschel died in 1972 at the age of sixty-five, journalist Carl Stern asked Heschel on the NBC religious television program *The Eternal Light* if he had a message for the youth. This was his response:

> I would say—let them remember that there is a meaning beyond absurdity. Let them be sure that every little deed counts, that every word has power, and that we do—everyone—our share to redeem the world, in spite of all absurdities, and all the frustrations, and all the disappointment. And above all, remember that the meaning of life is to live life as if it were a work of art.

Reading Comprehension

1. What were Rabbi Abraham Joshua Heschel's fundamental teachings?
2. Concerning Catholic-Jewish relations, what were two topics that Heschel wanted the Church to address officially?
3. In what two movements in the United States in the 1950s and 1960s were Abraham Joshua Heschel and Martin Luther King Jr. prophetic voices?

For Reflection

4. Write at least one paragraph in response to Heschel's words to the youth.

---

anti-Semitism Prejudice or hostility toward Jewish people.

Prayer

Traditionally, Jews recite this prayer—Aleinu—at the end of synagogue services. The prayer is believed to have been recited by Joshua after the death of Moses and prior to the entrance of the Israelites into the Promised Land.

It is our duty to praise the Master of all,
  to acclaim the greatness of the One who forms all creation.
For God did not make us like the nations of other lands,
  and did not make us the same as other families of the Earth.
God did not place us in the same situations as others,
  and our destiny is not the same as anyone else's.
And we bend our knees, and bow down, and give thanks,
  before the King, the King of Kings, the Holy One, Blessed is God.
The One who spread out the heavens, and made the foundations of the Earth,
  and whose precious dwelling is in the heavens above,
  and whose powerful Presence is in the highest heights.
The Lord is our God, there is none else.
Our God is truth, and nothing else compares.
As it is written in Your Torah:
  "And you shall know today, and take to heart,
  that the Lord is the only God,
  in the heavens above and on Earth below.
  There is no other."

3

CHRISTIANITY

Introduction

FOLLOWERS OF THE NAZARENE

The history of Christianity is rich and diverse. From its inception approximately two thousand years ago as a small Jewish sect to its present state as the world's largest religious tradition, Christianity has a history full of saints and sinners, expansion and division, music, art, and wars.

Witness the diversity of Christian ecclesial communities on Sunday morning television. As you surf the channels, you cannot help but see the differences. There are evangelists exhorting people to "receive Jesus into your hearts." Gospel choirs are singing in full voice. You may see a Christian preacher in a Jewish *tallit* and *kippah*. There is usually a Catholic Mass.

This chapter examines the various branches of Christianity, beginning with a brief overview of the history of the religion from its beginnings as part of Judaism to its expansion and splintering into various denominations. For all Christians, Jesus of Nazareth is the central figure of their faith. Through his Life, Death, and Resurrection, as recorded in the Christian Bible, Christians find meaning in their own lives and instruction on how to live. Major Christian feasts commemorate important events in the life of Jesus and the lives of his followers. These holy days are celebrated in both church and home, although the physical church building is considered the more sacred space.

Church is defined as both a people and a location; Christians define themselves by what they believe. Christianity has many **doctrines**—traditions and beliefs vary widely from denomination to denomination. Yet there is a set of

---

doctrines Principles, beliefs, and teachings of a religion.

From 1947 to 2005, Christian evangelist Billy Graham transitioned from preaching in smaller tent revival meetings to evangelizing thousands in stadiums around the world. His sermons were broadcast on the radio and on television.

core beliefs that almost every Christian can accept. For example, Christians believe Jesus is Lord of all and has risen from the dead. Christians also believe and follow the Great Commandment of love: to give full love and commitment to God and neighbor.

SECTION *Assessment*

Reading Comprehension

1. How do Christians find meaning in their own lives and instruction in how to live?
2. In what two ways is *church* defined?

For Reflection

3. Why might it be valuable to study Christianity in this course as an outsider who is not a Christian?

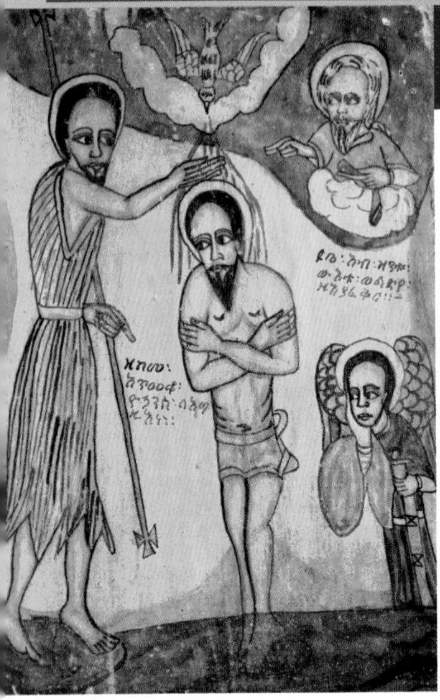

Section 1

A BRIEF HISTORY OF CHRISTIANITY

Most of what we know about the beginning of Christianity and its early years comes from sources written by followers of Jesus of Nazareth. These writings are both historical statements and theological interpretations of the actions and words of Jesus.

Jesus of Nazareth

The history of Christianity begins with Jesus of Nazareth. Stories of the birth of Jesus are recorded in the Gospels of Matthew and Luke. A point of agreement between the two accounts is that the birth of Jesus was in fulfillment of Jewish prophecy found in the Hebrew Bible. According to both Gospels, Mary, the virgin mother of Jesus, conceived him by the power of the Holy Spirit. According to historical records, Jesus was born around 4 BCE, shortly before the death of Herod the Great. Little is known about the childhood of Jesus other than that his family settled in Nazareth in Galilee. Joseph, from the lineage of King David, was a carpenter, so Jesus likely took up the same trade.

Jesus' baptism in the Jordan River by a Jewish baptizer named John inaugurated his public ministry. John's was a baptism of repentance and preparation for the long-awaited Jewish Messiah ("Anointed One"). After a period of temptation, Jesus returned to the region of Galilee, where he became known as a storyteller and miracle worker. His message included themes of repentance and reconciliation, love and justice.

Doubting Thomas, *1634, by Rembrandt Harmensz van Rijn.*

Jesus taught that the reign of God was at hand. The "Kingdom," as Jesus described it, was not an earthly, political kingdom. Instead, it was a kingdom of justice where the poor would not go empty-handed and the oppressed would be freed. Even more astonishing, prostitutes and tax collectors might enter the Kingdom before the righteous. Jesus also described the Kingdom as both present in the here and now and still to come in the future. Jesus' supernatural actions in the name of the Kingdom included healing, casting out demons, taming nature, and raising the dead to life.

Eventually, as Jesus' followers multiplied, some Jewish leaders and Roman authorities became alarmed. The Jewish leaders accused Jesus of **blasphemy.** He was brought before the Roman prefect, Pontius Pilate, as an insurrectionist. Pilate condemned him to death, and Jesus was tortured and crucified publicly on a Roman cross.

---

blasphemy Any word or deed that defames that which is considered sacred by a group of people. In Christianity, blasphemy is any thought, word, or act that expresses hatred for God, Christ, the Church, saints, or other holy things.

CHRISTIANITY: TIMELINE OF KEY EVENTS

BCE

ca. 4 .... Birth of Jesus

CE

30 .... Jesus is crucified and raised from the dead

50s–60s .... Epistles written by Paul of Tarsus

64 .... Persecution of Christians under Nero

90s .... Last Gospel written

96 .... Domitian persecution of Christians

ca. 150 .... Apostles' Creed written

166 .... Martyrdom of St. Justin

203 .... Martyrdom of Sts. Perpetua and Felicity

251 .... Birth of St. Anthony of Egypt

ca. 260 .... Birth of Eusebius of Caesarea

ca. 272 .... Birth of Constantine the Great

313 .... Edict of Milan

325 .... First Council of Nicaea

330 .... Constantine moves capital of Roman Empire to Byzantium

380 .... Christianity made official state religion by Theodosius I

381 .... First Council of Constantinople; completion of the Nicene Creed

431 .... Council of Ephesus

451 .... Council of Chalcedon

ca. 530	*Rule of Saint Benedict* written
1054	Great Schism
1075–1122	Investiture Controversy
1099	First Crusade captures Jerusalem from Muslims
1204	Western Christian crusaders take Constantinople
1377	Avignon Papacy ends
1483	Birth of Martin Luther
1484	Birth of Ulrich Zwingli
1509	Birth of John Calvin
1517	Luther posts his *Ninety-Five Theses* at Wittenberg
1534	King Henry VIII's Act of Supremacy
1563	Council of Trent ends
1720s	Methodist movement begins
1898	Birth of C. S. Lewis
1910–1915	Publication of *The Fundamentals*
1948	Establishment of World Council of Churches
1965	Second Vatican Council closes
1991	Orthodox Christianity restored in Russia
2008	Conservative Anglicans announce split from liberal Anglicans
2013	Pope Francis, an Argentinian, becomes first non-European pope in modern times

However, Jesus' story did not end there. Three days later, his followers found an empty tomb. Several of his followers, including Mary Magdalene and many of his **Apostles**, were visited by the Risen Jesus in the following days and weeks. This was more than resuscitation: Jesus transcended mortality. This was Resurrection. Their experiences of the Risen Jesus changed the lives of Jesus' followers forever. Those who had abandoned Jesus at the Cross were now willing to die horrible deaths for their convictions. Though hard to explain in human terms, something profound happened that first Easter morning that dramatically and forever changed the lives of rugged men and some women as well. Experiencing Jesus' Resurrection made his divinity and mission clear to his followers.

The Early Church

Forty days after his Resurrection, some of Jesus' disciples witnessed his return to heaven. Subsequently, they returned to Jerusalem for the Jewish spring harvest festival of Shavuot. As the disciples hid in an upper room for fear that the same people who had arrested and crucified Jesus would come for them, they experienced a phenomenon that they interpreted as the coming of the Holy Spirit. At this, the disciples lost all fear and went out into the streets of Jerusalem to preach. In their preaching, likely in Greek or Aramaic, Jews from the Diaspora heard, in their own languages, about Jesus for the first time. Several Jews became

The descent of the Holy Spirit at Pentecost, as described in Acts 2.

Apostles A term meaning "ones who have been sent"; originally, the twelve men whom Jesus chose to help him in his earthly ministry. The successors of the twelve Apostles are the bishops of the Catholic Church.

followers of Jesus on that day, known as Pentecost because it came fifty days after Passover. Pentecost has become known as the "birthday of the Church."

Christians believe that God made a new covenant through Jesus Christ in which the Church became the New Israel. Jerusalem became the first center of Christianity. From there, missionaries went to other places in Palestine, including the region of Samaria. They quickly moved beyond Palestine to other cities with Jewish populations, such as Antioch, Alexandria, and Rome. It was in Antioch that the followers of Jesus first became known as "Christians." In their view, they were not starting a new religious tradition. Rather, they saw the coming of Jesus as the fulfillment of God's promise to send a messiah to the Jewish people.

The spread of Christianity drew opposition from both Jews and Romans. Preaching about a Jewish messiah in a synagogue evoked a spectrum of responses—from acceptance to polite disagreement to outright hostility. Paul of Tarsus was initially a Pharisaic Jew who persecuted Christians. After a conversion experience on his way to Damascus, St. Paul helped found Christian communities in Asia Minor and Greece. He wrote letters called *epistles* to the fledgling communities to encourage their new life in Christ. Internal dissension was prevalent. One matter early Christians had to settle was which Jewish laws **Gentile** converts were required to follow. Eventually, a **council** in Jerusalem decided that Gentile Christians would not have to follow all the Mosaic Law. The council made the following decision:

Jesus as the Good Shepherd, from the early Christian catacombs in Rome, Italy, in the third century.

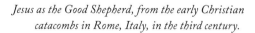

Gentile A person who is not of Jewish origin.

council The gathering of all bishops in the world in their exercise of authority over the universal Church. The pope usually calls a council.

> It is the decision of the holy Spirit and of us not to place on you any burden beyond these necessities, namely, to abstain from meat sacrificed to idols, from blood, from meats of strangled animals, and from unlawful marriage. If you keep free of these, you will be doing what is right. (Acts 15:28–29, NABRE)

As Christianity spread, it quickly became more a Gentile religious tradition than a Jewish one, though the Hebrew Scriptures and Jewish worship forms were maintained. As more Gentiles became Christian, it became less likely for Jews to convert to Christianity. By the middle of the second century, distinctions between Judaism and Christianity were clear.

Roman leaders decreed that Christianity was illegal throughout much of the religion's first three centuries. With such laws, many Christians were targets of various forms of persecution. The city of Rome was the most notorious in its persecution of Christians. Many Christians welcomed their fate, for their persecutions were opportunities to suffer for and witness their love of Jesus. Those who died for their faith were called **martyrs**. Some notable early Christian martyrs were Sts. Ignatius of Antioch, Polycarp of Smyrna, and Justin Martyr. The burial places of martyrs became destinations of Christian pilgrimage in the second and third centuries.

Things changed for Christians when the Roman emperor Constantine proclaimed in his Edict of Milan (313 CE) the official toleration of all religious traditions, including Christianity. Constantine was reportedly baptized a Christian on his deathbed. Emperor Theodosius I (347–395) made Christianity the Roman Empire's official religion in 380 CE.

Legalized Christianity

As the persecutions ceased, Christians organized themselves around bishops—successors of the Apostles—as leaders. Questions of Christian identity arose. Unlike Jews, who were identified by birth or by conversion, Christians were defined by a choice to profess belief, making self-definition ambiguous. Christians needed to delineate their beliefs. A central issue was to express a unified understanding of Jesus, the God Jesus called Father, and the Holy Spirit

---

martyrs Witnesses to the truth of faith who endure even death to be faithful to their beliefs.

The Holy Trinity, from a fifteenth-century Book of Hours.

he sent. Another issue involved the relationship between Jesus' divinity and his humanity.

Several Church councils gathered (for the most part, at the order of the Byzantine emperor in Constantinople) between 325 and 451 CE to address the nature of God and the nature of Jesus. The Nicene Creed, concerning Jesus' relationship with the Father and the Holy Spirit, was composed at the First Council of Nicaea (325) and the First Council of Constantinople (381). The Nicene Creed spells out what Christians believe about the nature of God. The doctrine of the Trinity states that God is Three Divine Persons in one substance: Father, Son, and Holy Spirit. The Council of Ephesus (431) declared that Mary was indeed the human mother of Jesus as well as the Mother of God, while the Council of Chalcedon (451) declared Jesus to be fully human and fully divine. Belief in these doctrines came to define a person as a true Christian.

As Christianity became more accepted, some men and women withdrew into the desert for an austere life of prayer and solitude. The word *monk* comes from the Greek word *monos*, meaning "alone," and began to be used to describe some of these men. Athanasius of Alexandria (ca. 296–373 CE), an important figure at the First Council of Nicaea, wrote a biography of the hermit Anthony of Egypt (251–356) that was widely read in both Greek and Latin. Anthony later became known as the "father of monasticism." Less austere but no less dedicated, Benedict of Nursia (480–ca. 547), the founder of the monastery at Monte Cassino, Italy, wrote a "rule" for his monks that became the foundation for Western Christian monasticism throughout the centuries. Later known as the *Rule of Saint Benedict*, it emphasized a balanced life of prayer, work, and study.

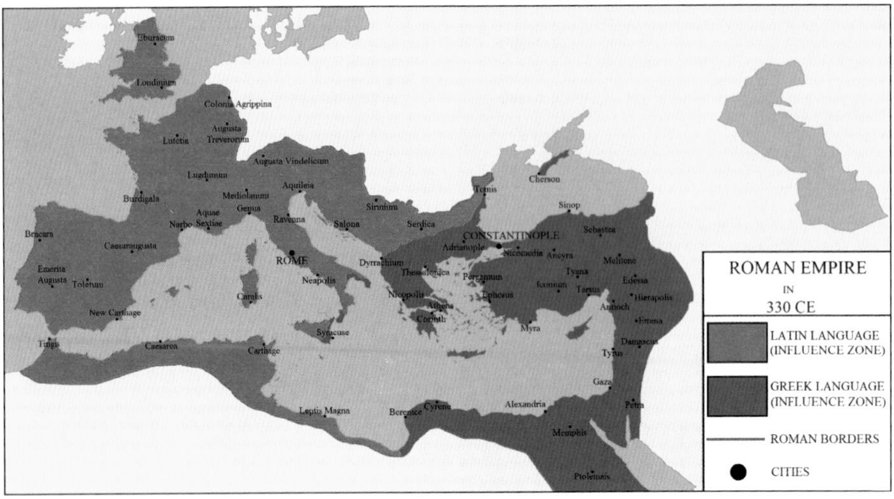

Growing Divisions

Constantine's decision to move the capital of the Roman Empire to Byzantium (renamed Constantinople) in Asia Minor in 330 gave the empire two political centers, exacerbating the existing differences between the Greek-speaking East and the Latin-speaking West. Christianity too was affected by this division. The Church became more easily separated into the Roman Church in the West and the Eastern Church in the Byzantine East. Differences in language, culture, music, art, architecture, government, and ritual between Christianity's eastern and western wings became increasingly pronounced.

The Council of Chalcedon established five major centers of Christianity. These **patriarchates** were Constantinople, Antioch, Alexandria, and Jerusalem in the East, and Rome in the West. Each center developed autonomously. The leaders of these Christian centers, called *patriarchs*, made up a loose confederation of equals. As the Roman emperor *decreased* in power, the patriarch or bishop of Rome *increased* in his own esteem. Believing that Rome was the burial place of Peter, the person on whom Jesus built his Church (see Matthew 16:18), the bishop of Rome claimed primacy over the other patriarchs. The

---

patriarchates The offices and jurisdictions of high-ranking bishops called patriarchs with authority over the other bishops within their territories. The five ancient patriarchates were Rome (which after 1054 became the only Western see) and Constantinople, Alexandria, Antioch, and Jerusalem (which became Eastern Orthodox sees).

Eastern patriarchs agreed to give respect to the point of "first among equals" to the bishop of Rome, but they disagreed that he should have primacy over them. The patriarch of Constantinople believed that his city was the New Rome because it was the seat of the emperor, though he did not believe that he had more authority than the other patriarchs.

As the Western Roman Empire collapsed in the fifth century, Germanic tribes moved toward Rome in great numbers. With no strong political leader in Rome, the bishop of Rome, called the *pope,* took on some of the temporal leadership. Many conversions to Christianity took place within these tribes. Often, the tribal leader's conversion meant the conversion of the entire tribe, as with the Frankish leader Clovis in 496. The more conversions, the stronger the Western Church became as an institution. On Christmas Day in the year 800, Pope Leo III crowned Charlemagne emperor of the newly established Holy Roman Empire.

Charlemagne (748–814), King of the Franks, King of the Lombards, Emperor of the Romans.

In the seventh and eighth centuries, Muslims, adherents of the new religious tradition called Islam, began conquering the Byzantine Empire, starting with Egypt, Syria, and Palestine. Thus, three of the four Eastern patriarchates—Alexandria, Antioch, and Jerusalem—were controlled by Muslims.

As time passed, the tension between the Eastern and Western Churches reached a boiling point. Both the claim of primacy by the bishop of Rome and the crowning of Charlemagne as emperor in the West were challenges to the East. The East's missionary efforts into Slavic lands were significant issues for the West. Other differences—for example, the use of leavened bread for Eucharist in the East and unleavened bread for Eucharist in the West, the ordination of married men in the East, and disparities in Lenten observances—compounded

Michael I Cerularius, Patriarch of Constantinople (left), and Leo IX, Bishop of Rome (right), excommunicated each other from the Church in the Great Schism of 1054. The schism led Christianity to a permanent split into the Catholic Church and the Eastern Orthodox Church.

the problem. Also, a council of Western bishops added *filioque* ("and the Son") to the Nicene Creed ("I believe in the Holy Spirit . . . who proceeds from the Father *and the Son*") without consulting Eastern patriarchs. Not happy with the addition or with having been excluded from the discussion, Eastern patriarchs found the statement heretical. The *filioque* controversy was the final straw. In 1054, the pope and the patriarch of Constantinople excommunicated each other. If that did not seal the split, the destruction of Constantinople by Western Christian crusaders in 1204 did. These events led to what is known as the *Great Schism*.

Though the emperors at the Second Council of Lyon (1274) and the Council of Florence (1431–49) attempted to reconcile East and West, Eastern Church authorities rejected the attempts. The patriarchs, who considered each other (including the pope) equals, could not accept the claim of papal superiority. Eastern Christianity became known as Orthodox Christianity, *orthodox* implying that apostolic teaching was transmitted in a "right" or "straight," traditional manner. The Christians of the East believed their form of Christianity came straight from Jesus and the Apostles.

Crusades A series of military expeditions by Western Christians in the eleventh through thirteenth centuries designed to take the Holy Land back from Muslims.

The Protestant Reformation

In both the East and the West, church-state relations were not always amicable. In the West, a controversy grew over who had the authority to appoint local bishops. Kings felt they had the power to do so, but Church leaders disagreed. By the late eleventh century, the controversy, known as the *Investiture Controversy*, became so great that the German king Henry IV and Pope Gregory VII clashed openly. The pope excommunicated the king. The controversy went on for nearly fifty years, through the reigns of two German kings and several popes. Eventually, the king gave in to the pope's sovereignty as long as the king had the right to approve the pope's choices for bishops.

Church and state and East and West were more likely to cooperate when they had a common enemy, such as Muslim invaders. To counter Muslim incursions, the **Crusades** were launched from Europe in 1095 and initially retook Jerusalem. However, after nearly three centuries of Crusades, Christians were unable to permanently restore Jerusalem to their possession.

In 1076, Pope Gregory VII excommunicated Henry IV, king of Germany, Italy, and Burgundy, and released his subjects from their allegiance. Henry was absolved in 1077.

The Western Church—commonly called the Roman Catholic Church—of the twelfth and thirteenth centuries had many temporal concerns. It exerted great political power, especially through the French pope, Clement V, who took up residence at Avignon, France, where the popes resided between 1309 and 1377. Arguments over who was pope and where the pope should reside, along with pockets of corruption within the institutional Church, all compromised the integrity of the Church but, at the same time, left the door open for reform.

Though there were others before him, the German Augustinian priest and monk Martin Luther (1483–1546) is generally recognized as the catalyst for the

Protestant Reformation. (The root of Protestant is *protest.*) On October 31, 1517, the eve of All Saints, Martin Luther nailed his *Ninety-Five Theses* to a church door in Wittenberg. This action began a serious clash between Luther and Roman Catholic officials. Luther had come to believe that authority within the Catholic Church should lie solely within the Bible and not within Church Tradition or the **Magisterium.** He believed salvation had no connection with a person's actions, only with a person's faith. He also believed in the priesthood of all believers, not just an ordained ministry. With the Bible as his sole source of authority, Luther left the priesthood, was excommunicated by the Church, and began organizing a new Christian denomination that came to be called Lutheran.

Leaders of the Reformation: Jan Hus (Bohemia, top left), Martin Luther (Germany, center), Ulrich Zwingli (Switzerland, top right), Philipp Melanchthon (Germany, bottom left), and John Calvin (France/Switzerland, bottom right).

The Protestant movement spread throughout much of northern Europe and North America. Luther's reform had a dramatic effect on Christians in Germany. Southern Germans tended to remain with the Catholic Church, while northern Germans tended to follow Luther. Following the Lutheran tradition, national churches soon sprang up in the Scandinavian countries of Norway, Finland, Sweden, and Denmark.

Other reformers in the sixteenth century included the French-born John Calvin and the Swiss-born Ulrich Zwingli, who began church reforms of their own in Zürich and Geneva, Switzerland. Along with Luther,

---

Magisterium The official teaching authority of the Church. The Magisterium is the bishops in communion with Peter's successor, the bishop of Rome (the pope).

Calvin and Zwingli retained some Catholic liturgical practices in their churches.

There were some more radical Protestant groups who believed that the reformers had not gone far enough. The Anabaptists and Mennonites abolished most liturgical practices, calling for still simpler forms of worship. They rejected infant baptism, insisting that baptism into Christ was an adult decision. They were also against the establishment of national churches. Starting in the seventeenth century, many Anabaptists and Mennonites, as well as some Puritans, escaped to America because of religious persecution by the more traditional Protestant groups such as the Calvinists and the Lutherans.

Henry VIII, in his quest for a male heir to the throne, had six wives. The marriage to his first wife (Catherine of Aragon) was annulled; his second wife (Anne Boleyn) was executed for treason; his third wife (Jane Seymour) died of childbirth complications; his fourth marriage (to Anne of Cleves) was annulled; his fifth wife (Catherine Howard) was executed for treason; and his sixth wife (Catherine Parr) outlived him.

As the Protestant movement grew, King Henry VIII of England was having his own problems with the Catholic Church. Once named "Defender of the Faith" by the pope, Henry received a papal dispensation to marry his dead brother's widow, Catherine of Aragon. Henry insisted his heir to the throne be male, but Catherine did not bear a son who lived to maturity. Henry petitioned Pope Clement VII to annul the marriage so Henry could marry the young Anne Boleyn. The pope would not grant the king his wish, so Henry countered by declaring himself head of the Catholic Church in England. Anyone who refused to accept his Act of Supremacy was considered a traitor to the throne. The Catholic Church in England declared its independence from papal authority and became a national church, known as the Church of England. Most of England's inhabitants accepted this change because there was little difference in the doctrine or practice of the faith. Initially, the difference came in who was in charge. Members of the Church of England are known as Anglicans, and another term for the faith of the Church of England is Anglicanism.

The English Reformation spread to other parts of the British Empire, each establishing a national church, such as the Church of Scotland and the Church of South Africa; many Anglicans in the United States are known as Episcopalians. The growing confederation of national churches associated with the Church of England is known today as the Anglican Communion.

Though it is difficult to generalize about the more than two thousand Protestant denominations existing today, those Protestant groups that began in the sixteenth century do continue in some broadly held beliefs articulated by Martin Luther. For example, most Protestants hold that salvation is by faith alone, defer authority on matters of faith to what is written in the Bible, and accept just two sacraments, Baptism and Communion.

The Council of Trent

The Council of Trent was presided over by three different popes: Paul III, Julius III, and Pius IV.

In 1545, the Catholic Church called a council to address the issues raised by the Protestant reformers. The decisions made at the Council of Trent (1545–1563) were to have lasting effects within the Roman Catholic Church and on its relationship to Protestant churches for the next four hundred years.

The Council of Trent reiterated Catholic teaching in several doctrinal areas. It reaffirmed papal supremacy. It said that *both* faith and good works are necessary for salvation. It named the Mass as a true sacrifice and reaffirmed (from the Fourth Lateran Council) **transubstantiation**, the doctrine stating how Jesus is truly present in the consecrated bread and wine. It emphasized its teaching that there are seven true sacraments.

Fr. Jacques Marquette, S.J., (1637–1675) was a French Jesuit missionary and explorer who traveled throughout the Great Lakes region—including what is now Michigan, Wisconsin, and Illinois—and down the Mississippi River.

The Modern Period

In the late seventeenth century, a revolution of ideas known as the Enlightenment inaugurated the Modern Period. *Rationalists* stressed the power of human reason. *Empiricists* taught that reality is perceivable only through the five senses. In this period, some Enlightenment views diminished the place of religious expression in people's lives by advocating the belief that people could determine their own destiny and had little need for God. There was a growing movement toward democracy and the separation of church and state.

At the same time, the Modern Period witnessed successes in the missionary efforts of Catholics and Protestants around the world. French Catholics went to North America, Indochina, and Africa. Spanish Catholics went to North and South America. Portuguese Catholics went to Brazil, Africa, China, and India. Dutch Reformers went to Africa and Indonesia. In the late eighteenth and early nineteenth centuries, various other Protestant groups made headway in Asia, Africa, and especially North America (except for Quebec, Canada). Anglicanism spread as the British Empire expanded.

In the East, the czars subordinated the Orthodox Church in Russia. In the early eighteenth century, Czar Peter the Great abolished the Russian patriarchate and had the church administered by the state. Though the

---

transubstantiation What happens at the consecration of the bread and wine at Mass when their entire substance is turned into the Body and Blood of Christ, even though the appearances of bread and wine remain.

Russian czar Peter the Great expanded the country's borders, modernized the army, and introduced Western dress and architecture. Peter is shown here trimming the beard of one of his subjects.

patriarchate was reestablished during the Russian Revolution in the early twentieth century, Communist governments persecuted all forms of religious expression, not only in Russia but wherever they ruled. It was not until the Soviet Union's breakup in 1991 that the Orthodox Church in eastern and central Europe and Russia regained some life.

A bright light within the vast diversity of Christianity is the *ecumenical movement.* This movement attempts to bring about understanding among the various Christian denominations. The World Council of Churches, based in Geneva, was founded in 1948 and presently has more than three hundred member churches from Orthodox and Protestant denominations. The Catholic Church is not a member of the World Council of Churches but does work closely with it. The Catholic Church's Second Vatican Council (1962–1965) also made significant strides in recognizing the validity of the existence of the various religious traditions in the world. The Church exhibited this openness by inviting members of the Eastern Orthodox churches, Anglican Communion, and some Protestant churches to attend the Second Vatican Council as observers.

SECTION *Assessment*

Reading Comprehension

1. What do Christians believe about Jesus of Nazareth?
2. Why is Pentecost significant to Christians?
3. What was the role of St. Paul in the spread of Christianity?

4. How was life different for Christians after the Edict of Milan?
5. Name two important Christian doctrines that were defined at Church councils in the fourth and fifth centuries.
6. Who was Benedict of Nursia?
7. Briefly trace the events that led to the Church's division between East and West.
8. What was the controversial issue between Pope Gregory VII and King Henry IV?
9. What major doctrines and beliefs do most Protestants share?
10. How did Anglicanism begin?
11. How did the Council of Trent respond to the Protestant reformers?

Vocabulary

12. What was the stated purpose of the Christian *Crusades*?

For Reflection

13. What does it mean to say "Jesus was not a Christian"?

Flash Search

14. Why is the Catholic Church not part of the World Council of Churches?

Section 2

SACRED STORIES AND SACRED SCRIPTURES

The Bible (from the Greek word *biblia*, meaning "books") is the collection of sacred Jewish and Christian writings, or Scriptures. The Christian Bible is a book of books. It includes the Hebrew Scriptures used by Jews, more commonly known to Christians as the Old Testament. The New Testament includes the *Gospels*, which are stories of the life of Jesus, and *epistles,* or letters, of the early Christian communities. In addition, one book is a history of the early Church, while the last book is an **apocalypse**. All Christians agree on the twenty-seven books of the New Testament. There are some differences among Protestant, Orthodox, and Catholic Bibles regarding accepted Old Testament books.

There are many important Christian writings outside of Scripture. One explained in this section is *apologetics*, from the Greek for "to speak in defense of." *Apologetics* is a style of writing that defends and explains the Christian faith.

The Christian Bible

The first Christians, who were Jews, already recognized the Hebrew Bible (see Chapter 2) as authoritative. The sacred books written by first-century Christians under divine inspiration came to be called the New Testament. According to the Second Vatican Council document *Dei Verbum*:

> In composing the sacred books, God chose men and while employed by Him they made use of their powers and abilities, so that with Him acting in them and through them, they, as true authors, consigned to writing everything and only those things which He wanted. (11)

The New Testament is a collection of twenty-seven books written in Greek in the first century. All but one author were Jewish: the author of the Gospel of Luke, who also wrote the Acts of the Apostles, was a Gentile. The books fall into four distinct literary genres: four Gospels, one narrative history, twenty-one letters, and one apocalyptic book. The Gospels are the New Testament's preeminent books, for they proclaim Jesus as the Son of God through the narration of his life, ministry, Death, and Resurrection (*CCC*, 139). The Acts of the Apostles is a history of the first Christians and their missionary efforts from Jerusalem to Rome. The epistles are formal letters written by individuals to Christian communities or to other individuals. The Book of

The four evangelists, writers of the Gospels, accompanied by their symbols (clockwise from top right): Matthew, a man; Mark, a lion; Luke, a bull; and John, an eagle.

---

apocalypse A prophetic or symbolic revelation of the end of the world. Several Jewish and Christian texts from around the second century BCE to the second century CE include apocalyptic writing.

Revelation, the last book of the Bible, is a highly symbolic and allegorical account of a vision a man named John of Patmos had of future earthly disasters and God's intervention to set up the reign of heaven on earth.

Several other Christian writings were written as Gospels, epistles, or apocalypses (for example, the Gospel of Thomas and the Apocalypse of Peter). However, these were written in the second or third centuries and were judged by early Church leaders not to meet the criteria to be included in the **canon** of the Bible. Early Christian leaders set up four criteria for a book to be included in the New Testament. A book must be

1. apostolic (attributed to an Apostle or one of his companions);
2. ancient;
3. widely read among the faithful; and
4. a source of the truth of God's Revelation and not **heresy**.

All branches of Christianity agree on what books are authoritative in the New Testament. They disagree on what books are authoritative in the Old Testament. All agree on the thirty-nine books in the Protestant Old Testament. Catholics include seven more books written during the Second Temple period, making the number of authoritative books in the Catholic Old Testament forty-six. Various Eastern Orthodox churches include more than forty-six Old Testament books in their Bibles. Catholics and Orthodox consider these additional Old Testament books to be *deuterocanonical*, meaning "of the second canon." Protestants typically consider any books beyond the agreed-upon thirty-nine books to be *apocryphal*, meaning "dubious" or "of dubious authority." For *ecumenical* discussion, or discussion related to all Christians, some Protestant Bibles include books they deem apocryphal, but they are separated out into their own section.

All Christians agree that the Bible is the inspired Word of God. However, while there is a consensus among Christians regarding the content of the Bible, this is not true about interpretation. Catholics, Eastern Orthodox,

---

canon An authoritative list of books accepted as Sacred Scripture. For Catholics, this is the twenty-seven New Testament books and forty-six Old Testament books that are accepted as inspired by the Church.

heresy For Christians, an obstinate denial after Baptism to believe a truth that must be believed with divine faith, or an obstinate doubt about such truth.

Among the deutercanonical books/books of the apocrypha are First and Second Maccabees, which tell the story of the attempted suppression of Judaism in Palestine in the second century BCE.

and Anglicans believe the Bible contains no errors regarding salvation but may include inaccuracies with respect to secular matters such as history and science. Many more Protestants believe that the Bible is the *literal* Word of God, who dictated it word for word in the native languages of the various writers over the centuries. For them, the Bible errs neither in spiritual nor in secular matters because God does not err.

Christians use the Bible in both public and private settings. Individuals may read the Bible as part of their prayer life. The Bible is often used as part of family devotions or Bible study groups. All Christians use the Bible in their worship services. Good homilies and sermons delivered by church ministers, ordained or not, have the potential to bring the power, nourishment, and support of the Word of God to all who hear it.

Apologetics

The second century saw a rise in Christian *apologetics*, a style of writing that defends and explains the Christian faith. The intended audience of apologetic writings is Christians, for the contents are meant to be tools Christians can use to explain and defend their faith in a world that does not always understand them. Influenced by Greek philosophical writings, early Christian apologists tended to appeal to a person's intellect in explaining and defending Christianity to Latin-speaking and Greek-speaking *polytheists* (believers in more than one god).

The best-known apologist of the second century was Justin Martyr. After calling himself a "disciple of Plato," he converted to Christianity and wrote numerous treatises on the faith. In his writings, Justin defended Christianity as a legitimate religious tradition and lifestyle in the wider pagan world. He was martyred for his Christian faith around 165 CE.

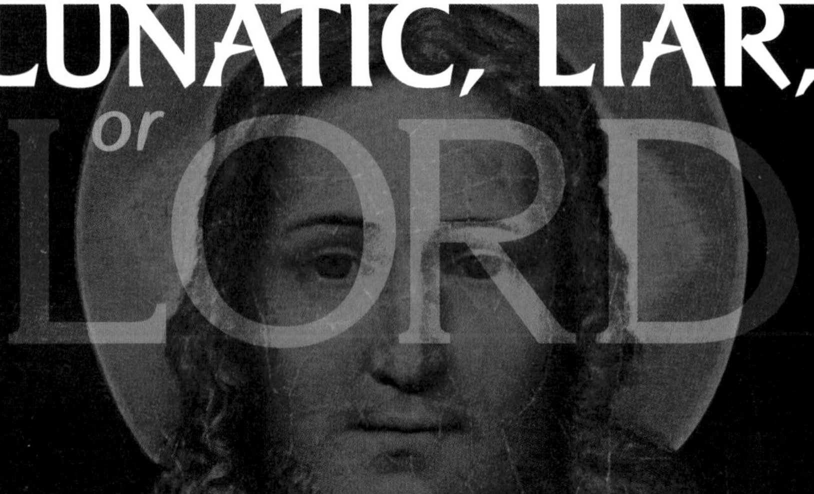

LUNATIC, LIAR, or LORD

The British writer C. S. Lewis (1898–1963) is known as a twentieth-century Christian apologist. In his book *Mere Christianity*, he included what is known as a trilemma of three possibilities regarding Jesus' identity to help people understand and form their own beliefs:

> I am trying here to prevent anyone saying the foolish thing that people often say about Him: I'm ready to accept Jesus as a great moral teacher, but I don't accept his claim to be God. That is the one thing we must not say. A man who was merely a man and said the sort of things Jesus said would not be a great moral teacher. He would either be a lunatic—on the level with the man who says he is a poached egg—or else he would be the Devil of Hell. You must make your choice. Either this man was, and is, the Son of God, or else a madman or something worse. You can shut him up for a fool, you can spit at him and kill him as a demon, or you can fall at his feet and call him Lord and God, but let us not come with any patronizing nonsense about his being a great human teacher. He has not left that open to us. He did not intend to. . . . Now it seems to me obvious that He was neither a lunatic nor a fiend: and consequently, however strange or terrifying or unlikely it may seem, I have to accept the view that He was and is God. (bk. II, chap. 3)

Another early author of apologetic literature was Irenaeus of Lyon. In 180 CE, he wrote *Against Heresies*, a treatise against Gnostic teachings. **Gnosticism** tended toward elitism, for its adherents set themselves up as purer than the Apostles because they possessed secret spiritual knowledge necessary for salvation.

SECTION *Assessment*

Reading Comprehension

1. Name the four literary genres represented in the New Testament.
2. How do the various Christian branches differ in their understanding of the Word of God?
3. List two ways in which Christians use the Bible in their lives.
4. What are the intentions of apologetic writings?

For Reflection

5. What do you think Church Father St. Jerome means when he writes, "Ignorance of Scripture is ignorance of Christ"? Turning the quote around, how would "Knowledge of the Bible is knowledge of Christ" be manifested in daily life?
6. What is your reaction to C. S. Lewis's trilemma quote?

Flash Search

7. What are some Jewish and Christian apocalyptic writings dating from between 200 BCE and 200 CE?
8. What is the oldest Bible in the world?

Gnosticism From the Greek word for knowledge; it is one of the earliest Christian heresies. It stressed the importance of secret knowledge passed on to a select few. It denied the goodness of creation and the material world.

Section 3
BELIEFS AND PRACTICES

For all Christians, Jesus is the central figure. He is the Son of God. The importance of his Life, Death, and Resurrection is not questioned. Many Christians articulate their beliefs in creeds. The *Apostles' Creed*, formulated about 150, is the most widely used among Christians. The Apostles did not write it, but it does articulate what the Apostles passed on:

> I believe in God, the Father Almighty, Creator of heaven and earth, and in Jesus Christ, his only Son, our Lord, who was conceived by the Holy Spirit, born of the Virgin Mary, suffered under Pontius Pilate, was crucified, died, and was buried; he descended into hell; on the third day, he arose again from the dead; he ascended into heaven and is seated at the right hand of God the Father Almighty; from there he will come to judge the living and the dead. I believe in the Holy Spirit, the holy catholic church, the communion of saints, the forgiveness of sins, the resurrection of the body, and life everlasting.

The *Nicene Creed*, formulated by bishops who attended the First Council of Nicaea in 325, is often recited at a Sunday worship service. It is longer than but similar to the Apostles' Creed in that it begins with a statement of belief in God the Father, followed by beliefs about Jesus, the Holy Spirit, and the Church. An explanation of some of the most prominent Christian beliefs and actions follows.

Blessed Trinity

The very complicated doctrine of the Trinity is an expression of how the first Christians experienced God through being in the presence of Jesus. They experienced God as Father, Son, and Holy Spirit, who are each fully God yet three distinct Persons of the same God. Another way to put it is that the Trinity, or the Triune God, is one essence in three Persons. Or, they are three distinct Persons in one substance.

Jesus

Jesus is the Second Person of the Trinity, making him God. According to the doctrine of the Incarnation, God became flesh in the person of Jesus. Christians state this in terms of the two natures of Jesus: fully human and fully divine. God became human so that human beings could share in God's divinity. Jesus was like all humans in everything but sin.

"The shepherds said to one another, 'Let us go, then, to Bethlehem to see this thing that has taken place, which the Lord has made known to us.' So they went in haste and found Mary and Joseph, and the infant lying in the manger" (Lk 2:15–16, NABRE).

Sin

An insight about sin helps to explain why Christians profess their need for Jesus. *Sin* is defined as an offense against God. For Christians, Adam and Eve were the first sinners. God commanded them not to eat from the tree of the knowledge of good and evil, but Adam and Eve disobeyed. Thus, the first sin was the sin of disobedience. Christians believe that the sin of Adam caused the loss of heaven for humankind and that this sin—known as the **Original Sin**—became a part of the human condition. Original Sin is removed in Christian baptism, though humans' propensity to commit actual sins remains.

Original Sin Adam and Eve's first sin of disobedience; also, the condition of sinfulness, resulting from Adam and Eve's sin, into which all humans are born.

"The woman saw that the tree was good for food and pleasing to the eyes, and the tree was desirable for gaining wisdom. So she took some of its fruit and ate it; and she also gave some to her husband, who was with her, and he ate it" (Gn 3:6, NABRE).

It must be noted that the doctrine of Original Sin is a tenet within Western Christianity only. Eastern Orthodox Christians believe that humanity bears the consequences of the sin of Adam and Eve but that humanity is not burdened with the guilt of that sin.

Salvation

God chose to redeem all humanity through Jesus. Though people sin, they can be reconciled to God. There is nothing more pleasing to God than one who turns away from wrongdoing and returns to God. There is no sin that God cannot forgive. Though nuanced among various Christians, most Christians believe that those who are baptized, truly follow Jesus and his way of living, and die in good graces are granted salvation. In other words, they are saved from the eternal punishment of sin. When they die, they will be fully united with Jesus in heaven.

Christ with the Cross, *ca. 1587–1596, by El Greco.*

Sr. Norma Pimentel, Executive Director of Catholic Charities of the Rio Grande Valley, Texas, greets asylum seekers from South America. Catholic Charities programs include emergency assistance, counseling, a pregnancy center, military family relief, housing, and homelessness prevention.

Christian Living

The Bible offers instruction on Christian living. Christians follow the Ten Commandments contained in the Old Testament. In answer to a question from a Jewish scholar on which is the greatest commandment, Jesus said, "You shall love the Lord, your God, with all your heart, with all your soul, with all your mind. This is the greatest and the first commandment. The second is like it: You shall love your neighbor as yourself" (Mt 22:37–39, NABRE).

Known as the "Great Commandment," Jesus' reply is the foundation of a Christian life, though Christians have interpreted it differently over the centuries. For example, some Christians believed that to love God, they must destroy what they perceive as God's enemies. Others interpreted loving God as loving all that God created, including imperfect human beings. Some interpreted loving God as abstaining from alcohol, dancing, or card playing. Nevertheless, the Great Commandment to love and the way Christians practice it have attracted many converts to Christianity. "See how the Christians love one another" has been a familiar refrain.

In his Sermon on the Mount in Matthew 5–7, Jesus offered a new interpretation of the Mosaic Law using the formula "You have heard it said . . . but I say to you . . ." Here are some examples from Matthew 5 (NABRE):

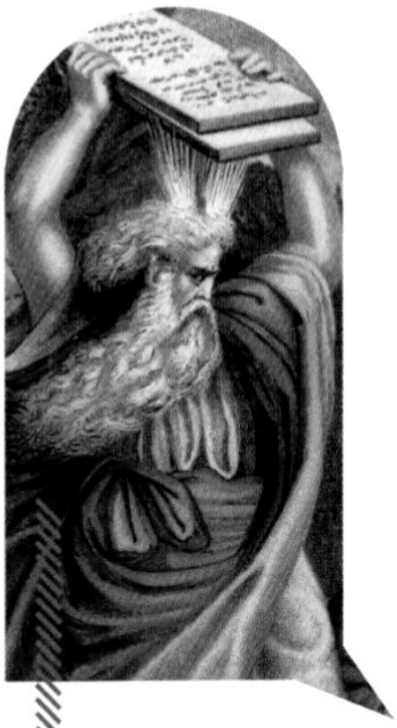

> You have heard that it was said to your ancestors, "You shall not kill; and whoever kills will be liable to judgment." But I say to you, whoever is angry with his brother will be liable to judgment. (21–22)
>
> You have heard that it was said, "You shall not commit adultery." But I say to you, everyone who looks at a woman with lust has already committed adultery with her in his heart. (27–28)
>
> It was also said, "Whoever divorces his wife must give her a bill of divorce." But I say to you, whoever divorces his wife (unless the marriage is unlawful) causes her to commit adultery, and whoever marries a divorced woman commits adultery. (31–32)
>
> You have heard that it was said, "An eye for an eye and a tooth for a tooth." But I say to you, offer no resistance to one who is evil. When someone strikes you on [your] right cheek, turn the other one to him as well. (38–39)
>
> You have heard that it was said, "You shall love your neighbor and hate your enemy." But I say to you, love your enemies, and pray for those who persecute you, that you may be children of your heavenly Father. (43–45)

Jesus states a commandment of the Mosaic Law and then reinterprets it in a more radical, personal manner. For example, according to Jesus, adultery is committed not only by action but by thought, whether one acts upon the thought or not. Not only should one not kill, which is prohibited in most societies, but one should not even be angry with another. Christian living calls people to go beyond the minimum and act as Jesus would act. Jesus not only loved his enemies but was willing to die an ignominious death on the Cross for them. When his enemies mocked and scourged Jesus, he offered no resistance.

For Jesus, the inner thought process is just as important as the exterior action. One's intentional bad thoughts are just as sinful as one's bad actions. To live in God as Jesus did, Christians are to "have the mind of Christ" (1 Cor 2:16, NABRE). In the concrete, Christians have the mind of Christ by performing such actions as loving their enemies; walking beyond the distance asked; and giving strangers coats when they are cold, washing their feet, and serving them with love. When Christians act in this way, they hear their neighbors say, "See how the Christians love one another."

Church

Christians are those who believe in the divinity of Jesus and who accept the Bible without adding or subtracting writings. The Church is a gathering of those who believe, under the guidance of the Holy Spirit, that Jesus is God.

"Church" is the name given to the convocation or assembly of God's people from every corner of the earth. Given the myriad divisions within Christianity, it would seem difficult to speak about one homogeneous group. Nevertheless, Christians proclaim their belief through the creedal formulation that they "believe in one, holy, catholic and apostolic church." It is a universal Church, striving for unity, not uniformity. The New Testament shows that being Church was never conditioned on uniformity.

Sunday morning service at New Bethel Baptist in Detroit, Michigan.

Sunday Mass at the Church of the Blessed Virgin Mary of the Rosary in Vladimir, Russia.

One can hear from time to time in some Protestant churches expressions such as "Isn't that right, church?" or "Let the church say 'Amen!'" As Jews are considered to be Israel in a spiritual sense, Christians would consider themselves spiritually the New Israel. As Jews are bound by a covenant with God established through Moses in the desert, Christians are bound by a new covenant established by Jesus. Christianity does not supersede Judaism. Instead, Christians believe that the coming of Jesus is the fulfillment of God's promise to the Jewish people.

SECTION *Assessment*

Reading Comprehension

1. According to the Apostles' Creed, what do Christians believe about God?
2. List the major Christian beliefs about the Trinity, Jesus, sin, and salvation.

3. Name two different ways Christians have interpreted the Great Commandment.

Vocabulary

4. What do Christians mean by *Original Sin*?

For Reflection

5. Explain the meaning of "church" as if to someone who is not Christian.

Flash Search

6. Who are some Christians who do not believe in evolution? Why don't they believe in it?
7. Explain the difference between "moral living" and "ethical living."

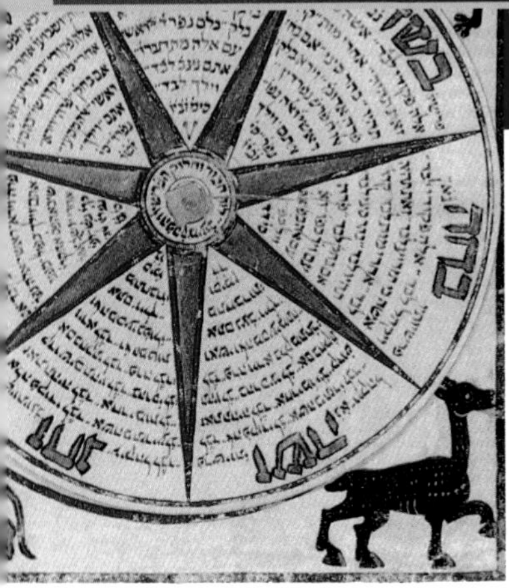

Section 4
SACRED TIME

Like Jews, Christians find that keeping sacred time is essential. The Christian calendar is centered on the life, ministry, Death, and Resurrection of Jesus. Whether celebrated daily, weekly, or annually, these sacred times can sanctify life. Christian festivals and holy days vary widely among the ecclesial communities. Generally, the more formal the worship service of a community, the more festivals and holy days it celebrates.

For all Christians, Sunday is a holy day. As the first Christians were Jewish, they kept Saturday as their weekly day of rest and commemorated Sunday as the Lord's Day. Early Christians associated Sunday with the Resurrection of Jesus, so they celebrated Sunday as a "little Easter." As the Christian population became less Jewish and more Gentile, Sunday became the official Christian day of worship.

All Christians celebrate Christmas and Easter. Many Christians expand their celebration to longer Christmas and Easter cycles. The Christmas cycle includes Advent, Christmas, and Epiphany, while the Easter cycle contains Lent, Easter, and Pentecost. More information on these annual Christian cycles follows.

Christmas Cycle

Advent

The calendars of many Christian communities—Catholic, Anglican, Lutheran, Methodist, and others—begin with the First Sunday of Advent, which falls four Sundays before Christmas. Advent is a season of preparation for the *advent*, or coming, of Jesus at his birth. Eastern Orthodox and Eastern Rite Catholic churches celebrate the "Nativity Fast," a similar season of preparation that begins on November 14, forty days before Christmas.

A suspended Advent wreath in the York Minster, an Anglican church in York, England.

Advent is not only a celebration of the first coming of Jesus more than two thousand years ago but also a preparation time for the coming of Jesus into the hearts of people today and a readying for Jesus' Second Coming at the end of time. In the northern hemisphere, the season of Advent is in the winter, a time when the light of day grows shorter and shorter until the winter solstice around December 21. To symbolize that the coming of Jesus is a light in the darkness, many Christians light candles on an Advent wreath every night during Advent. The wreath is decorated with a circle of evergreens and supports four candles; an additional candle is lit each Sunday and throughout the week of the four weeks in Advent.

Christmas

The Advent season concludes on Christmas Eve. Christmas, the second holiest day of the Christian year, celebrates the birth of Jesus. For most Christians, Christmas Day is December 25, but some Orthodox Christians celebrate it on January 7, the day after Epiphany. The actual date of the birth of Jesus is unknown. In the fourth century, Christians began to celebrate the birth of Jesus (the Son of God) on December 25 to contrast with the pagan celebration of the winter solstice.

Russians celebrate the Feast of the Epiphany every year on January 19 by bathing in ice-cold lakes and rivers to celebrate the baptism of Jesus in the Jordan River.

Epiphany

According to the Western Gregorian calendar, twelve days after Christmas is the Feast of the Epiphany. The word *epiphany* means "manifestation" or "revelation." In the early days of Christianity, Epiphany was associated with three moments in Christ's life in which he first revealed some aspect of himself to the world. Those three moments were his birth, baptism, and first miracle at the marriage feast at Cana. In the fourth century in the West, the birth of Jesus came to overshadow his baptism and first miracle as moments of initial Revelation. Thus, Christmas and Epiphany became two separate feasts in the West, while in most Orthodox churches, the more ancient celebration of Epiphany is maintained.

Easter Cycle

Lent

Easter, the greatest feast in the Christian year, is preceded by forty weekdays of Lenten preparation. The word *Lent* comes from an Old English word

Ash Wednesday at Our Lady of Lourdes Church in Mumbai, India.

for "springtime." The forty days of Lent are in remembrance of Jesus' spending forty days in the wilderness after his baptism. For many Western Christians, Ash Wednesday begins the Lenten season. On this day, a small cross of ashes is applied to the foreheads of the faithful, reminding them that their physical bodies are transitory. During Lent, Western Christians prepare for Easter's great feast by praying, doing penance, giving alms, fasting, and abstaining from other pleasures. Using slightly different calendaring, Orthodox Christians and Eastern Rite Catholics celebrate the Great Fast or Great Lent with practices similar to Lenten disciplines.

The last week of Lent is called Holy Week. This most solemn of weeks begins with Palm Sunday, remembering the occasion of great triumph when Jesus was welcomed into the city of Jerusalem by crowds waving palm branches. Holy Thursday, or Maundy Thursday, commemorates the Last Supper Jesus had with his disciples, at which he gave his disciples the commandment to "love one another . . . as I have loved you" (Jn 13:34, NABRE) and later washed their feet. The word *Maundy* comes from the Latin word meaning "commandment." Good Friday (Great and Holy Friday to the Orthodox) commemorates the Crucifixion and Death of Jesus. Holy Saturday, observed by quiet prayer until evening, remembers the day when Jesus descended to the abode of the dead.

Palm Sunday celebration in Krakow, Poland.

A Greek Orthodox Easter service at Annunciation Cathedral in Chicago, Illinois.

Easter

Easter, which celebrates Christ's Resurrection from the dead, is the holiest day of the year for Christians. It is a movable feast related to the date of the Jewish Passover. Most Christians celebrate it annually on the first Sunday after the first full moon of the vernal equinox.

Liturgical Christian churches such as Catholic, Orthodox, Anglican, and Lutheran churches have an Easter vigil service on Holy Saturday evening. These services recall the darkness of the tomb and Christ's breaking forth from that tomb, bringing light to the world. Several Protestant churches have an Easter sunrise service that begins in the early morning darkness and continues as the sun rises, symbolizing that Jesus is the Son who rose from the dead. Nearly all Christian churches have special Sunday services on Easter Day.

Pentecost

Pentecost means "fiftieth," and for Christians it refers to the fiftieth day after Easter. As described in the Acts of the Apostles, on the first Pentecost after the Resurrection, the Holy Spirit descended on the frightened disciples of Jesus like "tongues as of fire" (Acts 2:3, NABRE). This extraordinary experience enabled the disciples to go out into the streets of Jerusalem and proclaim the Good News of Jesus. Thousands of Jews accepted the Gospel and were baptized on that first Pentecost.

Life-Cycle Celebrations

Celebrations of sacraments are Christian sacred times that are not tied to a natural or liturgical season. A *sacrament* is defined as an "outward and effective sign of the Church given by Christ to give grace." The sacraments are signs authorized by Christ that transmit God's grace to the participant, usually through something tangible like water, bread, wine, or oil. Catholics and Orthodox celebrate seven sacraments: Baptism, Confirmation (Chrismation for the Orthodox), Eucharist, Penance (Confession), Anointing of the Sick (Holy Unction), Holy Orders, and Matrimony (Marriage).

Baptism is the only sacrament recognized by all Christians. Most Christians also acknowledge Eucharist (under various names) as a sacrament. Anglicans and Lutherans recognize Baptism and Holy Communion as sacraments; although they deem the remaining five sacraments not scriptural, they do have sacramental rites for them.

Celebration of baptism in Nyombe, Malawi, Africa.

Baptism is the sacrament that initiates a person into the Christian community. Whether the individual is immersed in a river or pool or sprinkled with water, the priest or minister proclaims the words, "I baptize you in the name of the Father, and of the Son, and of the Holy Spirit." Anglican, Catholic, Orthodox, and some more traditional Protestant groups such as Lutherans and Methodists baptize infants. Other Protestant ecclesial communities have "believer's baptism" in which a person is baptized only when old enough to proclaim a personal belief in Jesus. The Catholic Church recognizes "one baptism for the forgiveness of sins" and accepts as valid baptisms from most other Christian ecclesial communities.

Parishioners at the Cathedral of Saint John the Baptist in San Juan, Puerto Rico.

Eucharist, also known as the Lord's Supper or Holy Communion, fulfills Jesus' Last Supper command to break bread and share wine in memory of him. This sacred meal brings the partakers into communion not only with Jesus but with one another as the "Body of Christ" on earth. Catholics, Orthodox, Anglicans, and some other Protestants believe that Jesus is truly present in some way in the blessed bread and wine.

Prayer

Prayer is another sacred time for Christians. Prayer is a conversation or encounter between God and an individual or a group. Prayer can be formal or informal, long or short, verbal or silent. Prayer can involve singing and different postures and various gestures at different times. A person can pray anytime and anywhere.

The Bible contains many prayers. The Book of Psalms is a prayer book within the Bible. The Lord's Prayer, which Jesus taught to the disciples, is common to all Christians, though the wording may be slightly different:

> Our Father, who art in heaven, hallowed be thy name.
> thy kingdom come, thy will be done
> on earth as it is in heaven.
> Give us this day our daily bread,

and forgive us our trespasses
as we forgive those who trespass against us;

[or
and forgive us our debts
as we forgive our debtors;]
[or
forgive us our sins
as we forgive those who sin against us;]

and lead us not into temptation but deliver us from evil.
For the kingdom, the power, and the glory are yours,
now and forever. Amen.

SECTION *Assessment*

Reading Comprehension

1. Why did the early Christians change their day of worship from Saturday to Sunday?
2. What are the holy days in the Christmas cycle?
3. What are the holy days in the Easter cycle?
4. What are the two sacraments that most Christians celebrate?
5. Name some of the possible characteristics of prayer.

For Reflection

6. How can the Eucharist bring Christians together? How can the Eucharist pull Christians apart?
7. According to the Lord's Prayer, what do Christians believe?

Flash Search

8. Who are Eastern Rite Catholics?
9. Can a person be a Christian without being baptized?

Section 5

SACRED PLACES AND SACRED SPACES

A building called a *church* is the most sacred space for Christians. A church is a space where new members are initiated and significant moments are celebrated. Besides churches, Christians also hold the place on earth where Jesus lived and walked to be sacred. Christians call this area, in the modern-day State of Israel, the "Holy Land."

Church

Besides meaning "a gathering of people," a church is also a building. A church is the most sacred place for Christians. The exterior architecture of a church does not always clearly reveal the ecclesial community. For example, a Gothic-style church might be, among others, Catholic, Anglican, or Presbyterian. An urban storefront church could be Lutheran, Assembly of God, or Catholic.

The inside of a church is more telling. A church with an altar in the middle and a pulpit on the side is likely Catholic, Anglican, Orthodox, or perhaps Lutheran. If there are statues of Jesus, Mary, and the saints, then the church is likely Catholic. If instead of statues there are **icons**, the church is most likely Orthodox or Eastern Rite Catholic. Protestant churches tend to be simpler in ornamentation, some with just a pulpit in the sanctuary or on a stage.

---

icons Traditional religious images or paintings that are especially popular among many Eastern Christians.

Ebenezer Baptist Church in Atlanta, Georgia.

All Christian ecclesial communities would agree that the way they worship God is more critical than where they worship God. In times of war, persecution, or natural disasters, Christians have worshipped in any type of building available or even outside in a meadow, in a forest, on a seashore, or in the desert.

Holy Land

Since Jesus is the central figure in Christianity, the place where Jesus lived, ministered, died, and rose from the dead is sacred to Christians. Most of the Holy Land is in the present-day State of Israel. Bethlehem, where Jesus was born; Nazareth, where he grew up; and the region of Galilee, where he did much of his preaching and healing, are especially sacred. Jerusalem and areas surrounding it are also holy places for a number of reasons. Jesus preached and healed the sick there. Inside the walls of Jerusalem, Jesus was presented in the Temple when he was an infant; it's where he stayed behind at the age of twelve while his family headed back to Nazareth, celebrated Passover, and was tried

Jerusalem Old City.

as a criminal. Outside the walls of Jerusalem, Jesus died, was buried, was resurrected, and ascended to heaven.

SECTION *Assessment*

Reading Comprehension

1. How can the interior design of a church indicate which ecclesial community worships there?
2. Name and explain the significance of several sacred places in the Holy Land.

For Reflection

3. Describe a holy place that fills you with the presence of God.

Flash Search

4. Why are Protestant churches often less formally decorated than Catholic, Orthodox, or Anglican churches?
5. What is the difference between a cathedral and a basilica?

Section 6

CATHOLICS DIALOGUE WITH OTHER CHRISTIANS

The very word *catholic* means "universal" or "for everyone." The Church is catholic in two ways. First, it is catholic because Christ is present in the Church in the fullness of his Body; with the fullness of the means of salvation; with the fullness of faith, sacraments, and the ordained ministry that comes from the Apostles. The Church is also catholic because it takes the message of salvation to all people.

A traditional statement of the **Church Fathers** is that "outside the Church, there is no salvation." A positive way to reformulate the statement is that all people are called to this Church's catholic unity. However, although the Church is for everyone, not everyone belongs to the Church in the same way. There is a specific ordering of people in the Catholic Church: besides behaving lovingly, full members are validly baptized and they embrace the Gospel and all the essential teachings of the Catholic Church. The Catholic Church knows that

Pope Francis and Reverend Martin Junge, general secretary of the Lutheran World Federation, attend an ecumenical prayer service in 2016 to mark the opening of the five hundredth anniversary of the Protestant Reformation.

other Christians, who for various reasons do not profess the Catholic faith in totality or have had their unity under the pope severed, are still joined in many ways with the Catholic Church. Others who have not received the Good News of Jesus Christ are also connected to the Church in various ways.

The Catholic Church desires to recover the gift of the unity of all Christians. Unity is the charge of *ecumenism*, which seeks a visible unity of the Christian faith. Ecumenism is the responsibility of all Catholics. For Catholics to promote Christian unity, they must be committed to the following:

- a permanent renewal of the Church in greater fidelity to its vocation
- a conversion of heart—that is, a commitment to live a holier life
- praying with separated Christians
- growing in the knowledge of other Christians
- understanding the goals of ecumenism
- witnessing and learning from the dialogue between Catholic theologians and theologians of other Christian ecclesial communities
- collaborating in service to all people

The Catholic Church has engaged in official dialogue with several Christian ecclesial communities, including Anglican, Lutheran, and Orthodox Christians. Major topics include Baptism, the Eucharist, episcopacy, papacy, and mixed marriages. A starting point in many of the discussions is Sacred Scripture, since all Christians hold up the importance of God's Word in the life of the Church and world. This issue and some areas for dialogue that it offers are presented in the following subsections.

Book of the Church or Church of the Book?

While Catholics, Anglicans, and Eastern Orthodox understand the Bible as the "Book of the church," other Christian ecclesial communities consider that they belong to a "church of the Book." Catholics believe that the inspired text

---

Church Fathers Church teachers and writers of the early Christian centuries whose teachings are a witness to the Tradition of the Church.

A man lights his Bible with a smartphone during service at the Anglican Church of Redemption in southwest Nigeria.

of the Bible contains the fullness of God's Revelation and equally believe that the Church continues to guide the People of God through its integration and application of the truths of Scripture. Catholic belief is that God continues to guide the successors of the Apostles—the pope and the bishops—in every generation to preserve, expound on, and spread God's Word to all. This ongoing teaching is known as the Church's Tradition. Many Protestant ecclesial communities do not assign equal weight to Scripture and Tradition. For some Christians, the Bible is God's final Revelation to the world; they hold that answers to every human question imaginable can be answered in the pages of Scripture.

Historically speaking, the purpose of advocating *sola scriptura* ("scripture alone") was to limit the authority of the Catholic Church to what was in the Bible. For example, Protestant reformers denied the doctrines of papal primacy and veneration of images because neither was found in the Bible. Yet the Word of God cannot be limited to the printed word. The Word had a long history of oral tradition before it was written down. Reflecting on their experience of the God of history, both the Jewish people before the time of Jesus and the first followers of Jesus reinterpreted and revised the telling of God's actions among them. Note that the oral tradition of the Apostles existed before the first book of the New Testament was ever written down. The many writings of the early Christians of the first century that later became part of the New Testament came out of apostolic Tradition. This oral Tradition is no less the work of the Holy Spirit than is the written Bible.

Many Christians—Catholics included—misunderstand the role of the Bible in the life of the Church. Listening to evangelists on the radio or watching them on television adds to the confusion. Because personal interpretation of Scripture has been discouraged, the Catholic Church until recently did not

Reading the Bible during a service at Iglesia Maranatha in San Francisco, California.

encourage personal reading of the Bible. This attitude toward the Bible led to many Protestants calling Catholics nonbiblical Christians, even though Scripture is proclaimed during every Mass.

The Second Vatican Council document *Dei Verbum* encouraged Catholics to read, study, and pray the Sacred Scriptures. Since then, ecumenical dialogue has broken down many of the barriers established during the Protestant Reformation. Biblical scholars from all branches of Christianity have cooperated in the study of the Bible and published joint Bible translations and commentaries.

Understanding Biblical Inerrancy

Catholics, Orthodox, Anglicans, and some Protestants understand biblical *inerrancy* (freedom from error) quite differently from one another. All agree that there is no error in the Bible concerning those truths necessary for our salvation. For instance, it is necessary for a Christian to affirm that God, and no other god or gods, is the world's Creator.

Some Protestants believe the Bible is *completely* inerrant—that is, free from error not only in the areas of faith and morals but also in history, geography, and science. God's words are very clear to them, so interpretation is not necessary. They look to Scripture for answers to questions that the biblical authors never pondered and for truths that are not necessary for our salvation.

For example, neither how God created the world nor how long it took God to create the world is a truth necessary for our salvation. Similarly, it is unnecessary to know how many angels were at the empty tomb (one in Matthew 28:2, two in John 20:12). What is vital for salvation is faith in the Resurrection of Jesus. The Bible is meant to guide us in faith and morals, not in history, geography, or science. The former are necessary for our salvation, while the latter are not.

Interpreting the Bible

The Catholic Church continues to interpret the meaning of God's Word through the inspiration of the Holy Spirit and through the official teaching office of the Church, the Magisterium. Many Protestants see interpretation as necessary but encourage private and personal interpretation. There is a striking difference between the Catholic Church and most Protestant churches regarding views of who is able to interpret the Bible accurately.

Though Revelation from Sacred Scripture has ceased (no other writings can be added to the Bible), interpretation of God's Revelation has not. For example, there is nothing in the Bible that speaks against one human being enslaving another human being. Through the Holy Spirit, human history has shown us the egregious error of this human institution. Just because it is in the Bible does not mean God approves of human enslavement. The Catholic Church believes that such interpretation must take place under the Church's direction, particularly that of the Magisterium.

The Word of God is transmitted by human language and human history. The words printed in the Bible are not the author's property, limited to the time when they were written; they belong to the living Church, the People of God. One can find great meaning in a passage when one prays and reflects on the passage. The written word cannot be left to itself but must be interpreted with the Holy Spirit's guidance. It is God still speaking to the Church today.

When disputes about faith and morals arise, it is the Magisterium's duty and obligation to interpret, in the light of its long history of apostolic tradition, the writings of the Greek and Latin Fathers of the Church, the ecumenical councils, and the Bible itself. The Magisterium does not see itself as an entity

Movements within Protestantism

The words *fundamentalism*, *Evangelicalism*, and *Pentecostalism* are often used interchangeably in popular culture. However, though related, they are distinct movements within Protestantism.

Christian fundamentalism is a movement begun at the beginning of the twentieth century in the United States. The distribution of a series of pamphlets called *The Fundamentals* advocated returning to what the writers understood as Christianity's basics or fundamentals. Believing Protestantism was becoming too secularized, especially in relation to science, fundamentalists advocated the infallibility of the Bible on matters of history, science, and faith. In other words, fundamentalists held and still hold that everything written in the Bible is to be understood in its most literal sense. For example, God created the world in six twenty-four-hour days of a seven-day week.

The Evangelical megachurch Flatirons Community Church in Lafayette, Colorado, has about 19,000 weekly visitors.

Though related to fundamentalism, Evangelicalism is

Sunday service at Bay Ridge Christian Center Pentecostal Church in Brooklyn, New York.

more moderate. It too is a movement within Protestantism, based mainly in North America and northern Europe. The word *evangelical* comes from the Greek word for "good news." Evangelicalism emphasizes a personal faith in Jesus Christ and the Bible as an individual's sole religious authority. "Witnessing" or sharing faith with others is also vital in this movement. The Evangelical movement often manifests in such events as tent revivals and "crusades" in large public arenas.

Pentecostalism is one form of Evangelicalism. It is a movement that emphasizes the "gifts of the Holy Spirit" as referenced at the first Pentecost and in 1 Corinthians 12. These gifts may include speaking in tongues, healing, holy joy, and holy tears. Pentecostalism exhibits the widest spectrum of doctrinal beliefs and can be found in all branches of Christianity.

Writing Task

Distinguish among *fundamentalism*, *Evangelicalism*, and *Pentecostalism* in one paragraph of three to four sentences.

that opposes personal thinking. Instead, it sees itself as a servant safeguarding Scripture and Tradition from manipulation.

The Magisterium interprets Scripture based not on what the biblical author may have meant when he wrote it but on what a passage means to the Church community of each generation that follows. Some biblical passages may not seem clear to those reading the Bible millennia removed from when it was written. More than one interpretation may be valid if these interpretations are not in conflict with the Church's long Tradition.

SECTION *Assessment*

Reading Comprehension

1. What are the two understandings of inerrancy described in this section?
2. Distinguish between "Book of the church" and "church of the Book."
3. Why does the Catholic Church say that both Scripture and Tradition are sources of authority for Catholics?
4. What is the role of the Magisterium with regard to Scripture?
5. What is meant by *sola scriptura*?

Vocabulary

6. Who were the *Church Fathers*?

For Reflection

7. How many Christian ecclesial communities different from your own can you name?
8. What is one way you have personally experienced the division that exists among Christians of different ecclesial communities?
9. Agree or disagree: The division among Christian groups is a great scandal within Christianity. Explain your answer.

Flash Search

10. How many documents were produced at the Second Vatican Council?

Section Summaries

Introduction: Followers of the Nazarene

Christianity has its roots in Judaism. Christians are followers of Jesus, a first-century Palestinian Jew from a small village called Nazareth. Through the gift of faith, Christians believe that Jesus is not only a historical figure but also the Incarnate God who rose from the dead, Lord of all creation. Jesus gave his followers the Great Commandment to love God and one another.

- Explain in two to three sentences why the following statement is a fallacy: "I am not a Christian. I am a Catholic."

Section 1: A Brief History of Christianity

Jesus of Nazareth is the central figure in Christianity. Since Jesus was a Jew, the first followers of Jesus were Jews. Gentiles quickly grew to be the predominant adherents of Christianity in the Roman Empire. In the early years of the faith, Christians were often persecuted by Roman authorities. After Christianity was legalized, persecutions diminished. Several Church councils of the fourth and fifth centuries defined the major Christian doctrines. Growing divisions between Eastern and Western Christians led to a split between Christians centered in Rome and those centered in Constantinople. The Augustinian priest Martin Luther is credited with initiating the Protestant Reformation. Though late in coming, the Catholic Reformation centered on the teachings of the Council of Trent. The Enlightenment posed a threat to the faith of many Christians because of its emphasis on rationalism and empiricism. At the same time, Christian missionaries brought the faith to people all over the world. The ecumenical movement attempts to emphasize the similarities rather than the differences among ecclesial communities.

- Write a three- to four-paragraph explanation of the term *Christendom* as it refers to Europe's religious, cultural, and political realities in the Middle Ages.

Section 2: Sacred Stories and Sacred Scriptures

The Sacred Scripture used by Christians is the Bible. It is the Word of God, revealing to humankind God's divine plan. The Bible is a "book of books." The Christian Bible draws on its Jewish roots by including the Hebrew Bible. It is the sole source of authority for some Christians, while some ecclesial communities, including Catholics and Orthodox, recognize the authority of both Scripture and Tradition. Not all Christians recognize the same books in the Hebrew Bible as authoritative. While there may be consensus among the various Christian branches concerning the Bible's content, there is wide disagreement about its interpretation. Apologetic writings are those in which Christians explain and defend their faith, and they reflect this diversity of scriptural interpretation.

- All Christians accept the same twenty-seven books in the New Testament as authoritative. Research and list in a graphic design of your choice where Christian ecclesial communities are on the spectrum of which books should be included in the Old Testament.

Section 3: Beliefs and Practices

The most important Christian doctrines are in creedal statements such as the Apostles' Creed and the Nicene Creed. The doctrine of the Trinity—that God, though one, is Three Persons: Father, Son, and Holy Spirit—is central to Christianity. The doctrine of the Incarnation holds that in Jesus, God became human and that Jesus is both fully human and fully divine. Other important doctrines address sin and salvation. The Great Commandment—loving God and loving neighbor—is foundational for Christian living. Church is generally defined as a gathering of those who, under the Holy Spirit's guidance, believe Jesus is God.

- Look up and copy by hand the Athanasian Creed in an artistic style of your choice. Include a one-paragraph summary that explains its origins.

Section 4: Sacred Time

Christians keep Sunday, the day of Jesus' Resurrection, as a day of worship and rest. Many Christians observe the Christmas and Easter cycles of the

Christian liturgical calendar. Sacraments are outward signs of inward spiritual grace. Baptism and Eucharist are two sacraments celebrated by most Christians. Prayer is essential to the Christian life. Prayer is a conversation between an individual and God or between a community and God. The Lord's Prayer is the common prayer among Christians, though with some slight differences in wording.

- Create a color-coded graphic that compares the Catholic liturgical calendar with the Orthodox liturgical calendar.

Section 5: Sacred Places and Sacred Spaces

Exterior church architecture varies widely among churches. Church interiors provide insight into what is important to that worshipping community. Although churches are sacred spaces for Christians, Christians agree that how they worship is more important than where they worship. Places where Jesus carried out his ministry are sacred to Christians. Christians consider the modern-day State of Israel to be the Holy Land.

- Create a digital presentation on one of these holy sites in the Holy Land: Church of the Nativity, Church of the Holy Sepulchre, Golgotha, Capernaum, Nazareth, or the Mount of the Beatitudes. Your presentation should include photos, captions, and Scripture references and have at least five slides.

Section 6: Catholics Dialogue with Other Christians

The purpose of ecumenism is Christian unity. Catholics dialoguing with other Christians about Scripture has had a spectrum of responses from collaboration to nonengagement. While most Protestants believe the Bible is the sole authority for faith and morals, Orthodox and Anglicans join Catholics in believing Scripture and Tradition go hand in hand authoritatively communicating faith and morals. The teaching office of the Catholic Church, the Magisterium, sees itself as obligated to safeguard Scripture and Tradition from being manipulated.

- Research a Christian ecclesial community other than Catholicism. Include in a five-paragraph synopsis information on the community's history, central beliefs, and forms of worship.

Chapter Projects

Complete one of these projects by the conclusion of your study of this chapter.

1. Research Project on *Salvator Mundi*

   Research the painting *Salvator Mundi* (ca. 1500) by Leonardo da Vinci (1452–1519), and write a three-page essay that answers the following questions:

   - Who was Leonardo da Vinci?
   - What does *Salvator Mundi* mean in English?
   - Why do you think this painting is so named?
   - What medium does da Vinci use in this painting?
   - What do you think is the significance of the figure's gesture with his right hand?
   - What is the significance of the colors he is wearing?
   - Why was this artwork an international news story in 2017–2018?
   - Why is this painting a good model for this chapter on Christianity?

2. Examining the Avignon Papacy

   Research the Avignon papacy of the fourteenth century. Write a three-page essay or record a five-minute spoken video presentation that includes answers to the following questions:

   - What prompted popes to move to Avignon from Rome?
   - Why did the popes decide to remain in Avignon for so long?
   - What prompted the popes to move back to Rome?
   - Who were the popes who lived in Avignon?
   - What did the Avignon popes accomplish?

3. Replicating a Specific Christian Cross

   Using the medium of your choice, create a drawing of one of the following Christian crosses: Greek, Coptic, Orthodox, Latin, Franciscan Tau, Methodist, or Celtic. Include in the presentation a history of the cross and an explanation of its symbolism and meaning.

4. Presentation on Christian Symbols

   Create an art notebook or instructional slide presentation that includes all of the following symbols of Christianity: fish, anchor, alpha and omega, Chi-Rho, and the Agnus Dei. Include images of each symbol along with detailed captions with information on their history, meaning, and usage.

5. Song Performance: A Christian Hymn

   There are many hymns all Christians can sing together. Choose one from the following list, and write three to five paragraphs about its composer, history, and themes proclaimed, as well as appropriate settings and/or seasons for singing it. Then produce a solo or group video performance of the song on a platform you can share with your teacher.

   - "Amazing Grace"
   - "How Great Thou Art"
   - "It Is Well with My Soul"
   - "All Creatures of Our God and King"
   - "A Mighty Fortress Is Our God"
   - "Be Thou My Vision"
   - "Holy, Holy, Holy"
   - "Praise to the Lord, the Almighty"
   - "Go Tell It on the Mountain"
   - "Crown Him with Many Crowns"
   - "What a Friend We Have in Jesus"
   - "Joyful, Joyful, We Adore Thee"
   - "How Can I Keep from Singing?"

Key Image

Cross

The cross is the ubiquitous and nearly universal symbol of Christianity. It is found inside and outside places of worship. It can be seen hanging around a person's neck or from the rearview mirror of a car. It is worn in various forms of jewelry or as a tattoo. It is in movies, on television shows, on social media, in plays, in articles, in books . . . You can add to the list.

Unlike so many Christian religious symbols over the centuries that gained prominence and then faded from use, the cross endures. It seems rather odd that an instrument of torture, shame, and death remains the premier symbol of Christianity.

In the first few centuries of Christianity, the cross was not the great symbol it is today. Ancient graffiti has been found that ridiculed Christians, seemingly for allegedly worshipping the cross as an idol. It was dangerous to publicly display the cross before Constantine the Great (ca. 272–337 CE) had a wondrous vision of a cross of light in the sky with the inscription "In this sign, you will conquer" before his great battle at the Milvian Bridge near Rome in 312. Constantine embraced Christianity, and it became the favored religion of the Roman Empire.

It was not until around the sixth century that artists put a body on the cross. Even then, it was not a realistic portrayal of suffering and death. Though all the marks of crucifixion were present, the eyes of the serene Jesus were open and looking straight ahead. This was a reminder that Jesus was not dead and buried but resurrected and alive.

Other styles of crosses emerged in the early centuries of Christianity. Out of Egypt, the Coptic Christian cross developed as a fusion of a bare cross and the Egyptian hieroglyph *ankh*, meaning "life." The Celtic cross from the British Isles combined the plain cross with the pagan solar symbol of a cross within a circle.

It was not until around the ninth century that Christian art displayed a realistic depiction of a crucifixion. Common themes were Jesus crucified between the two thieves and Jesus crucified with his mother and the beloved disciple at the foot of the Cross.

Early in their history, Christians in Jerusalem began to celebrate the Feast of the Holy Cross, or the Feast of the Exaltation of the Holy Cross, to commemorate their salvation from sin and death through God's unconditional love. By the seventh century, that feast was celebrated in Rome. Early in the Medieval Period, Christians in Jerusalem began adding the ritual of venerating the cross to the Good Friday liturgy. By the eighth century, that movement found its way to Rome.

With the Protestant Reformation, the use of the cross as a symbol waned. Though many Lutheran communities kept the cross in processions and as decoration, most Protestant groups eliminated it altogether. If a cross was used, it was a plain one, for they eschewed artistic religious expression. However, the twentieth century saw a gradual return to religious art in Protestant churches. Especially toward the middle of the century, some more traditional Protestant ecclesial communities such as the Lutherans, Methodists, and Presbyterians undertook liturgical reforms that included using crosses to enhance religious services.

The cross has positive meanings, such as love, reconciliation, and redemption. Nevertheless, some Christians have misappropriated the symbol for malicious ends. In the Middle Ages, for example, Christian individuals and groups increasingly used the cross to pressure Jewish people to convert to Christianity. The pressure at times escalated to violence and sometimes even death. The cross was also a prominent symbol of the Western Christian crusaders. (The word *crusade* comes from the Latin word for *cross*.) With the cross prominently displayed on the armor of each crusader, the first Crusades devastated Jewish communities on their way to free Jerusalem from Muslim rule by means of a bloodbath.

White supremacist groups have misappropriated the symbol of the cross. For example, in the first half of the twentieth century, members of the Ku Klux Klan set out to terrorize people they did not like. They set ablaze tall crosses on lawns of Blacks, Catholics, and Jews, among others. To this day, some white supremacists still use the cross to promote their system of beliefs.

Through the retelling of the Crucifixion of Jesus, the cross is a dominant subject in the New Testament. The authors of the New Testament help us assign meaning to the cross. In the Gospel of John, the evangelist draws an analogy between Moses lifting up the bronze serpent attached to a pole (see Numbers 21:4–9) and Jesus being lifted up attached to a cross (see John 3:14). Those bitten by a serpent are to look upon the bronze serpent in order to be healed from the snake venom. In like manner, those who look upon Jesus on the Cross will be healed of sin's ravages. For John, the lifting up of Jesus upon an instrument of death is not the demise of Jesus but his Glorification. Jesus is exalted as the Son of God, not despised as a criminal of the state.

St. Paul also wrote about the cross in some of his epistles. For Christians, the Cross of Jesus Christ is always something about which to boast, not to be ashamed, for the instrument of torture and death was transformed into an instrument of victory over sin and death, and salvation for all (see 2 Corinthians 13:4; Galatians 2:20, 6:14). Through the salvific sacrifice of Jesus' Death on a cross, God's steadfast, unconditional love was revealed.

Christians believe in a mandate to take up one's cross and follow Jesus (see Matthew 10:38, 16:24; Mark 8:34; Luke 9:23, 14:27). What does it mean for a Christian "take up his or her own cross"? A classic story illustrates:

> People complained to God that the cross each was bearing was too heavy and burdensome. So God told everyone to gather in a giant circle and place their crosses in the center of the circle. Once all piled their crosses in the circle, God instructed everyone to test every cross until they found one that was the best fit. Unsurprisingly, everyone ended up with their cross.

Faithful Adherents

Perpetua and Felicity: Young Mothers of Faith

> There were then apprehended the young catechumens, Revocatus and Felicity, his fellow servant, Saturninus, and Secundus. With them also was Vibia Perpetua, nobly born, reared liberally, wedded honorably, having a father and mother and two brothers, one of them

a catechumen likewise, and a son, a child at the breast; and she was about twenty-two years of age. What follows here shall she tell herself; the whole order of her martyrdom as she left it written with her hand and in her own words.

Mary and the Christ Child with Sts. Felicity and Perpetua.

That which was "written with her hand" came to be known as *The Passion of Saints Perpetua and Felicity*. This ancient journal's unknown redactor briefly notes her familial circumstances in the above paragraph and explains that Vibia Perpetua is the author. It was most unusual for a woman at the beginning of the third century to be well enough educated to read and write. It is also noteworthy that all five apprehended were indeed **catechumens**, not yet in full communion with the Christian community. Perpetua writes that these five were taken into house arrest, where a few days later they were baptized. Soon after, they were moved to a dungeonlike prison.

The purpose of their arrest? They were apprehended not because they were Christians but because they were *converting* to Christianity. They were residents of the North African city of Carthage, an important city of the Roman Empire, in what is now Tunisia. The Roman emperor at the time was Septimius Severus. Realizing that it was futile to try to stop Jews and Christians from practicing their religious traditions, he instead outlawed conversion to Judaism and Christianity. Jews and Christians were both subject to suspicion and, at times, persecution. These religious traditions were under suspicion because they seemed to be exclusive groups, often gathering in homes. They worshipped one God only, and that God required a very high standard of moral living.

Perpetua starts her journal with the arrest and progresses to her imprisonment, trial, impending execution, and visions. She writes with great love and heartbreak about her pagan father, who tried several times to persuade her to recant her religious convictions. Perpetua also relates a vision she has of a brother who died at seven and tells about her infant son, who was nursing at the time of her arrest.

There were a couple of deacons who would visit the prisoners, providing food and water and bringing Perpetua her infant to be nursed. She was distraught when her son was away and joyful when he was with her. When condemned to death, she asked that her child be brought to her, but her father refused. Perpetua saw God acting in her life when at the time she was no longer permitted to nurse her son, her son no longer needed nursing.

Eight months pregnant when arrested with the others, Felicity was a mother-to-be. She and her companions did not want Felicity to be left behind and have to face execution later without them, so they prayed earnestly to God. Three days before they were to enter the arena in Carthage, Felicity "was delivered of a daughter, whom a sister reared up to be her own daughter." This meant that she could be with her companions when she died.

The execution of Perpetua and her companions was part of a full day of entertainment celebrating the birthday of the emperor's son Geta. (At this point, Perpetua handed her journal to someone else.) Joining them in the arena was a lion, a bear, a leopard, and a savage cow. Their encounters with the animals severely maimed most of the future martyrs, but none died. It was up to the executioners with swords to complete the task.

> They rose of themselves and moved, whither the people willed them, first kissing one another, that they might accomplish their martyrdom with the rites of peace.

The martyrdom of Perpetua, Felicity, and their companions took place around 203 CE. The redactor of *The Passion of Saints Perpetua and Felicity*

---

catechumens Unbaptized persons who are preparing for full initiation into the Church through the Sacraments of Christian Initiation by engaging in formal study, prayer, and spiritual reflection.

wrote the prologue and picked up the narrative when they went into the arena. Perpetua's account, written in Latin, was soon translated into Greek and quickly spread throughout much of the Roman Empire. Often it was read aloud to Christian communities on the day of the martyrs' death, March 7. Two hundred years after the account began circulating, Augustine was writing sermons about Perpetua. Today, many Christian churches, both Eastern and Western, celebrate March 7 as the Feast of Sts. Perpetua and Felicity. (The male martyrs seem to be ignored.) Even in Christian ecclesial communities that do not celebrate feast days of saints, Perpetua and Felicity are remembered as early Christian martyrs.

Reading Comprehension

1. Why were Perpetua and her companions arrested?
2. What was Perpetua's relationship with her father?
3. What was Perpetua's relationship with her son?
4. What is the legacy of *The Passion of Saints Perpetua and Felicity*?

For Reflection

5. Why do you think the title of Perpetua's journal only mentions the female martyrs even though there were male martyrs in the group?

Prayer

The following is offered as a prayer of ecumenism, for the spirit of unity among all Christians.

> Loving God, we ask that you would grant us the spirit of wisdom and unity so that we may be one, as you are one with our Lord Jesus Christ—and he with you.
>
> Enable all the members of the Body of Christ to live together in unity and fellowship with one another, and lead us into the paths of peace and righteousness—so that we may be well-pleasing in your sight.
>
> We ask you to teach us how to love one another as Christ loved us, and help us to show one another the unusual kindness that can only come from knowing your Son Jesus. May the Spirit stir up in our hearts a desire to be united as one in the bond of peace and fellowship. This we ask in Jesus' name. Amen.
>
> —Graymoor Ecumenical and Interreligious Institute

4

ISLAM

Introduction

SUBMISSION BRINGS INNER FREEDOM

Islam came on the world scene in the seventh century CE with the Arab prophet Muhammad's preaching. Like Judaism and Christianity, Islam is an Abrahamic religious tradition. All three religious traditions believe they are heirs of Abraham and his belief in the one God. Like Judaism and Christianity, Islam is a worldwide religious tradition with adherents on almost every continent and of almost every ethnicity. While there are more Christians in the world than adherents of any other religious tradition, Islam is not far behind in its number of adherents. In the twenty-first century, the rate of growth of Islam, measured by number of believers, is one of the fastest of any religious tradition.

The Arabic word *Islam* derives from the same root as the Hebrew word *shalom*, meaning "peace." *Islam* means "surrender" or "submission" (to God's will) and promises true peace with that surrender. An adherent of Islam is called a *Muslim*, which means "one who submits" (to God's will).

Islam is a monotheistic religious tradition. Muslims are so adamant about the oneness of God that some are uncomfortable celebrating the birthday of Muhammad because that celebration may take focus away from God. Muslims use the Arabic word **Allah**, meaning "the God," to address God. They believe all creation is Muslim—that is, all that Allah created naturally submits to God's divine will. While plants and animals instinctively submit to the will

---

Allah The Arabic word for God. The word's origins are from Semitic writings in which the word for god was *il*, *el*, or *eloah*. *El* and *eloah* were also recorded in the Hebrew Bible.

In the Sheikh Zayed Mosque in Abu Dhabi, United Arab Emirates, the wall facing Mecca is inscribed with the ninety-nine names of Allah.

of God, human beings have free will to choose to submit or not. Allah does not force anyone to submit. Muslims insist that surrendering to God is not confining or negative. Instead, it is a gracious surrendering to the all-compassionate, all-merciful Allah in whom true freedom lies.

According to Muslims, Islam has existed since the time of Adam. For this reason, Muhammad did not found Islam—he restored it. God's message had been revealed since the time of Adam to the Jews and Christians through the prophets, as seen in the Torah and the Gospels. While the people might follow a prophet's correct guidance for a time, eventually the prophet's message became corrupted, and God sent another prophet to guide the people back to the straight path. For Muslims, Abraham, Moses, and Jesus were simultaneously prophets and genuine Muslims who submitted to God's will. Their message was the true message, but followers of their guidance did not persist in the right path. Wanting to bring an end to the faith-apostasy-faith cycle, God called upon Muhammad to restore God's true message to the world once and for all. This message is shared in the Qur'an.

Muhammad was God's messenger with a message to all humanity to return to their true calling—to submit to Allah's will. He was also a political

Muslims in Lhokseumawe, Sumatra, Indonesia, perform Tarawih prayers—listening to and reflecting on the recitation of the Qur'an—on the first night of Ramadan.

leader and a spiritual leader. Just as it is incorrect to say that Muhammad founded Islam, it is also incorrect to call Muslims Muhammadans, for they are not followers of Muhammad.

Allah is at the center of Islamic life—physical, mental, economic, political, social, and spiritual. This chapter offers a brief history of Islam and an overview of Islamic beliefs and how Muslims express them daily. Islam is a universal community with members from all walks of life. Membership in the community carries with it specific obligations to God and to others.

SECTION *Assessment*

Reading Comprehension

1. What are the three Abrahamic religious traditions?
2. Why do Muslims not consider Muhammad the founder of Islam?

3. From what root is the word *Islam* derived?
4. What is the meaning of the word *Muslim*?

For Reflection

5. Name one thing you knew about Islam before reading this section.

Flash Search

6. What percentage of the population in your country is Muslim? In your state or province?

Section 1

A BRIEF HISTORY OF ISLAM

For Muslims, Islam has always existed. Islam began with Adam, the first man. Muhammad is known as the "Seal of the Prophets"—that is, the final messenger of God. According to a Muslim definition, he is not, therefore, the founder of Islam.

Muhammad: Messenger of God

Muhammad was born in approximately 570 CE in Mecca (Makkah), located in present-day Saudi Arabia. His father died before he was born, and his mother died when he was six years old. Orphaned, Muhammad was raised first by his grandfather and then by his uncle, Abu Talib, a caravan merchant. When Muhammad was old enough, he traveled with his uncle on the caravan excursions. In his travels, Muhammad often met with Jews and Christians and heard their stories. Muhammad also was introduced to Khadija, a widowed businesswoman fifteen years his senior. She employed him, and later they married and had children.

Muhammad was accustomed to going to a cave about once a month for a time of prayer and reflection. In the year 610, when he was in the cave, an angel, revealed to be Jibril (Gabriel), appeared to him. The angel commanded:

> Read, in the name of your Lord, who created.
> He created man from an embryo.
> Read, and your Lord, Most Exalted,
> Teaches by means of the pen.
> He teaches man what he never knew. (Surah 96:1–5, Qur'an)

Hira cave, where according to Muslim belief, Muhammad received the revelation of the holy Muslim book the Qur'an.

Since Muhammad was illiterate, he memorized the words that were spoken to him. According to Jibril, Muhammad was to be the messenger of Allah, the one God. Muhammad would receive many revelations throughout the rest of his life and share them with his wife and close friends. These revelations he received were later written down by his followers and became the Qur'an. His message was not unfamiliar to Jews and Christians: it centered on the belief in the one God, care for the poor and disadvantaged, and final judgment based on how people lived their lives on earth.

Yet few people believed Muhammad, for Mecca was a place of many gods. In the center of Mecca was a large, cube-like structure called the **Ka'bah**, which housed statues of more than 360 idols. Being asked to believe in only one God was too much for most of the people of Mecca. Belief in one God would also have destroyed the tribal structure, as tribes were aligned with specific gods.

Ka'bah The first Islamic shrine, which Muslims believe Abraham rebuilt on the spot in Mecca where Adam had originally built it. Destroyed by pagans, it was reclaimed and purified by Muhammad when he captured Mecca in the seventh century. The Ka'bah is currently enclosed within the Great Mosque of Mecca.

ISLAM: TIMELINE OF KEY EVENTS

CE

ca. 570 .... Birth of Muhammad

610 .... First revelation to Muhammad

622 .... Hijrah to Medina

630 .... Muslims return from Medina to capture Mecca

632 .... Death of Muhammad

632–661 .... Era of Rightly Guided Caliphs

638 .... Muslims conquer Jerusalem

656 .... Ali appointed fourth caliph

661 .... Ali assassinated

661–750 .... Umayyad caliphate

680 .... Husayn killed at the Battle of Karbala

732 .... Battle of Tours, France

750–1258 .... Abbasid caliphate

ca. 1100s .... Rise of Sufism

1187 .... Recapture of Jerusalem from Western Christian crusaders

1207–1273 .... Life of Jalāl ad-Dīn Muhammad Rumi

1299–1924 .... Reign of the Ottoman Empire

1453 .... Ottoman capture of Constantinople

1526–1857 .... Mughal Empire in southern Asia

1609 .... Muslims exiled from Spain

1924 .... Ottoman caliphate abolished in Turkey

1947 .... Founding of East and West Pakistan

1971 .... East Pakistan becomes Bangladesh

1979 .... Iranian Revolution

2001 .... September 11 attacks on the United States by Islamic extremists

Mecca

Eventually, Muhammad gained a small following in Mecca. His wife always believed him and was very supportive of him. His two friends, Abu Bakr and Uthman; his cousin and later son-in-law Ali, the son of his uncle Abu Talib; and a former enslaved person named Zaid were also among his first followers. Life became unbearable for these Muslims at Mecca, and they decided to move in 622 to present-day Medina. Their relocation became known as the **Hijrah**, or "migration." The Hijrah marks the beginning of the Islamic calendar: the Western calendar year of 622 is 1 AH (*Anno Hegirae* [Latin for "in the year of the Hijrah]) on the Islamic calendar.

Medina

Hijrah A term meaning "migration"; recalls the establishment of Islam in 622 CE, when Muhammad and his followers escaped from his enemies and left Mecca for Medina. The Hijrah marks the start of the Islamic calendar.

Initially, things went well for the Muslims in Medina. Not only was Muhammad a capable spiritual leader but his gifts as a political leader were also evident. As his following grew, so did his opposition. The Muslims of Medina fought and defeated Arabs and Jews in Medina and also defeated tribes from Mecca in battle. Strengthened by these victories, Muhammad and thousands of his followers made their way back to Mecca and captured it. He went immediately to the Ka'bah, the shrine where various tribes worshipped their gods, purified it by having all the statues removed, and rededicated it to the worship of the one God.

By the time Muhammad died in 632, many Arab tribes were calling themselves Muslim and submitting to Allah's will.

The Rightly Guided Caliphs

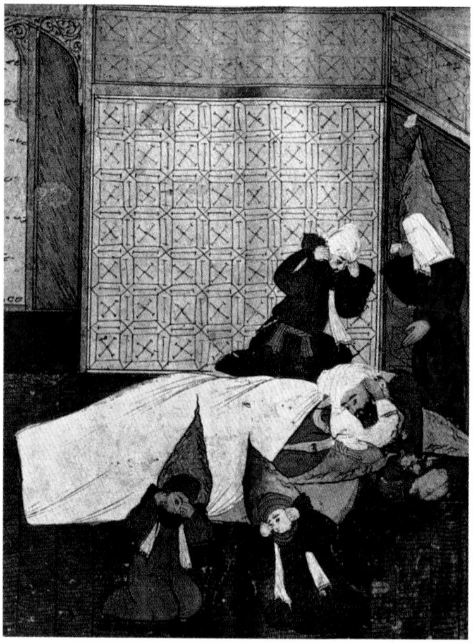

Death of the Prophet Mohammed. Many Muslims believe that Allah and Muhammad cannot be captured in an image by human hand and to attempt to do so is an insult to him. That is why Muhammad's face is covered here.

Muhammad's successors were called **caliphs**. The first to succeed Muhammad was Abu Bakr (632–634), one of Muhammad's original disciples. Though caliph for a mere two years, Abu Bakr consolidated through battle the loyalty of the Arabian Peninsula's newly Islamized tribes to the Muslim leadership and community. Umar (634–644) was chosen as Abu Bakr's successor. An enemy of Islam before his conversion in 616, Umar oversaw Islam's expansion to Persia, Damascus, and Jerusalem, often through military conquest. Before he was assassinated, Umar appointed a committee of six men to choose his successor. The committee chose Uthman (644–656).

---

caliphs Islamic temporal and spiritual leaders regarded by Sunni Muslims as successors of Muhammad.

The shrine of Ali ibn Abi Talib, cousin of Muhammad and fourth Rashidun caliph, in Najaf, Iraq.

As caliph, Uthman was instrumental in the publication and distribution of the **Qur'an**. However, Uthman's rule was marred by some weaknesses, which began a period of strife in Islamic history. Problems developed in the way he administered local provinces, and some groups felt that the governors he appointed were not responsive to their needs. A rival faction within Islam eventually killed Uthman, and Muhammad's cousin Ali (656–661) became the fourth caliph. Some members of Uthman's clan, the Umayyad, would not accept the legitimacy of Ali's **caliphate** because his selection was supported by some who were responsible for Uthman's death. Instead, they supported a caliphate with ties to the Umayyad.

Ali moved the Islamic capital from Medina to Kufah, in present-day Iraq, believing it a more central location. In the meantime, Uthman's cousin,

---

Qur'an In Muslim belief, God's final revelation, superseding the Jewish and Christian Bibles. The word means "recite" or "recitation." It is the holiest book for adherents of Islam.

caliphate A government under a caliph, who is at once a political and religious leader in Islam.

Mu'awiyah, a member of the Umayyad clan and governor of Syria, had also been proclaimed caliph. A power struggle ensued between the Ali caliphate and the Umayyad caliphate. Battles were fought, but neither side won a decisive victory. Both sides agreed to arbitration, and the decision was made in favor of Mu'awiyah and the Umayyad caliphate.

Ali could not accept the decision and continued ruling from Kufah, even though he lost some of his support. Ali was eventually assassinated, and his supporters elevated his son Hasan to caliph, but Hasan soon abdicated the position and recognized Mu'awiyah as caliph. Most of Ali's supporters concurred, and Mu'awiyah continued to rule from Damascus, Syria.

Unfortunately, the events surrounding the death of Ali opened a rift in the Muslim community that has never completely healed. In 680, not recognizing the legitimacy of the Umayyad caliphate, Ali's younger son, Husayn, attempted to claim the Muslim community's leadership. On their way to Kufah from Medina by way of Mecca, Husayn and his followers were massacred at Karbala in Iraq in what became known as the Battle of Karbala.

Those who became known as **Shi'ah** Muslims saw Husayn as a martyr whose death restored Islam to the purity given it by his grandfather, Muhammad. To this day, special events each year at Karbala commemorate the martyrdom of Husayn. Shi'ah Muslims continue to view Ali as the first **imam** and organize around an imamate, not a caliphate. Shi'ah Muslims do not recognize the legitimacy of the first three caliphs after Muhammad because they believe Muhammad gave exclusive authority or inspiration to his cousin Ali.

Though most of those who became known as **Sunni** Muslims accepted the rule of the Umayyads, they did not always approve. Sunni Muslims recognize all four of the first four caliphs, called the Rashidun, or Rightly Guided, Caliphs. Sunni caliphs administer the guardianship and promulgation of

---

Shi'ah The smaller of the two main branches of Islam that accepts the legitimacy of the successors of Muhammad starting with his cousin and son-in-law, Ali, whom they regard as the first imam.

imam A leader for prayer at a mosque who is chosen for his knowledge of Islam and his personal holiness; also, a spiritual leader of the line of Ali held by Shi'ah Muslims to be a rightful successor of Muhammad.

Sunni The larger of the two main branches of Islam that accepts the legitimacy of the leadership of all of the first four caliphs of Islam as successors of Muhammad.

The Umayyad Mosque was built in Damascus, Syria, from 706 to 715.

shari'ah, or Islamic law. Sunni and Shi'ah Muslims differ to this day on who is to lead the Muslim community, but there are no fundamental differences regarding Islam's beliefs and practices between the sects.

Classical Period

Within a century after Muhammad's death, the Umayyad caliphate had expanded into the Byzantine Empire and contributed to the fall of the Persian Empire. It spread farther to North Africa, Spain, and even France until Charles Martel pushed the Muslims out of France in 732 at the Battle of Tours. Though Muslims were rulers of these regions, it took most of the people living in these countries a long time to become Muslim because conversion to Islam was not accomplished on command or "by the sword." By the year 750, the Umayyad caliphate had expanded its empire to the borders of China and India.

---

shari'ah The revealed and canonical law of Islam based on the Qur'an, Sunnah, and Hadith that prescribes religious and temporal duties.

The rapid expansion of the caliphate brought many challenges, especially in an age when communication over long distances was slow. Gradually, Arabic became more widely used as an official language. The requirement to use Arabic in worship and the recitation of the Qur'an were also related to the gradual spread of Islam among a larger population. With a common language of administration and education, a unified culture began to emerge.

Arabic script on a milestone from the late eighth century, Riyadh, Saudi Arabia.

Umayyad rule began to weaken as the expansion of the caliphate slowed. New groups of Muslims asserted their right to a greater voice in society and government. Ruling a vast empire required the caliphs to put much energy into the temporal rather than the religious realm. Opposition to the worldliness of the caliphs grew at the beginning of the eighth century. A descendant of an uncle of Muhammad proclaimed himself the rightful caliph. Various opposition groups, including Shi'ah, merged and then defeated the Umayyads. Abu al-'Abbas al-Saffah took the caliphate in 750, replacing the Umayyad dynasty with the Abbasid dynasty. A remnant of the Umayyad dynasty escaped to Spain and set up a caliphate there.

Medieval Period or Golden Age of Islam

Under Abbasid rule, Muslim civilization and culture flourished, so much so that this period between the eighth and thirteenth centuries became known as the Golden Age of Islam. The Abbasids established a new capital at Baghdad, which became one of the largest and most magnificent cities in the world. Scientific, literary, and philosophical works from Greek, Persian, and Indian sources were translated into Arabic at Baghdad's House of Wisdom, a library and archive containing thousands of books. Muslim scholars' exposure to Greek and other traditions led to great intellectual ferment as Muslim scholars sought to reconcile reason and faith, science and religious teachings. Muslim scholars wrote critical commentaries that later passed in Hebrew and Latin translations into Europe, where, centuries later, Jewish scholars such as Moses Maimonides and Christian scholars such as Thomas Aquinas wrestled with the same questions and often quoted from the works of Muslim philosophers.

One of the most important and long-term contributions of Islamic civilization was the vast trade and communication network that developed within the expanding Muslim territory. Between the eighth and fifteenth centuries, the gradual but steady expansion of this region linked Malaysia, India, China, Arabia, Africa, the Middle East, and Europe. Trade routes created by Arab, African, and Asian traders became connected by a common language, belief system, and legal system in ancient times.

Politically, however, the Abbasids were unable to maintain a unified Muslim rule. Little by little, beginning in the ninth century, scattered provinces

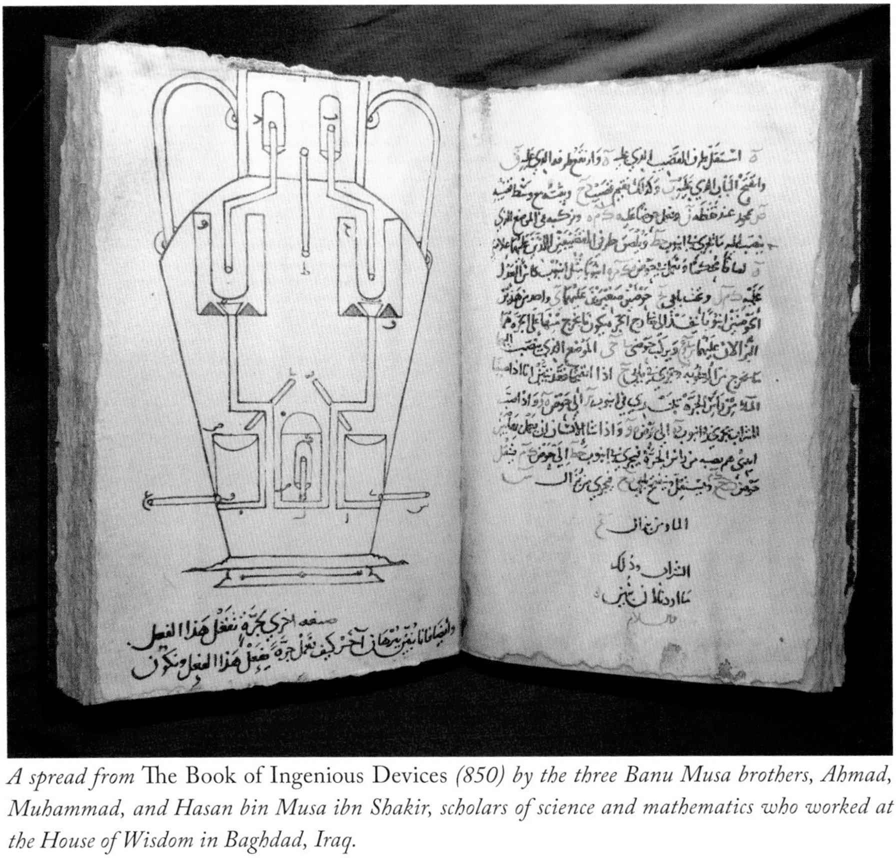

A spread from The Book of Ingenious Devices *(850) by the three Banu Musa brothers, Ahmad, Muhammad, and Hasan bin Musa ibn Shakir, scholars of science and mathematics who worked at the House of Wisdom in Baghdad, Iraq.*

began to proclaim their independence from the central government. Local rulers, military factions, and rival caliphates sprang up. By the twelfth century, there were several independent Islamic states. In the tenth century in Egypt, a Shi'ah group called the *Fatimids*, named after Muhammad's daughter and Ali's wife, Fatimah, founded the great city of Cairo and its famous Al-Azhar University, one of the oldest universities in the world.

The Great Mosque of Córdoba in Andalucia, Spain, built in the late eighth century.

Meanwhile, the remnant Umayyads, who had escaped to Spain, ruled from Córdoba, where they were free to develop religious scholarship and an attractive Islamic civilization of their own. Like Baghdad, Córdoba was a great intellectual center and boasted magnificent palaces, **mosques**, and libraries. Eventually a so-called Reconquest of Spain, a messy seven-hundred-year struggle of various Christian kingdoms, was undertaken to unify Spain under Christian rule. In 1492, the last great stronghold of the Muslims, the Alhambra in Granada, was captured. Until the seventeenth century, Muslims could stay in Spain, freely worship, own land, work, and even serve in the army. However, as the Spanish Inquisition (see Chapter 2, Section 1,

mosques Called *masjids* by many Muslims; buildings for personal and communal Islamic prayer and worship. Mosques can also be used for social, educational, and funerary events.

"Medieval Period") became more of a threat to Muslims, many left, and by the early seventeenth century, the remaining Muslims were exiled from Spain.

In the meantime, Christian crusaders from Europe captured Jerusalem from the Muslims in 1099, only to have it retaken by the Muslims in 1187. Though Christians embarked on later Crusades, none were militarily successful.

The Golden Age of Islam came to an end in the thirteenth century. The central Asian Mongols had captured China, Russia, and central Europe and were headed for the Middle East. They ended the Abbasid caliphate with the capture of Baghdad in 1258. The Mongols not only laid waste to cities wherever they went but also destroyed many of the scientific, literary, and scholarly works Muslims had amassed over the centuries. The Mongols were finally defeated in Palestine near Nazareth in 1260 by the Turkish Mamluks, a Muslim dynasty that ruled Egypt.

After a period of fragmented rule among Muslims, the next important regional power that developed, beginning toward the end of the thirteenth century in what is now Turkey, was the Ottomans. Although Muslim rule had expanded at the expense of the Byzantine Empire for centuries, control of the city of Constantinople had eluded Muslim rulers. However, the sacking

Worshippers perform Eid al-Fitr prayers during Ramadan at the Suleymaniye mosque in Istanbul, Turkey.

of the city by crusader armies in 1204 and the expansion of Turkish rule into Byzantine territory left Constantinople weakened. It finally fell to the Ottomans in 1453. The peak of the Ottoman Empire was in the sixteenth century under a sultan called Suleiman. However, at the same time, the power of European nations was on the rise, as many set up trading posts along the coasts surrounding the Indian Ocean to the disadvantage of the Muslims. By the beginning of the seventeenth century, both Europe's rise and the decline of the Ottoman Empire were apparent. However, this once great giant would not quickly disappear.

Modern Period

Christian missionaries accompanied the European traders as they broke into Muslim markets. While the missionaries saw their work as reclaiming people and land that had once been Christian back from Muslims, Muslims saw Christians as corrupting their lands and society. During the nineteenth century, a time when Muslim political influence had declined, European industrial, economic, and political dominance in the Middle East set up situations of conflict that are still present in the twenty-first century; European colonization is one source of the ongoing conflicts in Lebanon, Syria, Egypt, Israel/

From 1798 to 1801 France, under Napoleon Bonaparte, occupied Egypt, attempting to make it a French colony. This drawing depicts Bonaparte before the Great Sphinx of Giza.

Palestine, and Iraq. A great deal of ferment took place, leading Muslim leaders and intellectuals to reassess the foundations and traditions in their societies.

The political decline of Islam brought with it social and moral deterioration. The eighteenth to the twentieth centuries saw a marked rise in revivalism and reform movements to combat this decay. Islamic reform movements tended to go in two directions. One direction was an attempt to return to what was considered the pristine Islam from the time of Muhammad and the early Muslim community in Medina. It was believed that non-Islamic elements from colonial powers had corrupted Islam, which needed to be purified by returning to the literal teachings of the Qur'an and the **Sunnah**. The effects of these more fundamental reforms can be seen today in such countries as Saudi Arabia and Sudan.

A second direction for Islamic reform was to reinterpret Islam in light of the social and historical realities of the day. These reformers believed that the social and moral decline in Islam was due not only to European colonialism but also to personal, social, and moral decay within the Muslim community. These reformers believed that Muslims should accept the current political reality and embrace the movement toward separating religion and state. They also held that the best the West had to offer would strengthen Muslims in their faith and that Islam would regain the political prestige it once had. The effects of these more adaptation-minded reforms can be seen today in such countries as Malaysia and Indonesia.

At the beginning of the twentieth century, the Ottoman Empire was in such disarray that it was known as the "sick man of Europe." Reform was attempted but unsuccessful. Siding with the Germans during World War I, the Ottoman Empire was defeated and a nationalist movement arose in Turkey. It abolished the empire in 1922 and set up a secularized republic. Persian and Indian rulers were deposed or made into mere figureheads. In the aftermath of European colonial rule, artificial political borders were drawn more according to the desire for control of outside powers than in the interests or national groupings of people in these diverse regions. The continuing domination in the former Ottoman Empire by Western (Europe and the United States) and Eastern (China and the then-Soviet Union) powers created a great

---

Sunnah The body of traditional customs and practices of Muhammad that are models for observant Muslims and shared through the oral tradition.

With the prohibition of creating imagery of any living thing, Islamic calligraphy is a significant Muslim artistic expression. Various styles of Islamic calligraphy have been passed down through the centuries from master to student. This decorative handwriting is not merely an artistic and cultural endeavor. It is, above all, a spiritual practice, for most of what artists create are verses from the Qur'an.

deal of social and religious bitterness and economic inequity. The founding of the State of Israel in 1948 displaced thousands of mostly Muslim Palestinians from lands owned by their families for generations. This just added fuel to the fire.

The Western-initiated process of secularization, or marginalization of religious traditions in the former Ottoman Empire, created a great deal of uncertainty and social upheaval on the one hand and political repression on the other. The Iranian Revolution of 1978–1979, led by the Ayatollah Khomeini, was just one reaction to the perceived attack on Islam by the secularization movement and by what many Muslims thought of as the "godless" West.

The last Shah of Iran, Mohammad Reza Pahlavi, and his wife, Queen of Iran Farah Pahlavi, in 1971.

At the start of the twenty-first century, the second-largest religious tradition in the world, which had been almost entirely invisible to most persons living in the West just fifty years prior, drew sudden intense scrutiny. The hijacking by Muslim extremists of American planes to destroy buildings that were important symbols of the West and to end people's lives on September 11, 2001, brought unearned scrutiny to millions of Muslims' lives. A minuscule minority of Muslims had commandeered Islam by enflaming political, social, military, and economic grievances to legitimate violence against men, women, and children. These extremist groups claimed they were the only ones who practiced pure Islam. Some even seized land in the Middle East, attempting to reestablish a caliphate. The outsized attention seized by the few prompted ordinary Muslims to

Sayyid Ruhollah Musavi Khomeini, known as Ayatollah Khomeini, led the 1979 Iranian revolution that ended the monarchy in Iran. He then became the supreme leader of the Islamic Republic from 1979 to 1989.

Tunisia

Yemen

Algeria

In 2010–2011, after a series of public protests, the people of Tunisia ousted their longtime president, a move which ultimately lead to a new constitution and free and democratic elections. From Tunisia, the protests spread to Algeria, Libya, Egypt, Yemen, Syria, and Bahrain. Called Arab Spring, the rebellions resulted in civil wars and democratic and economic changes throughout these Arab countries.

ask themselves, "Who speaks for Islam?" The immense majority of moderate Muslim voices had a hard time being heard.

Many Muslim intellectuals are engaged in active efforts to retain important principles and find visual interpretations to keep their religious tradition vibrant while meeting the demands of modern life. In this, the efforts of Muslims are in many ways similar to the striving of members of other religious traditions around the world.

SECTION *Assessment*

Reading Comprehension

1. Explain how Muhammad received his first revelation.
2. What was Muhammad's chief message to humankind?
3. What was the primary cause of the division between the two major groupings of Muslims—the Sunni and the Shi'ah?
4. What is the importance of the Hijrah?
5. Name an accomplishment of Muslims during the Golden Age of Islam.
6. What were some major causes of the decline of the Muslim states in the Modern Period?
7. Describe the two directions of Islamic reform in the Modern Period.

For Reflection

8. What do you think it would be like to be ruled by a government that was entirely Catholic?
9. What do you think it would be like to be ruled by a government that espoused a religious tradition different from your own?

Flash Search

10. What is Wahhabi Islam?

Section 2

SACRED STORIES AND SACRED SCRIPTURES

The Qur'an is the most sacred book for Muslims. It is a collection of revelations Muhammad received directly from God in Arabic over a twenty-two-year period in Mecca and Medina. After the Qur'an, the Sunnah is the second authentic source of authority for Muslims. The Qur'an and the Sunnah are indispensable sources of instruction for living religious and moral lives.

Muslims also acknowledge the revealed writings of Judaism and Christianity. However, these books—the Torah, the Psalms, and the Gospels—are believed by Muslims to be only human words, not God's words; this means that they are corrupted by human error. Muslims believe the words of the Qur'an are God's words and thus infallible, uncorrupted by human intervention. The Qur'an is so sacred to Muslims that it should not be physically placed under any item and one should perform ritual washing before touching or reading it.

Qur'an

The word *Qur'an* means "recitation." Muhammad was unschooled, unable to read and write. As he received the revelations, he memorized them and then passed them on to his followers. They too memorized what they heard from Muhammad and wrote some of his words down. The third Rightly Guided Caliph, Uthman, did not want the sacred words lost; he wanted to make sure these words of Allah were passed on uncorrupted to the coming generations of Muslims. Also, as Islam spread, a growing number of its adherents spoke in

The University of Birmingham, in England, has carbon dated these pages from the Qur'an to the early seventh century, which makes it one of the oldest copies in the world.

other Arabic dialects and other languages, making changes to the text inevitable. Uthman charged Muhammad's scribe, Zayd ibn Thabit, with compiling the various copies and fragments of the revelations into one text and comparing it against the recitation of those who had memorized and recited the revelations in Muhammad's lifetime. The resulting authoritative text was what came to be known as the Qur'an. It was published and distributed to all the provinces.

Muslims commonly refer to the revelations Muhammad received in Mecca and Medina as **surahs**, which equate to chapters. The Qur'an is divided into 114 surahs. In general, it is arranged neither in chronological order according to when Muhammad received the revelations nor by theme or subject. However, some continuity can be detected: the last verse of one surah and the first verse of the following surah may have similar underlying themes.

---

surahs Chapters, or sections, in the Qur'an. Each surah is a separate revelation received by Muhammad.

The Dubai International Holy Qur'an Competition. The two-week competition involves multiple rounds, during which competitors answer questions and recite randomly selected passages of the Qur'an for judges.

The earlier Meccan revelations tend to speak about God's unity, power, and glory; right living; the end times; and Judgment Day. The later Medinan revelations add instructions on practical concerns such as what makes a good society, relations with non-Muslims, and financial and legal matters.

Since Muslims believe the Qur'an is a word-for-word message from God to Muhammad in Arabic, they remain hesitant to translate it into other languages. A translation into any other language would be an interpretation in which, even if the correct meaning were retained, the sacred words would not be.

From an early age, Muslim children learn to memorize and accurately recite the Qur'an as part of their religious duty. As noted, the task of memorizing the entire Qur'an dates to Muhammad's earliest followers. Those who accomplish such a task earn the honorary title of **hafiz**. Today, Qur'an memorizing contests are held in big stadiums in many parts of the Muslim world. Ironically, the winners are often not native speakers of Arabic.

Sunnah

The Sunnah records through the oral tradition Muhammad's customs and practices—that is, his way of life. For example, while the Qur'an may say that Allah commands all to pray, the Sunnah shows Muslims how to pray through the example of Muhammad. Since Muhammad is the best example for a Muslim life, Muslims need the Sunnah to help them emulate his actions. The Qur'an and the Sunnah go hand in hand. One needs both in order to understand Islam and live fully as a Muslim.

This Turkish album of calligraphies was written by Shaykh Hamdullah, a master of Islamic calligraphy. It includes quotations from the Hadith.

Hadith

The **Hadith** are similar but not identical to the Sunnah; Hadith record and support many of the customs and practices of the Sunnah. Muhammad's followers painstakingly recorded and transmitted oral and written accounts of his teachings and actions, which were compiled by the second century of the Islamic calendar. Not all Muslims believe Hadith accounts are divine revelation since they were written down centuries after Muhammad's death.

---

hafiz A Muslim who has memorized the Qur'an.

Hadith A word meaning "tradition"; the sayings and stories of Muhammad that are meant to form guidance for living out Islam.

In Baghdad, Iraq, this mural of Imam Ali ibn Abi Talib was painted over an image of overthrown Iraqi dictator Saddam Hussein.

Writings of the Shi'ah Imams

While the Qur'an and the Sunnah are sources of authority for all Muslims, Shi'ah Muslims have a third source of authority. For them, the teachings and writings of many early charismatic leaders called imams, descended from Muhammad's cousin and son-in-law, Ali, are an additional source of sacred literature. Shi'ah Muslims believe these descendants of Ali are infallible and consider their words and explanations nearly as authoritative as the Qur'an and the Sunnah.

SECTION *Assessment*

Reading Comprehension

1. Why is the Qur'an the most sacred writing for Muslims?
2. Why is there a hesitation to translate the Qur'an into other languages?

3. Why can it be said that the Qur'an and the Sunnah go hand in hand?

Vocabulary

4. What does the word *Qur'an* mean?

For Reflection

5. Give examples from Sacred Scripture that you have memorized or that readily come to mind when you pray.

Flash Search

6. How are the Hadith comparable to the Jewish Talmud?
7. What is the world's oldest complete Qur'an (not fragments)?

Section 3

BELIEFS AND PRACTICES

Belief in one God is at the core of Muslim belief. Along with Judaism and Christianity, Islam is a monotheistic religious tradition. Reciting the Arabic words *La ilaha illa Allah, wa Muhammadun rasul Allah* ("There is no god but Allah, and Muhammad is the Messenger of Allah"), Muslims proclaim this belief daily. Islam holds the following beliefs about God:

- God is the Creator and sustainer of the universe.
- God is all-loving, all-powerful, all-knowing, all-merciful, and present everywhere.
- Not only does God give life but God also takes life away.
- God is the judge of all. It is God who determines whether a person will spend eternity in heaven or hell.

Muslims believe in divine providence and that God is very involved as a guide in human history and human affairs. God knows what happened in the past, what is presently happening, and what will happen in the future. However, God does not predetermine what is going to happen. God allows free will for people to make their own choices. Free will is an integral part of what

---

Five Pillars of Islam The foundational principles and practices of Islam that were set forth by Muhammad and are practiced by all Muslims.

Shahadah The first, and most important, of the Five Pillars of Islam. It is a witness statement or a profession of faith that proclaims that there is no other god than Allah and that Muhammad is the messenger of Allah.

it means to be human. People are to be obedient to God but not coerced into submission. Surrendering to God's will brings freedom, not bondage.

Islamic understanding of "prophets" differs from the Judeo-Christian understanding. Most centrally, Muslims believe that Muhammad is the "Messenger (or Prophet) of God." Islamic teaching is that all the Judeo-Christian prophets were Muslims because they submitted to the will of God. Among the prophets mentioned in the Qur'an are Adam, Noah, Abraham, Moses and his brother Aaron, Jacob, Joseph and his brothers, Job, and Jesus.

Muslim behavior is guided by the **Five Pillars of Islam**, religious duties that each person is to perform. Muslims practice their religious tradition living in the community. The sections that follow explore these foundations of Muslim living in more detail.

The Five Pillars of Islam

Five specific acts and ways of performing them, found in the Qur'an and the Sunnah, form the basis of Muslim practice and worship. These acts are called the *Five Pillars of Islam* because the performance of these acts as perfectly as possible is the key to upholding one's religious life. More than just formalities, these acts purify believers in specific ways. Each has a physical and a spiritual, a worldly and an otherworldly, and a personal and a communal dimension. The Five Pillars of Islam, detailed below, have contributed significantly to defining the *ummah*, the name for the Islamic community.

✦ 1. Shahadah (Profession of Faith)

Reciting the Arabic words *La ilaha illa Allah, wa Muhammadun rasul Allah*, translated as "There is no god but Allah, and Muhammad is the Messenger of Allah," is the first and most important of the Five Pillars of Islam. The other four pillars are outward expressions of the first. This **Shahadah** is akin to the Jewish Sh'ma.

Muslims declare this belief in the absolute oneness of God several times a day. A "crier," called

Turkish muezzin Fatih Koca calls Muslims to morning prayer at Hagia Sophia in Istanbul, Turkey.

a **muezzin**, proclaims this creed from the **minaret** of every mosque. A father whispers these words into his newborn child's ears so that they are the first words the child hears on earth. A dying person attempts to have the Shahadah be the last words on his or her lips. A convert to Islam recites these words as a statement of belief. This public declaration of faith defines a person as a member of the Islamic community.

✦ 2. Salah (Prayer)

Submitting to God is at the heart of Islam. The Qur'an commands Muslims to pray or worship at fixed times during the day. The ritual prayer Muslims pray five times per day is called *salah*.

Ritual washing in Punjab, India.

Before Muslims pray, they must cleanse themselves physically and symbolically. The ritual washing, called **wudu**, opens and closes with a prayer. In addition to having a clean body, the person must be wearing proper clothing. Men must be clothed from the navel to the knees. Women must be dressed from head to toe. Shoes are not worn. To ensure that the place of prayer is clean, Muslims often use a prayer mat. Whenever a Muslim prays, he or she faces the direction of the Ka'bah in Mecca. This direction, marked in the mosque by a niche in the wall, is called the *qiblah*.

The five fixed times for prayer are (1) between dawn and sunrise, (2) after midday, (3) between late afternoon and sunset, (4) between sunset and the end of daylight, and (5) at night, between the end of daylight and dawn. Five times a day Muslims chant the following:

---

muezzin The man appointed at the mosque to call Muslims to prayer five times a day.

minaret A tall, slender tower attached to a mosque from which a muezzin calls Muslims to prayer.

God is most Great!
I bear witness that there is no god but God.
I bear witness that Muhammad is the Messenger of God.
Come to prayer.
Come to success.
[At morning prayer, the following line is added here: "Prayer is better than sleep."]
God is most Great!
There is no god but God.

In countries where Muslims are a minority, it is more difficult for them to stop and pray. However, many Muslims in school and work settings reserve times to fulfill this religious requirement. A Muslim may pray anywhere, as long as the place is clean. One might find Muslims stopping to pray in their homes, in a corner at the airport, out where they are tending the fields or flock, or in a library. In regions where Muslims are a minority, where it is more difficult for them to stop and pray, conscientious Muslims will still stop what they are doing and pray. With no muezzin about to call the community to prayer, modern technology may help. Today, computer applications, smartwatches, and unique clocks fill in for the muezzin. Whatever the difficulties, many Muslims take the obligation to pray seriously.

Friday is the special day of prayer for Muslims, though Fridays are not understood as the equivalent of a Sabbath. On Fridays, the second prayer time takes place in a mosque and is called *Jum'ah*, or "Assembly." In addition to the regular midday prayer, the imam or another prayer leader delivers a sermon. Since most of Islam has no clergy, anyone whom the community considers knowledgeable about Islam can be a prayer leader and deliver a sermon. As might be imagined, Muslims in non-Muslim countries find it challenging to attend Jum'ah in the middle of a Friday. In the United States, efforts are being made to make schools and businesses aware of this difficulty. At least in larger cities, small mosques are being built near business districts to accommodate Muslims working there.

---

wudu The ritual washing of the mouth, nose, ears, face, hands, arms, top of head, and feet that a Muslim must perform before salah, the Second Pillar of Islam.

✦ 3. Zakah (Almsgiving)

Men and women give alms to beggars after prayers at Baitul Mukarram National Mosque in Dhaka, Bangladesh.

Muslims give alms to the needy as an act of worship. Almsgiving is not an option but an obligation. Muslims believe that almsgiving or a "poor tax," called *zakah*, is one way a person can be freed from obstacles to a direct relationship with Allah. The Qur'an does not specify how much wealth one should share with others. Instead, it states, "They ask you how much they are to spend. Say: 'What is beyond your needs'" (Surah 2:219, Qur'an). However, 2.5 percent of one's income is the norm.

Other acts of charity are also encouraged. An act of charity can be anything from a smile to removing an obstacle from the road. Thus, in Islamic teaching, charity lies within reach of both the rich and the poor.

✦ 4. Sawm (Fasting)

All Muslims who have reached puberty and are not ill or traveling are required to keep a monthlong fast, called *sawm*, each year during the ninth Islamic lunar month, called **Ramadan**. It is the month in which Muhammad received his first revelation from God. The fast reminds Muslims to fulfill their obligations to care for the poor and needy. In Islam, to fast means to abstain from food, drink, and marital relations from dawn to sundown. A fasting person should also avoid arguments and try to focus on positive thoughts and deeds.

Ramadan The ninth month of the Islamic calendar, which is a month of prayer and fasting to commemorate the Night of Power, the first revelation to Muhammad by God. Ramadan fasting satisfies the Fourth Pillar of Islam.

Friends gather at Jama Masjid to break their first fast as the holy month of Ramadan begins in New Delhi, India.

During Ramadan, most Muslims have a light meal just before dawn. At the break of dawn, the first prayers of the day are recited. After sundown, the fast is broken with a meal. Later in the evening, special prayers are said, and passages from the Qur'an are read and shared at the mosque. Over the four weeks of Ramadan, the entire Qur'an is recited in the mosque. Ramadan ends with one of the two major feasts for Muslims, Eid al-Fitr, the Festival of Breaking the Fast. For Muslims, fasting is not a somber experience but a joyous event.

✦ 5. Hajj (Pilgrimage)

African Muslim women attend the annual Hajj in Mecca.

The **Hajj** is a pilgrimage to Mecca, Saudi Arabia, where Abraham submitted to the will of Allah. It is held annually in the twelfth month of the Islamic calendar. Hajj is required only once in one's lifetime and only of those Muslims who are physically and financially capable of completing it. The rituals performed on the Hajj reflect rituals and actions similarly performed by Abraham and his family during his migration from his native city of Ur in Mesopotamia.

For Muslims, some of the events of Abraham's life are different from those in the biblical account. In the Islamic tradition, Abraham left his

Hajj The annual Muslim pilgrimage to Mecca, Saudi Arabia. It is a mandatory religious duty for Muslims at least once in their lifetime providing they are financially and physically able.

> native city of Ur when he could not convince the inhabitants of that city to do away with their belief in many gods and believe in only one God. Abraham's caravan traveled through many parts of the Middle East before arriving in Egypt.
>
> After Abraham and his wife, Sarah, had grown old, unable to have children, Sarah offered Abraham her Egyptian servant, Hagar, hoping that Abraham might have an heir. Hagar bore their son, Ishmael. Not long after Ishmael's birth, Abraham called upon Hagar and Ishmael to prepare for a long journey. He led them to a valley in the desert of Arabia and left them there, trusting that God would care for them as promised. Their food and water soon dried up, and Hagar grew desperate for her young son's welfare. She ran up one hill and then a second, back and forth between the two hills, trying to hail a traveling caravan for help. Exhausted, she prayed to God for help, and soon water miraculously gushed from near the foot of Ishmael. Today, this place is called Zamzam. Over time, traders settled in that desert valley near the spring, which flourished into the city of Mecca.
>
> Meanwhile, Abraham came to visit from time to time. On one visit, when Ishmael reached puberty, Abraham told Ishmael he had had a dream in which God told him to sacrifice his son. Ishmael agreed to submit to God's will. When Abraham was just about to sacrifice Ishmael, he heard a voice from heaven saying that he would be rewarded for his good deed. So Abraham and Ishmael got a ram, slaughtered it, and celebrated. Desiring that the people of that desert valley worship the one God rather than many, Abraham and Ishmael rebuilt the Ka'bah once built by Adam to worship God. Through the angel Jibril, God showed Abraham the Hajj rituals, and Abraham spent the rest of his life calling upon the people to submit to God's will.

It is important to know how Muslims understand Abraham's story for the rituals of Hajj to make sense. Some of the rituals include circling the Ka'bah (located in the Great Mosque of Mecca) to mark its centrality to the Muslim community, running seven times between the two hills, drinking from the springs of Zamzam, and throwing stones at a pillar representing Satan, who tried to dissuade Abraham from sacrificing Ishmael. The Hajj centerpiece is for the pilgrims to go out to the Plain of Arafat, which surrounds the hill where Muhammad gave his last sermon. More than two million pilgrims spend the

Pilgrims circumambulating the Ka'bah, in Mecca.

day on the plain in prayer for forgiveness and intense devotion. Throughout the region, the array of pilgrims clad in white garments and offering prayers to God is believed to be a foretaste of the Day of Judgment. The pilgrimage ends with Eid al-Adha, or the Festival of Sacrifice, in which a lamb is sacrificed in commemoration of Abraham's willingness to sacrifice Ishmael.

Islamic Living

Muslims practice the Five Pillars of Islam as part of the *ummah* (community). There is no long process to become a Muslim. To be considered a member of the ummah, one merely has to state the Shahadah as a sign of belief and submission to Allah. Being a Muslim entails duties and responsibilities to other members and humankind as a whole as well as the right to the support of the community. Accepting Islam is not an end but a beginning. It is a lifetime endeavor to practice and perfect one's submission to and belief in Allah.

Islam entails a whole way of life, covering spiritual, social, personal, political, economic, and physical aspects. Allah is not only ruler of the earth but also the sovereign of every aspect of a Muslim's life. The Qur'an has much to say about what an Islamic society should look like overall, as well as in the day-to-day concerns of family life and the specific roles of women and men in family and community.

According to the Qur'an, Allah will provide for the needs of all creation. The Qur'an teaches that those who worry about money are losing sight of God. Besides, a mindset that charitable giving deprives the giver of basic needs is incorrect. The Third Pillar of Islam calls upon each Muslim to care for those in need. The zakah is a required contribution to charity. In some Muslim countries, the zakah is enforced by law.

Islamic law—called *shari'ah*, which means "revealed law"—is central to Muslim life. It is God's guidance on how to live. The primary sources of shari'ah are the Qur'an and the Sunnah. For example, the Qur'an teaches against murder, drunkenness, and sexual relations outside of marriage. It also spells out obligations for prayer, fasting during Ramadan, and giving to the poor. In other matters, Muslims look to the Sunnah for rules regarding Islamic practice and behavior.

However, many issues in a Muslim's life are not addressed in either the Qur'an or the Sunnah, neither of which is intended to be a code of law. For Sunni Muslims, Islamic scholars, called **ulama**, are responsible for the interpretation of shari'ah. They use consensus and analogous reasoning to come to decisions. The consensus opinion of the ulama often becomes law. One example of analogous reasoning concerns drinking alcoholic beverages. The Qur'an says one should not drink wine but mentions no other alcoholic beverage. By analogy, the ulama decided that a Muslim was not to drink any intoxicating beverage. As the centuries went on, further rulings were necessary to include other intoxicating materials such as recreational drugs.

While Shi'ah Muslims too have the Qur'an and the Sunnah as the primary sources for shari'ah, they do not use consensus or analogy. Rather, Shi'ah refer to the writings of imams to interpret what behavior God wishes from the people.

Recall that Islam sees no distinction between one's spiritual and temporal life. Hence, shari'ah covers all aspects of a Muslim's life, both personal and public; it contains the principles of how one is to live. Ulama do not see themselves as creators of Islamic law. On the contrary, God is the only lawgiver. Ulama see their role as interpreters of shari'ah, God's path for the believer.

Maulana Syed Arshad Madani, president of Jamiat Ulama-i-Hind in New Delhi, India.

---

ulama Muslim scholars trained in Islam and shari'ah.

As might be imagined, there are many variations of shari'ah. Not only are there differences between Sunni and Shi'ah, but there are geographic, cultural, and historical differences. While some want to reinterpret shari'ah for the age at hand, others see any change in interpretation as an abrogation of God's law. Whatever the differences, the goal is the same—teaching how to live one's life in accordance with the will of God.

SECTION *Assessment*

Reading Comprehension

1. Name and explain each of the Five Pillars of Islam.
2. How does one become a Muslim?
3. What are the sources of shari'ah, and what is its role in Islam?

For Reflection

4. Imagine you are a Muslim high school student beginning the school year the third week in August. The opening of school happens to coincide with Ramadan. Since a total fast from food and drink during daylight hours is mandated, what would your academic, social, extracurricular, religious, and family life be like for that month?
5. Compose three or more pillars that represent the essential practices of your religious tradition.

Flash Search

6. The word *jihad* is used a lot in the media. What are its two main meanings?
7. Why are there special Islamic banks?
8. Research how a college of your choice accommodates the dietary requirements of Muslim students.

Section 4
SACRED TIME

Muslims believe that all time is sacred because all time belongs to God. The five times reserved for prayer each day are even more sacred.

The Islamic calendar begins with the year of Muhammad's Hijrah. It is based on lunar months. The Gregorian calendar most people use is a solar calendar with 365 days and a leap year (extra day added) every four years. A lunar calendar is 354 days. The annual celebrations of the Muslim lunar calendar move back each year by about eleven days according to the secular calendar. For example, Ramadan in the year 2021 begins on April 12. In the year 2022, Ramadan begins on April 2.

This section explains sacred times that have special significance on the Islamic calendar. Two of the most important Islamic festivals are Eid al-Fitr (Festival of Breaking the Fast) at the end of Ramadan and Eid al-Adha (Festival of Sacrifice), which concludes the annual Hajj rituals at Mecca. Another unique holy day is Ashura, a day of atonement.

Eid al-Fitr (Festival of Breaking the Fast)

Eid al-Fitr marks the end of Ramadan, occurring on the first new moon twenty-nine or thirty days after the start of the month. Families come together, dressed in their finest clothes, for a festive meal in the homes of relatives. Cards are sent out, homes are decorated, and children receive presents. Those who are less fortunate are also remembered through charitable giving.

A family celebrates Eid al-Fitr at the end of Ramadan in Cotabato, Philippines.

A family shops at a market ahead of Eid al-Adha in Sana'a, Yemen.

Eid al-Adha (Festival of Sacrifice)

Eid al-Adha is the second of the major festivals in Islam. This feast, celebrated at the end of the Hajj, commemorates Abraham's willingness to sacrifice his son Ishmael (not Isaac, as in the Hebrew Bible) according to the will of Allah. As the angel Jibril substituted a ram for Ishmael, Muslims also slaughter an animal to commemorate their willingness to sacrifice their lives for God. Muslims like to clarify that the slaughter of an animal is not related to washing away sin, as in Judaism or Christianity. Instead, it is a symbol of their willingness to sacrifice themselves to live in God's will. It is usually a sheep or goat that is slaughtered, with most of the meat shared with those in need. In solidarity with those on pilgrimage to Mecca, Muslims not on pilgrimage celebrate this four-day Festival of Sacrifice from their homes with prayer and gift giving.

Ashura

Muslims mark Ashura as a day of fasting similar to the Jewish Yom Kippur, or Day of Atonement. The feast of Ashura marks the day God freed Moses and the Hebrew people from the grip of the Egyptian pharaoh. Muhammad fasted to commemorate this day and requested that his followers do the same.

Friends eat during the Ashura mourning feast in Bagh-e Malek, Iran.

Shi'ah Muslims especially mark Ashura as remembering the martyrdom at Karbala in 680 of Husayn, whom they consider to be the first imam. Adherents mourn the massacre of Husayn and reenact his death through passion plays. Some Shi'ah Muslims parade through the streets of Karbala wearing black, chanting, and striking their chests. A small number of Muslims strike themselves with ropes or chains, emulating the suffering of Husayn.

SECTION *Assessment*

Reading Comprehension

1. Explain the difference between the Gregorian calendar and the Islamic calendar.
2. What are the two great Islamic festivals, and what do they celebrate?
3. What are the two main significances of Ashura?

For Reflection

4. How do religious seasons and festivals contribute to the rhythm of your life?

Flash Search

5. What is a “whirling dervish”?

Section 5

SACRED PLACES AND SACRED SPACES

The mosque is the most sacred and most common space in Islam. There are mosques in almost every urban area and in some rural areas of the world. The holy cities of Mecca, Medina, Jerusalem, and Karbala have special significance to Muslims.

Mosque

The English word *mosque* comes from the Arabic *masjid*, which means "place of prostration in prayer." The mosque is the building of public worship for Muslims. The primary purpose of a mosque is as a space for prayer, either communal or private.

Traditionally, mosques are built in the form of a square and constructed from stone or brick. A mosque's distinctive exterior feature is the minaret, generally a tower where the muezzin proclaims **adhan**, the call to prayer.

Believers gather by the Kul-Sharif Mosque in Kazan, Russia, to celebrate Eid al-Fitr.

In some areas where Muslims are a minority group, the call to prayer of the adhan is confined to the area immediately near the mosque.

A mosque is also used for other social occasions such as weddings and meetings. In non-Muslim countries, the mosque is a place where Muslim children learn to recite the Qur'an in Arabic. The mosque can also be the place where funeral arrangements are made and a body is prepared for burial.

The holy city of Mecca, Saudi Arabia.

Mecca

Mecca, Saudi Arabia, is Islam's holiest city. Mecca is a symbol of Muslims' faith in the one God and God's faithfulness to the covenant with the prophets and, through them, all humankind.

Mecca is the birthplace of Muhammad and the location where he received his first revelations. Muhammad was forced to emigrate from Mecca for several years because of persecution but was later able to return in triumph. Mecca is the site of the Ka'bah and the pilgrimage (Hajj) destination for all Muslims who are able. For Muslims, the Ka'bah is similar in importance to the Holy of Holies for the ancient Jews. It is the geographic center of Islam and the symbolic place of the Divine Presence. After the death of Muhammad, a mosque called the Great Mosque was built around the Ka'bah.

---

adhan In Islam, the "call to prayer."

Medina

Medina, Saudi Arabia, is fewer than three hundred miles from Mecca. It is Islam's second holiest city. Medina was the city to which Muhammad emigrated due to the strong opposition he faced because of his preaching in Mecca. During their pilgrimage to Mecca, many Muslims today take the opportunity to travel to Medina to pray at the Prophet's Mosque, originally built by Muhammad; visit his burial place; and see other historical sites of the early ummah's development.

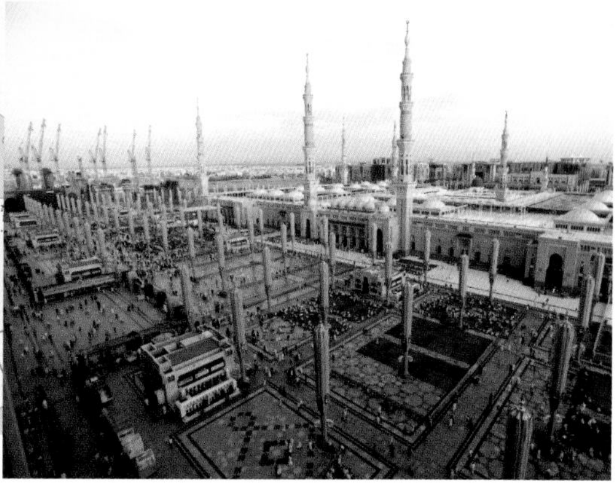

Pilgrims pray at Masjid al-Nabawi after completing the Hajj in Medina. After completing the pilgrimage in Mecca, pilgrims then travel to Medina, a distance of 210 miles.

Jerusalem

The city of Jerusalem is holy for Muslims as it is for Jews and Christians. Muslims believe Muhammad made his Night Journey to this sacred city around 621. The Night Journey refers to the night when Muhammad was taken miraculously on a winged horse to the Temple Mount in Jerusalem. This event includes Muhammad's brief ascension into heaven. There, Muhammad prayed at the head of the assembly of long-deceased prophets such as Abraham, Moses, and John the Baptist. It was during this ascension event that Muslims

The Dome of the Rock shrine in Jerusalem, Israel.

believe God called upon Muhammad to institute the practice of praying five times a day.

At the end of the seventh century, Muslims restored the ruined Temple Mount area, which they call Al-Haram ash-Sharif, or the Noble Sanctuary. Honoring Muhammad's Night Journey experience, Muslims built a shrine there called the Dome of the Rock, whose golden dome shines brightly in the skyline of the Old City. Later, they built the nearby Al-Aqsa Mosque, or "the Farthest Mosque," referring to the holy place that is farthest from the Ka'bah in Mecca. With a capacity of five thousand people, it is the largest mosque in Jerusalem.

Karbala

Karbala, Iraq, is the site of the massacre of Husayn, a grandson of Muhammad, and his family. On their way to Kufah, Iraq, to lay claim to the leadership of the Muslim people, they were besieged and killed by the Umayyad faction, who also claimed leadership. Shi'ah Muslims understand Husayn's

Shi'ah Muslims marking Ashura, which commemorates the slaying of Imam Hussein, in Karbala, Iraq.

death as the martyrdom of those upholding the purity of Islam shared with them by the prophet Muhammad. For this reason, some Shi'ah Muslims view themselves as a people persecuted for the true faith. A shrine with a golden dome surrounds the tomb of Husayn. To this day, Karbala is a significant place of pilgrimage for Shi'ah Muslims.

SECTION *Assessment*

Reading Comprehension

1. What are the various functions of a mosque?
2. How did Mecca become a holy place for Muslims?
3. Why are Medina and Jerusalem also holy cities for Muslims?
4. What is the significance of Karbala, Iraq, for Shi'ah Muslims?

Vocabulary

5. Define *adhan*.

For Reflection

6. In your opinion, how should a person prepare himself or herself before entering your place of worship?

Flash Search

7. Hagia Sophia was a beautiful Byzantine Christian cathedral. How did it become important to Muslims?
8. What is the significance of the color green for Muslims?

Section 6 CATHOLICS DIALOGUE WITH MUSLIMS

> The plan of salvation also includes those who acknowledge the Creator, in the first place amongst whom are the Muslims; these profess to hold the faith of Abraham, and together with us they adore the one, merciful God, mankind's judge on the last day. (*CCC*, 841, quoting *Lumen Gentium*, 16)

While visiting Morocco in August 1985, Pope John Paul II addressed a group of Muslim youth, telling them, "Dialogue between Christians and Muslims is today more necessary than ever." The truth of this statement has not dissipated. Dialogue between these two religious traditions with a common heritage and the two largest numbers of adherents in the world is late in coming. As children of Abraham, Catholics have more in common with Muslims than they may think.

In 1965, the Second Vatican Council instructed Catholics on the similarities between Catholics and Muslims:

> The Church regards with esteem also the Moslems. They adore the one God, living and subsisting in Himself; merciful and all-powerful, the Creator of heaven and earth, who has spoken to men; they take pains to submit wholeheartedly to even His inscrutable decrees, just as Abraham, with whom the faith of Islam takes pleasure in linking itself, submitted to God. Though they do not acknowledge Jesus as God, they revere Him as a prophet. They also honor Mary, his Virgin Mother; at times they even call on her with devotion. In addition, they await the day of judgment when God will render their deserts to all those who have been raised up from

> the dead. Finally, they value the moral life and worship God especially through prayer, almsgiving and fasting. (*Nostra Aetate*, 3)

An illumination from the Bible of Souvigny in the library at Moulins, France, shows Muslims, Christians, and Jews in Abraham's lap.

There are also significant differences between Catholic and Muslim beliefs. One major difference is in the understanding of the nature of God. Though Muslims believe in one God, Christians believe in one God who is in Three Persons—Father, Son, and Holy Spirit. The doctrine of the Holy Trinity is the central mystery of the Christian faith. The unity of Persons within the one God is foreign to Muslim understanding.

Catholics and Muslims also have a fundamental and essential difference in their understanding of Jesus. Catholics believe that Jesus the Christ is at once divine and human. Through the Paschal Mystery of his suffering, Death, and Resurrection, Jesus won redemption and salvation for humankind. Muslims believe Jesus existed, but they do not acknowledge his divinity. Instead, they hold that Jesus was a prophet second only to Muhammad. More particularly, Muslims believe Jesus was born of the Virgin Mary but did not suffer a human death by crucifixion. Instead, what seemed to be a crucifixion was an illusion created for some of Jesus' enemies. God would not let the crucifixion happen. According to the Qur'an, no death occurred. God raised Jesus to heaven.

For Catholics engaged in dialogue with Muslims, there are two things to remember about Muslims. First, Muslims are acutely aware that Catholics' understanding of Muslims is mostly gleaned from the Western media. The negative images of Muslims connected with the events of September 11,

2001, and other terrorist attacks overshadow the more than one billion Muslims in the world who subscribe to peaceful solutions and lifestyles. Second, Islam continues to react in many different ways to the Western colonialism of the seventeenth to twentieth centuries. Some Muslims believe the fall of the great Islamic empires was due to religious laxity. For this reason, they have attempted to purify their religious tradition, at least somewhat, by isolating themselves from dialogue with other religious traditions.

A family enjoys lunch during the festival of Eid al-Adha in Srinagar, the summer capital of Kashmir, India.

Productive dialogue between Catholics and Muslims begins with shared beliefs. The nature of the one God, the heritage of peoples descended from Abraham, and the sharing of positive and peaceful human values are good places to start. Another crucial area is the everyday struggle both religious traditions have with modern "isms" such as secularism and materialism. Family life is central to both Catholics and Muslims. Strategies for preserving religious values and practices while avoiding these clamoring outside pressures are worthy topics of discussion. Issues such as systemic prejudice, poverty, and the care of the environment also form common concerns. The Second Vatican Council "urges all to forget the past and to work sincerely for mutual understanding and to preserve as well as to promote together for the benefit of all mankind social justice and moral welfare, as well as peace and freedom" (*Nostra Aetate*, 3).

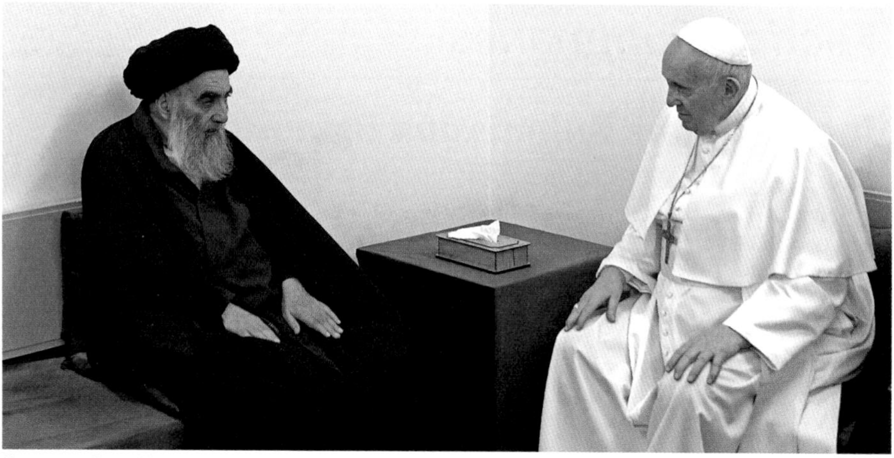

In 2021, Pope Francis met with Grand Ayatollah Sayyid Ali Al-Husayni Al-Sistani in Najaf, Iraq. The two men discussed the importance of cooperation and friendship between religious communities for the good of the region and the entire human family.

SECTION *Assessment*

Reading Comprehension

1. List some similarities between Catholics and Muslims.
2. Explain two significant differences between Catholic and Muslim beliefs.
3. What are two areas of concern when Muslims engage in dialogue with Catholics?
4. List some suggested areas of dialogue with Muslims.

For Reflection

5. What is the most surprising thing you learned in this chapter about Islam?

Flash Search

6. Since Muslims honor Jesus, what are some holy sites common to both Muslims and Christians?

Section Summaries

Introduction: Submission Brings Inner Freedom

Islam, which means "submission," is one of the three Abrahamic religious traditions. The followers of this monotheistic religious tradition are called Muslims. Though Muhammad was instrumental in its spread, Muslims believe Islam has existed since the time of Adam. Hence, Muhammad was not the founder but the restorer of Islam in the seventh century CE.

- In popular culture, the terms *Arab* and *Muslim* are used interchangeably. Explain, with examples, why this is a misrepresentation of both groups of people. Why do you think this confusion persists?

Section 1: A Brief History of Islam

The history of Islam began with a rapid expansion in all directions from its beginnings in Mecca under Muhammad's inspiration. Muhammad was the final messenger of God. He lived in present-day Saudi Arabia from about 570 to 632 CE. Under the first four Right Guided Caliphs, the Muslim caliphate expanded from the Arabian Peninsula to Northern Africa, China, India, and up to the Pyrenees in Europe. Muslim civilization and culture flourished between the eighth and thirteenth centuries, the Golden Age of Islam. In modern times, Western imperial powers eroded the Islamic caliphates and Islamic influence. In the twentieth century, the weakening and dismantling of Muslim states contributed to the erosion of Muslim influence. In current times, an intra-Islamic divide widened among Muslims concerning who has the authority to define a true Muslim.

- Share separate visual images of Islamic literature, poetry, philosophy, and historical events with a caption explaining each.

Section 2: Sacred Stories and Sacred Scriptures

Muslims believe that the Qur'an is the literal, infallible, direct word of God to humanity. For Muslims, it is the perfect scripture, although they read and respect the Torah, the Psalms, and the Gospels. The Sunnah is the example and lifestyle of Muhammad, much of it recorded in the Hadith. The Hadith are the recorded words and deeds of Muhammad.

- Create a two-column chart comparing and contrasting the Muslim view of Adam found in the Qur'an with the Judeo-Christian view of Adam found in the Hebrew Scriptures.

Section 3: Beliefs and Practices

Every Muslim's primary religious duties are the Five Pillars of Islam: the profession of faith, prayer, fasting, almsgiving, and pilgrimage. Attention to God and caring for others are the essential duties of a Muslim. The ummah is the name of the universal Islamic community. Shari'ah is the sacred law of Islam; its source is in the Qur'an and the Sunnah. Shari'ah is both a legal and a moral guide for Muslims. For Sunni Muslims, Islamic scholars called ulama are responsible for the interpretation of shari'ah. Shi'ah Muslims rely on the writings of the imams for interpretation of shari'ah.

- Create a word scramble, matching questions, or fill-in-the-blank sentences using at least six terms from this section. Print an answer key on the back of the paper. Exchange with a classmate and solve each other's vocabulary quizzes.

Section 4: Sacred Time

The two great feasts of Islam are Eid al-Fitr, the Festival of Breaking the Fast, which celebrates the end of Ramadan; and Eid al-Adha, the Festival of Sacrifice, which remembers Abraham's willingness to sacrifice his son Ishmael. Ashura is a day of fasting for all Muslims and a day of remembrance for Husayn's martyrdom for Shi'ah Muslims.

- Research and summarize in three to four paragraphs the conflict between Saudi Arabia and Iran over Mecca.

Section 5: Sacred Places and Sacred Spaces

The mosque is the place of public and private prayer for Muslims. Its primary use is communal prayer, but it also is used for other social, educational, and business functions. Mecca is the holiest city for Muslims. Medina is the second holiest city. Jerusalem and Karbala are other holy cities.

- Draw and label a simple floorplan of a mosque.

Section 6: Catholics Dialogue with Muslims

Similarities between Muslims and Catholics include their worship of the one Creator God and their submission to God's will. Two significant areas of difference between Muslims and Catholics concern the nature of God and the nature of Jesus Christ. Productive dialogue between Catholics and Muslims begins with shared beliefs. Other areas for discussion include family life, strategies for preserving religious values and practices in modern society, systemic prejudice, poverty, and care of the environment.

- Compare in three to four paragraphs the Islamic understanding of Isaac and Ishmael with the Catholic understanding.

Chapter Projects

Complete one of these projects by the conclusion of your study of this chapter.

1. Reading and Reporting on *The Kite Runner*

   Read the novel *The Kite Runner* by Khaled Hosseini. It is a story of friendship and family relationships set against the Russian invasion of Afghanistan in the 1980s, including the migration of refugees to Pakistan and the United States. Write a three- to four-page essay that includes the following:

   - the author's religious background
   - the historical context
   - the political context
   - how the main characters in the novel express Sunni and Shi'ah Islam (give specific examples from the novel)
   - the author's view of redemption as expressed in the novel's narrative (give examples)

2. Visual Presentation: The Taj Mahal

   Create a digital or slide presentation on the Taj Mahal, a mausoleum and a jewel of Muslim art in India. Write detailed notes for each image explaining the history and architecture shown. Your presentation should have ten to fifteen slides. Include these details:

   - the purpose of the building
   - the history of the building
   - its architecture
   - its exterior and interior designs and decorations
   - its place in the history of Islamic architecture
   - the Taj Mahal in modern times

3. Reading and Reporting on *I Am Malala* by Malala Yousafzai

   Malala Yousafzai is a Pakistani activist for human rights and education, especially for women. She is the youngest Nobel Peace Prize winner in history. Read her autobiography, and write a three- to four-page report that includes the following information:

   - the historical context
   - the political context
   - the religious context
   - her family background
   - examples from the book supporting Malala's statement "I'm a feminist and a Muslim."

4. Video Recorded Interview with a Muslim Neighbor

   Prepare and record a ten- to fifteen-minute interview with a Muslim adult neighbor. The video must be sharable with your class and teacher. Ask the neighbor to share the following:

   - background on his or her family and their place of origin
   - the attractiveness of Muslim life
   - the pluses and minuses of being a Muslim in Western society
   - a family heirloom
   - beliefs about the afterlife

5. Printing in Classical or Modern Arabic

   Print in classical or modern Arabic three of the "Ninety-Nine Names for Allah." Use a separate 8.5-by-11-inch sheet of heavy cardboard for each name. On a separate sheet of paper, write a brief explanation of the meaning of the names you have chosen as well as citations for where they occur in the Qur'an.

Key Image

Crescent Moon and Star

The crescent moon and star is the distinguishing symbol of Islam and identifies something as Islamic, but it is not a religious symbol. It is not mentioned in the Qur'an, Sunnah, or Hadith, the sacred writings of Islam. In fact, the crescent moon and star predate Islam by hundreds of years. Before the birth of Jesus, the symbol was used to decorate buildings, pottery, artworks, and coins in Mesopotamia and Persia.

The ancient Greek goddess Hekate was associated with the crescent moon and star. When Hekate was credited with protecting Byzantium from Philip II of Macedon's major, ultimately unsuccessful, siege (340–339 BCE), the city adopted these symbols in her honor. The crescent moon was on the city's flag, and both the crescent moon and star were on the city's coinage. In 330 CE, the Roman emperor Constantine moved the capital of the empire from Rome to Byzantium and renamed the city New Rome. To the crescent moon on the flag he added a six-pointed star in honor of Mary, the mother of Jesus.

Muhammad (ca. 570–632), who in Muslim understanding restored a religious tradition known as Islam, was so intent on the oneness of God that he prohibited any imagery of what God created. Muhammad would claim no symbol for Islam. In his military campaigns, flags were a solid black, white, or green. However, by the end of the seventh century, the crescent moon and star were on Islamic coins, and in the twelfth century on Islamic metalwork. But neither was exclusive to Islam. These same images could be found in Christian and secular contexts as well.

The Ottoman Empire was founded in Anatolia in about 1299 by Osman I. Legend tells of a dream Osman had in which the entire earth, from one end to the other, was umbrellaed with a crescent moon. For Osman, this dream was an affirmation of his caliphate, and he adopted the crescent moon as its symbol. However, the Ottoman Empire was a political entity, not a religious one. In 1844, the Ottoman Empire adopted a single flag that was red with a white crescent moon pointed to the right and a star. Today, with slight changes, it is the flag of Turkey.

A new Islamic movement emerged in the late nineteenth century with a desire to shed colonialism and foster a united and nationalistic Islamic community. The movement created a green flag with a white crescent moon and star. Several newly formed Muslim countries, some part of the Ottoman Empire and some not, adopted the crescent moon and star symbol. Variations included more than one star and the moon pointing in a different direction.

There are Muslims today who believe, like Muhammad, there should be no Islamic symbol at all. Yet for many other Muslims, the crescent moon and star identify a person, place, or thing as Islamic. Especially when Muslims are a minority in a community, they find it important to let others, both Muslim and non-Muslim, know that an establishment is Islamic. The crescent moon and star can be seen on many mosques and minarets; in Islamic community centers and Islamic schools; on storefronts, business buildings, and clothing; and as tattoos.

All Muslims agree that the crescent moon and star is not a religious symbol. Thus, the meaning ascribed to it is varied and personal.

Faithful Adherent

Rumi: Poet for Everyone

Rumi (1207–1273) was born Jalāl al-Dīn Muhammad Balkhi in Balkh in today's northern Afghanistan, a very religiously diverse region with Zoroastrians, Jews, Christians, Muslims, and Buddhists. He came from a long line of Islamic preachers. Rumi's father, Baha al-Din Walad, was a highly

Street vendors sitting under a sign bearing the image of Sufi mystic and poet Rumi in Mazar-i-Sharif, Afghanistan.

accomplished Sunni Islamic scholar, jurist, and mystic whom the people called the "Sultan of the Scholars." Rumi, religiously greatly influenced by his father, was raised a Muslim.

Mongol incursions under Genghis Khan (reigned 1206–1227) when Rumi was about eleven years old prompted Baha al-Din Walad to move his family and some of his followers out of danger. Their caravan was on the move for approximately eight years and covered about 4,500 miles. They traveled through such towns and cities as Baghdad, Jerusalem, Damascus, and Aleppo before settling in Konya, Anatolia, in present-day Turkey. Along the way, Rumi and his father fulfilled the Fifth Pillar of Islam by going on pilgrimage to Mecca.

Konya was in the empire of the Seljuks of Rum—hence the name "Rumi." Under the Seljuk sultanate of Rum, Baha al-Din Walad was appointed to a high government post and taught at a **madrasah**. Rumi studied Arabic,

---

madrasah A school or college of Islamic studies. Muhammad was the teacher of the first madrasah, which was in Mecca.

Sufism A mystical element of Islam. Practitioners seek a direct relationship with Allah through ascetic religious practices beyond those required for a Muslim.

Greek, the Qur'an, theology, shari'ah, philosophy, history, mathematics, and astronomy. He became a noted lecturer and preacher, thus gaining the Arabic title *Mawlana*, meaning "our master" or "our lord." Following in his father's footsteps, Rumi became an Islamic theologian, preacher, and jurist. After his father's death, Rumi took over his father's teaching post at the madrasah. He also began to fully immerse himself into the ways of **Sufism**. Rumi's great intellectual pursuits expanded to include the ways of the heart.

In 1244, when he was about thirty-seven, Rumi's life changed forever. That year he met a Sufi mystic named Shams of Tabriz, who became both a spiritual mentor and a spiritual companion to Rumi. After about three years, Shams disappeared, most likely murdered. Not believing such a thing could happen, Rumi set out to find his friend, going even as far as Damascus. It was at this point that Rumi had a breakthrough: "Why should I seek? I am the same as He. His essence speaks through me. I have been looking for myself!" Rumi realized his search for Shams was a far deeper search—a search for the God within.

From his profound loss of a great friend, poetry poured out of Rumi. A collection of his poems written in honor of Shams is called *Divan-i Kabir* or *Diwan-i Shams-i Tabrizi*. Rumi had immense love for his lost friend, but the poems were really about love of God. The reader can sense the release of Rumi's soul after so intense a loss. The love of God transcended the outward practices of Islam. He was ready to abandon his ego:

Whirling dervishes perform during a ceremony marking the anniversary of the death of Rumi.

I died as mineral and became a plant,
I died as plant and rose to animal,
I died as animal and I was human,
Why should I fear? When was I less by dying?
Yet once more I shall die human,
To soar with angels blessed above.
And when I sacrifice my angel soul
I shall become what no mind ever conceived.
As a human, I will die once more,
Reborn, I will with the angels soar.
And when I let my angel body go,
I shall be more than mortal mind can know.

Rumi never abandoned Islam in any way. He brought it to another level. The Qur'an was a significant theme for Rumi:

Flee to God's Qur'an, take refuge in it;
there with the spirits of the prophets merge.
The Book conveys the prophets' circumstances,
those fish of the pure sea of Majesty.

The writings by Rumi that are considered most important are found in the *Mathnawi*, a collection in six volumes of 26,000 couplets. There is no organization to the work other than its underlying topic of Sufi Islam. This work contains not only poetry but narratives, stories, anecdotes, and reflections. The stories and anecdotes, in particular, were developed from Qur'anic verses. It is written not only in Rumi's native Persian language but also in Arabic, Greek, and the local Oghuz Turkish language. As a scholar, he loved to teach, but Rumi wrote in a style accessible to all: simple, lyrical, and emotive; delightful, joyful, hopeful, humorous, and playful. He wrote in the second person. Rumi wrote of creation, wisdom, kindness, friendship, separation, loss, death, and most importantly love.

Rumi once wrote, "There are many roads which lead to God. I have chosen the one of dance and music." This was not a pleasing statement to more conventional Muslims for whom neither music nor dance were acceptable means of worship. Rumi was a "whirling **dervish**" who employed a meditation style of whirling in a circle with the head looking upward and arms

Rumi

outstretched. By this gesture, one opens one's whole self to the presence of God. As one whirls, simple music is played, particularly with a reed and a drum. After Rumi's death, his son Sultan Walad founded the Sufi Mevlevi Order, in which this dance is an integral part of worship.

For Rumi, nothing should be an obstacle to "turning" to God. He advocated the tolerance of all religious traditions. At his funeral, local Jews and Christians joined in the entourage that honored him. To this day, Rumi's tomb in Konya is a place of pilgrimage. One of Rumi's quotes is on his tombstone: "When we are dead, seek not our tomb in the earth, but find it in the hearts of men."

Reading Comprehension

1. What was the most significant turning point in Rumi's life?
2. What was Rumi's relationship with Islam?
3. What were some of the themes about which Rumi wrote, and which one was the most important?
4. Why is Rumi a model for interreligious dialogue?

For Reflection

5. How do you think Rumi's eight years as a migrant affected his writings?

---

dervish Another name for a Sufi; a Muslim who has taken a vow of poverty and austerity.

Prayer

Al-Fatihah ("The Opening") is often called the "Lord's Prayer of Islam." It is taken from the opening surah of the Qur'an.

In the name of **GOD**, Most Gracious, Most Merciful.
Praise be to **GOD**, Lord of the universe,
Most Gracious, Most Merciful,
Master of the Day of Judgment.
You alone we worship; You alone we ask for help.
Guide us in the right path;
the path of those whom You blessed; not of those who have deserved wrath, nor of the strayers.
(Surah 1:1–7, Qur'an)

5

HINDUISM

Introduction

IN PURSUIT OF ULTIMATE LIBERATION

Hinduism may be the world's oldest living religious tradition. It originated in approximately 1500 BCE on the Indian subcontinent. Though Hinduism moved beyond the Indian subcontinent in the nineteenth century, 94 percent of the world's Hindus live in India. Unlike Judaism, Christianity, and Islam, Hinduism had no founder or particular event that marked its beginnings. Instead, Hinduism is a synthesis of many elements, including the Vedic religion of the Indo-Aryans; the sacrificial rituals called **bhakti**; and the **asceticism** and meditation of, among others, the Jains and Buddhists.

The word *Hindu* comes from the **Sanskrit** word *sindhu*, meaning "river," specifically the Indus River in the northwest region of the subcontinent; it originally referred to people living in the Indus Valley region. In colonial times, the British designated *Hinduism* to refer to all the religious beliefs and practices of the people of India who were not Buddhists, Jains, Sikhs, Parsis, Muslims, Jews, or Christians. Hence, Hinduism is a foreign name imposed on its adherents in India. Most Indians would not call themselves Hindus; they might identify themselves by what **caste** they belong to, their family heritage,

---

bhakti In Hinduism, the devotional way of achieving liberation from the cycle of death and rebirth, emphasizing a devotee's loving faith in the gods.

asceticism The practice of self-denial and self-discipline, particularly for religious or spiritual reasons.

Sanskrit From a word that means "perfected"; an ancient Indo-Aryan language that is the language of Hinduism and the Vedas.

Millions visit the Sri Ranganathaswamy Temple of Srirangam in Tiruchirappalli, India, every year.

their town or village of origin, what philosophical school they adhere to, or what rituals they practice.

Hindus accept the premises or parts of several religious traditions. Nevertheless, Hindus hold that no one religious tradition can claim knowledge of the absolute Truth. To Hindus, the **Ultimate Reality** that other religious traditions may name as "God" is unknowable. Hinduism encourages its adherents to imagine a god that is best for them, even if that god comes from another religious tradition. Though Hinduism is mostly confined to India, its many practices and loosely held beliefs merit study because of Hinduism's long history.

---

caste One of the hereditary social classes in Hindu India that determines the occupation and social possibilities of its members.

Ultimate Reality In Hinduism, Brahman is the highest reality in the universe.

SECTION *Assessment*

Reading Comprehension

1. When and where did Hinduism originate?
2. What is the origin of the word *Hindu*?
3. How did people in India come to be called Hindus?

For Reflection

4. How would you feel about practicing a religion that did not originate with one founder?

Flash Search

5. Name and describe one famous Hindu who grew up in your state or province.

Section 1
A BRIEF HISTORY OF HINDUISM

Rather than addressing how Hinduism *began*, it is correct to speak about how Hinduism *emerged* as a religious tradition. What is now called Hinduism has grown and expanded over hundreds of centuries. The banyan tree, which is native to the Indian subcontinent, is often used as an analogy to explain Hinduism to non-Hindu people. A banyan tree does not only have branches that grow up; it has some branches that grow down into the ground, become roots, and sprout new trunks alongside the old. In an old banyan tree, it becomes difficult to distinguish which is the original trunk. Likewise, religious traditions in India have expanded and changed so much that there is no linear path to a beginning of what we call Hinduism.

Indus Valley Civilization (ca. 3300–1300 BCE)

The origins of Hinduism emerged in the greater Indus River region of southern Asia, in present-day Pakistan and northwestern India. Because scholars to this day are unable to decipher writings from the Indus Valley Civilization, archaeological finds are essential for revealing this vast and complex civilization. No place of worship or objects that might be for religious rituals have been found. However, archaeologists have discovered artifacts, such as female figurines, that have characteristics suggesting fertility and regeneration. Many seals that were pressed into clay have been found. Several seals depict male animals, also suggesting regeneration; other seals appear to show a man sitting in a meditative position. Still others portray a figure that could be a precursor of the Hindu god *shiva*. Other finds include jewelry charms, likely worn to

Excavated ruins of the city known in modern times as Mohenjo-daro in Sindh, Pakistan. Built in the twenty-sixth century BCE, it was one of the world's earliest major cities.

protect the wearer from evil spirits. The finds show that fire, water, and the sun all had religious significance.

Archaeologists have not located many weapons, which suggests a relatively peaceful civilization. Walls around the cities seem constructed more for flood control than for protection from enemies. Like the Nile River, the Indus River would seasonally flood its banks, leaving fertile silt for planting when the water receded. Inhabitants of the early Indus Valley Civilization engaged predominantly in herding and agriculture. At its peak, the Indus Valley Civilization was larger than the Egyptian, Mesopotamian, and Chinese civilizations of the same era.

Archaeological finds of the later years of the Indus Valley Civilization reveal well-planned urban societies. There was an elaborate water system, with each home having a bath with its accompanying drainage and sewer system. These baths suggest the value of hygiene and perhaps ritual purity associated with religious practice. Most astonishing is the seeming standardization of the layout of the cities, with their main north-south and east-west straight streets and the fired brickwork on buildings. Though cities were miles apart, their buildings contained many bricks of a uniform size.

Why the Indus Valley Civilization started to decline is unknown. It could have been a series of natural disasters, a gradual climate change, trade deficits, or a combination of factors. As it declined, inhabitants of the cities slowly

HINDUISM: TIMELINE OF KEY EVENTS

BCE

ca. 3300–1300............Indus Valley Civilization

ca. 2000–1300...........Aryan migration into northern India

ca. 1500......................Beginning of compilation of Vedas

ca. 500........................Beginning of compilation of *Bhagavad Gita*

ca. 900........................Beginning of compilation of Upanishads

ca. 500s.......................Buddhism and Jainism founded

ca. 400........................Beginning of compilation of the *Mahabharata*

ca. 400........................Composition of the *Ramayana*

CE

ca. 300–1500.............Composition of the Puranas

ca. 700s.......................Beginning of Muslim conquests in northwestern India

1175.............................Muslims establish capital at Delhi

1440.............................Birth of Kabir Das

1469.............................Birth of Guru Nanak, founder of Sikhism

1498.............................Vasco da Gama lands on Indian soil

1526.............................Beginning of Mughal Empire

1542–1605..................Life of Akbar

1666.............................Birth of Gobind Singh

1836.............................Birth of Ramakrishna

1858.............................British conquer Mughal Empire

1861 .... Birth of Rabindranath Tagore

1863 .... Birth of Vivekananda

1869 .... Birth of Mohandas Gandhi

1893 .... First World's Parliament of Religions held in Chicago

1897 .... Foundation of Ramakrishna movement

1947 .... Indian independence from Britain and founding of Pakistan

ca. 1965 .... Maharishi Mahesh Yogi brings his Transcendental Meditation Movement to the West

moved out, particularly toward the south and southeast, and began engaging in a simpler, more agrarian lifestyle. During this period, nomadic peoples known as Indo-Aryans slowly moved from central Asia into the Indus Valley region. Indo-Aryan society began to rise during an era called the Vedic Period. The two prominent contributions of Indo-Aryans to Hinduism may be their language and their scriptures.

Vedic Period (ca. 1500–500 BCE)

We know very little about the Indo-Aryan settlers of the Indus Valley except through a collection of their writings called the **Vedas**. First passed on orally, the Vedas were not written down for many years. The Vedic Period can be divided into the Early Vedic Period and the Later Vedic Period.

Vedas Ancient scriptures composed in Sanskrit that are the foundation of Hinduism. The word *Veda* means "knowledge." The most important Veda is the *Rig Veda*, which consists of 1,028 hymns praising the gods of the Aryan tribes who invaded India from the northwest starting around 2000 BCE.

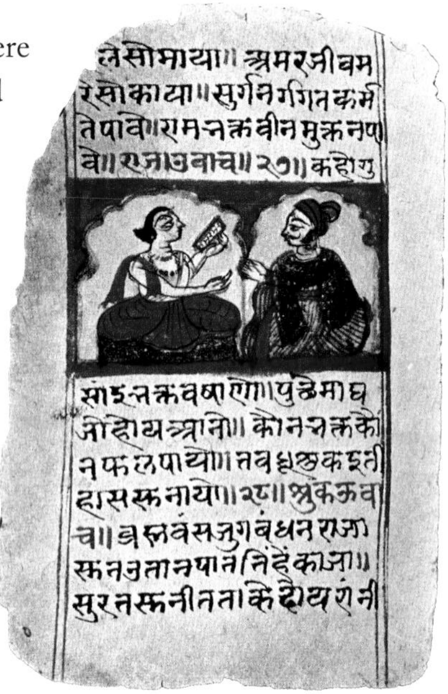

The Rigveda, or Rig Veda, is the oldest of the Veda texts. It contains a collection of hymns from between ca. 1500 and 1000 BCE.

Peoples of the Early Vedic Period were nomadic or seminomadic. They engaged predominantly in husbandry and agriculture, although there was also a warrior contingent adept at using horses. Later in the period, the people learned iron working, which enhanced their skill in battles and at working the land. They lived in villages, tribes, and clans. Each tribe was headed by a nonhereditary chief responsible for protecting the people and leading the local assembly or council. Though men and women had distinct tasks, women made more contributions in their societies than in the Later Vedic Period. Women had educational opportunities and could speak at communal assemblies. There was a class distinction based on the type of work in which one engaged, but distinctions were not so rigid that a person could not marry outside his or her class.

As the tribes were nomadic or seminomadic, the construction of permanent buildings was not practical. Both personal and communal worship occurred in the open. The people worshipped classical natural elements like earth (*Prithvi*), wind (*Vayu*), fire (*Agni*), water/rain (*Indra*), sun (*Surya*), and sky (*Varuna*). All was passed down orally, including prayers recited. Prayers mainly asked for what the people needed to survive. Offerings of simple food were part of the simple ritual.

In the Later Vedic Period, the Indo-Aryans spread to cover the whole of what is now northern India/Pakistan. As the people dispersed, their rulers, whose leadership became more singular and more powerful, claimed more territory. Growing kingdoms displaced the strong village ties and egalitarian assemblies. Settlements became more urban. Women lost representation and became more confined to household duties. Social stratification evolved into a rigid, hereditary caste system. The proper behavior of men and women at particular stages of life and within and between castes became more clearly regulated.

The education of boys—training under a **guru**—grew in importance, while the education of girls (except for the wealthy) declined. Gurus trained their disciples in many disciplines, including bhakti, a personal devotion to the gods. Two Hindu gods, Shiva and Vishnu, gained great prominence during this time. There was also a rise in people withdrawing for solitary personal prayer and other ascetical practices.

The trimuri is the three supreme deities of Hinduism: Shiva, Vishnu, and Brahma. This statue in the Elephanta Caves in Mumbai Harbor, India, is from the seventh or eighth century.

Classical Period (ca. 500 BCE–1200 CE)

The Classical Period is when Hinduism became recognized as a religious tradition. Ritual forms changed dramatically. Hindu temples were established even as home-based rituals continued to flourish. Rituals dealing with the cosmos became less important, and personal transformation came to the forefront. There was a shift in emphasis from the **transcendent** (e.g., the divine) to the immanent (e.g., the personal).

---

guru From the Sanskrit for "teacher"; a Hindu teacher and guide in philosophical and spiritual matters.

transcendent A term that means "lying beyond the ordinary range of perception."

The Hindu concepts of **karma** and reincarnation, the rebirth of souls in new bodies or forms of life, also arose during this time. Likewise, **samsara** came to the forefront. Meaning "to flow together," it is the belief in an ongoing migration between life and death and new life. In Hinduism, samsara is seen as ignorance of **Brahman**, or Ultimate Reality, and thus the soul is led to believe in the reality of the temporal, phenomenal world. Hindus established three nonexclusive ways to deal with samsara: the Path of Action, the Path of Knowledge, and the Path of Devotion (see Section 3, the feature "Three Paths to Liberation").

The Bhagvad Ghita *is written as a conversation between Prince Arjuna and his guide and charioteer Krishna, an avatar of Lord Vishnu.*

---

karma In Hinduism and Buddhism, the sum of a person's actions in this and previous states of existence, viewed as deciding their fate in future existences (reincarnations).

samsara In Hinduism, the endless cycle of birth, death, and rebirth or reincarnation until one has achieved oneness with Brahman (Ultimate Reality). Hindus believe that the illusion that a person is an individual rather than being one with Ultimate Reality fuels samsara. Buddhists believe much the same thing, but they believe that life is full of suffering.

Brahman In Hinduism, Ultimate Reality or Absolute Reality; the ultimate ground of all being.

Sanskrit, the liturgical and scriptural language of Hinduism that only a few understood, gave way to the use of vernacular. The **shruti** scriptures, which contained the Vedas and had been passed on orally, became the authoritative scripture believed to be divine revelation. Another emerging body of literature that the populace found more appealing was known as **smriti**. This

Mahavira founded Jainism in the sixth century BCE. Born a Hindu, Mahavira ("the Great Hero") reacted against some of Hinduism's practices, including the elaborate sacrificial rituals. Jainism contains some elements from both Hinduism and Buddhism. Jains are most noted for establishing ***ahimsa****, or nonviolence, an attitude that influenced many other Hindus, including Mohandas Gandhi, the famous Indian lawyer who led the peaceful revolution for India's independence in the twentieth century. Jains practice nonviolence or noninjury to the point that they will eat only those foods that will not kill plants or animals. Thus, they are vegetarians whose diet consists mainly of milk, fruit, and nuts. Most Jains reside in India, with others scattered in the United States and Canada, Europe, Africa, and East Asia.*

---

shruti From a word that means "that which is heard"; the most revered body of Hindu sacred scripture.

smriti Meaning "that which is remembered"; Hindu scriptures in the form of epics and stories that shed light on the more abstract and esoteric shruti scriptures. The *Mahabharata* and the *Ramayana* are smriti scriptures.

ahimsa In Hinduism, Jainism, and Buddhism, the intentional avoidance of violence or injury against another living thing by acts of omission or commission, be it word or deed.

included two great epics, the ***Mahabharata***, which includes the ***Bhagavad Gita***, and the ***Ramayana***.

Hindu-Muslim Period (ca. 1200–1600)

Muslim traders reached the borders of India at the end of the seventh century. By the early eleventh century, Muslims had conquered the northwest section of India. The newly arrived Muslim leaders did not try to convert Hindus to Islam. However, they did impose a tax on Hindus similar to the taxes they imposed on Jews and Christians they ruled in other places. Throughout the twelfth and thirteenth centuries, Muslim sultans moved into the northern and central sections of India, administering the region from Delhi.

In the sixteenth century, the Muslim Mughal Empire overran the Muslim rulers of Delhi and expanded Islam further into India. Some Mughal rulers were tolerant of Hinduism, while others took to destroying Hindu temples and statues. The Mughal emperor Akbar (reigned 1556–1605) attempted to combine different beliefs of the various religious traditions of India, even holding high-level discussions on the topic, but was unsuccessful. After Akbar, Muslim tolerance for Hinduism deteriorated,

Abū al-Fatḥ Jalāl al-Dīn Muḥammad Akbar.

Mahabharata Part of the Hindu smriti scriptures, an epic about the feud between the Pandava and Kaurava families over inheritance. Within the large epic are smaller stories, often philosophical.

Bhagavad Gita One of the stories within the *Mahabharata* epic, the most quoted of all Hindu scriptures throughout the centuries. It is a dialogue between Arjuna, a righteous warrior, and his charioteer, Krishna, an avatar of Vishnu, about personal detachment.

Ramayana Part of the Hindu smriti scriptures, an epic about the adventures of Prince Rama, who journeys to rescue his wife, Sita, from the demon-king Ravana.

and compromise on either side was negligible. For the most part, Hindus during this period established practices that clearly distinguished them from Muslims.

The tension between Hindus and Muslims contributed to great creativity. The Hindu poet Kabir Das (1440–1518) was influenced by Islamic mysticism, while his disciple Nanak (1469–1539) began a new religious tradition called Sikhism (see Section 3, the feature "Sikhism"), a synthesis of Hinduism and Islam.

Modern Period (1600–Present)

In 1858, the British defeated the Muslim Mughal rulers of India and made India a colony of Britain. With the arrival of the British in India came European culture, European values, and Christianity. European, and particularly British, colonialism was perhaps more disruptive to the social fabric of India and its inhabitants than the invasion of Muslims had been, especially in the cities. Hindus felt pressure to conform to the British way of life at least until 1947, when India gained independence from Britain, due in part to the work of Mohandas Gandhi (see Faithful Adherent, "Mohandas K. Gandhi: The 'Great Soul'").

British troops quelling the Indian Rebellion of 1857.

Meanwhile, tensions between Hindus and Muslims did not cease. Also in 1947, Muslims broke away from India and established East and West Pakistan, one nation with India sitting between its two regions. Not all Muslims chose to become part of Pakistan. To this day, there is a sizable number of Muslims in India, especially in the north. In 1971, East Pakistan became Bangladesh.

Though Christians have been on Indian soil since the late first century CE, it was not until the sixteenth century that a steady flow of Christian missionaries came to India. Some Hindus responded by taking the opportunity to reform their religion. Sri Ramakrishna (1836–1886) began the Ramakrishna movement to spread the idea that all religious traditions are paths to God.

Swami Vivekananda (1863–1902) was an Indian Hindu monk who toured the United States, Europe, and England in the late nineteenth century, introducing Hinduism to the Western world.

Very few people outside India knew of the existence of Hinduism until the late nineteenth century. A Hindu named Swami Vivekananda participated in the World's Parliament of Religions held in Chicago in 1893 and followed up by touring many parts of the United States as a missionary of Hinduism. Since then, a number of Hindu leaders have traveled throughout the world, especially to the West, preaching their understanding of Hinduism to whoever would listen.

In the 1960s, the British rock group The Beatles brought Maharishi Mahesh Yogi and his advocacy of **Transcendental Meditation** to the world's attention. In Transcendental Meditation, a person is given a mantra on which to meditate daily. During the 1960s and 1970s, A. C. Bhaktivedanta Swami Prabhupada (1896–1977) founded the International Society for Krishna Consciousness (ISKCON). Adherents are more popularly known as "Hare Krishnas" because of their continual chant using those words. Devotees are recognized in airports, on street corners, and on college campuses by their saffron-colored robes.

In 1968, The Beatles and their family and friends traveled to Rishikesh, India, to learn Transcendental Meditation from Maharishi Mahesh Yogi.

One reason Hinduism is so complex is that it is at once a religion and part of secular Indian society. In the twentieth century, as secularism grew in India and Western ideas became more influential, Hinduism overlapped even more between religion and the state.

India has 94 percent of the world's Hindus. At present, India is the largest democracy in the world and an emerging, future-driven economic powerhouse. The caste system is still practiced in India, often to the detriment of India's democratic principles. Some believe Hinduism is losing its soul. India has nationalistic goals and possesses nuclear weapons, the latter against the nonviolent roots of Hinduism. Most disturbing is the escalation of discrimination against non-Hindus, particularly Muslims and Sikhs.

Transcendental Meditation A trademarked meditation technique derived from Hinduism that promotes deep relaxation through recitation of a mantra.

SECTION *Assessment*

Reading Comprehension

1. What are some differences in how people lived between the Early Vedic Period and the Later Vedic Period?
2. How did Hinduism shift to emphasizing personal transformation during the Classical Period?
3. Describe the relationship in India between Hindus and Muslims between 1200 and 1600 CE.
4. Describe one movement that contributed to the expansion of Hinduism outside of India in the nineteenth and twentieth centuries.
5. Describe two considerable challenges Hindus encounter in India today.

Vocabulary

6. What was the purpose of a *guru*?

For Reflection

7. What images do you associate with Hinduism?

Flash Search

8. What is the Transcendental Meditation movement like today?
9. Besides dietary choice, list specific ways Jains practice ahimsa today.
10. Former Beatle George Harrison wrote a hit song called "My Sweet Lord." To whom does the song refer?

Section 2

SACRED STORIES AND SACRED SCRIPTURES

Of the two categories of Hindu sacred scriptures introduced earlier—shruti and smriti—shruti are considered the more sacred. *Shruti* means "that which was heard"; Hindus believe shruti texts contain what the gods revealed of the nature of all reality to ancient seers called **rishis**, and not one syllable is to be changed. *Smriti,* the second category of scriptures, is a word that means "that which is to be remembered." Though less authoritative, the smriti texts contain Hindu traditions initially passed down orally through the ages and are read more widely.

Shruti Scriptures

The earliest of the shruti scriptures—the Vedas—are from the Indo-Aryan era. They developed from an oral tradition transmitted only by Vedic priests. The priests believed that the timeless wisdom of the Vedas was revealed to rishis in the primordial past. They also believed the spoken word had the power for both good and evil and only the priests were to be the custodians of that force. The spoken word had to be pronounced correctly in order for it to be meaningful.

Originally, transforming the spoken words of the Vedas into written words was considered to be a defilement of the sacred. Even after the Vedas were in written form, they were still kept in the hands of the priests for centuries

---

rishis Hindu holy persons or sages.

before they became available as sacred scriptures for all Hindus. The Vedas were not translated from Sanskrit into European languages until after the British arrival in the seventeenth century.

The Vedas are made up of numerous hymns. Only the priests knew and chanted the hymns from memory. These hymns played a part in the sacrifice to the gods, the main form of worship for Indo-Aryans. There are four Vedas:

1. The *Rig Veda* is the oldest and most sacred. Compiled in the Sanskrit language about 1300 BCE, it contains more than a thousand hymns to various gods. There are multiple accounts of creation, hymns of praise to various gods, and mantras used in the fire sacrifice.

2. The *Sama Veda*, compiled around the eleventh century BCE, is a collection of hymns that were chanted at the **soma** sacrifices.

3. The *Yajur Veda* is a more prose form instructing the priests in the proper manner of fire and soma sacrifices.

4. The *Atharva Veda*, compiled around the ninth century BCE, is a collection of hymns intended for use in the home. This Veda also contains some charms, spells, and incantations to bring about healing or remove curses. Some of the healing is to correct the mistakes made during a sacrificial ritual.

There are four subdivisions within the Vedas. The *Brahmanas* are commentaries on the significance of the various rituals. *Aranyakas* are liturgies and rituals, *Samhitas* are hymns of praise to the forces of nature or mantras, and *Upanishads* are mainly philosophical texts.

The Upanishads merit more discussion. The word *upanishad* means "to sit down beside." These stories are often in the form of a dialogue between guru and student that attempts to reveal what is truly real and what is an illusion. More specifically, the Upanishads are concerned with the cycle of rebirth as it is contingent on a person's actions, liberation from the cycle of rebirth, and

---

soma A hallucinogenic beverage that was used in ancient India as an offering to Hindu gods and in Vedic ritual sacrifices.

the mystical relationship between Brahman, or Ultimate Reality, and **atman**, a person's soul/self. For example, the following story about a boy named Svetaketu is from the *Chandogya Upanishad* of the *Sama Veda*. Svetaketu's father is instructing his son on matters that cannot be seen, heard, or thought. The conversation between father and son continues in this way:

> "Place this salt in water, and in the morning, come to me." He did exactly so, and he said to him, "The salt that you put in the water last night, bring it hither."
>
> But while he grasped for it, he could not find it, since it had completely dissolved. "Take a sip from the edge of it. What is there?"
>
> "Salt."
>
> "Take a sip from the middle. What is there?"
>
> "Salt."
>
> "Take a sip from the far edge. What is there?"
>
> "Salt."
>
> "Set it aside and come to me." And [the boy] did exactly that, [saying,] "It is always the same."
>
> He said to him, "Being is indeed truly here, dear boy; but you do not perceive it here. That which is the finest essence, the whole universe has that as its soul. That is Reality that is the Self, that thou art, Svetaketu." (*Chandogya Upanishad* 6.13:1–3)

Over the centuries, the Upanishads became so important to Hindus that they were copied out of the Vedas and placed into their own book form. Thus separated, the Upanishads became the core spiritual teachings of Hinduism.

Smriti Scriptures

To many Hindus, the shruti scriptures seem very abstract and esoteric. In contrast, the smriti scriptures are epics and stories that bring the shruti scriptures to light.

The *Mahabharata* is a Hindu epic poem in the smriti category with more than two hundred thousand verses. The *Mahabharata* tells the story of the war between two families over an inheritance. Krishna, an **avatar** of the god

---

atman In Hinduism, the individual soul or essence.

In this illustration from the Mahabharata, *Jarasandha's army advances toward Krishna and Balarama.*

Vishnu, supports the righteous family. Included within the *Mahabharata* is the *Bhagavad Gita*, the most beloved Hindu scripture and the best-known outside Hinduism. The *Bhagavad Gita* focuses on Arjuna, one of the brothers in the righteous family, who is caught between his duty to fight as a member of the warrior caste and his dedication to nonviolence. He debates this dilemma with his charioteer, who turns out to be Krishna. The message of this epic is that one must cultivate disinterest—detachment from desires or personal agendas—in performing one's duties. According to Krishna (Vishnu), the benefits are these:

> But if a man will worship me, and meditate upon me with an undistracted mind, devoting every moment to me, I shall supply all his needs, and protect his possessions from loss. Even those who

---

avatar The incarnation of a Hindu god, especially Vishnu, in human or animal form. According to Hindu belief, Vishnu has been incarnated nine times. The tenth avatar will usher in the end of the world.

worship other deities and sacrifice to them with faith in their hearts worship me, though with a mistaken approach. For I am the only enjoyer and the only god of all sacrifices. Nevertheless, such men must return to life on earth because they do not recognize me in my true nature. (*Bhagavad Gita* 9:22–24)

Le Râmâyana. 1. L'exil de Râma.
LIBOX,
Extrait de viande assaisonné de la Cie Liebig.

This lithograph shows Rama's exile from the Ramayana.

The second of the great Hindu epics is the *Ramayana*. This epic is about Prince Rama, who is forced into exile with his wife and brother. When the evil Ravana kidnaps his wife, Rama goes on a long journey to find her and bring her home. After he rescues her, the three return to their kingdom, where Prince Rama becomes king.

The *Puranas* are smriti that tell stories about the three great gods of Hinduism—Brahma, Vishnu, and Shiva. Further, the Puranas contain stories and myths about creation and the history of the world. They are especially popular among people in the lower castes, in part because they contain miracle stories and emphasize personal devotions.

SECTION *Assessment*

Reading Comprehension

1. What is the difference between shruti and smriti Hindu scriptures?
2. What are the Upanishads concerned with?
3. What is the dilemma of Arjuna in the *Bhagavad Gita*?
4. What was the lesson Svetaketu's father was trying to teach him in the *Chandogya Upanishad*?
5. What are the Puranas?

Vocabulary

6. Name an *avatar* of the god Vishnu.

For Reflection

7. Share an example of when you thought you knew everything until intuition and experience taught you otherwise. How did you respond to your new insight?
8. Comment on Krishna's exhortation to Arjuna in the *Bhagavad Gita* to practice detachment. Is it possible? Is it practical?

Flash Search

9. The *Bhagavad Gita* influenced great writers and philosophers of the nineteenth and twentieth centuries. Name one of them and tell how.

Section 3
BELIEFS AND PRACTICES

While there are no absolute statements that all Hindus must believe, there is a set of beliefs and practices that most Hindus hold in common and accept as true. These are beliefs about gods and goddesses, the cycle of rebirth, and the sacredness of life. Hindu practices include participation in a communal experience that consists of the four pursuits of life, as determined by the caste system and an understanding of life stages. The following sections detail these beliefs and practices.

Deities

Ask a Hindu how many gods there are in Hinduism, and the answer is likely to be 330 million. This answer means to imply that there are so many gods and goddesses in Hinduism that they cannot be counted. Yet most Hindus also hold that all the gods and goddesses are the myriad images of the one Brahman, or Ultimate Reality. While the gods and goddesses have attributes (for the most part, human attributes), Brahman has no attributes. Brahman is transcendent, beyond reach.

The five senses combined cannot grasp Brahman. The mind, even that of a genius, falls short of fathoming Brahman. Brahman is the life force of the universe, permeating it with an all-pervading presence. All things in the material and immaterial world are of one essence, and that essence is Brahman. Brahman is manifested in creation as the many Hindu gods and goddesses.

Male Deities and Avatars

Three primary male forms of Brahman symbolize the cycle of life:

Brahma is the Creator.

Vishnu is the Preserver.

Shiva is the Destroyer.

Hindus worship these and other gods and goddesses as forms of the one Brahman (Ultimate Reality). Avatars too are forms of Brahman. (Recall that an avatar is the incarnation of a god or goddess who has descended from the heavenly world to earth.)

The two most popular avatars are those of the god Vishnu named Krishna and Rama (not to be confused with Prince Rama). Interestingly, Krishna himself is considered a god. Some Hindus consider Siddhartha Gautama, the Buddha and the founder of Buddhism (see Chapter 6), an avatar of Vishnu.

Female Deities

Brahman also assumes female forms. Parvati, the Divine Mother and goddess of fertility, love, harmony, beauty, marriage, and devotion, is represented in different forms. In one of her milder forms, she represents Devi, the Great Goddess. However, she can be represented with a wilder side as Durga, riding on the back of a tiger, or as Kali, the black or dark blue figure who is the deliverer of justice. She is often connected with Shiva. Saraswati, linked with Brahma, is the goddess of music, art, speech, wisdom, and learning. Lakshmi, associated with Vishnu, is goddess of prosperity, good fortune, and beauty.

Parvati in the Lakshman Temple, Rishikesh, Uttarakhand, India.

Atman

Hindus also believe that Brahman is identical to the innermost soul, the individual's essential nature, and each person's real self. The name for this "real self" is *atman*. The body, mind, and emotions of a person are not considered a person's real self. These are only illusion, or **maya**. Hindus strive for release from maya to recognize that atman and Brahman are the same. As Brahman is elusive and hidden, so too is one's true self. It is only through rigorous physical and mental discipline that an individual can achieve true self-realization, which is identical with the realization of Brahman. True self-realization is called **moksha**—that is, "liberation" from the endless cycle of rebirth.

Cycle of Rebirth

For Hindus, life is cyclical, not linear. Nature shows its cycle of birth, death, and rebirth every year. Every person is on a cycle determined by *karma,* the moral law of cause and effect. Under karma, who one is and how one now acts is determined by deeds in their previous lives. Also, how one acts now determines one's fate for the future.

Death and rebirth are part of samsara. In this cycle, a soul/spirit passes from one body to another. For example, one may transmigrate from a human body to that of an animal or insect. Though the physical body dies, the eternal atman lives on in another body.

A virtuous life contributes to a better future in this life and the next.

---

maya Sanskrit for "illusion"; a teaching of the Upanishads that only Brahman is permanent; everything else is only an illusion.

moksha In Hinduism, the transcendent state of ultimate liberation from samsara, the endless cycle of rebirth.

Three Paths to Liberation

Yoga is a type of training designed to discipline the entire human person—body, mind, and spirit. The goal of yoga for Hindus is to make the equality between atman and Brahman a reality, for then moksha, or liberation, is complete. The three paths to moksha are the Path of Action, the Path of Knowledge, and the Path of Devotion.

The Path of Action

The Path of Action is *karma yoga*, in which selfless service to others brings liberation from the endless cycle of rebirth. The devotee of this path resolves that his or her right actions and deeds will be performed not for personal gain but for Brahman. Even the person's desire for liberation must be purged, for Brahman is more potent than the noblest desire.

The Path of Knowledge

The Path of Knowledge is *jnana yoga*. This path involves three steps: learning, thinking, and viewing oneself in the third person. Learning is the information one receives from outside oneself. Thinking is the internal reflection on what one learned. Viewing oneself in the third person is like seeing from God's point of view. Meditation is the most common instrument in jnana yoga. Through meditation, a devotee sees the truth in how he or she is attached to this world.

The Path of Devotion

The Path of Devotion, *bhakti yoga*, is the path followed by most Hindus. Devotees of bhakti yoga perceive that Brahman is more immanent than transcendent. A pure, long devotion to Brahman can bring liberation.

Right actions merit transmigration to a better situation in the next life, while evil actions merit transmigration to a worse situation. There is no cosmic judge, no god who determines one's circumstances in the next life. Like a seed, the karma that one sows in this lifetime determines one's circumstances in the next.

Hindus believe there is liberation (moksha) from this samsara. Moksha is achieved by removing the karmic residue accumulated throughout countless deaths and rebirths. The three practices or "disciplines" that a person may choose to erode adverse karmic effects and move toward liberation are action, knowledge, and devotion. These three paths to liberation are called **yogas**.

The Sacredness of Life

With Brahman, or Ultimate Reality, present in all things, all things are sacred to Hindus. Hindus believe Brahman is in humans, plants, animals, insects, the cosmos, and the universe. Ahimsa, the desire not to harm any form of life, is the basis for the Hindu belief in nonviolent means as a solution to problems. It is because of ahimsa that most Hindus are vegetarians and that they consider the cow sacred. In the Vedas, the cow is associated with Aditi, the mother of all the gods. Mohandas Gandhi followed a form of ahimsa he called **satyagraha** in which he and his followers practiced peaceful resistance to British attacks when trying to free India from British rule in the mid-twentieth century.

The most famous advocate of the principle of ahimsa was the Indian lawyer and civil rights activist Mohandas Gandhi.

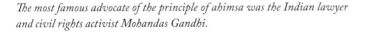

yogas Paths to moksha that endeavor to unite action (body), knowledge (mind), and devotion (soul). The three paths are karma yoga, jnana yoga, and bhakti yoga.

satyagraha The policy of nonviolent resistance initiated by Mohandas Gandhi in the first half of the twentieth century as a means of pressing for political reform.

Caste System

Hindus believe that there are four major life pursuits as well as four stages of life that apply to Hindu males. However, all discussions of Hindu living, pursuits of life, and life stages must be understood in light of the caste system. Castes make up the defined social order in Hindu society.

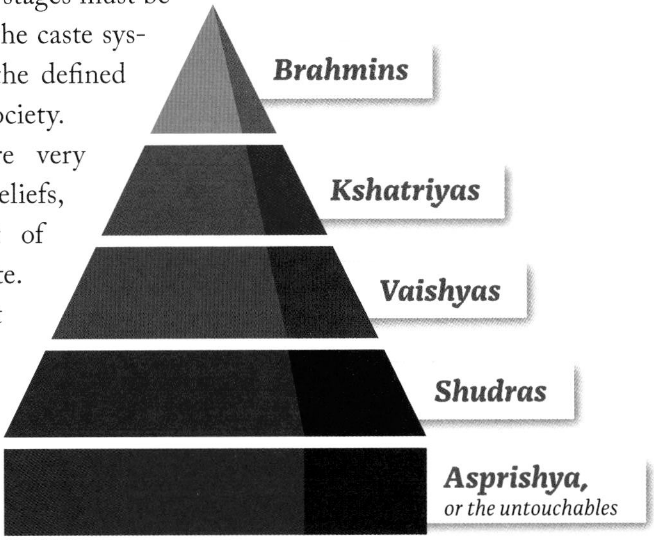

While Hindus are very tolerant of individual beliefs, they are less tolerant of straying from one's caste. The Indo-Aryans first introduced a threefold caste system into India, and later a fourth caste was added. The castes are related to karma and samsara in that one's caste is dependent upon actions in a previous life. The castes are ranked from highest to lowest:

1. ***Brahmins*** are priests, scholars, and teachers who make up the highest caste. They are from families who are considered the purest, wisest, and most learned.
2. *Kshatriyas* are rulers, warriors, and administrators. These families help protect and rule society.
3. *Vaishyas* are families of farmers and merchants.
4. *Shudras* are laborers and servants to the other three castes. Unlike members of the other three castes, families of the Shudra caste are not permitted to study the Vedas.

Besides these four caste levels, there is a fifth group that is deemed so low that it is not even part of the caste system. These are the *Asprishya* or "untouchables." These families are considered defiled because they have the degrading

---

Brahmins Hindu priests; also the highest social class in the Hindu caste system.

jobs in society such as cleaning up human waste. Also, to be born an untouchable means that one's actions in one's previous lives were in some way vile. There has been some movement in recent times to uplift the untouchables from their degraded status in society, but thousands of years of practice do not disappear easily.

Life Pursuits

Though how Hindus live differs widely depending on their caste, their goals in living are the same. For each caste, Hindus subscribe to four significant life pursuits:

1. *Dharma* is the pursuit of righteousness. It refers to a person's duties in life, especially those related to social obligations within one's caste.
2. *Artha* is the pursuit of both material and political wealth.
3. *Kama* is the pursuit of artistic, recreational, and sensual pleasure.

This Hindu monk's saffron-colored clothes symbolize his sannyasa, *or renunciation of material desires and prejudices. An individual in sannyasa is known as a Sannyasi (male) or Sannyasini (female).*

4. *Moksha* is the pursuit of liberation from the cycle of rebirth through action, knowledge, and devotion. Moksha was added as a fourth pursuit at the time of the Buddha (sixth to fifth century BCE), who is regarded by some Hindus as the ninth avatar of Vishnu.

The Stages of Life

The four stages of life, called *ashramas*, are general patterns for Hindu males of the first three castes to follow, though most progress through only the first two stages. Men are to fulfill their obligations to family and society before pursuing the more ascetic disciplines of the third and fourth stages. These are the stages for males:

1. *Brahmacarya* is the bachelor student stage for learning about the Hindu tradition, usually at the feet of a guru.

2. *Grihastha* is the stage of the householder, when he marries, raises a family, and contributes to society.

3. *Vanaprastha* literally means "retiring to the forest." This is the stage when a man begins to move away from ordinary family life to live as a hermit in order to pursue more otherworldly goals.

4. *Sannyasa* describes a spiritual pilgrim who renounces everything in this world to pursue moksha. In this stage, the man abandons the family and even the family name, and he lives as if he has no memory of his previous life.

Traditionally, Hindu women's identities are as daughters, wives, and mothers, and Hindu women live under the protection of a man.

SIKHISM

A religious tradition called Sikhism incorporates elements of both Hinduism and Islam. Sikhs would disagree with this assessment, however, believing their religious tradition to be unique. The word *Sikh* means "learner." Sikhs believe that God was revealed in an extraordinary way to Guru Nanak (1469–1539 CE), born a Hindu in a village of the Punjab area that is now in Pakistan. Nine other gurus, believed to be the reincarnation of Nanak, succeeded him. The last one, Guru Gobind Singh, died in 1708. The Sikh community considers Sikh sacred scripture (called the *Guru Granth Sahib*) the eleventh and final Guru.

Sikhism is like Islam in that it is a monotheistic religious tradition. God is transcendent but can be realized through nature and the experience of each person. God is Ultimate Reality, immanent, permanently pervading the universe, and eternally real. God is formless and eternal, having no beginning and no end. The *Mool Mantar*, the opening verse of the *Guru Granth Sahib*, is the statement of the Sikhs' belief in God:

A Sikh pilgrim reads the Guru Granth Sahib, *the central religious scripture in Sikhism, on the occasion of the 415th death anniversary of the fifth Sikh guru, Arjun Dev Jee.*

There is One God.
He is the Supreme Truth
He is the Creator
Is without fear
Is not vindictive
Is Timeless, Eternal
Is not born, so

He does not die to be reborn.
Self-illumined,
By Guru's grace
He is revealed to the human soul.
Truth was in the beginning,
and throughout the ages.
Truth is now and ever will be.

Similar to Hindus, Sikhs believe in karma, samsara, and moksha. However, Sikhs reject the caste system and hold that God created all people as equals, both men and women. They also reject ahimsa and any kind of idol worship.

According to Sikh scriptures, Sikhs perform several ascetic practices and Sikh men wear or carry with them the "five *K*s" as signs of devotion:

1. *Kesh* is uncut hair, a symbol of dedication to God (men wear a turban).
2. *Kanga* is a wooden comb, a symbol of cleanliness and purity.
3. *Kachha* refers to short pants of cotton usually worn under the outer garments, a symbol of chastity and moral living.
4. *Kara* is a steel bracelet worn on the right hand as a symbol of allegiance to the Guru.
5. *Kirpan* is a ceremonial short sword, the symbol of an unconquerable spirit.

Formal worship takes place in a Sikh temple, called a *gurdwara* ("gateway to the guru"). The service is generally led by a *granthi* (Sanskrit for "narrator"), though if one is not available, anyone knowledgeable in religious affairs may conduct the service. The service consists of singing and reading sacred scripture passages.

Sikhs do not have a homeland. When Indian Muslims founded Pakistan in 1947, many Sikhs moved out of the newly formed nation as Muslims moved in. Many Sikhs have a desire to establish their own homeland.

SECTION *Assessment*

Reading Comprehension

1. How are Brahman and atman related?
2. What are the three primary male forms of Brahman?
3. Describe how the Hindu cycle of rebirth relates to the three paths to liberation.
4. How are karma, samsara, and moksha related?
5. Name and describe each of the four Hindu castes. Also, describe the untouchables.
6. Name and describe the four stages of life for Hindu males.
7. What are the four life pursuits for a Hindu?
8. How is Sikhism similar to Islam? How is it similar to Hinduism?

Vocabulary

9. What is *maya*?

For Reflection

10. Of the paths to liberation mentioned in this section, which is most appealing to you? In what areas of your life or of society do you see a need for liberation?

Flash Search

11. What is the meaning and proper use of *Namaste*?

Section 4
SACRED TIME

Like Muslims and Jews, Hindus use a lunar calendar. To compensate for the eleven-day difference between the lunar and solar calendars, Hindus periodically add one month but do not name it. Instead, the added month bears the name of either the previous month or the next month. Cumulatively, about seven months are added approximately every nineteen years. Also, the Hindu calendar has six seasons rather than four. A simplified look at the Hindu calendar follows.

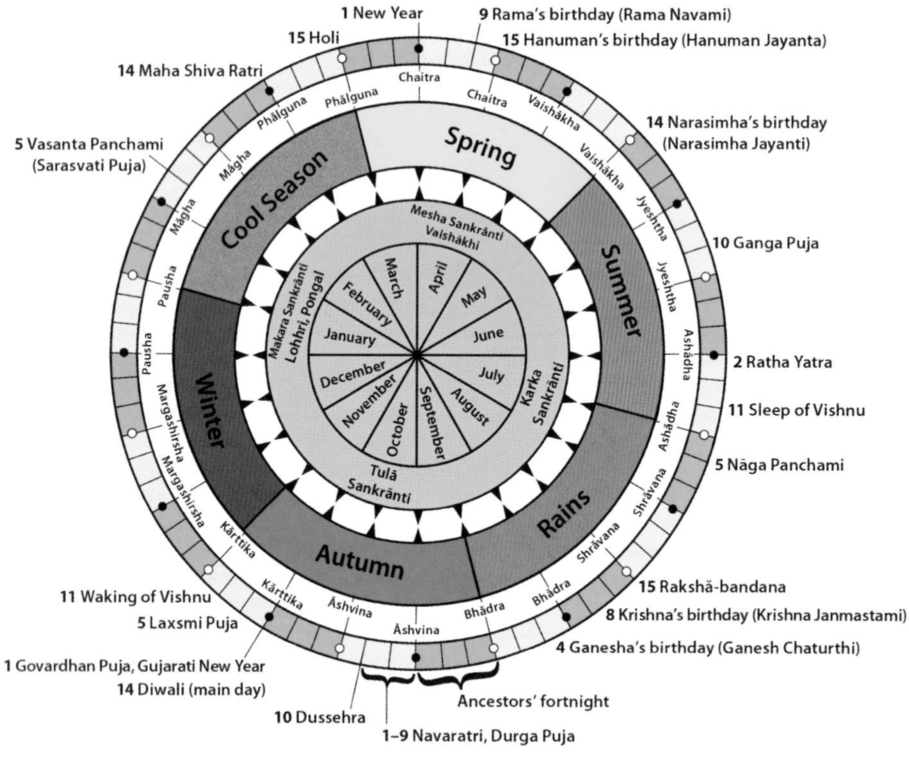

Hindus celebrate several annual festivals. They also mark various life-cycle events and rites of passage with celebrations and ceremonies.

Festivals

As Hinduism is a religious tradition of many gods and goddesses, there are also many Hindu festivals. There are a few festivals that all Hindus celebrate in common. Diwali and Holi are mentioned below.

Lighting candles outside the Golden Temple in Amritsar, India, to celebrate Diwali. During the five-day festival, Hindus, Jains, and Sikhs celebrate the victory of light over darkness.

Diwali (Divali, Dewali, Deepavali) is a "festival of lights" similar to Hanukkah for Jews and Christmas for Christians. There is no universal Hindu calendar, so there is no day that is standard for the beginning of the festival. In all parts of India, however, it is celebrated in the early autumn. The northern part of India tends to celebrate Diwali over five days, while parts of southern India celebrate it for one day. Diwali commemorates the return of Rama, the seventh avatar of Vishnu, to his kingdom after a fourteen-year exile. People light oil lamps to guide him and his companions on their journey home. In addition to lighting the path, the lights symbolically break through the darkness of evil. People celebrate by decorating their homes with colorful lights and candles. Diwali begins at the time of darkness, so the lights truly do break through the darkness. Some Hindus consider Diwali the start of the new year. In some regions, firecrackers are set off to frighten evil, while other regions make images of evil deities and throw them in a bonfire. No festival is complete without special foods and colorful clothes.

Holi is a lively spring festival also known as the "festival of colors" that commemorates the love between the deities Krishna and Radha. Often the division between castes is suspended during this time of celebration. Fun-loving pranks are part of this day as a reminder of the fun Krishna had as a boy. Hindus squirt each other with red-colored liquid or throw red powder on each other during the Holi festival. Another story associated with Holi is that of the demoness Putana attempting to kill the infant Krishna. Appearing as a lovely woman, Putana tried to feed Krishna poisoned milk from her breast, but Krishna sucked the blood out of her, exposing the dead Putana as the hideous demon she was. Her blood loss points to the loss of her life, thus the symbolic use of the color red.

Life-Cycle Celebrations

Hindus celebrate numerous occasions and rites of passage in the life cycle of birth, childhood, adulthood, and death. These celebrations are called *samskaras*. Hindus believe that if they are correctly observed, they can ward off bad karma and gain a better rebirth. Here are the sixteen samskaras of the life cycle:

Birth

1. *Womb placing.* This is the rite of conception where the husband and wife's physical union is consecrated to bring into the world a child with an advanced soul.

2. *Male rite.* This is a rite during the third month of pregnancy in which there are prayers for a male child and good health for mother and child.

3. *Hair parting.* Between the fourth and seventh months of pregnancy, the husband combs his wife's hair as a sign of love and support.

4. *Rite of birth.* At birth, the father welcomes and blesses the infant and gives the newborn a taste of ghee (clarified butter used in temple lamps) and honey.

Childhood

5. *Namkaran giving.* This rite welcomes the infant into the Hindu community of the family. It takes place anywhere between three and six weeks after birth. The given name is usually the name of a god or goddess. A person who converts to Hinduism also goes through the name-giving ceremony.

Parents carrying out the Namkaran, or naming ceremony.

6. *Feeding.* The first time the child eats solid food (usually rice) is marked.

7. *Ear piercing.* Boys and girls have both ears pierced and gold earrings inserted.

8. *First hair cutting.* This is a rite of passage for boys.

9. *Formal education.* The child marks his or her entry into formal education by writing the first letter of the alphabet in uncooked rice.

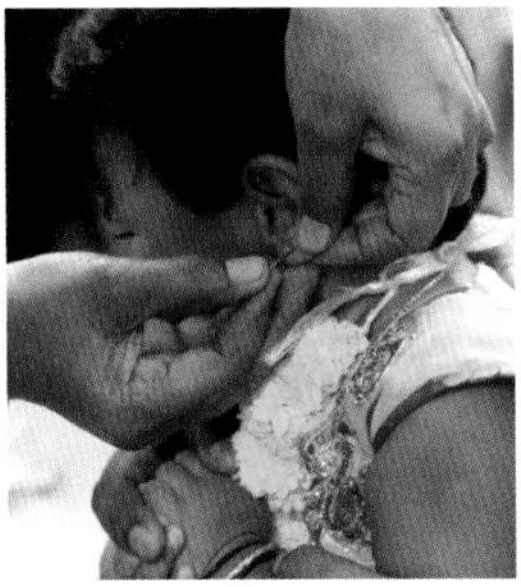

A Karnavedha, or ear piercing ceremony.

Adulthood

10. *Fit or proper season.* For girls, this is a purification ceremony after the first menstrual period. There is a home blessing marking their coming-of-age into adulthood.

11. *Beard shaving.* This home blessing ceremony marks the boy's first beard shaving and maturation into adulthood.

12. *Settlement of aim or word giving.* This is a betrothal ceremony where the man and woman pledge themselves to each other for marriage. A ring is given and presents are exchanged.

13. *Marriage.* Marriage is an elaborate ceremony that lasts for days. A ceremonial fire is present throughout, the gods are called upon, and vows are exchanged.

A couple performing a ritual during the vivaha, or wedding ceremony.

Death

14. *Preparation of body.* The eldest son usually washes, dresses, and adorns the body with flowers.

15. *Cremation.* The body is laid on a funeral pyre, usually located near a holy river. The fire is set, and ghee is poured on the fire. Prayers are recited, and people typically stay until the fire is out.

16. *Scattering the ashes.* The ashes are usually scattered over a sacred river near the funeral pyre. The Ganges River is the most popular river for this ceremony.

A couple scatters ashes from an urn into the Ganges River.

SECTION *Assessment*

Reading Comprehension

1. How do Hindus compensate for the different number of days in the solar and lunar calendars?

2. What do the festivals of Diwali and Holi celebrate? How are they celebrated?
3. Name and explain at least two of the sixteen Hindu ritual life-cycle celebrations.

For Reflection

4. What are some of the functions of festivals and holidays in a society?

Flash Search

5. Name and describe two Hindu festivals not mentioned in this section.

Section 5
SACRED PLACES AND SACRED SPACES

Temples, public shrines, and shrines set up in individual homes are among the sacred spaces for Hindus. As Brahman is present in all creation, natural sites like mountains and rivers are counted as sacred places. For Hindus, the Ganges River is the most sacred place.

Temples

Some villages may be too small to have a temple where a Brahmin (priest) can perform acts of worship, but most towns and all of India's major cities

Sri Veeramakaliamman Temple in Little India, Singapore.

Chidambaram Nataraja Temple in Tamil Nadu, India.

have temples. Temples have images of many gods and goddesses but are dedicated to one god in particular. That unique deity is often the god for a particular caste in that region.

Hindus seldom have congregational services at a temple where people participate in unified worship. Though a group of people may be in attendance, there is still a sense of individuality among the attendees. A Brahmin often performs **puja**, the practice of honoring a god or goddess in a devotional ritual, with minimum participation by the people. The deity is awakened by bells and then bathed, dressed, and offered incense, food, and flowers. Sometimes, there are special days for the deity when a statue, picture, or another image of the god or goddess, called a **murti**, is decorated and processed along the nearby streets.

Whatever their size or however complex, Hindu temples have a simple underlying structure. There is the outer hall, the temple proper, and the "womb chamber" where the main deity of that temple—usually Vishnu, Shiva, or Devi—resides. A Hindu temple is the temporary residence of a deity on earth. Each of these three areas has ambulatories so that devotees can circle in a clockwise direction as a sign of veneration.

---

puja The ritual worship of a god or goddess in both Hinduism and Buddhism.

murti The image of a deity in artistic form. Not an idol to be worshipped, it points to the deity.

A home shrine in London, England.

Home Shrines

Most Hindu families have a shrine or special place in their home where they perform puja. This place may be as large as a room or as small as a little table. Whatever the case, the household contains a murti of a god or goddess with special meaning for that family. Flowers or fruit may also be part of the shrine surrounding the murti. The puja can be performed individually or collectively. Usually, women conduct the home puja.

The simple ceremony involves welcoming the god or goddess into the house by calling upon him or her to dwell within the murti. It must be emphasized that Hindus do not believe the murti itself is the god or goddess. Instead, the murti represents the god or goddess. However, some Hindus believe the god or goddess dwells within the murti during the puja. The murti is also washed and dressed in fine clothes so that it is ready to receive guests. Fruits, flowers, and incense are offered to the murti. Prayers may be recited, hymns sung, and sacred texts read. In return for the offering, Hindus believe, the individual or family receives a blessing from the deity. After puja, those present eat the food offered to the deity.

Ganges River

Though Hindus usually frequent shrines and temples more often, the Ganges River is considered the most sacred of all places. Hindus consider a river—and the Ganges River specifically—the symbol of life without end. A festival called Kumbh Mela attracts millions to the Ganges River and four other rivers in a twelve-year cycle. Hindus participate in ritual washings as part of this festival.

The Ganges is considered the premier place for spiritual healing. Hindus perform ritual bathing in the river at all times of the year, believing the Ganges has the power to wash away the bad karma that destines them for

This occasion of the Kumbh Mela festival takes place at the confluence of the Ganges and the Yamuna rivers, in Allahabad, India, one of four river-bank pilgrimage sites. The Kumbh Mela is the world's largest religious gathering.

The Manikarnika Ghat is a holy cremation site in Varanasi, Uttar Pradesh, India.

another life on earth. Many Hindus request that, upon their death, their ashes be sprinkled into the Ganges River, especially near the holy city of Varanasi, also known as Benares. Hundreds of temples line the banks of the Ganges at Varanasi.

SECTION *Assessment*

Reading Comprehension

1. Why are natural sites sacred to Hindus?
2. Why do Hindus visit the Ganges River?

Vocabulary

3. How does a temple *puja* differ from a home *puja*?

For Reflection

4. Catholics often place flowers or other tokens around the shrines or statues of Jesus, Mary, and the saints. What do you think is the significance of these offerings?

Flash Search

5. Why are there so many Hindu temples in the city of Varanasi, India?

Section 6
CATHOLICS DIALOGUE WITH HINDUS

Diverse in its own practice, Hinduism has always had a reputation for tolerating religious diversity. In a similar spirit, the Second Vatican Council document on interreligious dialogue, *Nostra Aetate*, recognizes Hindu beliefs and practices:

> Thus in Hinduism, men contemplate the divine mystery and express it through an inexhaustible abundance of myths and through searching philosophical inquiry. They seek freedom from the anguish of our human condition either through ascetical practices or profound meditation or a flight to God with love and trust. (2)

Adherents of most of the traditions within Hinduism believe that there is one objective Truth but that the finite nature of the human condition is an obstacle to comprehending or attaining that pure, objective, many-sided Truth. Hindus believe that the prophets, sages, and contemplatives of various religious traditions over time have pointed their respective adherents to eternal Truth but that each tradition has only a piece of the Truth. While Hindus do not believe that if all of these truth statements and experiences were collected, the sum would equal the Truth, they do believe that the world would be closer to the Truth.

Tolerance for religious diversity finds Hindus comfortable in teaching fellow Hindus to be good Hindus—but also Jews to be good Jews, Buddhists to be good Buddhists, Christians to be good Christians, and the like. Tolerance does not imply minimizing one's individual religious tradition. On the contrary, in dialogue with various religious traditions, including Catholicism,

Austin Interfaith's annual Thanksgiving service in Austin, Texas, includes Catholic, Hindu, Sikh, Muslim, and Protestant religious leaders.

Hindus find clarity in the similarities and differences between them very important. They are anxious to resolve the many misconceptions others, especially in the West, have about Hinduism. In dialogue, all sides are reminded to keep an open mind, because a fragment of the Truth may be found in the religious tradition of the other. Simultaneously, dialogue enables each participant to delve ever deeper into the mystery of his or her own religious tradition, drawing the person to a more profound commitment to it.

Interreligious dialogue between Catholics and Hindus has focused on social issues essential to human dignity. Poverty and the lack of basic human necessities plague India; some of these issues are due to the caste system. There remains much mutual misunderstanding between Hindus and Catholics on two theological topics in particular. One topic is Jesus, and the other is religious images.

Jesus: The Incarnate God

Hindus gained continual exposure to Christianity starting with the coming of the British to India in the seventeenth century. However, Christianity has been present in India, especially southern India, since Christianity's infancy.

A mural of Jesus and the Hindu symbol Om in Chennai, India.

Legend has it that the Apostle Thomas went to India as a missionary and established a Christian community on the southwestern coast. St. Francis Xavier, a Spanish Jesuit missionary, ministered in southern coastal India in the sixteenth century. He would walk through the streets, ringing a bell to call children out of their homes to hear the Gospel.

Hindus have a wide range of views about Jesus. Some believe that Jesus spent his "hidden years"—that is, between age twelve and the beginning of his public ministry around age thirty—in India learning from Hindu sages and then incorporated what he learned into his ministry. Many Hindus see Jesus as a source of inspiration for moral or social reform or as a model for living an exemplary life. Some Hindus have gone so far as to commit themselves to Jesus, not as the Christian God but as one among many avatars like Rama or Krishna.

Some Hindus question Jesus' historical existence, believing that the stories of Jesus are myths like the stories of Hindu deities. Still other Hindus believe that Jesus was a **yogi**, someone who lived a disciplined, ascetic life.

---

yogi A practitioner of yoga, particularly in its meditative forms.

Whatever their view of Jesus, it is his teachings, especially those found in the Beatitudes, that most attract Hindus to him. To Hindus, Jesus is a man who is, as he describes in the Beatitudes, "clean of heart" (Mt 5:8, NABRE).

Catholics, and indeed all Christians, would agree with some views Hindus hold about Jesus. Love, compassion, kindness, sympathy, reconciliation, and justice are all virtues that each individual as well as social groupings and institutions need to perfect. Jesus' eating with sinners, healing people not of his religious tradition, and loving his worst enemies even to the point of dying for them—all of these are seemingly impossible behaviors that Catholics and Christians, as followers of Jesus, are called to emulate.

Images of Jesus and Mary are displayed alongside Shirdi Sai Baba, an Indian spiritual master from the turn of the twentieth century, and the goddess Lakshmi.

Yet the Catholic view of Jesus is much different from the Hindu perspective. Catholics view Jesus as a historical person, not a myth. He was born in Bethlehem in Judea during the time of Herod the Great and died at the hands of the Roman prefect Pontius Pilate. This biblical testimony is corroborated by independent sources such as the Jewish writer Josephus and the Roman historian Tacitus. There is no written mention anywhere within or outside the Bible that Jesus ever left ancient Palestine.

There is also no hint of Hindu beliefs such as karma, reincarnation, or the caste system in the teachings of Jesus. Rather, Jesus taught, often through parables, about God's coming reign and the need to prepare for that coming. Jesus performed miracles that showed his authority over both the natural and the supernatural realms. Jesus was a great teacher and wonder worker, but he was much, much more. Jesus is not one avatar among many avatars; Jesus is the only Incarnation of God. Jesus is God. As St. Paul tells us in his Letter to the Philippians:

> Have among yourselves the same attitude that is also yours in
> Christ Jesus,
> Who, though he was in the form of God,
> did not regard equality with God something to be grasped.
> Rather, he emptied himself,
> taking the form of a slave,
> coming in human likeness;
> and found human in appearance,
> he humbled himself,
> becoming obedient to death,
> even death on a cross.
> Because of this, God greatly exalted him
> and bestowed on him the name
> that is above every name,
> that at the name of Jesus
> every knee should bend,
> of those in heaven and on earth and under the earth,
> and every tongue confess that
> Jesus Christ is Lord,
> to the glory of God the Father. (Phil 2:5–11, NABRE)

Religious Images

Both Catholics and Hindus have a long history of depicting and appreciating religious images. They also share in being misunderstood by some who believe that religious imagery implies the worship of idols. Both Hindus and Catholics reject this notion. They find that such a charge represents a misunderstanding of the purpose and function of religious imagery.

Long before the Great Schism of 1054, both the Eastern and Western Christian Church had images of Jesus, Mary, saints, angels, biblical stories, and Christian historical events. Religious imagery—whether it be drawings or paintings or statuary of wood, metal, or stone—could be found in catacombs, basilicas, churches, chapels, castles, homes, monasteries, marketplaces, and fields.

(Left) An adorned Ganesh at a Tamil Hindu temple during the Vinayagar Ther Thiruvizha Festival in Ontario, Canada. (Right) A statue of the Virgin Mary of Medjugorje inside St. Jacob's Church, at Medjugorje, Bosnia-Herzegovina.

Beautiful icons in the Eastern Churches were destroyed in the eighth and ninth centuries as part of the Iconoclastic Controversy. The Protestant Reformation of the sixteenth century brought about another form of **iconoclasm**. Some Protestants destroyed religious statuary because they equated the presence of statues of Mary and the saints with idol worship rather than veneration.

Much of Hindu religious imagery is the depiction of its many gods and goddesses. A Hindu shrine may have images of only one deity, often the local village god or goddess. It seems the more massive the Hindu temple, the more religious imagery is found within. Hindu imagery can also be found in the home, on the streets, in stores and sidewalk shops, in government buildings, and along roads. As with Christian imagery, Hindu imagery has not always been completely safe. During invasions during the times of war, Hindus have

---

iconoclasm A term meaning "breaking of icons"; the belief that there should be no human depiction of the sacred, for it places the icon rather than what the image represents as the object of worship.

found their temples and shrines destroyed, which meant the religious objects inside were damaged as well.

Religious imagery has many functions. While it is ornamental, that is seldom its primary purpose. Religious imagery may be used to tell an inspirational story within a religious tradition. It may also be used to instruct adherents, especially those who are unable to read. Or a particular religious image may function as an object of veneration, which sometimes brings misunderstanding.

Religious images in Hinduism are not *worshipped* but *venerated*. They are accorded the same honor one would give to an extraordinary human guest—gifted with special food, candles, and perhaps flowers or incense. The veneration of a deity assists one in meditating on Ultimate Reality, which in Hinduism is unknown and unknowable. Yet the unknown and unknowable can be approached from the known: the many Hindu **devas**, which are known, reveal some aspect of Ultimate Reality. The more images depicting an aspect of the unknown, the more Ultimate Reality is revealed. The outrageousness of the images and their various components points to that for which language is lacking. A god or goddess represented anthropomorphically helps humans enter the mystery of Ultimate Reality.

Devotees carry a statue of Ganesha during the Ganesh Chaturthi festival in Mumbai, India.

There is a danger in Hinduism, however, in making the deities too human, too much like ourselves. Hindu artists avoid this danger by creating images that cannot be mistaken as representing finite human beings. For example, the more arms an image has, the more powerful the deity is. The more heads an image has, the more knowledgeable or wise the deity. What the figure wears, what it is holding in its many hands, whether an animal is integrated into the image—all these point to some aspect of the deity, which points to some element of Ultimate Reality.

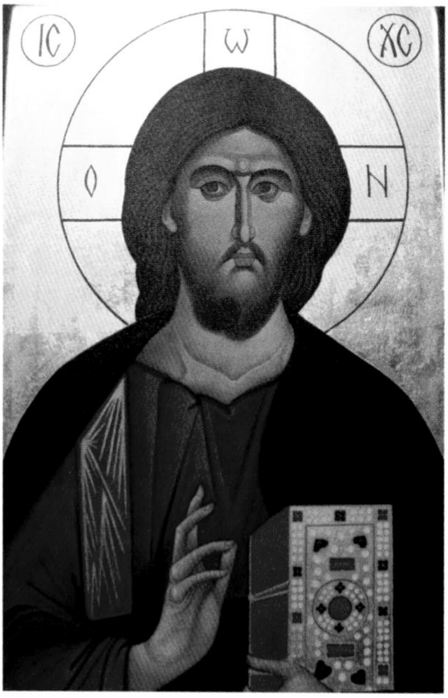

Jesus Christ Pantocrator icon.

In Christianity, while the Eastern Church has a long tradition of displaying religious icons (pictorials on flat panels of various materials), the Western Church has a tradition of displaying religious statues. In both cases, the religious images are overwhelmingly of historical figures. Jesus as the Good Shepherd, Jesus as King, the crucified Jesus in the arms of his mother, and Mary herself are all sources of inspiration.

Catholicism is a very incarnational religious tradition. In becoming human, Jesus raised the dignity of humanity. Catholics venerate those whom the Church deems closest to God and considers them exemplars on how to seek intimacy with God. Not only can religious imagery instruct and inspire but it also can form Catholics as a faith community. Placing flowers or lighting a candle in front of a statue is not an act of idol worship but a gesture of honor and veneration. Prayers to Mary and the saints are requests for intercession, not acts of worship or adoration. Catholics pray to, worship, and adore the Triune God alone. As art is translated into sacred images, so too are believers transformed into a holy people worthy of the promises of Christ.

---

devas From the Sanskrit for "shining ones"; celestial beings in the Hindu tradition.

SECTION *Assessment*

Reading Comprehension

1. What do Hindus believe each religious tradition has in regard to Truth?
2. Describe one view of Jesus that some Hindus hold.
3. Describe one similar view Catholics and Hindus have about Jesus.
4. Why are Catholics and Hindus accused of worshipping idols?
5. List three reasons for the use of religious imagery.

Vocabulary

6. Name two examples of *iconoclasm* in Christian history.

For Reflection

7. What is something you respect about Hinduism?
8. Why do you think some people persist in accusing Catholics and Hindus of idol worship even though they deny it?

Flash Search

9. Who are the three most popular devas in Hinduism?

Section Summaries

Introduction: In Pursuit of Ultimate Liberation

Hinduism is one of the oldest of the world's religious traditions and has more than a billion followers. Hinduism has no discernable beginning, no founder, no organization, no doctrinal statements, and a widely diverse group of adherents. It recognizes truths in other religious traditions but does not believe that anyone, including any Hindu, possesses the whole Truth.

- Explain in three to four paragraphs how you understand the following quote from the *Bhagavad Gita*: "Never was there a time when I did not exist, nor you, nor all these kings; nor in the future shall any of us cease to be" (*Bhagavad Gita* 2:12).

Section 1: A Brief History of Hinduism

Hinduism has its earliest roots in the Indus Valley region of India/Pakistan. The Vedic Period is so called because the Vedic scriptures of Hinduism emerged during that time. The Classical Period is the era when Hinduism emerged as a religious tradition. Muslim rule influenced Hinduism but not to the point of compromise. In 1947, a Muslim nation, Pakistan, split off from India. During the Modern Period, Hinduism expanded due to various unique movements, including those connected with Transcendental Meditation and the Hare Krishnas.

- Research the following question: In what ways did Hinduism influence the nineteenth-century American philosopher Henry David Thoreau? Answer in three to four paragraphs.

Section 2: Sacred Stories and Sacred Scriptures

There are two main categories of Hindu scripture—shruti and smriti. Among the shruti scriptures, the four Vedas, which contain various hymns, prayers, mantras, spells, and the like, are considered the most authoritative. The *Bhagavad Gita* is the most beloved of all Hindu smriti scriptures and the best known to non-Hindus. The Upanishads reveal the spiritual core of Hinduism.

- Read from the complete text of the *Bhagavad Gita*. Locate and copy three different sentences that represent a moral teaching.

Section 3: Beliefs and Practices

Hindus believe in countless gods and goddesses, yet all are manifestations of the one Ultimate Reality. Known as Brahman, Ultimate Reality is god, but not equivalent to the God of the Abrahamic religious traditions. Atman is the soul, spirit, or self of an individual. Atman is Brahman, but it takes millions of birth/death/rebirth cycles to move from maya, or illusion, to reality. Every human person is on a cycle determined by karma. Liberation from the cycle is known as moksha. Hindus are called upon to pursue four goals in life, with the fourth being moksha.

- Prepare a captioned photo display (printed or digital) of the three male and three female deities listed in the section.

Section 4: Sacred Time

Most Hindus use a lunar calendar that marks six seasons of the year. The diversity of Hinduism is so great that all Hindus celebrate only a few festivals in common. Most Hindus celebrate the festivals of Diwali and Holi, albeit in different ways. The vast majority of Hindus celebrate life-cycle rituals called samskaras, believing that a person can ward off bad karma and assure a better next life through them.

- Create your own artistic version of the Hindu lunar calendar. See Section 4 for an example.

Section 5: Sacred Places and Sacred Spaces

Brahmins perform devotional rituals called pujas at temples with minimal participation from other worshippers. Most homes have a special place or shrine for honoring a deity through a puja. Mountains, forests, and rivers are sacred places for Hindus. The Ganges River is the most sacred place for Hindus.

- Create a replica of a Hindu shrine in your home and take a photo to share with your teacher and class.

Section 6: Catholics Dialogue with Hindus

Hindus believe that partial Truth can be found in many religious traditions but that no religious tradition, including Hinduism, possesses the whole Truth. Hindus are happy to participate in interreligious dialogue, for they believe it is an opportunity to correct misunderstandings about Hinduism. Hindus hold a variety of views about Jesus, including that he is one among many avatars of Brahman, but according to Catholics, Jesus is the only Incarnation of God. Both Catholics and Hindus have a long tradition of using religious imagery, but the content of the images is radically different. Catholic depictions are mostly historical, while Hindu representations are predominantly mythical.

- What does religious tolerance mean to you? Write a four- to five-paragraph response.

Chapter Projects

Complete one of these projects by the conclusion of your study of this chapter.

1. Written Research Report on Hindu Sects

   There are three main sects in Hinduism: Shaivism, Shaktism, and Vaishnavism. Research and write a report on the following:

   - the beliefs of each sect
   - the worship practices of each sect
   - the relationship among the three

2. Reading and Reporting Orally on *Life of Pi*

   Read the novel *Life of Pi* by Yann Martel and prepare a five-minute oral report. Share examples of references to Hinduism in the novel. Also answer: In what ways do Pi's thinking and actions reflect Hinduism? Explain through specific examples. Record your report for your teacher on a sharable platform.

3. Contrasting Profiles on Hindu Women

   Write a three- to four-page comparison essay on two contemporary Hindu women—one who lives according to traditional roles of Hinduism and another who practices Hinduism from a modern perspective, eschewing the traditional roles.

4. Hindu Dance Demonstration

   Research the role of dance in Hinduism. Then plan a demonstration of a Hindu dance that you can video record. You can either do the dance yourself or record a friend performing. Include an opening narration giving the name, style, and history of the dance. Optional: Dress the dancer in traditional Hindu clothing.

5. Written Report on Rabindranath Tagore

   Research the life of Rabindranath Tagore (1861–1941) and write a three- to four-page report explaining how he was influenced by Hinduism in each of the following roles: poet, playwright, author, painter, and composer.

Key Image

Aum (Om)

Aum, also written as Om, is a sacred symbol in Hinduism. When it is spoken aloud, it is a sacred sound as well. Aum is the most widely chanted of all **mantras** in Hinduism. It is also found in Buddhism and Jainism. Adherents who say the sound claim it possesses great power. They have several beliefs about the sound: Within the vibrational frequency of pronouncing Aum, all of creation is encompassed. The past, present, and future of the entire universe are represented within Aum. The vibrations of pronouncing the sound have the potential to mirror the vibrational frequencies of the universe that were present since its creation.

mantras Sacred verbal formulas that are repeated in prayer or meditation.

Each letter of Aum has a meaning. The "ah" sound of the letter *A* represents beginning, newness, start, or birth. It is considered the primal sound devoid of cultural constraints. The second letter, *U*, is pronounced "oo," signifying all that is within life, between the beginning and end of the universe, between birth and death, or between creativity and destruction. The "mm" sound generated by pronouncing the letter *M* at the end of the word represents conclusion or destruction. It is the termination of all negativity or any obstacles that hold a person back from his or her numerous potentials. Since mantras are repetitive, the seamless chanting of "ah-oo-mm" concludes with the fourth sound—silence. This absence of sound is a moment for reflection before the mantra is repeated. Adherents believe that Aum is the source of all sound in the universe, beginning from the back of the throat and concluding with the lips.

The symbol Aum first appeared in the sixth century BCE. Different levels of consciousness are embodied within the printed symbol. The bottom left curve sweeping up toward the left represents the waking state, which is what people experience two-thirds of their lives. The bottom right curve signifies the dream state, which deals with one's inner world. The upper curve cascading down toward the left indicates the deep sleeping or unconscious state; it is neither the external of the waking state nor the internal of the dream state. The small dot at the top characterizes the transcendent or absolute consciousness, which in some ways can be described as stateless. It is neither internal nor external consciousness nor both. In this state, one experiences quietness, peacefulness, and blissfulness. Some call it enlightenment. The small curve under the dot signifies the Sanskrit word *maya*, or "illusion." Thus the waking, dream, and deep sleep states of consciousness are separated from transcendent or absolute consciousness by illusion. It is maya to think that the material is truly real. The more the scales of illusion dissipate, the more transparently an individual sees oneness with Ultimate Reality.

Aum is chanted at the beginning of many occasions in Hinduism: rituals, hymns, prayers, other mantras, class, birth, writings, letters, inscriptions, meditation, yoga practice, and more. Temples, public shrines, and home shrines usually display the Aum symbol. Books, films, and television shows make use of the Aum. Hindu art and even body tattoos portray the Aum symbol. As both sound and symbol, Aum has traveled far past its Indian roots.

Faithful Adherent

Mohandas K. Gandhi: The "Great Soul"

Few men of the twentieth century have left such a lasting legacy as Mohandas K. Gandhi (1869–1948). Though it is not substantiated, the great Indian writer and artist Rabindranath Tagore is credited with bestowing upon Gandhi the honorific title *Mahatma*, Sanskrit for "great soul." Gandhi was instrumental in liberating India from British colonial rule, gaining him the unofficial title of "Father of the Nation." Later civil rights activists such as Nelson Mandela and Martin Luther King Jr. derived their nonviolent tactics against oppression from Gandhi.

Gandhi was born in Gujarat in western India to a family that was part of the Vaishya (third-level) caste (see Section 3, "Caste System"). As Hindus, the family worshipped Vishnu. Though tied to an arranged marriage at age thirteen, Gandhi moved to London to study law and learn how to be an English gentleman. This move abroad was a clear violation of caste restrictions. As part of his education as an English gentleman, he read the Bible and was very taken by the Sermon on the Mount. Upon returning to India, Gandhi set up a law practice in Bombay (present-day Mumbai). His English persona was not an asset to him as an Indian man in a British-ruled society. His law practice failed. In 1893, Gandhi moved to South Africa.

For more than twenty years, Gandhi was a civil rights lawyer, defending immigrant Indians from discrimination in South Africa. Gandhi himself sometimes suffered discrimination at the hands of South African authorities. He was thrown off a train because a white man did not want a nonwhite man in his space. He was arrested several times for his leadership in peaceful resistance. At the same time, Gandhi was a community organizer, leading Indians in South Africa in *satyagraha*, or "peaceful resistance," which was

A statue of Mahatma Gandhi in Amritsar, India, is decorated on October 2, the anniversary of his birth. Gandhi Jayanti is a national holiday in India.

practiced through ahimsa, or in a nonviolent manner.

Gandhi returned to India in 1915 to assist in the movement for Indian independence from British rule. The "wannabe" English gentleman donned the clothing of a traditional Indian. Satyagraha was an integral part of his strategy. Through boycotts, tax revolts, sit-ins, civil disobedience, hunger strikes, noncooperation, protests, receiving beatings and arrests, writings, speeches, and example, Gandhi and his millions of followers wore down the British.

His religious beliefs spurred Gandhi's political actions. For him, God was Truth and Truth was God. Though a Hindu, Gandhi believed every major religious tradition was divinely inspired. The most influential scripture underpinning Gandhi's words and actions was the *Bhagavad Gita*. He strived to live by its major theme of detachment. One was to do one's best in everything and not be attached to outcomes. No matter how wonderful or how disastrous the outcome, one was to maintain equanimity. Whatever the outcome of a war, both sides suffer. In like manner, one is to be detached from all possession. Nonpossession is inner freedom, while possession is internal slavery.

Gandhi also worked to reform the status of the untouchables, the group of Indians who lived below the fourth caste, and of women. From a young age, Gandhi found the treatment of untouchables abhorrent. To Gandhi, all creation was divine. Treating people as poisonous, defiled, or polluted went against all his moral sensibilities. The untouchables had to endure not only constant discrimination but violence as well. Gandhi worked hard to abolish the practice of untouchability, including participating in a hunger strike. Untouchability was not legally abolished in India until 1950, two years after Gandhi died.

Sushma Swaraj, India's Minister of External Affairs in 2014, visits the Mahatma Gandhi Memorial in Washington, DC.

The treatment of women was another concern of Gandhi's. For him, men and women were companions and should be equal within the eyes of Hindu society. As per the custom of the day, Gandhi's marriage was arranged and took place at the age of puberty for each. Gandhi went off to London to study while his wife and child stayed home. The woman's family, no matter the financial situation, had to come up with a dowry for her marriage. Women were at a significant disadvantage, expected to play the traditional role of daughter, mother, and wife. Equally disturbing to Gandhi was the practice of *sati*, in which a widowed woman sacrificed herself by throwing herself upon the funeral pyre of her husband. Sati was outlawed in India in 1987.

British rule ended in India in 1947. That same year, India was partitioned along religious lines with the creation of Muslim-dominated East and West Pakistan, a move that Gandhi opposed and that sparked deadly religious riots. A few months later, in January 1948, Gandhi was assassinated by a Hindu nationalist dissatisfied with Gandhi's promotion of religious reconciliation and tolerance.

Reading Comprehension

1. What prompted Gandhi to become involved in politics in South Africa?
2. Why did Gandhi choose to change his clothing from that of an English gentleman to a traditional Indian style?
3. How was the practice of satyagraha successful against the British?
4. Why was Gandhi so adamant about abolishing "untouchability"?
5. What practices of Hinduism during his time did Gandhi view as depriving women of social and economic equality?

For Reflection

6. Seldom does one have a chance to interview a "great soul" in one's life. Cast yourself as a journalist with the privilege of interviewing Gandhi. List at least seven questions you will ask in the interview.
7. Imagine and discuss how you would like to see ahimsa and satyagraha practiced today.

Prayer

The Gayatri Mantra, the mother of all the Vedas, the foremost Hindu mantra, inspires wisdom. The meaning of this prayer of the same name may be summarized as "May the Almighty God illuminate our intellect to lead us along the righteous path."

Oh God! Thou art the Giver of Life,
Remover of pain and sorrow,
The Bestower of happiness,
Oh! Creator of the Universe,
May we receive thy supreme sin-destroying light,
May Thou guide our intellect in the right direction.

6

BUDDHISM

Introduction

THE CALL TO WAKE UP

Buddhism—from the Sanskrit word *budhi*, meaning "to wake up"—is a human-centered rather than god-centered religious tradition. The responsibility for spiritual development in Buddhism rests totally upon the individual. The purpose of a Buddhist is to be awakened or enlightened about that which is real.

Unlike Hinduism, Buddhism has a founder: Siddhartha Gautama, a Hindu born in the sixth century BCE into the warrior caste in what was then India and is now Nepal. Called simply "the **Buddha**," meaning "the Awakened One," Siddhartha taught that people could be enlightened and attain **Nirvana** by following his teachings. Siddhartha was neither a god nor a messenger of a god; he was a human being who pointed to his teachings, not to himself. Though some Buddhists believe Siddhartha Gautama had some divine element to him, what appears to be their worship of him is instead a sign of their deep respect for the man whom Buddhists believe to be the most compassionate person in history. For some, bowing to the Buddha image is bowing to the Buddha-nature within each individual.

Buddhism is more than 2,500 years old. Over the centuries, Buddhism grew into two main branches, Theravada and Mahayana Buddhism, with a vast array of subdivisions in Mahayana Buddhism. The history of Buddhism is complex, and its library of sacred texts is vast. Ritual and meditative practices

---

Buddha When capitalized, the term refers to Siddhartha Gautama. It is from the Sanskrit word meaning "to awaken," or one who has attained enlightenment.

Nirvana A term meaning "extinction" or "blowing out"; refers to the release from suffering, impermanence, delusion, and all that keeps the cycles of rebirth (samsara) going. Nirvana is the spiritual goal for all Buddhists.

Siddhartha Gautama, the Buddha.

cover the spectrum from the simple to the elaborate. Though most Buddhists live in Asia, a steadily growing number of Buddhists are found on the continents of Europe, Australia, and North America. There are approximately 520 million Buddhists in the world today.

SECTION *Assessment*

Reading Comprehension

1. What makes Buddhism different from all the other religions you have studied in the previous chapters?
2. What is one difference between Buddhism and Hinduism?
3. What are the two main branches of Buddhism?

For Reflection

4. As you begin your study, what are two things you already know about Buddhism?

Section 1
A BRIEF HISTORY OF BUDDHISM

Buddhism began with the birth of Siddhartha Gautama in approximately 560 BCE in what is now Nepal. The religious tradition continued with the preservation of the Buddha's teachings through four succeeding "councils" of his followers. It then spread in several directions across Asia. Though Buddhism began on the Indian subcontinent, it spread to central, eastern, and southeastern Asia. Today, there are Buddhists worldwide, including in the Western world, where many are attracted to Buddhism's focus on meditation, spirituality, and wisdom.

Siddhartha Gautama

Siddhartha Gautama, sometimes called Shakyamuni, meaning "sage of the Shakya clan," was born a Hindu of the warrior caste around the middle of the sixth century BCE. His father was king of a small village in present-day Nepal. Many stories and legends are associated with Siddhartha's birth. His mother, Queen Maya, dreamed that an elephant touched her right side, and she conceived. Brahmins, of the priestly Hindu caste, interpreted the dream for her: she would bear a son who would be either a king or a holy man.

According to Buddhist tradition, Queen Maya traveled to her father's house to prepare for the birth. Along the way, she stopped at the Lumbini Garden. When she stepped off her chariot, she held the branch of a tree for support and to rest. Immediately, her child emerged from her right side without any help and took seven steps. He then stopped and said, "No more births for me." He was named Siddhartha. Seven days later, Queen Maya died.

The birth of Buddha in the Lumbini grove, from the Chua Ho Quoc pagoda in Phu Quoc, Vietnam.

Siddhartha's father went to great lengths to shield him from the world's pain and suffering, including his mother's death. He lived the life of a pampered prince, having as many women and servants at his disposal as he desired.

At age sixteen, Siddhartha married Yasodhara, and they had a son named Rahula. When he was twenty-nine, Siddhartha had his charioteer take him beyond where his father permitted. On these travels, Siddhartha saw things his father had tried to shield him from. Siddhartha saw an older man, a very sick man, a corpse, and a wandering holy man without possessions. These became known as the **Four Sights**, and each made a dramatic impression on Siddhartha, changing the course of the prince's life. The first three taught him about aging, sickness, and death; the sight of the holy man showed Siddhartha that riches were not the path to inner liberation.

The next night, Siddhartha quietly kissed his sleeping wife and son and had his charioteer take him to the forest's edge. There, Siddhartha donned the

---

Four Sights The four encounters that Siddhartha had on an unannounced journey outside of his father's palace that each taught him something about the world: an old, crippled man (old age); a diseased man (illness); a decaying corpse (death); and finally an ascetic (riches do not lead to inner liberation). These were the inspiration for Siddhartha to become a monk.

BUDDHISM: TIMELINE OF KEY EVENTS

BCE

ca. 560 .... Birth of Siddhartha Gautama

ca. 483 .... Death of Siddhartha Gautama

ca. 483 .... First Buddhist Council

ca. 383 .... Emergence of Theravada Buddhism in India

304.............................. Birth of Indian emperor Ashoka

ca. 100......................... Emergence of Mahayana Buddhism

29 .... Compilation of *Pali Canon*

CE

ca. 100......................... Emergence of Buddhism in China

ca. 400s....................... Translation and editing of Tripitaka into Pali

ca. 500s....................... Emergence of Ch'an Buddhism in China

ca. 500s....................... Introduction of Buddhism in Japan

618 .... Beginning of T'ang dynasty in China

ca. 800s....................... Introduction of Buddhism in Tibet

ca. 800s....................... Founding of Tendai and Shingon schools of Buddhism in Japan

1203 .... Destruction of final Buddhist institutions in India by Muslim ruler Muhammad Ghori

ca. 1300s..................... Emergence of Zen, Pure Land, and Nichiren Buddhism in Japan

ca. 1400s..................... Abolishment of Buddhism in India

1578.............................. Sonam Gyatso first to be named Dalai Lama in Tibet

1852	First Chinese Buddhist temple established in the United States in San Francisco
1930	Founding of Soka Gakkai in Japan
1935	Birth of fourteenth Dalai Lama of Tibetan Buddhism
1949	Communist takeover of China
1959	Tibetan Buddhists flee to India and Nepal
1989	Fourteenth Dalai Lama wins Nobel Peace Prize
1998	Terrorists commit a deadly suicide attack on the Temple of Tooth in Sri Lanka where the Buddha's tooth relic is enshrined
2013	Twenty Tibetan Buddhist nuns become first women to earn geshe degrees

simple robes of a holy man and had his charioteer take all his princely clothes and jeweled possessions back to his father. For the next six years, Siddhartha lived as a wandering **ascetic**, meditating for hours each day and eating only enough to stay alive. He became so emaciated that he said he could put his finger in his belly button and feel his backbone.

At one point, Siddhartha sat under a **bodhi tree** and sought answers to questions about life, especially suffering. Mara, a demon associated with death

---

ascetic A person who renounces material comforts to live a self-disciplined life, especially in the area of religious devotion.

bodhi tree The large, sacred fig tree at the Mahabodhi Temple at Bodh Gaya where Siddhartha the Buddha achieved enlightenment. *Bodhi* means "awakening" or "enlightenment."

A statue of the Buddha sitting under a Bodhi tree in Wat Phan Tao, Chiang Mai, Thailand.

and desire, tempted Siddhartha. Mara tempted Siddhartha with thirst, lust, discontent, and sensuality, but to no avail. Going deeper into meditation about suffering and the cycle of rebirth, Siddhartha finally reached the **enlightenment** he sought. He was awakened to the cause and cessation of suffering. Siddhartha struggled with whether to share his new insights with others.

Returning to the Deer Park near where he lived, Siddhartha delivered his first sermon to five ascetics who had once traveled with him but later abandoned him. He told them that neither indulgence nor asceticism could release people from samsara, the endless cycle of birth, death, and rebirth. Instead, it was the **Middle Way**, life in the middle of the spectrum between indulgence and asceticism, that led to freedom from samsara. Living the Middle Way consists of following the Four Noble Truths, the fourth of which is the Noble Eightfold Path, eight practices dealing with wisdom, morality, and

---

enlightenment The state of being awakened about life's illusions and removed from the cycle of rebirth.

Middle Way The Buddhist teaching that liberation from samsara comes neither through severe ascetical practices nor through wild indulgences but in the middle of the spectrum between those two opposites.

meditation. You will read a fuller explanation of the Four Noble Truths and the Noble Eightfold Path in Section 3.

Those first five wandering ascetics to whom Siddhartha preached in the Deer Park decided to follow him, and they formed a monastic community. Siddhartha continued his travels and preaching and gained many followers. He returned to his homeland, where he converted many of his tribe, including his wife, son, and cousin, to his Middle Way.

At age eighty, Siddhartha died, possibly of food poisoning. As he lay on his right side dying, he asked the gathering crowd whether anyone had any questions. There was no response. He told the people that nothing in the world was permanent and that they had to work out their own salvation with diligence. When Siddhartha died, his followers believed he entered Nirvana. The year was about 483 BCE. He was cremated, and his **relics** were divided and distributed to places where he had traveled. *Stupas* (dome-shaped monuments) were later erected over his relics, and they became destinations of Buddhist pilgrimages.

The Buddha passed away to final Nirvana, or parinirvana.

The Four Councils

Siddhartha left his followers neither a successor nor personal writings. His legacy was the **dharma** (teachings of the faith), which he shared with all who would listen. After his death, the Buddha's followers shared his teachings and practices informally, but there was a concern for preserving the purity of them. Shortly after the Buddha's death, a council of his longtime followers—five hundred monks—gathered to preserve his teachings. They recited their memories of him in their group and tried to come to an agreement on

---

relics Items of religious devotion, especially pieces of the body or personal items of an important religious figure.

dharma From the Sanskrit meaning "uphold." In Hinduism, it is that which is in accordance with the laws of the cosmos and of nature—for example, righteous acts. In Buddhism, it is the teachings of the Buddha.

In life, the Buddha shared his knowledge with his sangha, or company.

his teachings. After this First Council, the monks held periodic recitation gatherings to maintain the purity of the memories and as a means of sharing them with others.

Members of this community of monks (known as the **sangha**) called a Second Council to address questionable practices involving some "liberal" monks who sought a relaxation of monastic discipline, including permission to store salt, eat after noon, drink palm wine, and accept silver and gold. The Second Council found these practices unlawful, but the decision was likely

---

sangha Originally the name for the Buddhist monastic community. Later it came to describe the entire community of monks, nuns, and laypersons.

Theravada Buddhism The more traditional of the two main branches of Buddhism, claiming their roots in the historical life of Siddhartha Gautama. It is found mainly in Thailand, Laos, Cambodia, Myanmar, and Sri Lanka. Mahayana Buddhists sometimes uncharitably call it Hinayana Buddhism, meaning "Lesser Vehicle."

Mahayana Buddhism Literally the "Greater Vehicle," a branch of Buddhism that accommodates a greater number of people from all walks of life toward enlightenment. It is strongest in Tibet, China, Taiwan, Japan, Korea, and Mongolia.

a seed for a major split between the conservative Sthavira Buddhists and the liberal Mahasanghika Buddhists. These two groups continued to subdivide over the next few decades until there were eighteen sects, ten belonging to the Sthaviras and eight belonging to the Mahasanghikas. From the Sthavira group, only **Theravada Buddhism** survives to this day, and the Mahasanghikas were forerunners of today's **Mahayana Buddhism**.

The Third Council occurred when Emperor Ashoka of the Maurya dynasty of India converted to Buddhism in the third century BCE. Disenchanted with the devastation war left on people, communities, and the environment, he began to rule his empire by the Buddhist ideals of moral living and pacifism. Ashoka also continued to support Hinduism and Jainism.

Ashoka is known for creating the original stupas as places to honor Siddhartha. He subdivided the relics of the Buddha into minuscule elements so that he could create thousands of stupas as pilgrimage sites. Buddhist tradition holds that Ashoka's son, a Buddhist monk, and companions were sent to Ceylon (modern-day Sri Lanka) as missionaries. There, King Tissa and many of his nobility converted to Buddhism. Buddhist missionaries also went deep into the Hellenized (Greek) world of the West. Edicts of Ashoka inscribed on rocks and pillars indicate that missionaries met with the Seleucid king

The Great Stupa constructed by Ashoka at Sanchi, Madhya Pradesh, India.

Antiochus II, the Egyptian pharaoh Ptolemy II, and several other Western rulers in the third century BCE. The growth of Buddhism was so swift under Ashoka that some questionable teachings emerged and flourished without correction. The purpose of the Third Council was to purify the sangha of its various irregularities.

Two separate Fourth Councils reflected the divisions within Buddhism by the first century BCE. The Theravada sect held a council in Sri Lanka after a famine caused the deaths of several monks; the remaining monks gathered to preserve memories from the period so they would not be lost. The Sarvastivada tradition, a sect established during the time of Emperor Ashoka, is said to have convened a council in the first century CE.

Around 100 CE, Mahayana Buddhism, with its emphasis on lay participation, emerged as a distinct branch of Buddhism. Increased lay participation brought other new interpretations of Buddhist scripture.

Buddhism in India

Thankfully, Ashoka's efforts preserved Buddhism and extended it beyond India; by the time Muslims invaded India in the twelfth century, Buddhism had mostly disappeared from India, the land of its birth.

The ruins of Nalanda, a fifth-century monastery and center of learning, in Bihar, India.

Buddhism had made great strides in India during the first few centuries of the Common Era, especially during the reign of the Gupta dynasty in the fourth and fifth centuries CE. It was during the Gupta dynasty that Buddhist universities became a prominent part of monastic centers. The universities boasted an extensive curriculum, with students taking courses not only in Buddhism but also in logic, science, mathematics, medicine, and music. They also became training places for missionaries. One of the most famous Buddhist universities was Nalanda, located not far from where the Buddha first attained enlightenment. The rise in the number of universities prompted the rise of the Mahayana tradition as a dominant expression of Buddhism.

A negative factor of large monasteries and universities was that they tended to make the monks more elitist. Consequently, the laity began to drift away from Buddhism and move toward the resurgent bhakti movement in India. This attrition, coupled with the Huns' invasion of India in about 470 that destroyed thousands of monasteries, rendered Buddhism in India nearly extinct. Though the Huns were defeated in 528, Buddhism never fully recovered in India.

Buddhism was able to revive itself to some extent in India with the foundation of the Pala dynasty in the eighth century. Kings of the Pala dynasty were patrons of Buddhism, building many great monastic centers. With the end of the Pala dynasty and Muslim invasions in the twelfth century, Buddhism disappeared from India until the twentieth century, with the exception of only a few remnants.

Surprisingly, after centuries of absence, Buddhism is slowly returning to India. With the positive and inspirational example of the Tibetan Buddhists exiled to India due to persecution by Communist China and as a statement of protest against the caste system, conversions to Buddhism continue to experience a revival in twenty-first-century India.

Buddhist Expansion beyond India

Not long after the death of Siddhartha Gautama, Buddhism found its way to central Asia and eventually into regions now known as Afghanistan, Uzbekistan, Tajikistan, Pakistan, and parts of Iran. Buddhism shared these places with Hinduism, Christianity, and Islam.

Buddhism came to China around the beginning of the Common Era. It took a while to find a home there, but when it did, it became, along with

The Dambulla cave temple, located in Dambulla, Matale District, Sri Lanka, dates back to the first century and is home to a series of Buddhist statues and paintings as well as a monastery.

Confucianism and Taoism, very much part of the religious landscape. To the many schools of Buddhism, China contributed **Ch'an** and **Pure Land Buddhism** (see Chapter 7, Section 1). From China, Buddhism moved by the fourth century to Korea, where the **Tripitaka**, a compilation of early Buddhist scriptures, was highly revered.

Ch'an Buddhism A monastic Chinese school of Mahayana Buddhism that teaches that all can reach enlightenment but must be directed by a spiritual master. Meditation is the dominant method of spiritual cultivation.

Pure Land Buddhism An East Asian school of Mahayana Buddhism with a great devotion to the buddha Amitabha. Pure Land Buddhists believe that chanting "Amitabha" with great sincerity of heart will gain one entrance into the realm of the Pure Land. Pure Land Buddhism holds belief in more than one buddha.

Tripitaka From the Sanskrit meaning "Three Baskets"; the compilation of three collections of early Buddhist texts. The Tripitaka is also known as the Pali Canon.

Buddhism was introduced to Southeast Asia via Sri Lanka in the third century. In what is now Malaysia and Indonesia, it joined Hinduism to provide two strong religious traditions in the region until around the twelfth and thirteenth centuries, when Islam eclipsed both religious traditions except among the Chinese minority. Present-day Thailand and Myanmar were predominantly Theravada Buddhist strongholds. Influenced by China, present-day Cambodia and Vietnam were dominated by Mahayana Buddhism. In the last few centuries, European colonialism overwhelmed Buddhism in Southeast Asia, and the spread of Communism in the twentieth century devastated it. However, Buddhism was never wholly lost, and there are small signs of revival today.

The first Dalai Lama was Gendün Drubpa.

Japanese Buddhism was and remains unique. Around the sixth century CE, Ch'an Buddhism, called **Zen Buddhism**, as well as two sects of Buddhism that became distinctly Japanese, came to Japan. Rulers of Japan readily adopted Buddhism, but the practitioners of Shinto, the indigenous religious tradition of Japan (see Chapter 8, Section 1), were at first less welcoming. Eventually, it became difficult to distinguish between Shinto and Buddhism.

The fourteenth and current Dalai Lama is Tenzin Gyatso.

In Tibet, **Vajrayana Buddhism**, also known as Tantric Buddhism, emerged as a branch of Mahayana Buddhism in the eighth century. Vajrayana Buddhism puts a great emphasis on the practitioner doing mantras, rituals, and meditations to strive for

---

Zen Buddhism The Japanese version of Ch'an Buddhism.

Vajrayana Buddhism Literally meaning "Diamond Vehicle," the prominent branch of Buddhism in Tibet.

enlightenment. In the fourteenth century, Tibetan Buddhists came to believe that the leaders of their monasteries were reincarnations of great **bodhisattvas** who chose to postpone their own opportunity to enter Nirvana so that they could assist others to enter Nirvana themselves. Leaders of monasteries in Tibet became known as **lamas**. Since the fifteenth century, the head of Tibetan Buddhist monastic leaders has been called the **Dalai Lama**. In the twentieth century, the Dalai Lama was also the political leader of Tibet until the Chinese Communist government forced him out of Tibet in 1959. The Tibetan Buddhists set up their exiled community in Dharamshala, India.

Buddhism in the Modern Era

Buddhism did not take hold in the West until the modern era. There had been earlier, sporadic encounters between the West and Buddhism, mostly with Christian missionaries. St. John of Damascus (ca. 675–749) wrote a translation of the Buddha's life for Christians around the beginning of the eighth century. It is titled *Barlaam and Josaphat*. The main character, Barlaam, was a legendary Christian saint. Jesuits such as St. Francis Xavier (1506–1552) in Japan and St. Matteo Ricci (1552–1610) in China also encountered Buddhism in their missionary efforts.

A page from Barlaam and Josaphat *by St. John of Damascus.*

---

bodhisattvas In Mahayana Buddhism, people who compassionately refrain from entering Nirvana in order to help others enter first.

lamas In Tibetan Buddhism, teachers and often heads of monasteries.

Dalai Lama The head lama of Tibetan Buddhism who was the spiritual and political leader of Tibet until the Communist Chinese takeover forced his exile to India.

As the British sent merchants to set up trade routes to build their empire, a sustained interaction between Buddhism and the West came together. The translation of Buddhist texts into European languages brought Buddhism even deeper into the West, especially among Western intellectuals. In the United States, the poet Henry David Thoreau published a French translation of one of the **sutras** into English in the mid-nineteenth century. Also, the expansion of the railroads during the nineteenth century brought thousands of Chinese immigrants, some of whom were Buddhists, to the western part of the United States to work on that endeavor. At the end of the nineteenth century, one could find Japanese Buddhists among Japanese immigrant field laborers in Hawaii and California. The 1893 World's Parliament of Religions held in Chicago was another opportunity for Buddhists to make their religious tradition known to the West.

Soyen Shaku, abbot of the Engaku-ji Buddhist monastery in Kamakura, Japan, spoke at the 1893 World's Parliament of Religions. His translator was a young monk named D. T. Suzuki.

D. T. Suzuki

In the middle of the twentieth century, the Japanese Zen master D. T. Suzuki (1870–1966) translated his books on Zen Buddhism into English. Suzuki's version of Buddhism influenced American authors Allen Ginsberg and Thomas Merton, a Catholic Trappist monk, both of whom kept in contact with him.

The rise of Communism triggered attempts to eradicate Buddhism in several countries, first in Russia. After World War II, the Communist takeover in Asia affected Buddhism in China, Tibet, and parts of southeastern

---

sutras Discourses in Buddhist scriptures that are attributed to Siddhartha Gautama.

An Amitabha Empowerment ceremony at Meditation Mount in Ojai, California.

Asia. However, as history attests, Buddhism's decline in one region created an opportunity for its rise in another.

Buddhism's worldwide popularity grew even more at the start of the twenty-first century. Many Westerners find some aspects of Buddhism, with its emphasis on individualism, self-help, and self-realization, interesting and even helpful. Some appropriate aspects of Buddhism into their religious tradition, while others journey to conversion. Buddhism is one of the fastest-growing religious traditions in select areas of the world, including England and California.

SECTION *Assessment*

Reading Comprehension

1. Briefly summarize the birth, enlightenment, and death of Siddhartha Gautama.
2. What were the main issues addressed by each of the early Buddhist councils?

3. What attracted Emperor Ashoka to Buddhism?
4. How did the rise of Communism in China impact Buddhism?
5. What attracts some Westerners to Buddhism?

Vocabulary

6. Differentiate between a *sangha* and *stupas*.
7. In English, what does the term *Tripitaka* mean?

For Reflection

8. Which is more appealing to you: a life of indulgence, a life of asceticism, or a life based on the Middle Way? Why?

Flash Search

9. Besides Buddhist Zen, there is Jewish Zen, Christian Zen, and Muslim Zen. Explain the similarities and differences between them.

Section 2

SACRED STORIES AND SACRED SCRIPTURES

Siddhartha Gautama wrote no texts, nor did his immediate followers. Rather, for several generations after the death of the Buddha, his followers kept both stories about him and his teachings alive by passing them on orally at recitation gatherings.

Like the scriptures of other religious traditions, Buddhist sacred texts developed over many centuries. There is now an enormous corpus of Buddhist writings in a wide variety of literary genres. Texts were initially translated into various languages with little regard for accuracy. The literal translation of texts and the addition of other texts tended to bring tension and sometimes division within Buddhism. Thus, there is no agreement among, or even within, the various branches of Buddhism as to which texts are authoritative. Nevertheless, a review of Buddhist scripture is necessary for a better understanding of this religious tradition.

Scriptures of Theravada Buddhism

The early Buddhist scriptures known as the Tripitaka, or "Three Baskets," were passed down orally in Sanskrit before being written down around the first century BCE in the Pali language. Thus, another name for the Tripitaka is the **Pali Canon**. The "Three Baskets" to which the Tripitaka refers are the Vinaya Pitaka, the Sutra Pitaka, and the Abhidharma Pitaka.

- The Vinaya Pitaka is the code of monastic rules for monks and nuns. There are 227 rules for monks and 311 rules for nuns. The rules highlight

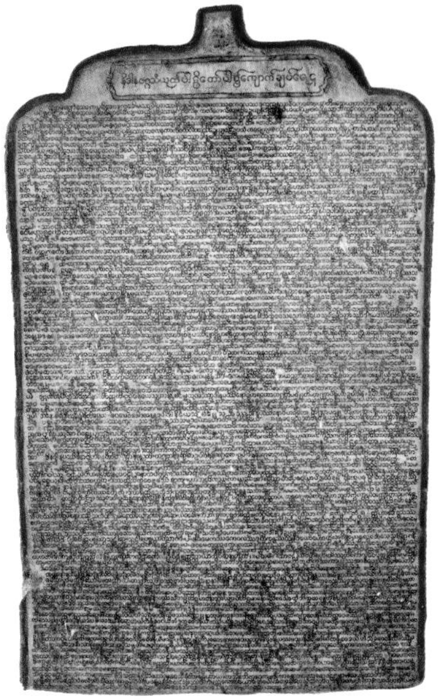

One of 729 two-sided stone tablets that contain the words of the entire Pali Canon at the Kuthodaw pagoda in Mandalay, Myanmar.

offenses in descending order of seriousness. Each rule is accompanied by a story that explains the reason for the rule. This basket also includes records of the life and ministry of Siddhartha Gautama.

- The Sutra Pitaka is made up primarily of discourses attributed to Siddhartha Gautama. Many of the topics of the discourses, such as morality, later became part of Buddhist doctrine. This basket contains the story of the Buddha's birth and attainment of Nirvana.
- The Abhidharma Pitaka examines the Buddha's psychological teachings and analyzes Buddhist doctrine in detail. The Abhidharma Pitaka is of more interest to monks or serious students than to the average lay Buddhist. The Mahayana and Vajrayana versions of this basket contain additional essays.

The Tripitaka in total is the authoritative scripture for Theravada Buddhists. Theravada Buddhists believe the Tripitaka contains the words of the historical Buddha.

Scriptures of Mahayana Buddhism

Besides their own version of the Tripitaka, Mahayana Buddhists hold numerous other texts sacred. Most popular is The Lotus of the True Law, more widely known as the **Lotus Sutra**. Mahayana Buddhists attribute the Lotus Sutra to the Buddha, but it was more likely composed over several generations

---

Pali Canon The authoritative Buddhist scripture of Theravada Buddhists, written in the Pali language. It is an important but not definitive scripture for Mahayana Buddhists. The Pali Canon is another name for the Tripitaka.

Lotus Sutra A Mahayana Buddhist text teaching that enlightenment is available to all Buddhists because of the great compassion of bodhisattvas.

Chapter 25 of the Lotus Sutra by calligrapher Sugawara Mitsushige in 1257.

between 100 BCE and 200 CE. Mahayana Buddhists believe the Lotus Sutra contains the Buddha's final teachings.

The popularity of the Lotus Sutra is due to the universality of its message. With its concept that all living things possess what scholars call Buddha-nature, the Lotus Sutra teaches that all people, not just religious professionals or monastics, can attain enlightenment. The Lotus Sutra also advocates the bodhisattva ideal in which, while working on one's own Nirvana, a person helps others attain Nirvana through the sharing of wisdom and compassion.

The Lotus Sutra contains a story that departs dramatically from what Theravada Buddhists believe about Siddhartha Gautama. For Theravada Buddhists, Siddhartha was a human person who was born, who lived on earth, and who died a natural death. The Lotus Sutra describes Siddhartha as an emanation of a divine Buddha who appeared on earth in human form to teach people the path to liberation.

The other very popular Mahayana work is the *Perfection of Wisdom* sutras, a treatise on how to achieve the perfection of wisdom of a bodhisattva. It teaches that to attain perfect wisdom, one must go beyond ordinary and rational knowledge. One must transcend the world of existence and resolve seeming contradictions by treating them as paradoxes. For example, many would say that light and darkness are opposites. According to the *Perfection of Wisdom* sutras, light and darkness are virtually the same, for both are ultimately nothing.

Scriptures of Vajrayana Buddhism

Like Theravada and Mahayana Buddhism, Vajrayana Buddhism has scriptures of its own. Vajrayana Buddhists use Mahayana scriptures but add to them their **tantric** texts from India and China. The Kanjur ("Teachings") contains both the teachings of the Theravada and Mahayana scriptures and scriptures unique to Vajrayana Buddhism. It includes a number of sutras, or discourses, on the Buddha's teachings.

Unlike Theravada and Mahayana Buddhism, Vajrayana Buddhism places a high value on the tantric tradition of India. In Hinduism, tantrism employs some forms of worship and ritual to appropriate and harness the powerful energies of Ultimate Reality in order to be one with Ultimate Reality someday. In Vajrayana Buddhism, tantric texts include instructions on how to perform the rituals or meditations to gain enlightenment. Buddhists also have the Tanjur, or Translation of the Treatises, which is a collection of commentaries on the Kanjur.

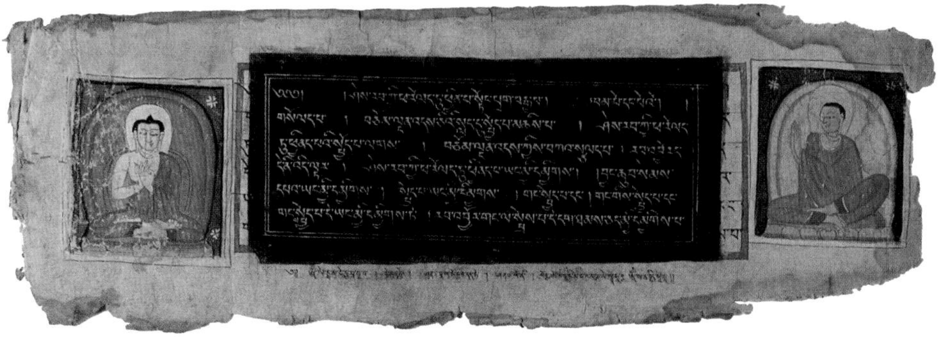

A stack of pages from a Tibetan copy of the Kanjur.

Two examples of Vajrayana tantric techniques are the use of **mandalas** and mantras to help focus one's personal meditation. As in Hinduism, a mantra is a repeated, often chanted, sacred word or phrase that assists one in focusing during meditation. The mandala is a sacred geometric symbol of the universe.

---

tantric A word to describe literature written in Sanskrit that is concerned with ritual acts of body, speech, and mind.

mandalas In both Hinduism and Buddhism, geometric figures representing the universe. Their construction may be part of ritual and/or meditation.

The Way to Happiness

Examine these statements on happiness from the *Dhammapada*, a collection of sayings of the Buddha found in the Tripitaka:

Let us live happily, then, not hating those who hate us! Among men who hate us let us dwell free from hatred!

Let us live happily, then, free from (moral) ailments among the ailing! Among men who are ailing let us dwell free from ailments!

Let us live happily, then, free from greed among the greedy! Among men who are greedy let us dwell free from greed!

Let us live happily, then, though we call nothing our own! We shall be like the bright gods, feeding on happiness!

Victory breeds hatred, for the conquered is unhappy. He who has given up both victory and defeat, he, the contented, is happy.

There is no fire like passion; there is no losing throw like hatred; there is no pain like this body; there is no happiness higher than rest.

Hunger is the worst of diseases, the body the greatest of pains; if one knows this truly, that is Nirvana, the highest happiness.

Health is the greatest of gifts, contentedness the best riches; trust is the best of relationships, Nirvana the highest happiness.

He who has tasted the sweetness of solitude and tranquility is free from fear and free from sin, while he tastes the sweetness of drinking in the law.

The sight of the elect (Arya) is good, to live with them is always happiness; if a man does not see fools, he will be truly happy.

He who walks in the company of fools suffers a long way; company with fools, as with an enemy, is always painful; company with the wise is pleasure, like meeting with kinsfolk.

Therefore, one ought to follow the wise, the intelligent, the learned, the much enduring, the dutiful, the elect; one ought to follow a good and wise man, as the moon follows the path of the stars. (Chap. 15, 197–208)

Writing Task

Answer in two to three paragraphs: What is one lesson about happiness you learned from this reading?

The Paradise of Shambhala from the Bardo Thödol, or the Tibetan Book of the Dead.

One of the most popular scriptures within Vajrayana Buddhism is the Tibetan Book of the Dead. It contains various writings on death, dying, and rebirth. It describes what life—specifically consciousness—is like between death and rebirth. The popularity of the Tibetan Book of the Dead stems partially from the fact that it is read either by a dying person or by a relative around the time of death.

SECTION *Assessment*

Reading Comprehension

1. What is the most popular sacred text among Mahayana Buddhists?
2. How does Mahayana Buddhism differ from Theravada Buddhism regarding beliefs about the nature of Siddhartha Gautama?
3. What is one of the most popular Vajrayana sacred texts? Why?

Vocabulary

4. The *Pali Canon* is also known as what?

For Reflection

5. Christians have a closed canon, meaning they are not able to add books to the Bible. Buddhists do not have a closed canon.

What do you think are the advantages and disadvantages of each practice?

Flash Search

6. Why is the Tibetan Book of the Dead appreciated in the West?

Section 3 BELIEFS AND PRACTICES

The center of all Buddhist beliefs is the Four Noble Truths, which originate from Siddhartha Gautama's earliest sermons. Buddhists believe that those who are ignorant of the Four Noble Truths will remain in samsara (recall that samsara is the endless cycle of suffering through death and rebirth and that karma is the cause of samsara). Understanding the Four Noble Truths leads to the Noble Eightfold Path and perfection of the Middle Way—avoiding extremes and taking everything in moderation. These beliefs and subsequent practices are at the heart of Buddhism.

The Four Noble Truths

These are the Four Noble Truths:

1. Life is filled with suffering.

Suffering in this case refers not only to physical suffering but also to the mental suffering that comes with facing the various traumas of life. We begin this life with the trauma of birth. As life goes on, we experience physical, mental, and emotional pain; illness; injury; old age; and fear of death. The reasons for suffering include our struggles with impermanence, incompleteness, imperfection, and discontent.

Physical beings, both earthly and heavenly, are continually changing. In fact, all material things change: human beings age, wood rots, and stars form. Our thoughts, feelings, and attitudes change too. That is why all life is impermanent. The Buddhist doctrine associated with impermanence is known as **anatman**. While Hindus understand the self or soul (atman) as Brahman (Ultimate Reality), Siddhartha Gautama taught that if the soul is purely God, then it is not a soul at all. Therefore, it is really "no soul" or "no self." The existence of a soul implies permanence, and nothing is permanent to Buddhists. To them, the notion of having a separate self or soul is an illusion, which causes suffering.

2. The cause of suffering is desire.

Because we believe our individual selves are real, we have cravings. We continuously want things. When we do not get them, we are frustrated or disappointed. Even if a person receives what he or she wants, the resulting happiness is impermanent. Ignorance of the reality of the not-self (believing the self to be real, permanent, and unchanging) is the fundamental cause of suffering.

3. To cease suffering, one must cease desiring.

The only thing permanent, and thus real, is the end of suffering. When we free ourselves from the bondage of desires and cravings, and stop believing that our individual self is real, suffering ceases. This freedom brings people happiness and contentment. Nirvana extinguishes the suffering of samsara. Nirvana is what is real in Buddhism.

4. The path to the end of suffering is the Noble Eightfold Path.

The Noble Eightfold Path is the moral standard of Buddhism. The Noble Eightfold Path (see the subsection "The Noble Eightfold Path" in this section) is the Middle Way between indulgence and self-denial.

While both Buddhists and Hindus believe in the cycle of samsara, their concept of how samsara ends differs significantly. The cessation of

---

anatman The Buddhist doctrine of "no soul" or "no self," stating that a permanent, unchanging, independent self does not exist, though people act as if it does. Ignorance of anatman causes suffering.

samsara for Hindus is moksha, while for Buddhists it is Nirvana. Recall that moksha is liberation from samsara and the realization that the individual self—atman—is one with Ultimate Reality, Brahman. While there is immortality in Hinduism, there is no immortality in Buddhism because there is no self, no soul. Nirvana means extinguishing the flames of desires, cravings, or passions. This extinction is neither a positive nor a negative experience. Instead, Nirvana *is*. In achieving Nirvana, one is awakened to the reality of the human condition, no longer ignorant or delusional.

The Noble Eightfold Path

As the fourth of the Four Noble Truths, the Noble Eightfold Path is the central path of life that leads to liberation from samsara. When a person has perfected these eight practices, he or she is awakened or enlightened and attains Nirvana.

The elements of the Noble Eightfold Path can be divided into categories of morality, meditation, and wisdom. Moral conduct brings about meditation, meditation brings about wisdom, and, completing the circle, wisdom gives rise to moral conduct.

◆ *1. Right Understanding*

The first step of the Noble Eightfold Path requires that we see things as they truly are. Right understanding means understanding the causes of suffering, the end of suffering, and how one endures suffering. In short, this step is a summation of the Four Noble Truths.

◆◆ *2. Right Thought*

The mind must be purified of all that moves it away from enlightenment. Right thought is not just getting rid of wrong thoughts. It is replacing wrong thoughts such as hatred and desire with right thoughts such as loving-kindness and renunciation. Right thought is equated with the Christian beatitude of being clean of heart.

◆◆◆ *3. Right Speech*

We must eliminate all forms of lying, slandering, gossiping, and using harsh words. Instead, a person must speak truthfully and kindly about others.

4. Right Conduct

Right conduct exhorts us not to cheat, steal, murder, or engage in any kind of sexual misconduct. We are to act generously, not greedily.

5. Right Livelihood

Right livelihood demands that we do not earn a living through actions that harm other living things. We should not make our livelihood by slaughtering animals, doing anything involving weapons, or manufacturing or selling any kind of intoxicant, such as drugs or alcohol.

6. Right Effort

This path has to do with a person's thoughts. We must be diligent in getting rid of bad or delusional thoughts while cultivating good, wholesome thoughts.

7. Right Mindfulness

We must monitor all that we think and do. Awareness of thoughts, feelings, and actions at all times assists in dispelling illusions. Right mindfulness means knowing oneself.

8. Right Concentration

This final element is a form of meditation in which a person might concentrate on one object, such as a flickering candle, to give full attention to the object and dispel other distractions. This attentiveness enables us to see things as they really are and thus gain enlightenment.

Community

Buddhist belief and practice are marked differently by monks, nuns, and laypeople. Recall that *sangha* refers to a Buddhist community of monks or nuns. Buddhists traditionally believed that only in the monastic life could one properly practice the teachings of the Buddha. The role of laypeople was to take care of the material needs of the monastics, thereby gaining themselves merit for a better rebirth. Recent developments expanded *sangha* to mean the community of all Buddhist practitioners: monks, nuns, and laypeople. The sangha

Nuns wait in line to receive donations at a monastery in Sagaing, Myanmar.

is one of the **Three Jewels of Buddhism**. The two other jewels are the Buddha and the dharma. The Three Jewels are considered the core of Buddhism. In becoming a Buddhist, one proclaims refuge in these Three Jewels as follows:

> I take refuge in the Buddha.
> I take refuge in the dharma.
> I take refuge in the sangha.

Though the monastic and lay lifestyles are very different, they depend on each other. For example, Theravada monks are celibate and provide spiritual direction to the laity by their example. The laity provide physical nourishment to monks, who seek their daily food through begging at the households of Buddhist devotees.

The goal for all Buddhists is to be enlightened and reach Nirvana. For Theravada Buddhists, **arhat** ("worthy one") is the name for such an enlightened

---

Three Jewels of Buddhism The ideals at the heart of Buddhism: the Buddha, the dharma, and the sangha.

person. However, only those who have heard the teachings of the Buddha can become arhats.

Mahayana Buddhists likewise accept the status of arhat as an ultimate goal. However, the exemplary person in Mahayana Buddhism is a bodhisattva who has chosen to defer full enlightenment until all other humans have reached Nirvana. Because of their great compassion for all persons, bodhisattvas, who are not necessarily monks or nuns, transfer merit they have gained to others so that others reach Nirvana. The bodhisattva will enter Nirvana last.

Mahayana monks abide by the same rules as Theravada monks. However, they add to the rules by witnessing about Siddhartha Gautama and his way of life and emulating his attitudes of peace and compassion to others. Monks of the Japanese Mahayana Buddhist sect of Zen Buddhism do not beg for alms. Instead, they earn their livelihood. Another Japanese Mahayana sect known as Shin (a school of Pure Land Buddhism) permits monks to marry and raise families.

Sivali, an arhat who is venerated by Theravada Buddhists. He carries a walking stick and folded umbrella and is the patron saint of travel.

---

arhat From the Sanskrit for "worthy one"; a concept of Theravada Buddhism that refers to one who has attained Nirvana in his or her present lifetime and is thus liberated from the cycle of rebirth.

Ksitigarbha is one of the four principal bodhisattvas in Mahayana Buddhism. He is the guardian of children.

SECTION *Assessment*

Reading Comprehension

1. Name and explain the Four Noble Truths.
2. List the three major categories of the Noble Eightfold Path.
3. What are the Three Jewels of Buddhism?
4. What differentiates Zen Buddhist monks from other Mahayana Buddhist monks?

For Reflection

5. How would you go about the process of "ceasing of all desires"? Is the desire to cease all desires itself a desire? Explain your response.

6. How would your peer group be different if it followed the Noble Eightfold Path?

Flash Search

7. What do Buddhists believe about heaven and hell?

Section 4
SACRED TIME

Buddhists do not have a special day of the week to worship together. Theravada Buddhists can make offerings to images of the Buddha at a temple at any time. Because the Buddha is not a god, bowing to his image is a sign of profound respect rather than submission to a deity. Mahayana Buddhists do the same and also make offerings to images of bodhisattvas. In places where there are no temples, Buddhists worship at home.

At both home and temple, the items offered usually are flowers, candles, or incense. The scent of incense reminds Buddhists of the influence of good virtue. Flowers, which soon wither, remind people of the impermanence of everything. A recitation of the Three Jewels is usually part of the offering.

Meditation

Meditation is central to every branch of Buddhism. The last three elements of the Noble Eightfold Path concern meditation. By engaging in right effort, right mindfulness, and right concentration, Buddhists believe they are well on their way to enlightenment. Meditation is also a means of heightened awareness. Meditating helps people cultivate awareness of their dreams, goals, and self-identities, as well as the means to engage in good karma. Siddhartha Gautama taught his disciples several types of meditation. Two of the most commonly used are Mindfulness of Breathing and Meditation of Loving-Kindness.

As might be imagined, Mindfulness of Breathing focuses on the ebb and flow of our breathing. As you breathe in and out, you try not to let other thoughts and distractions intrude. The person who persists in practicing this form of meditation over a long period finds that the power of concentration becomes stronger, and inner calm enters not only the mind but the whole person.

Visitors pray and meditate at the Yonghe Temple in Beijing, China.

The Meditation of Loving-Kindness, like most Buddhist meditations, begins with Mindfulness of Breathing. When the mind is calmed, a person then focuses on the self and says loving intentions about himself or herself. Here are some examples:

> May I be a loving person.
> May I have a heart filled with love.
> May I be a peace-filled person.
> May I be a fulfilled person.

After focusing on the self, a person then turns his or her attention to others: first to one whom the person loves, then to one toward whom the person is neutral, and finally to one whom the person dislikes. The person meditating then wishes each of these three people well over a long time.

Puja

As with Hindus, puja is part of the daily life of practicing Buddhists. Recall that for Hindus, puja is a worship service held in homes and temples to honor a deity. For Buddhist monks, puja takes place in monasteries, while for Buddhist laity, puja generally takes place at home shrines.

A home shrine in Vietnam.

What makes up a shrine in a Buddhist's home? Components generally include an image of the Buddha and, in some countries, representations of family ancestors. In a typical puja ritual, participants offer flowers, fruit, a bowl of water, incense, and lighted candles to revere, respect, and honor the Buddha. Buddhists offer reverence and gratitude to the Buddha through gestures such as removing one's shoes before beginning, folding one's hands and bowing, and, in some traditions, prostration. Prayers are said, a mantra may be chanted, and meditation on some aspect of the dharma may be included. In addition, the Three Jewels and the **Five Precepts** are recited.

Honoring the Buddha and his dharma are not confined to the home. Public shrines and temples are also places for puja. In predominantly Buddhist nations, images of the Buddha are everywhere, cast in bronze, stone, wood, metal, or other materials on different structures and surfaces. A Buddha replica may be two inches or two stories tall. Images may be in the form of paintings of many styles and mediums. Images of the Buddha are in small

A public shrine across the street from the Strand Hotel in Yangon, Myanmar.

Five Precepts The basic moral standard by which all Buddhists are to live. The Five Precepts are (1) do not take the life of any living creature; (2) do not take anything not freely given; (3) abstain from sexual misconduct and sexual overindulgence (for monastics, abstain from any sexual activity); (4) refrain from untrue or deceitful speech; and (5) avoid intoxicants.

shrines on street corners, in shops, on roadsides, in public parks, and the like. In countries where adherents are predominantly Mahayana Buddhists, images of bodhisattvas are also displayed. These images are not only reminders of exemplary lives but also sources of power and good karma.

Festivals

There are two types of Buddhist festivals. The first is centered around the Buddha's life. Celebrated on the full moon day of May, Vesak, or "Buddha Day," is the holiest day of the year for Theravada Buddhists. For them, Siddhartha Gautama was born, became enlightened, and died all on the same date. The emphasis of this festival is enlightenment. Theravada Buddhists light colorful lanterns and candles around the monasteries where the celebrations occur and lovingly decorate an image of the Buddha. Customarily, a monk gives a sermon on some aspect of the Buddha's life.

Celebrating Vesak at Pagode du bois de Vincennes in Paris, France.

Many Mahayana Buddhists commemorate the birth, enlightenment, and death of the Buddha on three separate days throughout the year. For Mahayana Buddhists, the celebration of the Buddha's life may entail bathing the sacred image, followed by a procession. The bathing not only signifies great reverence for the Buddha but also reminds practitioners that everyone's life has faults that need washing away.

A second type of Buddhist sacred celebration is the three-month period known as the Rains Retreat. It began as a retreat for mendicant (begging) monks who preached the dharma through their wanderings during all but the three months of the monsoon season. Though it is still primarily a monastic retreat, lay Buddhists also consider the Rains Retreat a time of great holiness. The end of the retreat is celebrated with a great festival put on by the laypeople. At a special ceremony, monks are presented with new robes. Laypeople believe that the monks gain high spiritual power during the Rains Retreat and hope some of the holiness radiates onto them and shortens samsara.

There are also minor festivals that mark the seasons, particularly spring and autumn. However, these are not specifically religious in nature, and they are connected more with countries and regions than specifically with Buddhism.

Life-Cycle Celebrations

Buddhism plays little role in most rites of passage, except those at the time of death. The Tibetan Book of the Dead characterizes dying as a sacred act. Death rituals are important in Buddhism because of the religious tradition's great interest in life after death and the rebirth of the person. The most important concern is to help a person move from samsara to Nirvana.

A grandmother and granddaughter in Bhutan.

There are no specific Buddhist initiation ceremonies for infants. The initiation of a newborn into a community is based on local customs. Buddhists connect birth with suffering and samsara. They believe a newborn had previous existences and that the karma of previous lives may influence the character of the person in this life.

Like birth ceremonies, marriage ceremonies are performed according to local customs. Any aspect of Buddhism in a marriage ceremony is at the discretion of the planners of the event. A Buddhist couple often marries in a civil ceremony and asks a monk or the local sangha to bless the marriage afterward. The marriage blessing may take place at a temple, shrine, or home. The blessing may include chanting from sacred scripture and perhaps a sermon on married life.

SECTION *Assessment*

Reading Comprehension

1. Why is meditation important to Buddhists?
2. Briefly describe Mindfulness of Breathing meditation.
3. How do Theravada and Mahayana Buddhists celebrate the birth of the Buddha?
4. What is the origin of the Rains Retreat?

Vocabulary

5. Compare the Ten Commandments with the *Five Precepts* of Buddhism.

For Reflection

6. What are obstacles in your life that keep you from gaining the benefits of meditation?
7. What are similarities among home shrines in the Hindu, Buddhist, and Catholic traditions?

Flash Search

8. Why is the practice of mindfulness so popular in the West these days?

Section 5
SACRED PLACES AND SACRED SPACES

Monasteries, temples, and places connected with events in the life of the Buddha are among the sacred places and sacred spaces in Buddhism.

Monasteries

Buddhist monasteries are often attached to temples. In Theravada Buddhism, men especially must spend part of their lives in a monastery. They may leave the monastery when it is time to marry but often return when their children

The Tibetan Buddhist Hemis Monastery, in Hemis, Ladakh, India.

are grown. Also, laypeople share in the merit of the monks by providing them food and maintaining the monasteries through their monetary donations.

Temples

The temple is especially sacred for Theravada Buddhists. Monks live at the temple complex and perform certain religious rites there. Laypeople come to the temple for religious devotions, meditation, and instruction on Buddhist teachings. At a temple, there are usually images of the Buddha and stories

Hoi Duc Temple in South Portland, Maine (left), and Ruwanwelisaya Stupa in Anuradhapura, Sri Lanka (right).

of his life depicted in paintings or statues. A stupa containing relics from the Buddha or his followers is usually present. Mahayana Buddhist temples often have several enshrined images of people from the past who became enlightened and bear the title "buddha." Mahayana and Vajrayana temples sometimes have shrines venerating bodhisattvas. A temple usually has a place for a monk to deliver a sermon on a special occasion.

Originally, stupas were small mounds made of stone or brick, usually located near a temple, that housed the relics of the historical Buddha. As Buddhism expanded, relics of the Buddha gave way to relics of other important Buddhist figures and other religious objects. As the small mound of a stupa expands, it becomes a towering, elaborately decorated dome called a **pagoda**. Stupas and pagodas connected with temples naturally become pilgrimage sites.

---

pagoda An eastern Asian tower, usually built with roofs curving upward at the division of each of several stories and erected as a temple or memorial.

Buddha statues in the Lumbini Garden in Hpa-An, Kayin State, Myanmar.

Places of Pilgrimage

Other sacred places for Buddhists are those that are in some way connected with the life and ministry of the historical Buddha. They are located in present-day India or Nepal.

The Lumbini Garden is the traditional site of the birth of Siddhartha Gautama. Located in Nepal, it became a place of pilgrimage shortly after the death of Siddhartha. In the third century CE, Emperor Ashoka had a twenty-two-foot pillar erected there as a memorial to the Buddha.

The descendant of the bodhi tree where the Buddha reached enlightenment at Mahabodhi Temple, Bodhgaya, Bihar, India.

Bodh Gaya, a village in the state of Bihar in northeastern India, is the site of the bodhi tree under which the Buddha meditated and gained his enlightenment. The tree now there is said to be a descendant of the original bodhi tree. Near the tree is a sandstone slab marking the place where Gautama became enlightened. A stone under the present tree has a footprint said to have been imposed by the

Buddha. Buddhist pilgrims often make offerings of flowers and decorate the area. Saplings from the original bodhi tree are planted throughout India, and they too are places of pilgrimage.

Sarnath is a site near the confluence of the Ganges and Varuna rivers in Uttar Pradesh in northern India. The Deer Park in Sarnath is where Siddhartha Gautama preached his first sermon about the Four Noble Truths and where he gained his first disciples. Emperor Ashoka constructed a stupa there. Deer still roam the park today. More than 1.5 million tourists visit the park annually.

Kushinagar is the traditional place of the death of Siddhartha. The Kushinagar Nirvana Temple was built in 1956 to commemorate the 2,500th year of the Buddha's entrance into Nirvana. There is also a 1,500-year-old red stone statue of a reclining Buddha at Kushinagar.

SECTION *Assessment*

Reading Comprehension

1. Name a difference between a Theravada temple and a Mahayana temple.
2. How does a pagoda differ from a stupa?
3. What is the significance of each of the four pilgrimage sites related to the life of Siddhartha Gautama?

For Reflection

4. What are symbolic "relics" in your life that you revere?
5. Name a holy place or shrine you have visited. What is one impression you had of this place?

Flash Search

6. Buddhists are well known for their discipline of nonviolence. Nevertheless, some Buddhists in Myanmar have recently resorted to violence. Why?

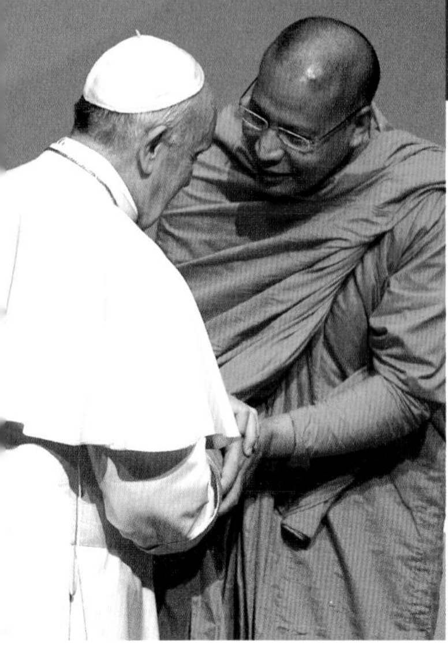

Section 6
CATHOLICS DIALOGUE WITH BUDDHISTS

Both Catholics and Buddhists look to "walk gently upon the earth rather than trample the earth with heavy boots." The most common areas of agreement between Catholics and Buddhists are related to peace and compassion. One way that compassion is practiced in both traditions is through nonviolence. While Christianity *preaches* peace and compassion and speaks out against the injustice of war, Buddhists point to the fact that seldom in their history have their adherents ever *engaged* in war.

Another similarity between the two traditions is monasticism. Living in a climate with a monsoon season, Buddhist monks began establishing monasteries in the fourth century BCE to shelter themselves from the harsh weather for months at a time. In Christianity, the monastic lifestyle developed in the fourth century CE when hermits populated the desert caves of the Middle East before forming great monasteries throughout both the eastern and western portions of the Roman Empire.

Thomas Merton

Meditation, part of the monastic traditions of both Catholicism and Buddhism, is a major topic of interreligious dialogue. While the content is different, some practices are similar. Since the 1960s, Buddhists and Catholics have engaged in interreligious dialogue in monastic settings. In 1968, Trappist monk and internationally known spiritual author Thomas Merton attended an international meeting of Buddhist and Catholic monks in Bangkok, Thailand.

As with any two religious traditions, several differences exist among similarities in belief and practice. More information on similarities and differences between Catholicism and Buddhism follow.

Jesus Christ and Siddhartha the Buddha

There are striking similarities between the accounts of the lives of Jesus and Siddhartha Gautama. Both had miracles associated with their conception. Both were tempted before they began their public life. Both had a group of followers and shared a message and a way to spiritual freedom. Both were founders of a worldwide religious tradition. However, Buddhism originally spread to the East, while Christianity spread primarily to the West. During modern times, Buddhism is newly flourishing in the West while Christianity is making new inroads in the East. Ironically, very few Christians now reside in modern-day Israel, where Christianity originated, and very few Buddhists live in India, where Buddhism originated.

The differences between Jesus and Siddhartha are just as striking as the similarities. Siddhartha never claimed to be divine, while Jesus is both human and divine. Jesus was born of humble means, while Siddhartha was born into royalty. Siddhartha was married, and Jesus was not. While Jesus' message was about the Kingdom of God, Siddhartha's message was about the cessation of suffering.

The Theme of Suffering

Catholics and Buddhists have very different perspectives on suffering. In general, all Buddhists who have not reached enlightenment and Nirvana are suffering. Destructive attitudes and activities such as greed, hatred, and stealing subject them to return to another life of suffering. To escape samsara—the endless cycle of birth, death, and rebirth—Buddhists must stop the desires and cravings of the heart and practice the Noble Eightfold Path.

Buddhist monks and Catholic priests attend a memorial prayer service on the anniversary of the 2011 Great East Japan Earthquake and Tsunami. More than 15,000 people died in the two tragedies.

Buddhists recognize three categories of suffering. The first category is physical suffering. Violence inflicted by one person on another is part of this category. So is getting in a car or motorcycle accident or having an illness.

A second category of suffering is related to change or transition in one's life. The amount of suffering experienced in such transitions directly relates to one's attachment to another person or to an object. For example, a best friend moving away would cause more suffering than an acquaintance moving away. And more suffering results when a home is destroyed in a fire than when a shirt is permanently ruined by ink or soil.

A third category of suffering seems counterintuitive; it is pain brought about amid pleasure. Buddhists believe that suffering lurks within the pleasure of an accomplishment. The suffering comes from the fact that, since all things are impermanent, the pleasure of feeling a sense of accomplishment—for example, receiving a good grade or scoring a goal—is impermanent and illusory. The disconnect between that which is real and that which is illusory causes suffering. In essence, Buddhists would say that suffering comes when one possesses the illusion that something or someone will bring pleasure. Though this seems to be a negative or pessimistic view, Buddhists would say that their perception of suffering is ultimately life giving, for looking squarely at and accepting wholeheartedly that which is real and turning away from illusion brings deep peace and true happiness.

Catholics understand suffering as part of the finite human condition. Some suffering, such as that caused by natural disasters and disease, comes through no fault of one's own. Other sufferings are brought upon us by others and ourselves, for one of the consequences of Original Sin is an inclination to evil. The greatest moral evil ever committed—the Crucifixion of God's only Son—brought about a good for all humanity. However, evil and suffering themselves never become a good.

It is a mistake to think that God created suffering or that God wants people to suffer. On the contrary, God desires the end of suffering, and sometimes we are the instruments to help alleviate the suffering of others. Suffering is a mystery. "Why must people suffer?" is a question that we all must live with and even hold in awe. The most important thing to remember about suffering is to trust God. God is in control. God knows what is happening. God is always with all creation and provides what people need to get through life's many sufferings. It is Jesus on the Cross who gives strength to those who know the promise of the Resurrection. As was the case with Jesus, all suffering ceases at one's resurrection when one experiences eternal life with God and the saints. You should not be surprised if, at the Final Judgment, you are asked, "Did you help alleviate the sufferings of your brothers and sisters?"

SECTION *Assessment*

Reading Comprehension

1. Describe the similarities and differences between Jesus and Siddhartha Gautama.
2. Why would Buddhists say that there is no such thing as pure pleasure?
3. Compare the Catholic and Buddhist concepts of suffering.

For Reflection

4. The perennial question of the problem of evil goes something like this: "If God is all-good, all-loving, and all-powerful, why is there so much suffering in the world?" How would you answer this question?

Flash Search

5. When, where, and how did Thomas Merton die?

Section Summaries

Introduction: The Call to Wake Up

The root for *Buddha* and *Buddhism* means "awaken." The founder of Buddhism, Siddhartha Gautama, is given the title the Buddha, or "Awakened One." The goal of Buddhism is Nirvana. To reach that goal, one must be awakened from the illusion of desires, for they bring only suffering. Theravada and Mahayana are the two major branches of Buddhism.

- Find out when Buddhism came to your country. In what ways does Buddhism appear in your country's religious landscape?

Section 1: A Brief History of Buddhism

Siddhartha Gautama, sometimes called Shakyamuni by his followers, was the founder of Buddhism. As Siddhartha was a Hindu born in what is now Nepal, Buddhism has its roots in Hinduism and India. The first councils of early Buddhism were convened to codify monastic discipline and unify Buddhist scriptures. Buddhism received imperial patronage from Emperor Ashoka. Two major branches of Buddhism are Theravada and Mahayana. The Muslim invasion of India eventually drove Buddhism from India by the end of the twelfth century, though Buddhism is reemerging there today. In its first few centuries of existence, Buddhism spanned much of the continent of Asia. Though there were sporadic Western encounters with Buddhism over the centuries, Buddhism did not take hold in the West until the modern era.

- Research and answer in three to four paragraphs: Why did Siddhartha Gautama reject any notion about God or any deities?

Section 2: Sacred Stories and Sacred Scriptures

The various branches of Buddhism have scriptures they share as well as scriptures that are unique to the respective branches. The one scripture shared by all major branches of Buddhism is the Tripitaka. One of the most popular scriptures in Mahayana Buddhism is the Lotus Sutra. Vajrayana Buddhism has a number of tantric texts.

- Research the Lotus Sutra. Why is it so popular among Mahayana Buddhists? What teachings does it contain? Answer in three to four paragraphs.

Section 3: Beliefs and Practices

The foundations of Buddhist teaching are the Four Noble Truths and the Noble Eightfold Path, which leads to the end of suffering, or Nirvana. The Three Jewels are considered the core of Buddhism. The sangha is the Buddhist community of monks, nuns, and laypeople. Monastic and lay lifestyles are different but interdependent.

- Draw and label three images that represent Theravada, Mahayana, and Vajrayana Buddhism.

Section 4: Sacred Time

Buddhists do not have a special day of the week to worship together. They can make offerings to images of the Buddha (and for Mahayana Buddhists, to images of bodhisattvas) at a temple or at home. Meditation is common to every branch of Buddhism. The two most common forms of meditation are Mindfulness of Breathing and Meditation of Loving-Kindness. Buddhists celebrate only a few festivals. All Buddhists celebrate the birth of Siddhartha Gautama in one form or another. Buddhists have no specific life-cycle ceremonies for birth and marriage, but they do have special funeral rituals.

- Find a short Buddhist meditation. Practice reciting it, and then record yourself. Send the recording to your teacher.

Section 5: Sacred Places and Sacred Spaces

Monasteries are often connected to Buddhist temples. Besides images of the Buddha, Mahayana temples include images of other buddhas and bodhisattvas. A stupa contains relics or other sacred objects of Buddhism. The most popular places for Buddhist pilgrimage are those connected with events in the life of the Buddha. These sacred places are located in India or Nepal.

- The pagoda has a unique style of architecture. Research and answer: What is the symbolism of the architecture? Create a digital presentation with five or six slides to demonstrate. Use the notes feature to explain each slide.

Section 6: Catholics Dialogue with Buddhists

Compassion and peace are held in high regard in both Buddhism and Christianity. Both Christianity and Buddhism have strong, vibrant monastic traditions and place emphasis on meditation. There are both striking similarities and vast differences between Jesus and Siddhartha. Suffering is a significant topic in both Catholicism and Buddhism, but each religious tradition sees the meaning of suffering very differently.

- Research the similarities and differences between Buddhism and Christianity regarding the role of relics. Share images of two relics from each tradition with a detailed caption for each.

Chapter Projects

Complete one of these projects by the conclusion of your study of this chapter.

1. Creating a Mandala

   Draw your own mandala. You will need, at minimum, art paper, pencil, compass, and ruler. Examine several mandalas online. Consider ways to emulate a favorite mandala and adapt it to make it your own. Use directions from a "how to draw a mandala" website to help you get started.

2. Drawing or Photographing Buddhist Symbols

   Research and draw the following symbols of Buddhism. For each, relate a brief history, describe the symbol's meaning(s), and suggest various uses. You can create your images digitally or on art paper. Optional: Create a photographic display of Buddhist symbols.

   - lotus flower
   - lion
   - bell

- mala
- parasol
- two fish

3. Buddhist *Jeopardy!*-Style Questions

   Use index cards to record answers to questions about Buddhism with the questions on the other side of the card. Write ten answers and questions in each of three categories: easy, medium, and hard (a total of thirty questions). The questions and answers should all be able to be found in this chapter. Separate the cards into stacks by level of difficulty. Arrange to lead a game of *Jeopardy!* for your classmates for review or duplicate the questions so that they can review the chapter material on their own.

4. Buddhist Word Search

   Use vocabulary words and other key terms from this chapter to create a word search grid. Your grid should contain at least twenty searchable words. Provide your own instructions as to which directions the words may run (frontward, backward, diagonal, etc.). List the words at the bottom of the word search. Make copies and share with your classmates.

5. News Story on Buddhist Nuns

   Write a two- to three-page newspaper-style article with the headline "Buddhist Nuns in Western Society Today." Include answers to the following questions in your article:

   - What was the traditional role of Buddhist nuns for centuries?
   - In what ways do Buddhist nuns contribute to Buddhism and to Western society today?
   - What challenges do they face in Buddhism and in greater society today?

Key Image

Dharma Wheel

The dharma wheel is the ancient universal symbol of Buddhism. Buddhists believe this symbol has the power to bring people to enlightenment, for it instructs people how to follow the Buddha's teachings. Practicing the dharma (the teachings of the Buddha) and working toward that awakening will bring an individual to Nirvana.

The existence of the dharma wheel precedes Buddhism. It is found in depictions of the Hindu god of protection, Vishnu. There are multiple interpretations within Buddhism regarding symbolism within the dharma wheel. However, there seems to be agreement on the symbolism of the wheel itself. Circular in shape, the wheel represents the perfection of the dharma, the precision of the Buddha's teachings. For the hub, rim, and spokes, interpretations diverge.

The hub represents ethical or moral discipline. It can represent integrity as well. The three shapes within the hub most often symbolize the Three Jewels of Buddhism—the Buddha (the enlightened one and founder of Buddhism), the dharma (the teachings of the founder), and the sangha (the Buddhist community). The rim represents meditation and mindfulness, concentration, or attentiveness, which preserve the teachings as one entity and hold the practice together. There can be any number of spokes, which are disciplines of wisdom. The dharma wheel with eight spokes is the most popular dharma wheel by far. It represents the Noble Eightfold Path, which is the path one must trek to reach liberation from the birth-death-rebirth cycle and step into Nirvana.

In art depicting the Buddha, the dharma wheel is sometimes inscribed on his hands or his feet, symbolizing great power. There are portrayals where the Buddha is holding his hands in the shape of a wheel. Painting buildings with and getting tattoes of the dharma wheel are popular for Buddhists. Groups undertake the creation of Buddhist mandala geometric patterns based on the dharma wheel, as well as beautiful artistic renderings in paintings and murals. Ordinary life is not left out, for the dharma wheel can be found on such everyday items as bedspreads and T-shirts. Buddhists believe the dharma wheel has power, and they like to be in its presence.

Faithful Adherent

The Dalai Lama: The Happiness Monk

The Dalai Lama has been one of the most recognizable religious leaders in the world from the twentieth and into the twenty-first centuries. The fourteenth Dalai Lama, born Tenzin Gyatso in 1935 in a small village in Tibet, was chosen as the reincarnation of the thirteenth Dalai Lama at the age of two after reported signs and visions led a search party of Tibetan Buddhists to find him.

From humble beginnings in a farming family, he moved with his family to the capital, Lhasa, and at age six began his studies as a Tibetan Buddhist monk. After Communist China invaded Tibet in 1950, the Dalai Lama, at age fifteen, took over full political leadership from the temporary regent. There was a national uprising in Tibet against Communist China in 1959, and Chinese troops brutally suppressed it. The Dalai Lama and many others

The Dalai Lama and Pope John Paul II in a 1982 visit at the Vatican.

escaped to India, where the prime minister, Jawaharlal Nehru, welcomed the refugees. To this day, the exiled Tibetan government has its headquarters in Dharamshala, India. China has not allowed Tibetans to demonstrate any allegiance to the Dalai Lama.

Through his many speeches and books, a preeminent message of the Dalai Lama is the first of the Four Noble Truths: life is filled with suffering. Yet, he acknowledges, no human person wants to suffer. Instead, people want happiness. The titles of many of his books attest to that truth: *The Art of Happiness*; *All You Wanted to Know from His Holiness the Dalai Lama on Happiness, Life, Living, and Much More*; and *The Leader's Way: Business, Buddhism, and Happiness in an Interconnected World.* In addition to his books and speeches, the Dalai Lama's whole being exudes happiness. His grand smile and infectious laugh witness to his inner happiness.

For the Dalai Lama, life is made happier through acknowledging and practicing the human values of compassion, forgiveness, forbearance, serenity, and self-discipline. Living out these values brings self-confidence and inner strength, eliminates pitting one group of people against another, and shares hope for one global family. When we think beyond ourselves, our individual problems become quite small, and we begin to achieve inner peace.

The Dalai Lama received the 1989 Nobel Peace Prize in recognition of his nonviolent campaign to end the Communist Chinese government's policy of genocide and persecution in his homeland. The Nobel committee praised him "for advocating peaceful solutions based upon tolerance and mutual respect in order to preserve the historical and cultural heritage of his people." Receiving the prize, he modestly said, "I feel honored, humbled, and deeply moved that you should give this important prize to a simple monk from Tibet. I am no one special."

In 2011, the Dalai Lama stepped down as political leader of the exiled Tibetan government in order that the people could democratically elect a leader. He maintained his role as spiritual leader.

Reading Comprehension

1. What role did the Dalai Lama hold in Tibet after Communist China took over the country?
2. Why is happiness the major theme in so many of the Dalai Lama's books?
3. Why did the Norwegian Nobel Committee grant the Dalai Lama the Nobel Peace Prize in 1989?

For Reflection

4. What personal characteristics do you think are needed to stand against an enemy nonviolently and with compassion? Explain.

Prayer

Buddhists do not believe in God or gods, so their prayers are not addressed to God or gods. Rather, traditional Buddhist prayer is a way of practicing the Noble Eightfold Path, including right understanding and right mindfulness.

> With every breath I take today, I vow to be awake;
> And every step I take, I vow to take with a grateful heart—
> So I may see with eyes of love into the hearts of all I meet,
> To ease their burden when I can,
> And touch them with a smile of peace.

7

CHINESE RELIGIOUS TRADITIONS

三聖圖

Introduction

MANY TRADITIONS AND PRACTICES

As you can decipher from the plural in the chapter title, "Chinese religious traditions" does not equate with just one religion. Rather, they are a commingling of Chinese folk religion, Confucianism, **Taoism**, and Buddhism. Before the Communist takeover of China in 1949, every one of these religious traditions was an integral part of Chinese life and culture. After years of religious oppression in China, a small light is flickering again to allow some religious expression to take place. There is hope for some rebirth of Chinese religious traditions in China. Also, Chinese religions are still celebrated by Chinese people in Hong Kong and many other countries around the world.

Unlike other religious traditions, Chinese religious traditions do not have strict membership rules, and the Chinese often blend practices of one religion with another. For example, many religious practices in China include a deep reverence for ancestors. Several include practices in astrology and incorporate **yin and yang**. And a person may live according to Taoist principles yet regularly visit Buddhist temples.

Another complication in studying Chinese religious traditions is that it is sometimes difficult to determine whether each is a religion, a philosophy,

---

Taoism From the Chinese root word *Tao*, meaning "Way," a Chinese mystical philosophy founded by Lao-tzu that teaches conformity to the Tao by "action without action" and simplicity. The Tao is considered to be the driving force of the universe.

yin and yang Meaning "shaded and sunny"; opposite but complementary energies in Chinese religious traditions, philosophy, and culture.

or merely an intellectual exercise. Taoism, for example, operates like other traditional religions with an organized structure including priests, monks, nuns, and temples. Yet Taoism, like Confucianism, also has a rich philosophical tradition.

This chapter provides a sketch of religious traditions in China through the centuries and explains how these various religious practices and expressions commingled and yet stood apart through so many centuries.

This Chinese zodiac wheel is based on the lunar calendar and shows which animals are assigned to each year in a repeating twelve-year cycle.

SECTION *Assessment*

Reading Comprehension

1. Why does this chapter cover Chinese religious traditions in the plural and not the singular?
2. What are some of the various Chinese religious traditions that have blended together over the years?
3. Besides the blending of religious traditions, what is another complication in studying Chinese religions?

For Reflection

4. What are the advantages and disadvantages of belonging to a religion without strict membership rules?

Section 1

A BRIEF HISTORY OF CHINESE RELIGIOUS TRADITIONS

The history of Chinese religious traditions parallels Chinese dynasties. We know about religious practices during the Shang dynasty (ca. 1600–1046 BCE) from archaeological finds from that era and others that followed. For example, artifacts from the graves of the ruling class point to a belief that the afterlife would be like earthly life. Archaeologists have found horses, chariots, servants, dogs, food, pottery, medicine, and the like in Shang-era graves.

Rulers of the Shang dynasty venerated their ancestors, believing they mediated between the gods and the ancestors' descendants on earth. Ancestors also had powers of healing and fertility. Hence, maintaining their happiness was necessary to continue the flow of good fortune. The people also venerated nature gods for good fortune in weather and farming. In the Shang dynasty, the highest god was Shangdi, translated as "Lord on High."

More information on the development of particular traditions of Chinese religious traditions follows.

Ancient Chinese Folk Religion

As in most ancient cultures, the ancient Chinese did not distinguish between religious and secular practices. All aspects of life were closely entwined. Popular Chinese religion—called "folk religion" to distinguish it from the later,

A woman prays at her ancestor's resting spot during the Qingming Festival, also known as Tomb-Sweeping Day, in Hong Kong.

organized religious traditions of Confucianism, Taoism, and Buddhism—was rich in its breadth of religious experiences.

Ancestor veneration played an integral part in folk religion from the beginning of the Zhou dynasty, which followed the Shang dynasty and lasted until the eighth century BCE. Ancestors were not so much worshipped as deities but revered as older, wiser members of the family. The older a person was at the time of death, the more he or she was honored. The Chinese believed their ancestors had two souls. One soul would disappear at death, while a second soul was immortal. This second soul was the object of reverence. It was the responsibility of the male head of the household to make sure ancestors received appropriate care. Failure to offer proper reverence to ancestors could anger them to the point that they might destroy crops, send illnesses, or cause mental distress, including nightmares.

---

ancestor veneration A religious practice referring to various ways of showing respect and reverence for family ancestors after their deaths. It is based on the belief that deceased family members are still living in some fashion.

CHINESE RELIGIOUS TRADITIONS: TIMELINE OF KEY EVENTS

BCE

ca. 1600–1046............Shang dynasty

1046–256....................Zhou dynasty

ca. 600..........................Lao-tzu believed to have lived

ca. 551..........................Birth of philosopher K'ung Fu-tzu (Confucius)

ca. 369..........................Birth of philosopher Chuang-tzu

206 BCE–220 CE.........Han dynasty

CE

ca. 100..........................Buddhism comes to China

ca. 100..........................Formation of Taoist communities

581-618.........................Sui dynasty

618–907........................T'ang dynasty

ca. 638..........................Islam comes to China

ca. 650..........................Emergence of Ch'an Buddhism

960-1279.......................Song dynasty

ca. 1000s......................Emergence of neo-Confucianism

1215..............................Mongols conquer China

1275..............................Marco Polo in China

1368–1644....................Ming dynasty

1583..............................Mateo Ricci in China

1644–1911....................Qing dynasty

1645-1742.................... Chinese Rites Controversy

1949.............................. Communists take over China

1966-1976.................... Cultural Revolution

1982.............................. Document 19 declares religion a negative force

Ancestors were not the only ones ancient Chinese people revered; there was also an elaborate pantheon of gods and goddesses. While the high god during the Shang dynasty was Shangdi, the high god of the Zhou dynasty was T'ien, meaning "heaven." The names "Shangdi" and "T'ien" are often used interchangeably. T'ien ruled over several lower gods and goddesses. Intrinsically connected to human nature as a source of goodness, T'ien governed the destiny of both the ruling class and the ordinary people. Royal ancestors were intermediaries between T'ien and their royal descendants on earth.

King Wu of Zhou (d. 1043 BCE) was the first king of the Zhou dynasty in China.

All ancestors had the power to grant good health, longevity, prosperity, and fertility to their families on earth. Receiving effective results from deities and ancestors required properly executed sacrificial rituals by family members. Some people also offered sacrifices to their local agricultural or household gods. The proper time for the ritual was sometimes determined through a form of divination. While the Chinese all honored their ancestors, during the Zhou dynasty, only the ruler was allowed to offer sacrifices to the high god T'ien.

A completely new religious concept during the Zhou dynasty was the notion of the **Mandate of Heaven** (recall that T'ien means "heaven"). The Mandate of Heaven was intended to assure the people of a kind and just ruler, and the sacrificial rituals were to assure the people of a good harvest.

T'ien desired peace and harmony throughout all creation. Kings were called upon to represent heaven on earth by maintaining personal integrity, ruling the people with care and concern, and appointing government officials based on merit rather than heredity. If the kings behaved in an immoral, cruel, or corrupt fashion, T'ien took the mandate away from them and transferred it to another dynasty. At least, that is how the theory went, but theory and practice often diverged. Corrupt leaders, general warring factions, social disarray, and moral decline led to the eventual demise of the Zhou dynasty.

Ancient Chinese people used **divination** to discern the messages of the gods. They may have discerned messages regarding future events from cloud formations in the sky or from the cracks on a tortoise's shell. Astrology was a common form of divination; the configuration of the stars and planets were omens for good or evil.

Confucius

It is impossible to talk about Chinese religious traditions without including the teachings of Confucius and his followers. Confucius was a Chinese philosopher whose sayings and ideas in the collection *Analects* were popularized and followed after his death. "Confucius" is the Latinized form of the Chinese K'ung Fu-tzu. Known more as a moral philosopher than as a religious figure, Confucius was more interested in helping cultivate sages for a better world on earth than in preparing souls for a world to come. Nevertheless, there were religious elements within his philosophy.

Confucius lived from around 551 to 479 BCE during a time in the Zhou dynasty when different factions were fighting for leadership of the imperial government and its territory. He was born in the small

Confucius

A display of translations of the Analects of Confucius in different languages at the National Museum of China in Beijing, China.

feudal-like state of Lu, a product of the union between his seventy-year-old father and a teenage concubine. Confucius's father died when the boy was three years old, and he and his mother found themselves shunned by his father's family. Poor and without social ties, they moved to a nearby town, where his mother worked and instructed the eager Confucius in all aspects of education.

As a teenager, Confucius took a minor government post keeping books for warehouses. He married at age nineteen, and his beloved mother died when he was about twenty. However, nothing could get in the way of Confucius's education. For Confucius, learning was not merely an accumulation of knowledge but also an important means of building moral character. As he continued his studies, Confucius shared his knowledge with other young men, though teaching was not his first love.

Mandate of Heaven The Chinese concept used to morally legitimize the rule of the kings of the Zhou dynasty and the early emperors of China. T'ien (meaning "heaven") would bless the authority of a just ruler but would give the mandate to another if the ruler proved unjust.

divination The attempt to ascertain hidden knowledge or foretell future events by the interpretation of omens or through supernatural means (e.g., the analysis of cloud formations or the casting of bones).

Rather, Confucius spent his entire adult life aspiring to public office. He went on a twelve-year trek with a few of his students, searching for a region that would hire him as a public official. However, since Confucius held the view that governments needed reform, existing governments saw him as a threat to their administrations. He did hold positions in the Lu government—minister of works and minister of crime—but had to resign. Confucius spent the last years of his life teaching and compiling ancient Chinese texts. Included in his writings were the *Analects*. Though the teachings were slow to catch on, later generations of Chinese rulers and people read and adopted them.

Confucius's writings reveal that he saw chaos all around him. He believed that if society returned to the values of the ancients, chaos would disperse. Confucius was especially interested in those values that were transmitted through rituals such as ancestor veneration, worship of the high god T'ien, and death rites. He believed that it was his duty to recapture these lost elements of ancient civilization and reintroduce them into his world. Proper ritual observance and moral persuasion were Confucius's formula for success. Near the time of his death, because his ideas had yet to catch on, Confucius thought himself a failure. He was very wrong.

Confucianism

Confucius regarded himself as a transmitter of ancient Chinese social values rather than as a founder of a religious tradition or a philosophical school. He studied ancient Chinese scriptures and attempted to revive their wisdom in his society. Confucius was not inventing anything new; he was simply putting his contemporaries in touch with their ancestors.

It was not until about two centuries after Confucius's death that two of his disciples, Meng-tzu (ca. 371–289 BCE) and Hsun-tzu (ca. 310–230 BCE), were able to make significant inroads in communicating Confucian teachings to the political elite. However, the two men promoted opposite reasons for adopting Confucius's ideas. Meng-tzu advocated the intrinsic goodness of human nature, teaching that if one did not cultivate one's good nature, evil would slowly take over. He maintained that by following the Confucian teachings of cultivating one's best self, a person could manifest intrinsic goodness. Hsun-tzu, on the other hand, asserted the intrinsic evil of human nature, teaching that it was necessary to learn how to live morally to avoid evil and become good.

Confuscius and his disciple Meng-tzu.

During the Han dynasty (206 BCE–220 CE), the teachings of Confucius became the state belief system by imperial decree. Confucianism was taught in all the schools, and the Confucian Classics (see Section 2) were required reading for all who aspired to public office. The Confucian ideal of education centered not only on the accumulation of knowledge but also on the building of moral character. Confucianism began to move toward a society of equality by claiming that a person was made noble not by birth but by character. Character building was a lifelong process of education and self-discipline. By the beginning of the Common Era, the moral idealism of Confucianism could not be separated from overall Chinese society. Around this time, a **cult** honoring Confucius as a semidivine figure emerged. By the sixth century, temples to Confucius dotted the landscape.

The influence of Confucianism decreased with the collapse of the Han dynasty (third century CE), while the influence of Taoism and Buddhism increased. By the eleventh century, however, Confucianism was again gaining prominence. This resurgence, called **neo-Confucianism**, integrated within

---

cult An external religious practice, observance, or devotion surrounding a deity, holy person, or religious object of a particular religious tradition.

neo-Confucianism A movement in China in the eleventh century that promulgated the resurgence of Confucianism while reinterpreting it in the light of Taoist and Buddhist influences.

The Temple of Confucius, built at the location of his house in 611 CE in Qufu, Shandong, China.

it elements of Buddhism and Taoism. Scholars of neo-Confucianism, well versed in all three religious traditions, sought to integrate Taoist beliefs about the universe and Buddhist beliefs about human nature into the Confucian scholarly tradition.

This trend reversed again during the Qing dynasty (1644–1911), when there was a move to return to the "purer" Confucianism of the Han dynasty. Because of the introduction of many European elements into Chinese society during this period, the reform of Confucianism was unsuccessful. Also, honoring Confucius as a deity mostly ended in the sixteenth century. Statues of Confucius himself were replaced with plaques bearing inscriptions of some of his teachings. Though there was another attempt to form a cult around Confucius in the twentieth century, the advent of Communism in China put that to rest.

The Chinese Communist revolution of 1945–1949 placed Confucianism in disfavor. The Chinese monarchy and traditional family structures and rituals, which helped support Confucianism, were gone. After Mao Zedong and the Communists came to power, Confucianism, along with all other religious traditions, was officially banned. All religious expression was considered elitist, outdated, and a threat to personal freedom.

Presently, interest in Confucianism is again stirring among the Chinese elite. In their attempt to counter the Westernization of China, they are rethinking Confucianism as an important part of Chinese heritage. To many Chinese people today, Confucius is known as the "father of Chinese culture."

Lao-tzu and Taoism

Lao-tzu was a Chinese philosopher believed to have lived around the sixth century BCE. (He may be a legend to the Chinese and not a person in history.) He is credited as the founder of Taoism, a religious tradition with roots going back to 2000 BCE. What little is known about the life of Lao-tzu was written by Ssu-ma Ch'ien in his *Records of the Grand Historian* around 100 BCE.

According to this account, Lao-tzu's family name was Li, and his given name was Erh. Lao-tzu was in charge of sacred books at the court of the Zhou dynasty. Disillusioned with the political and moral decline, he rode west to the Chinese wilderness. It is said that the guard at the frontier pass, Yin Hsi, asked Lao-tzu to write down his wisdom. Lao-tzu wrote what became known as the *Tao Te Ching*, or "The Book of the Way and Its Power," addressing it to sage-kings.

By the third century BCE, Taoist writings emphasized individuals more than rulers. A follower of Lao-tzu, Chuang-tzu (ca. 369–ca. 286 BCE), wrote

This Lao-tzu statue on Lao Mountain in Qingdao, Shandong, China, is 164 feet tall.

a text promoting the process of self-perfection. In 142 CE, Chang Tao-ling claimed he received a revelation from Lao-tzu and was named the first "celestial master" of Taoism. His successors were the spiritual leaders for Taoist priests who ministered in Taoist "churches." The celestial masters emphasized both political renewal and self-perfection.

In the third century CE, after the fall of the Han dynasty, Chinese rulers turned to Taoist leaders for advice in political and spiritual matters. However, as with Confucianism, the ritual aspects of Taoism tended to focus on the elite and not attract common people until the fourth century, when Taoism gradually incorporated some elements of folk religion.

In the centuries since, Taoist priests have encouraged practicing methods of self-perfection. Like every other religious tradition in China, Taoism was discredited by the Chinese Communist rulers of the twentieth century.

A Taoist priest blesses food offerings at Dalongdong Baoan Temple in Taipei, Taiwan.

However, elaborate Taoist rituals are still conducted in Taiwan, and elements of Taoism continue to influence Chinese spirituality and culture.

Buddhism in China

Buddhism was slow to take hold in China. In the first few centuries of the Common Era, some Chinese pilgrims went to India, brought back scores of Buddhist sacred texts, and translated them into Chinese. In its early stages in China, Buddhism was tied closely with Taoism, with its various ascetical practices, the use of magic, and the emphasis on the attainment of enlightenment. Borrowing Taoist vocabulary to explain difficult Buddhist concepts, translations of the Buddhist sacred scriptures enjoyed recognition from both the elite and the peasantry. Buddhism's initial appeal in China was to the poor because of its strong emphasis on family. During the Sui dynasty (581–618), the Chinese government steadily patronized Buddhism.

However, it was under the T'ang dynasty (618–907) that Buddhism flourished the most, though the perception remained that it was a "foreign religion." The number of Buddhist monasteries expanded substantially during this period, but the ordination of monks remained under the control of the state. As the monasteries accumulated wealth through landholdings, a backlash against Buddhism boiled up to the point that in 845, the Chinese imperial government destroyed Buddhist temples, monasteries, and shrines. Over the next two centuries, Buddhism united even more closely to Taoism, and the two religious traditions converged with Confucianism and Chinese folk religion to form the underpinnings of Chinese religious traditions. Though the Buddhist and Taoist scholars tended to remain separate, Chinese culture experienced a multitraditional religious landscape. Many Mahayana Buddhist schools

Emperor Wen of Sui (541–604), the first emperor of the Sui dynasty.

An Amitabha Buddha in Longxing Temple in Zhengding, Hebei, China.

dotted the religious landscape of China, but only two dominate today—Pure Land and Ch'an Buddhism. Over the centuries, Pure Land Buddhism and Ch'an Buddhism existed side by side, often to the point of nondistinction.

Pure Land Buddhism

Pure Land Buddhism came to China from India in the fifth century. Though not very popular in India, it became prevalent in China, especially with poor people. Unable to spend the time in meditation or to work for good karma, the working poor found Pure Land Buddhism to be adaptable to their lifestyle.

Pure Land Buddhism developed from the Mahayana belief that there is more than one buddha. According to tradition, Amitabha was a great bodhisattva for many lifetimes. He was able to make a series of forty-eight vows by which he would bring all sentient beings to Nirvana through his accumulation of an infinite amount of merit. To accomplish this task, Amitabha, now a buddha, went to one of the celestial realms and created a Pure Land where there was no evil, pain, or suffering. This Pure Land is perpetually ideal: there are no natural disasters, the trees have jewels on them, and anything one wants is granted.

A person only needs to recite the name "Amitabha" ("Amituofo" in Chinese) with great faith and devotion throughout life in order to be reborn into the Pure Land. Though an individual has less moral responsibility in this form of Buddhism, rebirth into the Pure Land is made possible because of the infinite merit of Amitabha Buddha, who enables devotees' entrance into Nirvana. From China, Pure Land Buddhism spread to Vietnam, Korea, Japan, and Tibet.

Ch'an Buddhism

Ch'an, meaning "meditation," is a Chinese form of Buddhist meditation begun in India. It emerged in China around the seventh century CE with two opinions about the attainment of enlightenment. One faction believed enlightenment happened suddenly, while the other believed enlightenment came only gradually. In both approaches, it was through a master-student relationship

Shaolin Monastery, a Chán Buddhist temple on Mount Song that was founded in the fifth century in Dengfeng, Zhengzhou, Henan, China.

that one learned how to meditate correctly and how to deal with questions, insights, and challenges that arose.

One common technique for meditation in Ch'an Buddhism is the use of a gong'an, more commonly known in the West by its Japanese name, koan. A *gong'an* is a paradoxical statement or story used to clear the mind of its many obstacles, so that insight and enlightenment can transpire. A traditional gong'an is one you may have heard: "What is the sound of one hand clapping?"

SECTION *Assessment*

Reading Comprehension

1. Briefly describe these elements of Chinese folk religion: ancestor veneration, divination, and astrology.
2. What did the celestial masters of Taoism emphasize?
3. How is Buddhism linked with Taoism?
4. Differentiate between Pure Land Buddhism and Ch'an Buddhism.

Vocabulary

5. What is *neo-Confucianism*?

For Reflection

6. Recall a time when, like Confucius, you thought your ideas would remedy a problematic situation, but people rejected them. How did you feel?
7. Name some modern people who gained esteem after their deaths, as Confucius and Lao-tzu did after theirs.
8. Chinese history contributed to a blending of religious traditions. How has the history of some Western nations contributed to a blending of various religious traditions?

Flash Search

9. How is Confucianism being promoted in China today?

Section 2

SACRED STORIES AND SACRED SCRIPTURES

As neither Confucius nor Lao-tzu considered himself the founder of a religious tradition or claimed to have received or recorded revelations from any deity, the writings attributed to them and their followers are not considered divinely inspired.

Confucius drew from the wisdom of the ancient sages. He is credited with compiling and creating several volumes of Chinese literature to add to what was already in place. After his death, a large body of Confucian scriptures became sources of inspiration and the means to train students in Confucianism for centuries.

While the *Tao Te Ching* is attributed to Lao-tzu, it is doubtful that he wrote any of it. Instead, the *Tao Te Ching* is the work of followers of Lao-tzu several centuries after his death, drawing from age-old writings that predated the birth of Lao-tzu. For this reason, it is accurate to say Taoism predates Confucianism.

Information about scriptures and stories of these Chinese religious traditions follows.

Confucian Classics

The sacred writings of Confucianism are commonly called the *Confucian Classics*, though some of them predate Confucius. The Confucian Classics are divided into two main groups, the **Five Classics** and the **Four Books**. A person

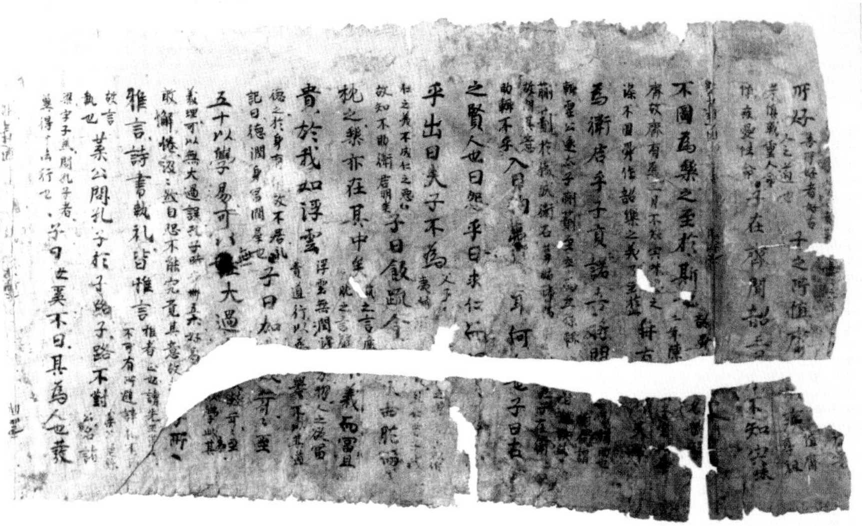

Part of a Tang Dynasty manuscript of the Analects of Confucius, circa seventh century, China.

who wanted to work within the Chinese government had to master these nine texts in order to pass civil exams and secure government employment.

Confucius considered the Five Classics to be from a golden era of Chinese history. These were the primary documents used by Confucius to teach his students. Though they predate him, the Five Classics are attributed to Confucius. They include historical documents; an anthology of poems; the *I Ching*, a manual for divination; records of the state of Lu where Confucius was born; and texts on the principles of **li**, or proper conduct.

Followers of Confucius compiled the Four Books. They are texts of wisdom inspired by Confucius and Meng-tzu, a disciple of Confucius. The Four Books include the *Analects* (sayings of Confucius), the *Great Learning* (philosophical utterances systematically arranged with commentaries by the compilers of the

---

Five Classics A collection of five ancient Chinese books used by Confucians for study. They were written or edited by Confucius.

Four Books During the Ming and Qing dynasties, the accepted curriculum that needed to be studied and passed in order to hold civil office.

li From the Chinese meaning "proper" or "rites"; the Confucian practice of proper behavior specific to one's relationship to another. It includes the rituals that must be properly performed in order for one to be called a chun-tzu, or "superior one" or "gentleman."

text), *Doctrine of the Mean* (details how the way of perfection can benefit adherents), and *Book of Meng-tzu* (dialogues of the great follower of Confucius).

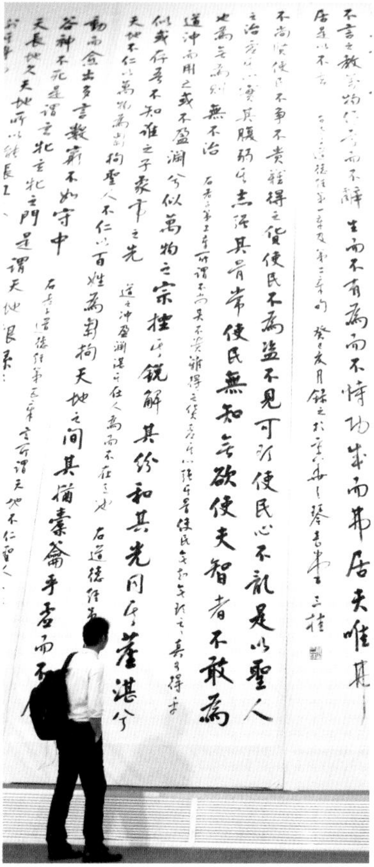
The Tao Te Ching *by Chinese calligrapher Luo Sangui in Nanjing, China.*

Tao Te Ching

The *Tao Te Ching* is one of the most widely read pieces of Chinese literature in the world. Translated into many languages, the *Tao Te Ching* is the centerpiece and the source of Taoist beliefs. Though its authorship is attributed to the sage Lao-tzu, it is more likely that a group of people authored it several centuries after his lifetime. The following is an excerpt from the *Tao Te Ching* explaining the Tao itself:

> The tao that can be told is not the eternal Tao.
> The name that can be named is not the eternal Name.
> The unnamable is the eternally real.
> Naming is the origin of all particular things. . . .
> The Tao is like a well: used but never used up.
> It is like the eternal void: filled with infinite possibilities.
> It is hidden but always present.
> I do not know who gave birth to it.
> It is older than God. . . .
> The Tao is called the Great Mother: empty yet inexhaustible.
> It gives birth to infinite worlds.
> It is always present within you.
> You can use it any way you want. . . .
> The Tao is infinite, eternal.
> Why is it eternal?
> It was never born; thus, it can never die.

> Why is it infinite?
> It has no desires for itself; thus, it is present for all beings. (*Tao Te Ching*, 1:1–2; 4; 6; 7:1)

To summarize, the Tao is the nature of things. All that emanates from the Tao returns to the Tao. There is power of action without action. All are called to live a life of simplicity in harmony with the Tao.

SECTION *Assessment*

Reading Comprehension

1. What are the two main categories of the Confucian Classics?
2. What are the *Analects*?
3. Who likely authored the *Tao Te Ching*?
4. What is the Tao?

For Reflection

5. Read and reflect on the quote from the *Tao Te Ching* at the end of this section. What does it mean to you?

Flash Search

6. A number of films incorporate Taoist principles. Name one film and explain the principle.

Section 3
BELIEFS AND PRACTICES

It is possible that Confucius and Lao-tzu were contemporaries, so it is not surprising that they had some of the same ideas about human nature, society, sovereignty, eternal life, and the universe. The difference was their emphasis. While Confucianism emphasizes the cultivation of a virtuous life to train political leaders who could help create an ideal society, Taoism is more concerned with acceptance of "the way life is." Tao means "way."

Beliefs Associated with Confucianism

Confucius could be called a follower of Chinese folk religion. He believed in the high god T'ien and various other Chinese deities and also engaged in other folk rituals and practices of his time. But Confucius was wary of the various cults that were part of Chinese society. He thought that the various gods and goddesses should be kept at a distance.

For Confucians, perfection comes not from relationships with the gods but through relationships with others and with society. As T'ien was perfect, so humans should strive for perfection. In many ways, Confucianism is a form of character formation. The one who attains perfection was a **chun-tzu**, a "superior one" or "gentleman." In Confucius's time, only aristocratic men were educated, but Confucius chose to teach any male he considered intelligent enough to engage in learning and character building. The period of formation included the principles of li and **jen**. Though not explicitly religious, these principles were representative of Chinese culture and thought.

---

chun-tzu According to Confucius, a person who lives by the ideals of li and jen and is not petty, arrogant, mean-spirited, or vengeful.

jen The virtue of altruism. It has to do with one's humanness.

WHAT IS LI?

禮

Li was the practice of the proper way to live, calling for courtesy, etiquette, formality, and respect. Li was witnessed by a person's polite gestures, which flow from the essential goodness of the person. Li focused on an ideal way of behaving for five common relationships in Chinese society:

1. *Emperor to subject.* The emperor was to be an example to his subjects, calling them to live the same virtuous life he lived.
2. *Father to son.* The father was to be a model to his son, who was in turn to honor his parents in this lifetime and revere them in the next.
3. *Husband to wife.* The husband was to head the household and preserve the memory of his family's ancestors; the wife was to bear sons and obey her husband.
4. *Elder brother to younger brother.* The younger brother was to respect his older brother, for the older brother was responsible for carrying out the family rituals of ancestor veneration.
5. *Friend to friend (males).* Friends were to respect each other, with the junior friend showing deference to the elder one.

WHAT IS JEN?

仁

While li pointed outward to behavior, jen pointed inward to one's heart. Jen refers to humanity or benevolence. According to Confucian thought, a person should be transformed from a life ruled by the passions to one guided by enlightened wisdom. Religious and ethical rituals helped a person achieve jen.

A person who combined li with jen was in position to be a chun-tzu. A person cannot fake being a chun-tzu. Being a chun-tzu means being so filled with jen that one's benevolence flows into action.

Beliefs Associated with Taoism

To know the way,
we go the way,
we do the way.
The way we do,
the things we do,
it's all there in front of you.
But if you try too hard to see it,
you'll only become confused.
I am me, and you are you.
As you can see;
but when you do
the things that you can do,
you will find the way.
The way will follow you.

—*The Tao of Pooh* by Benjamin Hoff

Taoism is a return to simplicity and harmony with all creation, for the Tao is the ultimate source of all creation—an impersonal God. Though the word *Tao* can be defined as the "way," "path," or "course," in reality, all definitions fall short. Slightly more accurately, Taoism can be thought of as the way or the nature of things. The goal of humanity, then, is to move in harmony with the Tao. A "go-with-the-flow" attitude permeates all creation, so creation flows with the Tao.

ACTION WITHOUT ACTION

Taoists believed that the force through which the Tao acts is **wu wei**, or "nonaction." Wu wei may be more precisely explained as "action without action." For example, the emotion a painting evokes by hanging in a gallery is a form of wu wei. Another is the wordless nonaction of a newborn whose various needs are fulfilled. The non-action evokes action. That is the way of the Tao.

無為

IMMORTALITY

陰陽

To Taoists, life is a delicate balance between yin and yang. Maintaining that balance enables one to avoid death and achieve immortality. The goal of a Taoist is immortality. Taoists believe that actual physical immortality is a reachable goal. Immortality is expressed through union with the Tao. To attain immortality, a Taoist engages in several practices; breath control, good hygiene, certain elixirs, meditation, and proper rituals all contribute to immortality. Those who are believed to have reached immortality are known as **hsiens**.

DEITIES AND OTHER SPIRITS

玉皇

By the ninth century, Taoists believed in a whole pantheon of gods and goddesses, including Lao-tzu. The high god of the pantheon was known as Yu Huang (for Confucians, T'ien). Taoists were known for their celebrations of gods and goddesses that included lavish costumes and elaborate rituals often performed in temples. Taoists also celebrated the Buddha, bodhisattvas, and gods and goddesses of other Chinese religious traditions.

Chinese Living

For average Chinese people, the religious traditions discussed in this chapter are not distinguishable within their own practice of religion. For example, it is not unusual to see statues of both Lao-tzu and the Buddha in the same temple and equally revered.

---

wu wei Meaning "nonaction," but often interpreted as "action without action"; a Taoist concept that centers on allowing the Tao to unfold without human interference.

hsiens Meaning "immortals"; Taoists who have reached their ultimate goal—physical immortality.

Visitors at an altar inside the multi-religious A-Ma Temple in São Lourenço, Macau, China.

Confucius assured his followers that the best way to live was as a superior person who combined li with jen. Taoists and Buddhists would say that the most virtuous person practices wu wei, or action without action. Each practice is a part of the fabric of Chinese culture. The average Chinese person who practices them is likely unaware of whether one religious tradition is being emphasized over the other.

With such diverse practices and beliefs, one would think that forming a community rooted in religious beliefs would be impossible. Yet for centuries, Chinese society was rooted in family structures including Confucian ancestor veneration. Monasticism was also a vital part of Buddhism and Taoism. How could these three very different religious traditions combine and merge to form one Chinese community? One saying may explain: "Chinese people are Confucian in public, Taoist in private, and Buddhist concerning death." The Chinese have a broad spectrum of beliefs and practices woven so tightly into Chinese culture that the only way to make distinctions is to take the threads out one by one. However, systematically removing the threads would weaken the fabric of Chinese society. That is why distinctions can be made and clarified only in the course of study like this one.

Who Knows What Is Good or Bad?

Yin and yang demand balance. Similarly, the Chinese concept of what is good and what is bad may not be fixed. However, in Chinese religions, "good" and "bad" do not refer to moral judgments; they describe whether an event is lucky or unlucky. Read this story and answer the questions that follow.

> Once upon a time there was a farmer whose horse ran away. A neighbor came to console him, since it was the farmer's only horse. The farmer replied, "Who knows what is good or bad?"
>
> The next day the horse returned with a herd of wild horses close behind. Hearing the thunderous noise of the horses' hooves, the neighbor returned to the farmer gleefully rejoicing. The farmer only said, "Who knows what is good or bad?'
>
> The third day the farmer's son went into the corral to break one of the horses. But the horse threw the son off so fiercely that the son broke his leg. Again the neighbor came by to give the farmer his condolences. The farmer replied, "Who knows what is good or bad?"
>
> Several months later some government officials came to the property of the farmer seeking to draft his son into the military. However, because of the son's broken leg, his draft was deferred. Once more the neighbor came by to congratulate the farmer on his good fortune. The farmer again replied, "Who knows what is good or bad?"

Writing Task

- What is the point of the farmer's words, "Who knows what is good or bad?"
- What does the story say about harmony and balance?
- Tell about an experience you had that at first seemed to be bad but turned out to be good.
- Tell about an experience you had that at first seemed to be good but turned out to be bad.

SECTION *Assessment*

Reading Comprehension

1. What are the five crucial male relationships in Confucianism?
2. How do Taoists understand immortality?
3. How does the saying "Chinese people are Confucian in public, Taoist in private, and Buddhist concerning death" help describe the Chinese commingling of religious traditions?

Vocabulary

4. Explain the meanings of *li* and *jen*.
5. Explain *wu wei* and give an example.

For Reflection

6. What understanding did you elicit from the excerpt from *The Tao of Pooh*?

Critical Thinking

7. Why would Confucian character formation prohibit someone from being phony or "two-faced"?

Flash Search

8. In *The Tao of Pooh*, what Taoist principle or principles does Winnie the Pooh represent?

Section 4
SACRED TIME

You've probably heard of the traditional Chinese calendar or the Chinese New Year. Chinese religious traditions and culture operate on a unique, complex lunar calendar. The Chinese lunar calendar has 354 days. The Chinese name their years by combining one of the ten celestial stems with one of the twelve terrestrial branches. The stems and branches are arranged so that the name of a year will reoccur only once every sixty years. The twelve terrestrial branches also have animals associated with them. It is with the animal name of the year, such as "the Year of the Dragon," that Westerners are most familiar.

There are many traditional festivals on the Chinese calendar. Recently, Communist China has permitted the resumption of some of the festivals, though each has been celebrated regularly outside mainland China for years. Descriptions of the main Chinese festivals follow.

Chinese New Year

Chinese New Year, also called Lunar New Year, is the most important of all Chinese festivals. It takes place sometime between late January and late February, depending on the lunar calendar. It is celebrated over fifteen days. A few weeks before the new year, the Chinese prepare by thoroughly cleaning their homes and purchasing items such as tangerine trees, flower displays, Chinese paintings, and calligraphy. Major celebrations occur in Hong Kong, which was under British rule from 1842 to 1997. Hong Kong is festooned with brightly colored decorations, and stores are packed with shoppers.

On New Year's Eve, the Chinese say prayers and pay homage to Tso Kwan, the kitchen god or "Stove Master," who returns to heaven to report on the behavior of humans for the year. On New Year's Day, family members exchange small gifts, often money wrapped in a red packet. Another traditional part of the festival is Kai Nien, or "Squabble Day," so called because it is

The Chinese New Year parade in Chinatown in New York City.

believed that if you argue on that day, many arguments will follow during the rest of the year. On the fourth day of the festival, Tso Kwan is welcomed back, and families hang new pictures of Tso Kwan in their kitchens. On the final day of the festival, lantern celebrations take place. Lanterns are hung in homes to promote good fortune, health, and happiness. The lantern celebration ends the New Year's festivities.

Ching Ming

Ching Ming, meaning "Remembrance of Ancestors Day," is celebrated in early April. It is a day devoted to honoring deceased relatives. Chinese people gather at cemeteries to clean and care for the graves of their relatives. Also, willow branches are hung in doorways to ward off evil spirits. Legend has it that those who do not hang willow branches will appear as dogs in the next life.

During Ching Ming, Chinese families visit the tombs of their ancestors to clean the gravesites, pray, make ritual offerings of food dishes, and burn joss sticks.

Tin Hau

The Tin Hau Festival is celebrated on the twenty-third day of the third lunar month (late April, early May). The day is set aside to honor a young girl known as Tin Hau, the "Queen of Heaven." She is known as the mother of boat people and sailors. The legend dates from the eleventh century when Tin Hau dreamed that her brothers were drowning and she flew over the waters on clouds and rescued them.

A young man lights joss sticks during the Tin Hau Festival in Hong Kong, China.

There are numerous shrines and temples dedicated to Tin Hau. Chinese boat people, sailors, and those who live on the waterfront sail to the Tin Hau Temple in Joss House Bay in Hong Kong on Tin Hau's birthday, paying respect to the goddess and asking for safety in the coming year.

The Dragon Boat Festival

The Dragon Boat Festival is held in late spring. The day honors Qu Yuan (340–278 BCE), a famous Chinese patriot who wrote many classical poems

Competitors in the annual dragon boat race in Hong Kong, China.

espousing Chinese nationalism. At the end of his life, Qu Yuan became disillusioned and drowned himself in the Milo River. The local people were so upset that they went out on the river in boats and began to beat the water with their paddles to keep the fish from eating his body. They also threw rice in the water to draw the fish away. The Dragon Boat Festival consists of a variety of decorated, colorful boats, including the fierce head of a dragon. The dragons symbolically search the waters for Qu Yuan's body.

The Dragon Boat Festival takes place on the fifth day of the fifth lunar month, which Chinese people consider to be unlucky, with natural disasters and illnesses taking place more often at this time than other times of year. Therefore, many families also hang things such as garlic or pomegranates in their doorways to ward off evil spirits during this festival.

Mid-Autumn Festival

The Mid-Autumn Festival is second in popularity to the Chinese New Year Festival. It recalls a time during the T'ang dynasty when Chinese rulers carefully studied and worshipped the moon. Today, to celebrate this festival, Chinese people—citizens of Hong Kong especially—travel to high places in the region to make sure they have a good view of the moon. The hills of the city of Victoria in Hong Kong and the area beaches shimmer in the glow of lantern lights.

Women show the mooncakes they have made during the Mid-Autumn Festival in Hefei, China.

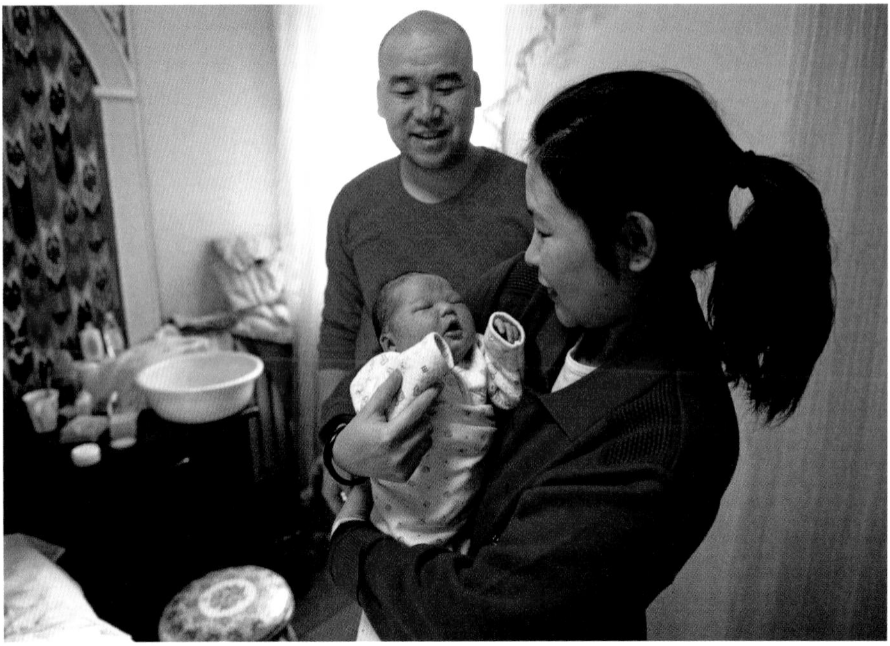

A newborn baby girl in Beijing, China.

Life-Cycle Celebrations

The Chinese mark four life stages: birth, coming-of-age, marriage, and death.

Boys are preferred over girls in Chinese culture. It is a boy who carries on the family name, takes care of the parents in old age, and sees that ancestors have proper care. In 1979, the Chinese government enacted a policy limiting births to one per family in an attempt to slow population growth. Since then, girls have frequently been aborted selectively or placed for adoption due to this policy. In 2015, the policy was revised to permit two children instead of one.

Regarding birth celebrations, Chinese mothers are first allowed one month to rest after giving birth while other family members care for her and her child. At the end of the month, there is a celebration in which the newborn is given symbolic gifts representing good health and prosperity. As a sign of good luck, family members and friends eat eggs on that day.

Food also plays a part in the celebration of the coming-of-age of a teenager. The celebrants eat chicken as a main course, believing chicken is a sign of maturity.

There are six stages to a traditional Chinese marriage:

1. *Proposal.* A determination is made about whether or not the man and woman are a good match. There is the exchange of the "eight characters" taken from the terrestrial and celestial branches of the horoscopes of the man and woman. The eight characters represent the year, month, day, and hour of each person's birth. Also, if any inauspicious event occurs in the family of the bride-to-be three days after the proposal, it is taken as a sign that the proposal was rejected.
2. *Engagement.* After the wedding date is determined with the help of Chinese divinations, the woman's family announces the engagement with invitations and the gift of cookies made in the shape of the moon.
3. *Dowry.* The woman's family delivers the dowry in a procession to the house of the groom-to-be. The man sends gifts equal in value to the dowry to the woman.
4. *Procession.* The man goes to the family home of the woman to escort her to his home.
5. *Wedding.* On the wedding day, vows are exchanged and a grand banquet takes place.
6. *Morning After.* The day after the wedding, the new bride serves her parents-in-law breakfast, and they reciprocate. Gifts of dried fruit are given to the newly married couple as a symbol of a good marriage and fertility.

The bride's dowry is prepared to be delivered to the groom's home before their wedding.

Mourners attending a funeral in Jinzhai County, Anhui Province, China.

The last stage of life is death, which Chinese people commemorate with several rituals. At death, the body is washed and placed in a coffin. Food and objects significant to the deceased person are placed in the coffin to assist in the entrance to the next world. Family members cry out to inform the neighbors of the death and put on clothes made of coarse material. Mourners bring incense and money to aid with the funeral expenses. A Taoist or Buddhist priest performs the funeral rites, though sometimes a Christian minister assists. Mourners follow the coffin to the cemetery carrying willow branches, symbolizing the soul of the person who died. A branch is then carried to the family's ancestral altar and placed there to honor the spirit of the deceased.

SECTION *Assessment*

Reading Comprehension

1. Describe the Chinese New Year celebration.
2. Why is Ching Ming an important Chinese celebration?

3. How do Chinese people celebrate the Mid-Autumn Festival?
4. Why is the birth of a boy preferred over the birth of a girl in Chinese culture?
5. Name and describe the six stages of a typical Chinese marriage.

For Reflection

6. Name a coming-of-age ritual in Western society. What is its purpose and value?
7. What advantages do you see in having such a structured marriage process?

Flash Search

8. What is the role of feng shui in celebrating the Chinese New Year?

Section 5
SACRED PLACES AND SACRED SPACES

The number of sacred places and sacred spaces in China diminished significantly after the Communist revolution. Since 1949, many Chinese temples have been destroyed, abandoned, or turned into government facilities. Temples left for religious practice are heavily regulated. The Chinese government always monitors and often selects the religious leaders in the various religious traditions practiced in China.

Temples

Of the temples that remain in China, there are several different kinds: Taoist, Buddhist, and even some Confucian temples. Temples are further defined as local or state temples. At local temples, people make offerings to the regional gods and goddesses as well as to ancestors. Before the twentieth century, the state temples were places where the emperor made sacrifices on behalf of his subjects, usually to T'ien, to lesser deities, and at times to Confucius.

Tourists visiting the Buddhist Giant Wild Goose Pagoda, Xi'an, Shaanxi, China.

A couple presents offerings to a home ancestral shrine before their wedding.

Shrines of Ancestors

Within Chinese temples are typically shrines to local gods and ancestors of the local family or families. In addition, most Chinese families maintain a home ancestor shrine, where they make offerings of food and incense to ancestors, sometimes daily.

Ancestor Gravesites

For the Chinese, the world of the dead is a mirror image of the world of the living, and the needs of the deceased are similar to the needs of the living. The Chinese take choosing a burial site very seriously because they believe that evil powers and bad spirits inhabit a poorly chosen gravesite. **Feng shui** is the art

---

feng shui The Chinese practice of positioning objects—especially gravesites, buildings, and furniture—to achieve harmony based on belief in yin and yang and the flow of chi, the vital life force or flow of energy.

A symmetrical cemetery in Dagantangcun, China.

of divining a harmonious place or date that has a positive spiritual aura. Feng shui has recently become popular in the West as an aspect of interior design.

The Ch'u Fou Temple is the burial place of Confucius. As Chinese revere their familial ancestors, they also revere their spiritual ancestor Confucius.

SECTION *Assessment*

Reading Comprehension

1. Why are there fewer temples in China today than there were before 1949?
2. Why is the location of a burial site so important to the Chinese?

Vocabulary

3. What is *feng shui*?

For Reflection

4. How do you honor your ancestors?

Flash Search

5. What are the Mogao Grottoes, and what is their significance?

Section 6
CATHOLICS DIALOGUE WITH ADHERENTS OF CHINESE RELIGIOUS TRADITIONS

It is in the rituals surrounding death and the remembrance of those who have died that elements of four Chinese religious traditions—folk religion, Confucianism, Taoism, and Buddhism—most align with Christianity and Catholicism. The folk devotional practice of ancestor veneration incorporates elements of Confucian li (the father-to-son aspect), Taoist afterlife, and Buddhist karma.

Ancestor Veneration in Chinese Religious Traditions

This textbook uses the term *ancestor veneration* rather than *ancestor worship* for this Chinese practice. The former is more appropriate because the Chinese do not treat their ancestors as deities. Family members do not worship, pray to, or ask favors of their ancestors; they revere them. Ancestors are part of the social fabric of Chinese culture. Though they are no longer visible on earth, Chinese tradition holds that ancestors are the living dead. They are still part of the family but located in another realm. Wherever the deceased are now, they influence the fortune of a family or community and can assist their descendants. They too have needs and grow anxious or restless when their needs are not met. Forgetting about ancestors or showing little or no reverence brings

These Chinese graves in Thailand follow the rules of feng shui.

misfortune to their descendants. Those who died untimely or violent deaths also bring misfortune to the family or community.

In Chinese religious traditions, when a person dies, a feng shui master is called upon to determine the proper environment, date, and placement of the body. For the environment, the surrounding nature is essential. Are the mountains favorable or inauspicious? Does the river flow in the correct direction or pattern? For a proper date of burial, the feng shui master consults the position of the stars and the date of the birth and death of the person. There can be no conflict between the present astrological orientation and the Chinese astrology of the deceased. The yin and yang of the environment must support balance between the living and the dead. As for the placement of the corpse, the feng shui master determines which direction is most favorable for the body to face. Adherents of Chinese religious traditions believe that if the environment is not proper, the date of the burial is wrong, or the orientation of the body is incorrect, misfortune befalls the family and their descendants. If they are all correct, great fortune comes.

After the funeral rituals, the ancestor is cared for by way of a **spirit tablet** bearing the deceased person's name and other information that is particular

---

spirit tablet A placard placed in a household shrine or temple to honor ancestors.

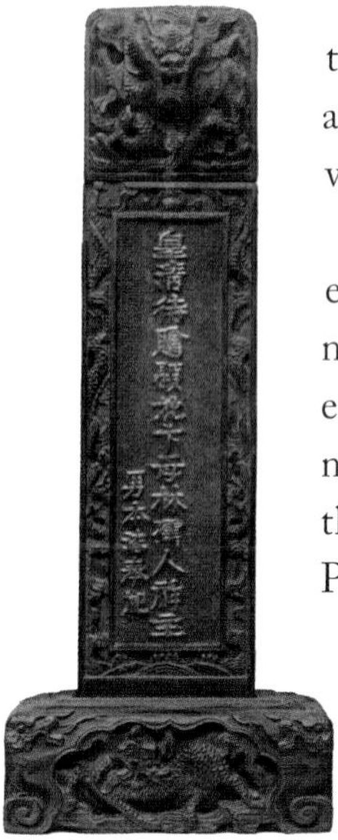
A Chinese ancestral tablet.

to a region. Many spirit tablets also have a photo of the ancestor. The spirit tablet is placed on the family altar, where family members revere the soul of the ancestor.

The realm in which the soul resides is similar to the earthly realm. Hence, the ancestor has the same material needs in the realm of the living dead as they did while on earth. The eldest son is responsible for taking care of the needs of the ancestors. Offerings are placed in front of the spirit tablet. Food, especially fruit, is most common. Paper or small-scale representations of other items, such as cars, kitchen appliances, and money, are included on the family altar. There may even be tools of the trade in which the person engaged while on earth. At certain times during the year, family members go to the gravesite to care for the grave. The annual Ching Ming Festival is one such occasion for caring for the gravesites of ancestors.

Catholic Belief in the Communion of Saints

In the Apostles' Creed, which predates the Nicene Creed, Catholics profess that they believe in the **Communion of Saints**. The Communion of Saints includes all those who are "in Christ," both living and dead (*CCC*, 954).

Catholics are sometimes accused of "worshipping" saints. This is just as inaccurate as saying that adherents of Chinese religious traditions "worship" their ancestors. Catholics *honor* saints, both living and dead. They also pray to saints for **intercession** on their behalf with the Triune God. However, only God is worthy of worship. It is common for Catholics to ask other Catholics on earth to pray for them. Therefore, Catholics who ask the saints in heaven to pray for them are doing nothing out of the ordinary (see *CCC*, 956–957).

As those who follow Chinese religious traditions show reverence to their ancestors by placing items such as flowers and candles on the family altar, so

---

Communion of Saints In Christianity, refers to the unity in Christ of all those living on earth (the pilgrim Church), those being purified in purgatory (the Church suffering), and those enjoying the blessings of heaven (the Church in glory).

intercession An offering or prayer of petition to God on behalf of another.

The Communion of Saints tapestries in the Cathedral of Our Lady of the Angels, Los Angeles, California.

too do Catholics show reverence to a saint by placing flowers or candles before an image of the saint, sometimes on a family altar. As people of Chinese religious traditions show reverence by bowing with folded hands, Catholics show reverence by kneeling with folded hands. Neither the adherents of any of the four Chinese religious traditions nor Catholics worship deceased family ancestors or ancestors in faith. They reverence them.

To many Protestant Christians, however, these gestures of reverence by both the Chinese people and Catholics seem like idol worship. Protestants do not deny the existence of saints in heaven. However, they believe that prayer should be directed to God alone. They believe that Jesus is the only Mediator. Catholics also believe that Jesus is the only Mediator. Nothing is stopping Catholics from praying directly to God. Professing belief in the "Communion of Saints" is acknowledging a communal rather than an individualistic relationship between the pilgrim saints on earth and the eternally living saints in heaven (*CCC*, 955).

Ancestor Veneration in Catholic Ritual

When a new group of Catholic missionaries reached the shores of China in the seventeenth and eighteenth centuries, ancestor veneration had already been practiced in Chinese folk religion for millennia. Some missionaries found the practice more secular than religious and saw no need to ban it among newly converted Chinese Catholics. But other missionaries found the practice contrary to Catholic belief and sought to ban it. For more than a century, what became known as the **Chinese Rites Controversy** went back and forth between permission and prohibition of ancestor veneration for Chinese

A Catholic woman's grave in Hong Kong, China.

Chinese Rites Controversy A dispute within the Catholic Church during the seventeenth and eighteenth centuries over whether Chinese folk religion rites and offerings to ancestors constituted idolatry. The Jesuits believed the rites were compatible with Catholicism; the Dominicans did not. Pope Clement XI decided in 1704 in favor of the Dominicans, but his teaching was relaxed in the twentieth century to allow for some participation in those rites by Chinese Catholics.

Catholics greet Bishop Joseph Li Shan at a government-approved Catholic church in Beijing. On September 22, 2018, the Vatican announced a historic accord with China on the appointment of bishops in the Communist country as Pope Francis recognized seven Beijing-appointed bishops.

Catholics, ending with permanent prohibition in 1742. In 1939, the Holy See revisited the issue under the papacy of Pope Pius XII and determined that veneration of ancestors was permissible for Chinese Catholics as long as there was no veneration element contrary to Catholic doctrine nor any hint of superstition.

Further, the Second Vatican Council taught that in some circumstances, liturgical and sacramental rituals could be adapted for some cultures, especially in "mission lands." In April 1998, a Special Assembly for Asia of the Synod of Bishops met at the Vatican. The bishops saw **inculturation** as an important but daunting task before them. For the bishops of Asia, one way

---

inculturation Defined by Pope John Paul II as "the incarnation of the Gospel in native cultures and also the introduction of these cultures into the life of the Church" (*Slavorum Apostoli*, 21).

inculturation is expressed is by introducing the veneration of ancestors into the Church's ritual life. The bishops of Vietnam, where there is a Chinese minority, were especially encouraged to begin the process. They saw inculturation not as accommodating Catholicism to a particular culture but as a means of evangelization.

In 2018, Pope Francis struck a deal with the Chinese Communist government. The deal called for China to formally recognize the pope's authority within the Church and his final say in choosing bishops in China. The Vatican, in return, had to recognize bishops the Chinese government had previously installed and who had been excommunicated by the Church.

SECTION *Assessment*

Reading Comprehension

1. Why do Chinese families use feng shui masters upon the death of a loved one?
2. Why can it be said that people who practice Chinese religious traditions do not worship their ancestors?
3. Why is it important to the Catholic bishops of Asia not to dismiss the Chinese practice of venerating ancestors?

Vocabulary

4. Explain the *Chinese Rites Controversy*.

For Reflection

5. What is your own experience of inculturation?
6. How do you see inculturation enriching Catholic liturgical experiences?

Flash Search

7. What is the status of Catholicism in China today?

Section Summaries

Introduction: Many Traditions and Practices

Chinese religious traditions are primarily a commingling of ancient folk religion, Confucianism, Taoism, and Buddhism. The line between the religious and the philosophical is often blurred as well. Religious expressions were largely suppressed in China by the Communist takeover of that vast country in 1949. Private devotions continue.

- Research the practice of tai chi. Write about the name's etymology, its popularity in the West, and its connections with Chinese religious traditions.

Section 1: A Brief History of Chinese Religious Traditions

Chinese folk religion has elements of ancestor veneration, divination, and astrology. Confucius attempted to revitalize society through reviving the wisdom of the ancient Chinese sages. The two significant themes of his teachings were learning and relationships. Attributed to Lao-tzu, Taoism refers to "the Way" (the Tao), or that which is foundational to the temporal and spiritual. Its emphasis is on the self-perfection of the individual. Buddhism united with these other Chinese religious traditions to form the multitraditional Chinese religious landscape. Pure Land and Ch'an are the dominant forms of Buddhism in China.

- Create a chart or diagram comparing the following aspects of Confucianism and Taoism: major teachings, what is needed for living well, literary genre of the sacred texts, view of human nature, and view of spiritual nature.

Section 2: Sacred Stories and Sacred Scriptures

Lao-tzu did not create any writings and Confucius only a very few, but their followers did. Of all the Confucian Classics, the *Analects* is the most closely associated with Confucius. The Confucian Classics are a set of nine works, divided into two groups; some of the writings predate Confucius. The main sacred writing of Taoists, the *Tao Te Ching*, is one of the most-read works of Chinese literature in the world.

- Research the *I Ching*, a classic Chinese text. Write three to five paragraphs explaining its name, history, symbolism, and usage.

Section 3: Beliefs and Practices

Confucianism is concerned with character formation. In Confucianism, li (proper conduct) and jen (benevolence) are two of the most important virtues leading to perfection. Taoists believe that actual physical immortality is a reachable goal. The Tao permeates all creation—it is an impersonal god. Wu wei is "action without action," the force through which the Tao acts. The li and jen of Confucius, the wu wei of Taoists, and the Buddhist concept that all life is suffering weave together to form the fabric of Chinese living.

- Create a poster or media slide(s) portraying in images and words three ways a person can form his or her character from a Confucian perspective.

Section 4: Sacred Time

Though there are numerous traditional Chinese festivals, few are celebrated in mainland China. The Chinese New Year is the most important Chinese festival. The Mid-Autumn Festival is second in importance to the Chinese people. The Chinese mark important life-cycle events with practices drawn from a variety of Chinese religious traditions.

- Create a chart listing at least ten Chinese festivals in the first column. In a second column, include a brief description of each festival. In a third column, give the approximate time of year when each occurs.

Section 5: Sacred Places and Sacred Spaces

Many Chinese temples were destroyed or taken over by the government after the Chinese Communist takeover in 1949. Chinese people honor their ancestors at local temples, home shrines, and gravesites. Ch'u Fou is sacred because it is the burial place of Confucius.

- Research and write two to three paragraphs explaining how feng shui has become part of contemporary Western culture.

Section 6: Catholics Dialogue with Adherents of Chinese Religious Traditions

Chinese people do not worship their ancestors but venerate them. Neither do Catholics worship their "ancestors in faith." The Communion of Saints is the unity of the Church on earth, in purgatory, and in heaven. In the seventeenth and eighteenth centuries, there was controversy over whether ancestor veneration would be permitted to Chinese Catholics. Recently, the bishops of Asia have been looking at introducing the veneration of ancestors into the liturgical and sacramental rituals of the Catholic Church in their countries.

- What does the Church teach about the veneration of images? Quote your answer directly from paragraph 2141 of the *Catechism of the Catholic Church.*

Chapter Projects

Complete one of these projects by the conclusion of your study of this chapter.

1. Essay on the Values of Harmony and Competition

   Harmony is a high value in Chinese religious traditions and culture, while competition is a high value in Western culture. Write a two-page essay on the advantages and disadvantages of each value. Are they "competing" values, or can they at times be "harmonious"?

2. Podcast Script and Presentation

   Write a podcast script in which you (the narrator) are interviewing Confucius, Lao-tzu, and Siddhartha on ways to live a happy, fulfilled life. Write three questions followed by answers to each question from each religious leader. Make a video or audio recording of your podcast. You may choose others to play the parts or record each part in your own voice(s).

3. Reading and Reporting on a Chinese Novel

   Read and report on *The Kitchen God's Wife* by Amy Tan or another novel approved by your teacher that features Chinese religion and culture. Write a three- to five-page report on how the novel portrays Chinese folk religion and Chinese religious traditions. Include themes such as luck, duty, marriage, and patriarchy.

4. Artistic Rendition of Yin and Yang

   Come up with a list of pairs of opposites (e.g., success and failure, young and old, freedom and constraint) that illustrate the concept of yin and yang. Illustrate at least five of the opposite pairs using images and words in a slide presentation or on a poster.

5. Essay on Your Choice of Topic

   Write a three- to five-page essay on one of the following topics or on a topic of your choosing that your teacher approves:

   - American Society Needs to Put More Yin in Its Yang
   - The Chinese Custom of Female Foot Binding
   - Choosing Catholic Bishops in China Today
   - Urban Chinatowns in the United States

Key Image

Yin and Yang

The symbol representing yin and yang is familiar to many. It is a circle where half is dark with a light spot, while the other half is light with a dark spot. The curvy line through the center of the circle indicates that the two sides are not absolute opposites. Instead, the opposites complement each other. One is not superior to the other, for superiority or inferiority imbalances the harmony desired. Both halves are needed for wholeness.

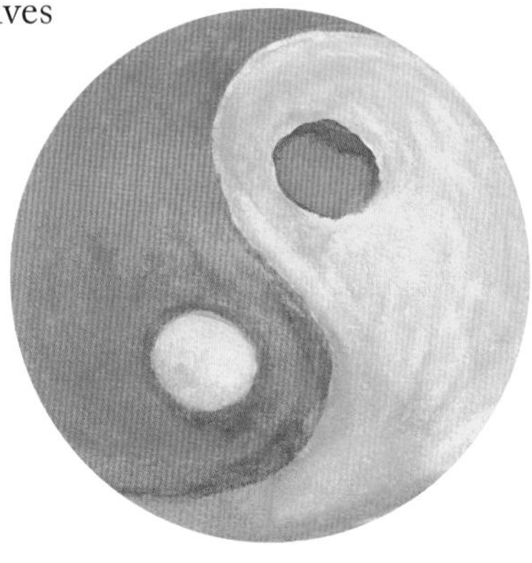

Yin and yang originally referred to the shaded and sunny sides of hills and valleys. While yin signifies "dark/shady side," yang indicates "sunny side." Valley slopes on the sunny side tended to have the name "yang" in them, while slopes on the shady side tended to have the name "yin."

Yin and yang symbolize the complementary, harmonious play of pairs of opposites in the universe. They are interdependent in the sense that one has no meaning without the other. For example, good has no meaning without evil, high has no meaning without low, light has no meaning without dark, and cold has no meaning without hot. One defines the other. There is no antagonism between the pairs, for both are needed. Everything contains a seed of its opposite, as the light and dark spots within the symbol indicate. Good has an element of evil; high has an element of low, light has an element of dark, and cold has an element of hot, and vice versa. The opposition is not total but relative. The opposites are two sides of the same coin. For adherents of ancient Chinese religions, nature is in a continual dance to remain balanced between the yin and the yang.

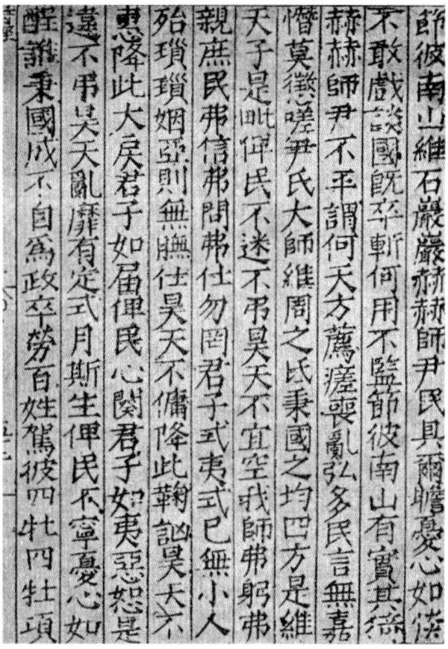
節彼南山維石巖巖赫赫師尹民具爾瞻憂心如惔
不敢戲談國既卒斬何用不監節彼南山有實其猗
赫赫師尹不平謂何天方薦瘥喪亂弘多民言無嘉
憯莫懲嗟尹氏大師維周之氐秉國之均四方是維
天子是毗俾民不迷不弔昊天不宜空我師弗躬弗
親庶民弗信弗問弗仕勿罔君子式夷式已無小人
殆瑣瑣姻亞則無膴仕昊天不傭降此鞠訩昊天不
惠降此大戾君子如屆俾民心闋君子如夷惡怒是
違不弔昊天亂靡有定式月斯生俾民不寧憂心如
酲誰秉國成不自為政卒勞百姓駕彼四牡四牡項

A Song Dynasty–printing from the I-Ching *(Book of Changes) from between 960 and 1269.*

The yin-yang symbol goes back thousands of years. It is believed to have emerged from the activity of measuring shadows with poles in order to mark the seasons. Yang is correlated with the winter solstice when the length of daily sunlight increases. With the length of daily darkness increasing, yin is allied with the summer solstice. Yin is associated with the moon, while yang is linked with the sun.

While the concept of yin and yang can be dated to the fifteenth century BCE, the first written mention of it appears in the ***I Ching***, written during the Western Zhou dynasty in the ninth century BCE. In the later *Tao Te Ching*, we read,

All things carry yin yet embrace yang.
They blend their life breaths in order to produce harmony. (42:2)

According to Chinese mythology, yin and yang were both born from the chaos that created the universe. In their dance of harmony, they created humans and deities. Yin and yang are immortal, living at the center of the

---

I Ching Meaning "Book of Changes"; an ancient Chinese book of wisdom and divination manual; one of the Five Classics of Confucianism.

earth in perfect balance. If circumstances of life are full of conflict, one's physical, mental, and spiritual being lacks harmony. If there is too much stress (yang), one needs to find avenues of peace (yin). The principles of yin and yang help to remove stress. Yin and yang underlie Chinese medicine, martial arts, literature, science, and everyday living.

Faithful Adherent

Matteo Ricci, S.J.: First Western Missionary in China

Matteo Ricci, S.J.

It is not accurate to call Matteo Ricci (1552–1610), an Italian Jesuit priest, an adherent of Chinese religious traditions. However, there is no doubt that Ricci was very familiar with the Chinese religious landscape of his time. In 1582, the Jesuit superior sent Ricci to the Portuguese colony of Macao on the coast of the South China Sea. It was the only part of China that Western missionaries had been permitted to visit.

While in Macao, Ricci took up an extensive study of the classical Chinese language. Not only did he master speaking Chinese but he also learned how to write in Chinese script. He also studied Chinese culture. In 1583, Ricci and his Jesuit companion Michael Ruggieri entered China. They brought with them several Western items such as clocks, musical instruments, and tools for studying math and astronomy. Because of Ricci's extraordinary skills in math and astronomy, he was invited to the court of Emperor K'ang-Hsi in Beijing in 1601. He remained in the court of the emperor for nine years, hoping to facilitate the beginning of a Chinese-Christian civilization.

Ricci's study of Chinese culture led him to a new approach in missionary work. Versed in Confucianism, he decided to use existing Confucian principles to explain Christianity. He explained to the Chinese that Christianity was the completion of their Chinese faith, not something completely new. He

Ricci traveling in China.

also taught that ancestor veneration was a legitimate memorial to family members and was compatible with the Catholic faith. Later Catholic missionaries to China were not as well versed in Chinese culture as Ricci and questioned what he had taught the Chinese about ancestor worship. They also complained to the Vatican. In 1704, the Vatican taught that ancestor worship was not compatible with Christianity. In 1721, the Chinese emperor banned Catholic missionaries from China.

At the time of Ricci's death in Beijing in 1610, there were about 2,500 Catholics in China. By code of Chinese law, Westerners who died in China were required to be buried in Macao. However, because of Ricci's accomplishments in China, another Jesuit missionary made a plea to the emperor for his burial in Beijing. The emperor granted the request and marked Ricci's gravesite in Beijing with a Buddhist temple.

Reading Comprehension

1. What were two skills that made Ricci an effective missionary in China?
2. How did Ricci use Confucianism to help explain the Christian faith?
3. Why was Ricci invited to meet with Emperor K'ang-Hsi?
4. What complaint about Ricci did later missionaries make to the Vatican?

For Reflection

5. How might St. Paul's words, "I have become all things to all, to save at least some" (1 Cor 9:22b), apply to Ricci's missionary approach?

Prayer

Reflect on these words of the Chinese Buddhist "Universal Love Aspiration."

Through the working of Great Compassion
in their hearts.
May all beings have happiness
and the causes of happiness.
May all be free from sorrow
and the causes of sorrow.
May all never be separated from the
sacred happiness, which is sorrowless.
And may all live in equanimity,
without too much attachment
and too much aversion;
and live believing in the equality of
all that lives.

8

JAPANESE RELIGIOUS TRADITIONS

Introduction
HEAVENLY ORIGINS

Japanese people have long felt that their island nation has heavenly origins. In fact, Japanese people believe that gods (called **kami**) inhabited the land and were very much a part of the created world. In a traditional Japanese story, the heavenly gods Izanagi and Izanami (see above) create Japan when they descend to bring order out of the chaos of the earth:

> Many gods were thus born in succession, and so they increased in number, but as long as the world remained in a chaotic state, there was nothing for them to do.
>
> Whereupon, all the heavenly deities summoned the two divine beings, Izanagi and Izanami, and bade them descend to the nebulous place, and by helping each other, to consolidate it into terra firma. "We bestow on you," they said, "this precious treasure, with which to rule the land, the creation of which we command you to perform." So saying, they handed them a spear called Ama-no-Nuboko, embellished with costly gems. The divine couple received respectfully and ceremoniously the sacred weapon and then withdrew from the presence of the deities, ready to perform their august commission.
>
> Proceeding forthwith to the Floating Bridge of Heaven, which lay between the heaven and the earth, they stood awhile to gaze on that which lay below. What they beheld was a world not yet condensed but looking like a sea of filmy fog floating to and fro in the

---

kami The Japanese name for any kind of spiritual force or power.

> air, exhaling the while an inexpressibly fragrant odor. They were, at first, perplexed just how and where to start, but at length Izanagi suggested to his companion that they should try the effect of stirring up the brine with their spear. So saying he pushed down the jeweled shaft and found that it touched something.
>
> Then drawing it up, he examined it and observed that the great drops which fell from it almost immediately coagulated into an island, which is, to this day, the Island of Onokoro. Delighted at the result, the two deities descended forthwith from the Floating Bridge to reach the miraculously created island. In this island they thenceforth dwelt and made it the basis of their subsequent task of creating a country. (Japanese creation myth quoted from an article by Alan Watts)

Like Chinese religious traditions, Japanese religious traditions are a commingling of traditions: the Japanese indigenous tradition of Shinto as well as Buddhism, Confucianism, and Taoism. Placed in a Japanese setting, these religious traditions have a very thin, often transparent, line separating them. Since the other religious traditions are discussed elsewhere in this text, this chapter will place more emphasis on Shinto and its relationship with other religious traditions of the Japanese people.

SECTION *Assessment*

Reading Comprehension

1. Why do Japanese people believe their nation has heavenly origins?
2. Briefly summarize the story of the heavenly gods Izanagi and Izanami.

For Reflection

3. Write two things you know about the island of Japan.

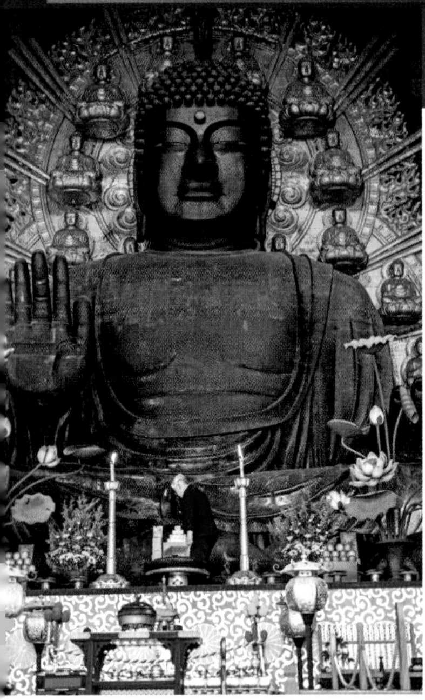

Section 1
A BRIEF HISTORY OF JAPANESE RELIGIOUS TRADITIONS

The exact origin of purely Japanese religious traditions is difficult to determine. Japan's written history began around the sixth century CE when Koreans introduced Chinese Buddhism to Japan along with the more sophisticated Chinese culture. Written language first came to Japan in the form of the systematic Chinese written characters, which the Japanese adopted. Prior to that period, the Japanese kept no written history. It is only through archaeological finds that historians have been able to piece together a vague idea of what Japanese life was like before the sixth century CE.

As in so many cultures, ancient Japanese people made no distinction between religious, social, and economic aspects of life. The Japanese people organized themselves by clans, and worship and ritual took place through the clan structure. Burial sites reveal a concern for what happened to family members in the afterlife. Other artifacts suggest that the Japanese people prayed to nature spirits for the blessing of children and the growth of crops, especially rice. They also held festivals, especially in spring and autumn, the time of planting and harvesting.

Japanese Creation Myth

Throughout their history, the Japanese believed that their land and their emperor had divine origins, setting them apart from the rest of the world.

JAPANESE RELIGIOUS TRADITIONS: TIMELINE OF KEY EVENTS

CE

5 .... Establishment of Grand Shrine at Ise

ca. 500s .... Buddhism comes to Japan

594 .... Buddhism encouraged by Prince Shotoku

ca. 700s .... Composition of *Kojiki* and *Nihon Shoki*

1175 .... Pure Land Buddhism established

1185–1333 .... Kamakura shogunate

ca. 1200s .... Rise of samurai

1549 .... Jesuit missionary Francis Xavier arrives in Japan

1600–1868 .... Tokugawa shogunate

1868 .... Meiji Restoration and creation of State Shinto

1870–1966 .... Life of D. T. Suzuki

1946 .... Emperor Hirohito forced to publicly deny his divinity after Japan defeated in World War II

Japan's rulers were believed to be direct descendants of the sun goddess, Amaterasu. Their origins are explained in an ancestor myth in which spirits called kami emerged just after the formation of heaven and earth. These first kami in turn created other kami.

Eventually, the kami couple Izanagi and Izanami arrived. As creators, they dipped a jeweled spear into the ocean of the amorphous earth, and solid masses formed. These solid masses became the islands of present-day Japan.

Amaterasu Omikami, goddess of the sun.

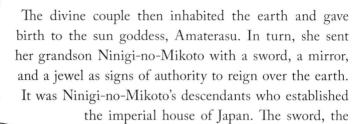

The divine couple then inhabited the earth and gave birth to the sun goddess, Amaterasu. In turn, she sent her grandson Ninigi-no-Mikoto with a sword, a mirror, and a jewel as signs of authority to reign over the earth. It was Ninigi-no-Mikoto's descendants who established the imperial house of Japan. The sword, the bronze mirror said to be housed at Ise, and the jewel are to this day symbols of imperial rule in Japan. Not only did the land of Japan and the rule of its emperors have a divine origin but the Japanese people did as well. According to the myth, kami also created the Japanese people.

Influence of Chinese Religious Traditions

Buddhism, Taoism, and Confucianism were introduced to Japan in the middle of the sixth century. The Japanese imperial court became interested in these new religious traditions because they came from China, a place they perceived as having a culture superior to Japan's.

Eager to learn all things Chinese, the Japanese ruling class adopted the Confucian model of education. They found Confucian social conventions helpful in forging a national identity. Of particular interest to the Japanese emperors was the Confucian notion of li (see Chapter 7, Section 3), as it directly addressed the relationship between the emperor and his subjects and the relationship between father and son. While the subject and son were to be loyal and obedient, the emperor and the father were to be benevolent. For the ruling class, these attitudes and expressions of loyalty and obedience were an excellent formula for social stability.

A Confucius statue at Yushima Seido Temple, Tokyo, Japan.

The introduction of Chinese culture also brought Taoism to Japan. The Taoist traditions of harmony with nature and divination were not foreign to the Japanese people. Taoists used techniques of divination for some of the same purposes as the Japanese people. Divination was one way of making sacred and godly the various signs within nature. People employed divination to determine the best time for an event to take place, among other things.

Confucianism and Taoism did not become separate religious traditions in Japan. Instead, aspects of each were adopted and adapted into unique, indigenous Japanese religious expressions. Buddhism was graciously accepted as a form of religious expression for the Japanese people as a whole.

Shitennō-ji in Osaka, Japan; the original temple on this site was commissioned by Prince Shōtoku in the late sixth century to promote Buddhism in Japan.

When Buddhism was introduced into Japan, Japanese leaders were the first ones attracted to it. They were particularly interested in Buddhism's philosophy, elaborate doctrine, well-organized priesthood, art, and literature. During worship, they sometimes venerated the buddhas and the kami side by side. Buddhist rituals for the dead and memorials for ancestors were also of great interest to the royal household. The Buddhist practice of cremation began in India and became acceptable in Japanese Buddhist burial rites. In 594, Prince Shotoku made Buddhism the state religion. During the next few centuries, Buddhists built many temples and monasteries.

Nevertheless, the Japanese indigenous religion did not disappear, for the creation myth of Japan's divine origins was told and retold. With the influx of new religious traditions, it became necessary to give a name to the indigenous religion. The Chinese called Japanese religious expression Shinto, which means "the way of the kami," as the Japanese believed that the kami were everywhere. At first honored in natural settings, kami eventually became enshrined at various local clan sites.

Expansion of Buddhism

During the Heian Period (794–1185), Japan moved from a centralized to a feudal form of government, and Buddhism became the prominent religious tradition in Japan. In the ninth century, two new Buddhist sects, Shingon and Tendai, were introduced via China. Yet Japanese Buddhism remained unique. Most Japanese Buddhist sects were forms of Mahayana Buddhism that saw no problem claiming kami and bodhisattvas as the same thing. During the Kamakura **shogunate** (1185–1333), several new sects of Buddhism, including Pure Land and Zen, flourished.

Daishō-in Temple, a Shingon Buddhist temple in Hatsukaichi, Japan.

Shingon Buddhism is a form of Vajrayana Buddhism. The Japanese nobility was particularly interested in Shingon, with its elaborate rituals, secret transmission of insight, and instructive scriptures. Central was its belief that enlightenment could be attained in this lifetime if one were

---

shogunate A form of military government that ruled Japan while emperors were the nominal leaders from the twelfth until the nineteenth century.

Sensō-ji, a Tendai Buddhist temple in Tokyo, Japan.

willing to undergo the strict discipline of ritual and study. Shingon Buddhism also strived to blend with the indigenous religion of Japan by venerating both kami and Buddhist deities.

Chinese Tien-tai Buddhism became known as Tendai Buddhism in Japan. Focusing on the Lotus Sutra for inspiration, Tendai members gave great faith and devotion to Amitabha Buddha (known in Japan as "Amida Butsu") from Pure Land Buddhism. The Lotus Sutra taught that enlightenment was universal, not just for monastics. A further adaptation of Tendai Buddhism was the addition of the worship of nature kami.

It was inevitable that Pure Land Buddhism would also reach the shores of Japan. This took place during the Kamakura shogunate. As in China, the Pure Land Buddhism of Japan advocates great devotion to Amida Butsu as a way to be reborn in the blissful Pure Land. One way of showing great devotion to Amida Butsu is to recite "Namu Amida Butsu" ("I take refuge in Amitabha Buddha") like a mantra or to, in some other way, always keep Amida Butsu present in one's mind.

One of the most popular forms of Buddhism in Japan was, and remains, Zen Buddhism, which had its origins in Chinese Ch'an Buddhism. Rather than statues and images of the Buddha or bodhisattvas, Zen Buddhism was more interested in a direct vision of nature. Gardens, rocks, mountains, and birds were the most popular subjects of Zen Buddhist art. The Zen connection between religion and nature was truly seamless.

The two most noted schools of Zen Buddhism are Rinzai Zen and Soto Zen. At the heart of each is meditation. While Rinzai Zen believes a person could gain immediate enlightenment, Soto Zen believes enlightenment is a gradual process. And while Soto Zen emphasizes a method of *zazen*, or "sitting meditation," Rinzai Zen places more emphasis on the use of the **koan**. These are meant to break through logic and intellect to allow an intuitive flash, called a **satori**, to emerge and eventually lead to enlightenment. These are two notable koans:

If a tree falls in a forest where no one is present to hear it, does it make a sound?

What did your face look like before your parents were born?

Meanwhile, Shinto, the indigenous religious tradition of Japan, continued to flourish during the Kamakura shogunate. As people from other East Asian countries visited Japan, Shinto adopted from and adapted to other religious traditions and cultures. From Confucianism, Shinto borrowed li; from Taoism, the calendar, divination, some festivals, and balance with nature; and from Buddhism, various rituals, philosophical systems, and ancestor veneration. To many Shinto adherents, Buddhist deities were just other forms of kami. Buddhist deities, Buddhist scriptures, Shinto kami, and Shinto prayers

---

koan A paradox used in Zen Buddhism to train the adherent to abandon ultimate dependence on reason, opening the opportunity for enlightenment.

satori The name for sudden enlightenment as advocated by the Rinzai school of Zen Buddhism, as opposed to gradual enlightenment taught by the Soto Zen school.

fit quite naturally together for the ordinary Japanese worshipper. It was common to have both Shinto and Buddhist worship services in Shinto shrines. This mutual arrangement continued until the nineteenth century, when the Meiji government forced a separation between Shinto and Buddhism.

Modern Era

In 1549, the first Christian missionaries, including the Jesuit St. Francis Xavier, came to Japan. The missionaries were able to win Christian converts due in part to Japanese interest in Western beliefs and culture, as well as some initial support from the Japanese government. However, this support did not last long. Fearing the missionaries had a political agenda, the government issued an edict in 1587 banishing Catholics from Japan. In 1597, twenty-seven European and Japanese Catholics were executed at Nagasaki, making them the first Christian martyrs in Japan.

The Tokugawa shogunate came into power in 1600. The new rulers were military leaders, called *shoguns*. They reorganized a fragmented government and society in a manner influenced by Confucian values. An overall theme of this shogunate was to purify Japan from all outside influences. To ensure the

The Twenty-Six Martyrs Museum in Nagasaki, Japan.

banishment of Christianity from Japan, the Tokugawa reformers required citizens to register with a Buddhist temple at birth, marriage, and death. More Buddhist temples were built as part of this regulation. Some reformers even attempted to return Japan to a time before the influence of Chinese religious traditions and culture. The scholar Motoori Norinaga (1730–1801) was the most famous of these reformers seeking a pure Shinto. However, other religious traditions were so embedded in Japanese culture that "pure Shinto" was impossible.

State Shinto of the Meiji Period (1868–1912) restored some of the imperial power lost under the shogunates. Meiji emperors forced a separation between Shinto and Buddhism, and there was a concerted effort toward nationalism and toward restoring a time when the emperor was a kami and the Japanese people were of divine origin with a divine mission. The movement toward nationalism included removing any trace of Chinese culture, Confucianism, Taoism, and Buddhism. As with the efforts at "pure Shinto," purifying Japan of the other religions was impossible because of their long presence in the fabric of Japanese society. In particular, since Buddhism was an integral part of Japanese heritage and culture, the people of Japan revolted against its suppression, and the government acquiesced.

When the emperor gave in and allowed people to practice their religious traditions, Catholic Christians, who had continued to practice their faith secretly for more than two hundred years, came out into the open. However, the persecutions of Christians continued, and the Western world reacted with protest against Japan. Because Emperor Meiji did not want to lose Japan's burgeoning economic and trade relationship with the industrial West, his government lifted the ban on the practice of Christianity in 1873. With the ban lifted, Christian missionaries, this time including Protestants, returned to

A nineteenth-century Japanese Shinto priest.

Japan. However, with the rise in nationalism, the number of Japanese people converted to Christianity were few.

At the beginning of the twentieth century, there was a tremendous surge in what became known as "new religions." They were not really *new* religions, for they integrated elements of Japan's existing religious traditions into what are better described as movements or societies. Individuals claiming divine revelation or divinity founded these new groups. **Soka Gakkai** is an example of a Japanese new religion.

(Left) Emperor Hirohito of Japan, at his coronation. (Right) Hirohito with American Army General Douglas MacArthur in 1945 after Japan's surrender in World War II.

The defeat of Japan in World War II in 1945 was devastating to a nation that believed itself to be at the center of creation. At the end of the war, the Allies forced Emperor Hirohito to renounce his claim of divinity, leaving the Japanese people to practice any religious tradition they chose. Religious

---

Soka Gakkai A Japanese Buddhist "new religion" founded in 1930 that emphasizes the power of the Lotus Sutra and advocates nonviolence. Today, it is not only the largest of Japan's new religions but also an international organization.

freedom weakened both State Shinto and nationalism, leaving room for the new religions to advance. Recently, however, the more ancient forms of Shinto and Buddhism have attracted some Japanese devotees. Surpassing all religious revivals, however, has been the revival of Japanese nationalism. Deprived by the Allies of the option of building another powerful army, Japan has forged an economic powerhouse that offers nationalistic pride to its people.

SECTION *Assessment*

Reading Comprehension

1. What role does the Japanese creation myth play in Japanese identity?
2. Who were Japan's rulers traditionally believed to be descended from?
3. Describe the differences between Rinzai Zen Buddhism and Soto Zen Buddhism.
4. What did the Meiji government attempt to restore?
5. What happened to Emperor Hirohito after World War II?
6. How does the derivation of *Shinto* relate to *kami*?

Vocabulary

7. Explain the Japanese new religion named *Soka Gakkai.*

For Reflection

8. What is a national myth of your country? How does it help define the nation, its leaders, and its people? If you live in a country that does not have a national myth, do you think you are missing something? Why or why not?
9. In what ways do you think meditating on a koan might help you in your spiritual life?

Flash Search

10. How is Japanese sumo wrestling related to Shinto?

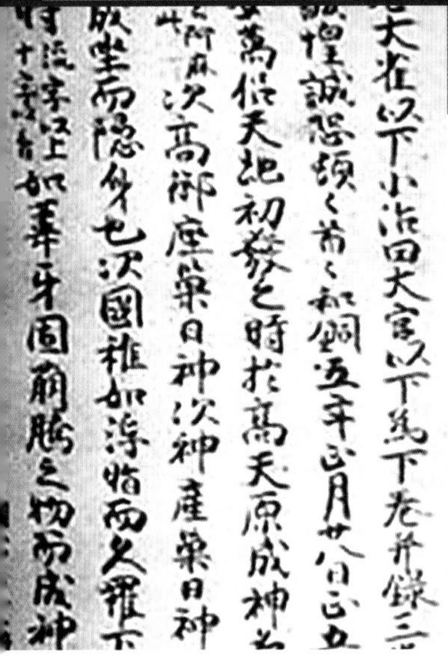

Section 2
SACRED STORIES AND SACRED SCRIPTURES

Japanese indigenous religion, or Shinto, does not have any official sacred texts inspired or revealed by the gods. However, two texts are considered authoritative and significant for the Japanese people's religious and historical heritage. In the eighth century, the Japanese imperial government commissioned the Japanese people's compilation of the oral myths and legends. Written in Chinese characters, the *Kojiki* (*Record of Ancient Matters*) was completed in 712. It includes the creation myth of Japan and the ancestral genealogy of emperors from the beginning to Emperor Tenmu, who commissioned the work.

A second writing—the *Nihon Shoki* (*Chronicles of Japan*)—was compiled as a chronicle of Japan's history. Finished in 720, it begins with the Japanese creation myth and covers Japanese history through the end of the seventh century.

The Goddess Uzumé.
From Hokusai. Reproduced for this Work by a Japanese Engraver.
To face page 34, Vol. I.

Ame-no-Uzume, the goddess of dawn, mirth, meditation, revelry, and the arts.

As with so many documents written in ancient times, these two portray the elite classes, not the ordinary people. They were written to legitimize the imperial rulers as direct descendants of the sun goddess, Amaterasu, so that they could claim a form of sacred kingship.

SECTION *Assessment*

Reading Comprehension

1. Name the two ancient texts that contain the national myths and history of Japan. What important stories are in these texts?
2. Why did the imperial government commission the writing of these texts?

For Reflection

3. Imagine if the Christian Bible were considered authoritative but not revealed by God. How do you think that would affect Christian history, doctrine, liturgical life, and prayer life?

Flash Search

4. Name and explain a national myth and its origin from a country of your choice. Name, if possible, the source of the myth.

Section 3
BELIEFS AND PRACTICES

Though Shinto is the indigenous religious tradition of Japan, there is fluidity between Shinto and Buddhism. It is common to find both kami and buddhas honored in the same home.

Shinto Beliefs about Kami

In the Shinto tradition, kami are not gods in the sense that they are transcendent or all-powerful. Rather, they have to do with whatever is sacred. Shinto sees the natural world as good. Kami inhabit this world in trees, mountains, holy people, the emperor, and anything else deemed sacred or powerful. However, there are also destructive kami. An erupting volcano is a destructive kami.

Redemption is possible because the world is imbued with the goodness of kami. Redemption comes not through good works of helping others but through proper rituals associated with kami or the compassion and mercy of a buddha like Amida. In the past, the imperial leader of Japan, as the representative of the sun goddess, Amaterasu, manifested kami. His presence reminded the Japanese people that all was well in this world. The focus of kami is to aid and protect.

A stone fox statue representing Inari Okami—the kami of foxes, fertility, rice, tea, and saki—at the Fushimi-Inari shrine in Kyoto, Japan.

A home shrine, or kamidana, in a backyard in Kawagoe, Japan.

People worship kami in local or national shrines, at their home **kamidana**, or in nature. Some Japanese people worship the kami that inhabit a specific mountain or other forms of nature. Praying to a kami may involve praise, thanksgiving, appreciation, or acknowledgment of its power. It is customary to save a request of the kami for the end of the prayer. Requests are commonly for blessing of children, a good harvest, a good job, good health, protection of family members, or prosperity.

Buddhism in Japan

As noted, Shinto and Buddhism are closely related in the Japanese religious landscape. Buddhism began in India, but as it expanded throughout the continent of Asia, it was adapted to local situations. Japan was no exception. Some Japanese people believe buddhas and bodhisattvas are just another form of kami. Likewise, some Japanese Buddhists believe kami are manifestations of

---

kamidana Japanese for "kami shelf"; a home shrine dedicated to a kami.

Hyogo Great Buddha in the Nofukuji Temple in Kobe, Japan.

various buddhas. Statues of various buddhas are found everywhere in Japan. It is also not unusual to find buddha statues within Shinto shrines or for a home to possess both a kamidana and a **butsudan**. Similar to Chinese religious traditions, it is at the butsudan that ancestor veneration takes place.

Japanese Living

As Shinto made no distinction between religion and politics or between religion and nature, *harmony* is an apt word to describe Japanese living. This virtue further points to the fact that, for the Japanese, people and kami dwell together. Shinto maintains its harmony with other religions partly because it does not possess any rigid system of doctrines that might bring it into conflict with other parts of Japanese life.

Besides harmony, another strong virtue important to the Japanese people is loyalty. In the five relationships of li, loyalty is the glue. Loyalty once went to the extreme when **samurai** were willing to die by ritual suicide, or **harakiri**, rather than humiliate their ruler. It has always been clear in li that the subordinate is loyal to the superior, but in Japan there is also mutual loyalty. Today, the virtue of loyalty is still exhibited in corporate Japan, where loyalty to the clan until death is replaced with loyalty to the corporation until retirement.

Contrasting with "rugged individualism" of the West, in Japan, the individual takes a back seat to the family, region, and nation. Religious expression is exhibited in two primary ways. The clan or extended family is the most important social structure for Japanese living. The family belongs to a local Shinto shrine based on where they live and to a local Buddhist temple for ancestor veneration. Second, Japanese people are part of the national clan. At one time, the emperor was the head of the clan and made offerings to the sun goddess, Amaterasu, at the Grand Shrine at Ise on behalf of the Japanese people. Though initially a kami for the imperial family, Amaterasu became the national kami.

An extended family visits Sensō-ji Temple in Asakusa, Tokyo, Japan.

---

butsudan In Japanese households, the Buddhist family altar, generally containing memorial tablets for deceased ancestors. Historically, it was maintained in addition to the kamidana.

samurai From a word meaning "to serve"; a member of a hereditary feudal warrior class that served Japanese rulers. Samurai cultivated such virtues as loyalty, honor, and courage.

harakiri Ritual suicide by disembowelment by sword formerly practiced by Japanese samurai or decreed by a court in place of the death penalty.

SECTION *Assessment*

Reading Comprehension

1. Describe various ways in which kami are manifested.
2. Why are harmony and loyalty valued virtues in Japanese religious traditions?
3. What kind of religious expressions may be found in a Japanese home?

Vocabulary

4. What is *harakiri*?

For Reflection

5. Do you consider yourself preordained to accomplish something worthwhile with your life? What is it?
6. What are the advantages and disadvantages of living in a governmental system that separates church from state?

Flash Search

7. What is the samurai belief system?

Section 4
SACRED TIME

Matsuri is the name for Japanese festivals. As shrines and their kami are mostly local or regional in nature, so are most Japanese festivals. Though most matsuri are connected with Shinto, all the religious traditions of Japan participate in the annual cycle of festivals.

The Japanese use a lunar calendar similar to the Chinese lunar calendar for calculating times of many of their festivals. However, during the Meiji Period, when Japan's interest in collaborating with the Western world in business heightened, the Gregorian calendar grew in use; it is in general use in Japan today.

Information follows on some of the main Japanese festivals and life-cycle celebrations.

Omisoka and Shogatsu

Omisoka—a name for the last day in the twelfth month of the Japanese lunar calendar—is the year-end festival in preparation for New Year's Day. In preparation for the new year, people clean their homes, especially their butsudan and kamidana. They also purify the local shrines and temples and ancestors' graves.

The New Year, called Shogatsu, is the most important celebration in Japan. It is a three-day event held on January 1, 2, and 3. At Buddhist temples, bells are rung eight times on New Year's Eve and one hundred times on New Year's Day to purify the people of the 108 sins in Buddhism.

---

matsuri Japanese for "festivals"; term refers to Shinto festivals predominantly celebrated at local or regional shrines.

kimonos Long robes with wide sleeves traditionally with a broad sash as an outer garment typically worn by Japanese women.

New Year's Eve and New Year's Day are spent overnight at the Shinto Nishinomiya shrine in Nishinomiya, Hyōgo, Japan.

Hina Matsuri

Hina Matsuri, or "Girls' Day," is celebrated on March 3. Though Hina Matsuri is not a public holiday, most Japanese families with daughters celebrate the occasion. Parents dress up male and female dolls in traditional Japanese court costumes and set them up on a tiered stage to symbolize a royal wedding. The emperor and empress dolls are placed on the top of the tier, and the other dolls are placed on descending levels down in rank to the court musicians at the bottom. Offerings of rice cakes, peach blossoms, and sweet white sake are set before the stage. Japanese daughters dressed in **kimonos** gather and celebrate a wish for health and happiness with their families.

Hina Matsuri, or Girls' Day, is celebrated on March 3 each year, and it is a traditional custom for the families with young girls to have the dolls on display at home weeks prior to the holiday.

Kodomo no Hi

Kodomo no Hi, or "Children's Day," celebrated on May 5, was once Boys' Day as a counterpart to Girls' Day. Now it is a public holiday celebrated by all children. The tradition of this day goes back to ancient Japan, but it became popular during feudal Japan when samurai was an estimable career for Japanese boys. Today, windsocks shaped like carp fly in the skies of Japan on Kodomo no Hi. The carp was chosen for its characteristics of courage and fortitude, as a carp can swim upstream and, amazingly, up waterfalls. These are characteristics parents wish for their children so that they will find success in life.

Carp kites fly over Japan for Children's Day.

Obon

Obon is a three-day festival, rooted in Buddhism, celebrated in mid-August, during which the Japanese people believe the spirits of ancestors return home for a short time. Families go to the gravesites of their ancestors and light candles, lanterns, and bonfires to give the spirits of their relatives light by which to see their way back to the family home. The highlight of this festival is the folk dances performed at temples or shrines.

The Obon Festival is also known as the Festival of Souls. As part of the festival, families float lanterns to honor the spirits of their deceased ancestors.

Life-Cycle Celebrations

Several festivals of the different Japanese religious traditions are celebrated to mark the life cycle from birth to death.

Between thirty and one hundred days after birth, a newborn is taken to the local shrine to be presented to the local kami. Japanese people traditionally believe the kami watches over the child for the rest of his or her life.

Japanese weddings are traditionally held at shrines. However, an increasing number of weddings occur at Christian churches, even if the couple is not Christian. There are still some Shinto elements to the wedding, but more brides prefer to wear a white gown rather than a traditional kimono on their wedding day.

The Japanese people greatly respect their ancestors and mark various death rituals. Generally, after the funeral or cremation, a series of memorial services is held over months and years until the fiftieth year, when the deceased is considered truly an ancestor in the Japanese tradition. Most cemeteries in Japan are Buddhist cemeteries.

A family visits the Meiji Shrine in Tokyo, Japan, for a traditional ritual of prayers for good health and for newborn babies.

SECTION *Assessment*

Reading Comprehension

1. Why did Japan move to the Gregorian calendar?
2. How do Japanese people prepare for the New Year?
3. Describe what takes place on Hina Matsuri.
4. What is the significance of flying carp-shaped windsocks on Kodomo no Hi?
5. Why is there growing desire among Japanese people to celebrate a wedding in a Christian church, even though neither party is Christian?

6. What happens on the fiftieth anniversary of a Japanese person's death?
7. What does Obon commemorate?

For Reflection

8. How can sitting with a dying person be a sacred time?

Flash Search

9. What is kabuki theater, and how is it related to Japanese religious traditions? Why is the term sometimes used disparagingly about politics?

Section 5
SACRED PLACES AND SACRED SPACES

Because of Japan's divine origins, there is no place in Japan that is not sacred. However, the Japanese people do designate sacred spaces. Home shrines seem to possess particular holiness, often giving both a Shinto kamidana and a Buddhist butsudan places of honor. While the kamidana recalls the presence of kami, the butsudan is a place for both the Buddha and ancestor spirits to reside. The head of the family makes offerings on behalf of the family to the kami or the Buddha in order to seek blessings and protection from evil. While Shinto emphasizes things of life such as birth, marriage, agriculture, or even a new job, Buddhism places emphasis on the end of life and the afterlife.

Besides sacred spaces in the home, there are also local and national shrines, temples, and monasteries. Some businesses also have a kamidana and a butsudan. Mountains, rivers, trees, and boulders are also considered sacred places.

Shinto Shrines

Lacking for the most part formal scriptures, doctrines, and ethical codes, Shinto places great emphasis on ritual. These rituals take place at home, local, or national shrines. Since there is no specific day of the week for worship, devotees generally perform their home rituals on any morning they wish, either as individuals or as a family. Japanese people also visit the local shrine any day of the week to honor the local kami. There are thousands of Shinto shrines in Japan, though very few have priests.

Ryuko-ji Temple in Uwajima, Ehime, Japan. Ryuko-ji stands on a hillside up a steep flight of stone steps in a valley.

The local Shinto shrine is designed simply and blends into the Japanese landscape. Believing that kami exist in nature, the Japanese find it important that flowers and foliage surround the shrines. Even in the densest cities of Japan, a Shinto shrine is an oasis of tranquility and beauty, an environment fit for a kami. Since Shinto and Buddhism are closely connected in Japan, a Shinto shrine is generally located near a Buddhist temple.

Both individual and communal worship at the shrine is simple. Devotees first perform a purification rite where they wash their hands and face and rinse their mouth. They then enter a hall, pray, and make an offering. Today, the offering is usually money, but when Japan was more agricultural, the offerings were the fruits of the harvest. Within each shrine, there is a small chamber where the **kami body** is kept. The kami body is usually something quite simple, like a mirror, a sword, or a pebble. It is considered sacred and emits such spiritual power that a priest rarely looks inside the chamber. If the door to the chamber is opened, a screen still blocks the kami body from view. The occasion for opening the chamber is usually a festival in which the kami is invited to participate.

---

kami body An object into which it is believed the kami descends during a Shinto worship service. Often the object is a mirror or sword.

The Ise Grand Shrine in Ise, Mie, Japan, is a Shinto shrine dedicated to the sun goddess, Amaterasu.

Grand Shrine at Ise

Ise, in the Kansai region of the main island of Japan, was the location of the shrine for the imperial family in ancient Japan. Since the imperial family believed they were direct descendants of the sun goddess, Amaterasu, they dedicated this shrine to her and placed a bronze mirror as a kami body in its inner chamber. When the Japanese sun goddess, Amaterasu, fled to a cave, the world was plunged into darkness; it was only when the goddess of mirth, Ame-no-Uzume, performed an erotic dance outside the cave that Amaterasu left the cave for a better look. Then, while Amaterasu was distracted by her reflection in the mirror Ame-no-Uzume had hung outside the cave, the other kami sealed the cave so she could not reenter it, and sunshine was returned to the world. Hence, Amaterasu was the kami of the imperial family.

Eventually, the shrine of the imperial family became the national shrine of Japan. The emperor acted as the priest of that shrine, making offerings on behalf of his country. Today, the Grand Shrine at Ise still has many pilgrims and visitors. It is one of the major symbols of Japanese religious, political, and cultural heritage.

Mount Fuji

The tallest mountain in Japan at 12,390 feet, Mount Fuji is a symbol of Japan that contributes to Japan's physical, cultural, and spiritual geography. It is located sixty-two miles from Tokyo, Japan's capital and largest city. Mount Fuji is also an active volcano, sitting atop the convergence of three tectonic plates. The last time Mount Fuji erupted, in 1707, more than an inch of volcanic ash fell on Tokyo.

Mount Fuji is also the single most popular tourist site in Japan for both Japanese and foreign tourists. More than two hundred thousand people climb to the summit every year, mostly during the warmer summer months. Huts on the route up the mountain cater to climbers, providing refreshments, basic medical supplies, and room to rest. Many people start climbing Mount Fuji at night in order to experience sunrise from the summit. The sunrise from Mount Fuji has a special name: *Goraiko*.

Mount Fuji has been a sacred site for adherents of Shinto since at least the seventh century. Many Shinto shrines dot the base and ascent of Mount Fuji. Shinto shrines honor kami, the supernatural deities of the Shinto faith. The kami of Mount Fuji is Princess Konohanasakuya, whose symbol is the cherry blossom. There is an entire series of shrines to her, called *Asama shrines*. The main Asama shrines are at the base and summit of Mount Fuji, but there are more than a thousand across Japan.

SECTION *Assessment*

Reading Comprehension

1. Why do many Japanese home shrines have both Shinto and Buddhist elements?
2. Describe the typical elements of Shinto worship.
3. Why is the Grand Shrine at Ise significant?
4. What is the purpose of the bronze mirror?
5. Who is the kami of Mount Fuji, and what is her symbol?

Vocabulary

6. Why is the kami body in the Grand Shrine at Ise a bronze mirror?

For Reflection

7. How does connection with nature deepen your spiritual well-being?

Flash Search

8. What is the relationship between bonsai and Japanese religious traditions?

Section 6 CATHOLICS DIALOGUE WITH ADHERENTS OF JAPANESE RELIGIOUS TRADITIONS

A point of comparison between Japanese religious traditions and Catholicism is sacred time. Every religious tradition has its calendar, and sometimes various groups within a tradition use different calendars. In any case, sacred time is usually oriented around the core beliefs of a religious community and essential to the practice of the religious tradition. Sacred time is marked in a regular, periodic fashion such as weeks, months, and years. Individual and communal observances, as well as **feast days** and religious festivals, also mark sacred time.

Sacred Time in Japanese Religious Traditions

Japanese religious traditions have used three different calendars to mark sacred time: the lunar calendar of 354 days in a year, the Gregorian solar calendar with 365 days in a year, and the complex Chinese calendar. However, Japan's religious festivals are based not on the three calendars but around the four

---

feast days Periodic commemorative festivals; for Christians, days celebrated with special liturgies to commemorate the sacred mysteries and events tied to Christian redemption or to honor Mary, the Apostles, martyrs, or saints.

Participants in swan costumes perform a dance during the Sanja Festival in Tokyo, Japan. The three-day event starts with a grand parade with people in traditional costumes performing dances before mikoshi (portable shrines) from the local communities are carried to and from Asakusa Temple.

Hanamatsuri, or flower festival, is held on April 8 and celebrates the Buddha's birthday as well as the return of spring.

seasons of the year. The three combined calendars of Japanese religious traditions are thus filled with numerous festivals. When local and regional festivals are included, the number of religious festivals seems overwhelming. With Shinto and Buddhism intertwining, the celebration of the festivals is often more important to the Japanese than any religious meanings they might have.

Sacred Time in Catholicism

Catholics mark sacred time in a very different manner from those who practice Japanese religious traditions. Rather than using the four seasons of nature to aid in designating sacred time, Catholics look to Easter, the day that marks

The Procession of Silence in Mexico commemorates the Crucifixion of Christ on Good Friday.

Christ's Resurrection, as the preeminent and central event of the Christian year and base other important dates around other significant events in the life of Christ.

Though discrepancies in dating Easter occurred between Eastern and Western Christianity when Western Christianity moved to the Gregorian calendar in 1582, the liturgical seasons' sequence within the liturgical year remains the same. Throughout the Church Year, special feast days honor the lives of Christian saints. Mary, the Mother of God, is the foremost saint. In addition to the designation of feast days for Mary and the saints on the Church's universal calendar, regional or diocesan calendars are created as well.

SECTION *Assessment*

Reading Comprehension

1. How many calendars do Japanese religious traditions typically rely on to designate their sacred time?

2. Why do Eastern and Western Christians use slightly different calendars?

For Reflection

3. How do Christian celebrations of special seasons and feast days help to counterbalance secularism?

Flash Search

4. What are the religious underpinnings of a Japanese tea ceremony?

Section Summaries

Introduction: Heavenly Origins

It is part of the Japanese creation myth that heavenly gods (kami) created Japan when they descended to earth to bring order out of the chaos of the earth. A kami is any spiritual or sacred power or presence. Japanese religious traditions are a commingling of Chinese religious traditions and their various aspects with the indigenous Japanese religion. *Shinto*, "the way of the kami," is the name given to the Japanese indigenous religion.

- Research and briefly summarize the popularity and practice of Japanese religious traditions in your country today.

Section 1: A Brief History of Japanese Religious Traditions

It is difficult to know when the indigenous Japanese religious tradition, Shinto, began because Japan's written history began only around the sixth century CE, when Koreans introduced Chinese culture and Buddhism to Japan. Shinto centers around the many kami that inhabit the natural world. The rulers and people of Japan absorbed elements of Buddhism, Taoism, and Confucianism into their religious and cultural practice. There are several branches of Japanese Buddhism. At various times in history, Japanese governments have supported Shinto or Buddhism as the state religion.

- Find and share an image of nature created by a Zen Buddhist. Write a caption for the image that gives its creator, date of creation, and title.

Section 2: Sacred Stories and Sacred Scriptures

The eighth-century *Kojiki* and the *Nihon Shoki* are the closest Shinto has to sacred writings, though neither is considered a divine revelation. They contain myths, history, and genealogies of ancient Japan. These authoritative texts were commissioned by emperors to legitimize imperial leadership.

- Examine a map of Japan, a nation made up of more than six thousand islands. Answer in three to four paragraphs the following: What role do you think geography plays in the Japanese understanding of themselves as a divine people? How do you think this self-understanding contributed to Japan's imperial overreach before and during World War II?

Section 3: Beliefs and Practices

Shinto and Buddhism are closely intertwined in Japan's religious expressions. The major focus of Shinto is the kami, who imbue the natural world with goodness. People worship kami in local or national shrines, at their home kamidana, or in nature. Some Japanese believe buddhas and bodhisattvas are another form of kami, or vice versa. Harmony and loyalty are the most valued virtues in Japanese life.

- Research the creation of kamidanas. Write at least five steps for creating your own home kamidana.

Section 4: Sacred Time

Three types of calendars are used to mark sacred time in Japanese religious traditions. *Matsuri* is the name for Japanese festivals. Most matsuri are connected with Shinto, though all religious traditions play a part. New Year's Day is the most celebrated festival in Japan, though it is not strictly a religious festival. Buddhism, Shinto, and Christianity are all part of Japanese life-cycle rites.

- Research the meaning and list names and descriptions of three Japanese matsuri that are celebrated today.

Section 5: Sacred Places and Sacred Spaces

It is common for a Japanese home to have both a kamidana and a butsudan. The local shrine is where much of Shinto individual and communal worship takes place. The kami body is an object—often a mirror or sword—into which it is believed a kami descends during a Shinto worship service. The greatest shrine in Japan is the Grand Shrine at Ise, dedicated to the sun goddess, Amaterasu, by the imperial family.

- Search a travel website for the Grand Shrine at Ise. Plan a trip from your home to this shrine. Break down in writing the cost for airfare, three nights at a hotel, and three tourist activities you would undertake during your visit.

Section 6: Catholics Dialogue with Adherents of Japanese Religious Traditions

Though designated in different ways, sacred time is a dimension of all the world's religious traditions. For Japanese religious traditions, sacred time is influenced by nature's four seasons, while for Catholics, sacred time focuses on Easter and events in the life of Jesus.

- How is the Paschal Mystery central to all Catholic religious seasons? Write a two- to three-paragraph explanation.

Chapter Projects

Complete one of these projects by the conclusion of your study of this chapter.

1. Reading and Reporting on *Shogun*

   Read the novel *Shogun* by James Clavell. Write a three- to four-page essay on it that includes the following information, using specific examples.

   - historical context
   - religious context
   - themes of death and karma
   - role of the samurai

2. Martial Arts Demonstration

   Research one form of Japanese martial arts (e.g., karate, judo, aikido, jujitsu, sumo, or several others). Write a two-page essay on the martial art that includes the following:

   - the origin of the martial art
   - the relationship of the martial art and Japanese religious traditions
   - the physical and mental training needed
   - the rituals that are performed before, during, and/or after the event

   Also, learn, practice, and demonstrate two moves from the martial art you chose. Have someone video record your demonstration and add a brief audio narration explaining and naming the moves you demonstrated.

3. Creating a Zen Garden

   Create your own Zen garden, in which rocks are arranged in paths or bridges leading to a focal point to aid in meditation. Zen gardens incorporate the basic landscape where they are placed. The basic items you will need are rocks and stones. Your Zen garden can be inside or outside. Take photos of your Zen garden, and video record yourself narrating the meaning of the pattern and items you have chosen for your Zen garden. In addition, write a one-page essay detailing the history of Zen gardens in Japan and their presence today. Include information about why gardens in general are considered Zen in nature.

4. Writing Your Own Koans

   Recall that a koan is a paradoxical statement or story used to clear the mind of its many obstacles, so that insight and enlightenment can transpire. Review the examples in the Section 1 subsection, "The Expansion of Buddhism," and then do one of the following:

   - Write ten of your own koans that meet the definition.
   - Write three koans that meet the definition and decorate them with symbolic drawings that accentuate their meaning.

5. Essay on Your Choice of Topic

   Write a three- to four-page essay on one of the following topics or on a topic of your choosing that your teacher approves:

   - The Popular Appeal of Japanese Religions in America
   - The Various Methods and Symbols of Ritual Purification
   - The Influences of Chinese Culture on Japan
   - The State of Religion in Japan Today
   - Japanese Art, Architecture, or Literature and Its Relationship to Religion

Key Image

Torii

The torii is the most recognizable symbol of Japanese religious traditions. It is a gate found at the entrance of every Shinto shrine, and it is not unusual to find one at the entry to a Japanese Buddhist temple. The torii separates the space of the ordinary from sacred space where the kami are at once present and protected. The shrine is where religious rituals and practices honoring the kami take place. While a torii in Japan separates the common from the sacred, outside Japan it is a symbol of Japan and Japanese culture. For example, large and small torii are a common feature in home gardens.

The torii characteristically has two vertical posts topped by a crossbeam that is either straight (*shinmei* torii) or slightly curved (*myōjin* torii). There are other styles of torii, but these two are the most common. A second straight crossbeam below the top one acts as a structural stabilizer. Wood or stone are the traditional materials for the torii, but today they may also be made of concrete or metal. Torii made from wood are often painted bright red, symbolizing vitality and offering protection from evil. Also, red has mercury in it, which protects the materials from decay.

It is customary to bow one's head before passing through a torii. Since the torii is the gateway for the kami, one is not to enter through the middle but along the side. Though torii are prevalent at Shinto shrines, they are more generally speaking gateways to the spirit world. A torii sometimes marks a place with a deep spiritual meaning, such as a mountain, river, lake, or island.

The origins of the torii are ambiguous. The first documentation of its existence in Japan is in the tenth century. Some think it arrived on Japan's shores with the coming of Buddhism from either India or China. Others believe it originated in Japanese mythology.

Faithful Adherent

D. T. Suzuki: The Zen Way

Zen Buddhist scholar D. T. Suzuki wrote more than one hundred books and articles, taught at universities, and lectured widely in Japan and the United States. He could speak and write not only in his native Japanese but also in Chinese, German, French, and English. With these skills, Suzuki crossed social, cultural, and generational boundaries and introduced Zen Buddhism to the modern world. Suzuki was not a spiritual leader like Gandhi or Mother Teresa of Calcutta, for his style was more intellectual than pastoral. Though he was comfortable around the intellectual elite, he was just as comfortable around working-class people.

D. T. Suzuki

Born in Kanazawa, Japan, in 1870, Teitarō Suzuki began his life as the Meiji government began its rapid reforms toward modernity. Moves to Westernize and industrialize Japan were well on their way. His father's death when Suzuki was young plunged him and his mother into poverty, but his mother found ways to get her son a good education. His mother died in 1890. Soon after her death, Suzuki began the practice of Zen with a Zen master. Though not a monk, he lived a monk's life at the Zen Buddhist temple in Kamakura.

Because of his expertise in languages, Suzuki was asked in 1893 to translate into English his abbot's speech on Zen Buddhism at the first-ever World's Parliament of Religions in Chicago. Along with Zen Buddhism, several Asian religious traditions made their global debut that year.

In 1894, Suzuki received his Zen name, Daisetsu—hence the abbreviated form D. T. Suzuki. By 1897, Suzuki was in LaSalle, Illinois, working at Open Court Publishing Company translating Eastern religious texts, including the

Tao Te Ching, into English. He published his first English-language work, called *Outlines of Mahayana Buddhism*, in 1907. He returned to Japan in 1909 and taught at the university level. In 1911, Suzuki married Beatrice Erskine Lane, a scholarly Scottish-American **Theosophist**. Together they founded in 1921 the Eastern Buddhist Society and began publishing the English-language journal *The Eastern Buddhist*. Both the society and the journal thrive today.

Suzuki's wife died in 1939. By then, he had mostly retired. He spent World War II in Kamakura meditating, writing, and publishing. After the war, Suzuki returned to teach in colleges in both the United States and Japan. By then, the name D. T. Suzuki had become synonymous with Zen Buddhism worldwide. He became a celebrity, in great demand for speeches, public appearances, and interviews. D. T. Suzuki died in Japan in 1966 at the age of ninety-five.

Reading Comprehension

1. What did Suzuki's mother value?
2. What skills of Suzuki's were most useful in introducing Zen Buddhism to a Western audience?

For Reflection

3. Why might people be attracted to Zen Buddhism?

Theosophist An adherent of Theosophy, a late nineteenth-century esoteric philosophical movement with roots in Western philosophy, Hinduism, and Buddhism. Theosophy is the belief that one can have profound insight into God and the universe through ecstasy and other phenomena. Helena Blavatsky, a Russian immigrant to the United States, is credited with founding the movement.

Prayer

This Shinto Prayer for Peace was one of twelve prayers prayed at a World Peace Day in Assisi, Italy.

> Although the people living across the ocean surrounding us,
> I believe, are all our brothers and sisters,
> why are there constant troubles in this world?
> Why do winds and waves rise in the ocean surrounding us?
> I only earnestly wish
> that the wind will soon puff away all the clouds
> which are hanging over the tops of the mountains.

EPILOGUE

Prayers of Pope Francis

These two prayers for universal solidarity are found at the conclusion of Pope Francis's 2020 encyclical, *Fratelli Tutti* (*On Fraternity and Social Friendship*).

A Prayer to the Creator

Lord, Father of our human family,
you created all human beings equal in dignity:
pour forth into our hearts a fraternal spirit
and inspire in us a dream of renewed encounter,
dialogue, justice, and peace.
Move us to create healthier societies
and a more dignified world,
a world without hunger, poverty, violence, and war.

May our hearts be open
to all the peoples and nations of the earth.
May we recognize the goodness and beauty
that you have sown in each of us,
and thus forge bonds of unity, common projects,
and shared dreams. Amen.

An Ecumenical Christian Prayer

O God, Trinity of love,
from the profound communion of your divine life,
pour out upon us a torrent of fraternal love.
Grant us the love reflected in the actions of Jesus,
in his family of Nazareth,
and in the early Christian community.

Grant that we Christians may live the Gospel,
discovering Christ in each human being,
recognizing him crucified
in the sufferings of the abandoned
and forgotten of our world,
and risen in each brother or sister
who makes a new start.

Come, Holy Spirit, show us your beauty,
reflected in all the peoples of the earth,
so that we may discover anew
that all are important and all are necessary,
different faces of the one humanity
that God so loves. Amen.

A

APPENDIX A
Religions with Christian and American Roots

FOR THE WORSHIP OF GOD
AND THE SERVICE OF MAN

Introduction
CLOSE TO HOME

Hopefully, this course broadened your understanding of some of the world's religious traditions, beginning with those traditions more familiar to you (Judaism, Christianity, and Islam) before widening the circle to include religious traditions with roots far away in both time and location (Hinduism, Buddhism, Chinese religious traditions, and Japanese religious traditions). In our increasingly close-knit world, even these traditions had likely entered your consciousness before this class.

This appendix draws the circle more tightly to your own experience as we examine five American religious traditions with roots mostly in nineteenth-century Protestant Christianity, though they advocate some beliefs that fall outside traditional Protestant Christianity. They are religious traditions to which some of your neighbors, friends, relatives—or perhaps even you—subscribe. We will briefly look at the various traditions' historical backgrounds and some of their beliefs and practices, which are often misunderstood. The sections for each tradition will conclude with at least one topic for dialogue with Catholicism.

RELIGIONS WITH CHRISTIAN AND AMERICAN ROOTS: TIMELINE OF KEY EVENTS

CE

1782 .... Birth of William Miller, Adventist movement

1805 .... Birth of Joseph Smith, Church of Jesus Christ of Latter-day Saints (Mormons)

1821 .... Birth of Mary Baker Eddy, Church of Christ, Scientist

1827 .... Birth of Ellen White, Seventh-day Adventists

1846 .... Brigham Young brings Mormons to Salt Lake area of Utah

1852 .... Birth of Charles Russell, Watch Tower Bible and Tract Society (Jehovah's Witnesses)

1869 .... Birth of Joseph Rutherford, Watch Tower Bible and Tract Society

1961 .... Unitarian and Universalist Churches combine to form the Unitarian Universalist Association

Section 1
CHURCH OF JESUS CHRIST OF LATTER-DAY SAINTS

A Brief History

The Church of Jesus Christ of Latter-day Saints, commonly called the Mormon Church, traces its origins to Joseph Smith Jr. (1805–1844). At age fourteen, Smith was praying in a grove near his family's farm in upstate New York, seeking guidance about which church to join after attending a church revival. Two figures he took to be God the Father and Jesus Christ appeared to him in a vision and directed him not to claim membership in any church because they had all become corrupted.

Smith was told the church founded by Jesus would be restored to its original purity in teachings and priesthood. In 1823, a heavenly being named Moroni appeared to Smith and directed him to a hill where metal plates containing ancient hieroglyphics were buried. Over the next four years, Smith translated the plates into what is known as the Book of Mormon. (The term *Mormon*, used to describe both the church and its members, comes from this text.) These sacred scriptures contain religious texts of an ancient American civilization, including the appearance of the Risen Jesus on American soil. The Church of Jesus Christ of Latter-day Saints was established in 1830, the same year the Book of Mormon was published.

Followers of Smith were persecuted. Finding it necessary to move several times, in 1839 the Mormons built their first temple in Nauvoo, Illinois. However, the community found opposition even there. One reason for the persecution was that the Mormons practiced **polygamy**, arising from a revelation

This engraving shows the angel Moroni delivering the plates of the Book of Mormon to Joseph Smith.

of Smith's. A more practical reason for opposition was that the Mormons had established a powerful voting bloc in Nauvoo, thereby wiping away the locals' political control. In 1844, Smith and his brother Hyrum were killed by an angry mob after being imprisoned in nearby Carthage.

Brigham Young succeeded Joseph Smith as leader of the Mormons. Some members of the church believed that only a descendant of Joseph Smith—in this case, his son Joseph Smith III—should head the church. A splinter group of those followers formed the Reorganized Church of Jesus Christ of Latter-day Saints, now called the Community of Christ, with headquarters to this day in Independence, Missouri. Because of continuing persecution, Brigham Young led the Mormons on a 1,300-mile journey across the Great Plains and into the Salt Lake basin of Utah. Salt Lake City, Utah, continues to be the center of the Mormon Church.

Today, the Church of Jesus Christ of Latter-day Saints is among the fastest-growing religions in the world. There are about seventeen million members worldwide, with approximately half living in the United States. Chile, Uruguay, and several South Pacific nations have a higher percentage of Mormons than the United States, in which Mormons make up about 2 percent of the population.

---

polygamy The practice or religious custom of having more than one wife or husband at the same time.

Beliefs and Practices

Mormons hold that primitive Christianity, founded by Jesus, was corrupted through **apostasy** around the second century. To restore the church of Jesus Christ, Mormons believe there is a need for a new revelation, a new scripture, and a new priesthood, all found in the church restored by Joseph Smith. Though Mormons accept that elements of truth are found in all religious traditions, they also believe that they alone are the true Christians. Mormons do not consider themselves Protestants but Christians according to the purest form of Christianity as founded by Jesus. These are other essential Mormon beliefs:

- Salvation is possible only within their church. To save ancestors, Mormons hold a service that allows for the baptism of dead relatives of church members.
- Native Americans are descended from one of the ten lost tribes of Israel.
- Jesus is not God (though Mormons do name the traditional Trinity).
- Jesus will return to earth and set up a new Jerusalem and a thousand-year reign in America.

Salt Lake Mormon Temple in Salt Lake City, Utah.

apostasy The abandonment of one's religion.

As Mormons also hold that God's revelations did not stop with the last page of the Bible, neither do revelations cease with the Book of Mormon. The president of the church (the name for the foremost Mormon leader) is seen as a prophet, no different from the biblical prophets. Mormon presidents succeeding Joseph Smith have received new revelations. For example, President Wilford Woodruff ended the Mormon practice of polygamy at the end of the nineteenth century after receiving a revelation. In 1978, President Spencer Kimball received a revelation to allow males of African descent to be ordained to the Mormon priesthood. Blacks had been denied the priesthood because the church claimed they were descendants of Cain, the murderer of his brother Abel.

In addition to the Book of Mormon, the Pearl of Great Price (writings and revelations of Joseph Smith) and Doctrine and Covenants (writings and revelations since the restoration in 1830) are considered sacred writings of the Mormon church.

The Mormon worship service is simple: prayers, singing of hymns, listening to sermons delivered by laypeople, and a celebration of the Lord's Supper using bread and water. Water is used instead of wine as Mormons are forbidden to use all drugs, including alcohol, tobacco, and caffeine.

Baptism by immersion happens at the age of eight or older. Proxies are baptized on behalf of dead ancestors. Mormons spend a lot of time investigating and maintaining family genealogies to include relatives who were not baptized when alive in this type of baptism.

The church is very involved in missionary work. It is common for young people around the age of twenty to participate in two years of missionary work, often in another country. About fifty thousand people engage in missionary work annually.

Catholics Dialogue with Mormons

There is little common belief between Catholicism and the Church of Jesus Christ of Latter-day Saints. Most fundamentally, Catholics and other Christians believe that Jesus Christ is the Son of God and the Second Person of the Blessed Trinity. Mormons believe that Jesus was the first spirit born to heavenly parents. By not believing in the divinity of Jesus, Mormons place themselves outside orthodox Christianity.

Catholics believe in one God who is a unity of Three Persons—Father, Son, and Holy Spirit. Mormons believe in three separate Gods in one Godhead and that Elohim and Jehovah are separate gods. Catholics do not believe in a baptism of the dead; while Jesus affirms that baptism is necessary for salvation, God "himself is not bound by his sacraments" (*CCC*, 1257). Mormons believe that their church is the only true and living church. Catholics hold that the Catholic Church was founded by Christ and made manifest on the day of Pentecost.

Mormon missionaries walk to Sunday lunch in Colonia Juárez, Mexico.

While there are many differences between the two faiths, both Catholics and Mormons see evangelization as an intrinsic aspect of their respective religious traditions. Both are quite involved in missionary activities throughout the world. Both are also active in caring for the poor and disadvantaged. It is not unusual for Mormon communities to use Catholic Relief Services to get food, money, and other material for people in need. Finally, Catholics and Mormons (and all people) alike are dependent on God's grace and mercy for their life and salvation.

SECTION *Assessment*

Reading Comprehension

1. From where does the term *Mormon* come?
2. Why is the Church of Jesus Christ of Latter-day Saints not considered a Protestant church?
3. Why do Mormons allow baptism of the dead by proxy?
4. What is one essential difference between Catholicism and Mormonism?

Vocabulary

5. When was *polygamy* removed as an official practice of Mormonism?

For Reflection

6. What do you think about the Mormon practice of baptism by proxy?
7. If members of a new religion descended on a rural town today, what do you think would be the reaction of the local people?
8. Why do you think the Church of Jesus Christ of Latter-day Saints is one of the world's fastest-growing religions?

Flash Search

9. What criteria does one have to meet in order to audition for the world-famous Mormon Tabernacle Choir?

Section 2

SEVENTH-DAY ADVENTISTS

A Brief History

Adventist is the name for those who believe the Second Coming, or Advent, of Jesus is imminent. The Seventh-day Adventist Church emerged from a nineteenth-century millennialist movement. *Millennialism* is the belief that at Jesus' Second Coming, he would reign on earth for one thousand years.

William Miller (1782–1849), a Baptist preacher, taught that the Bible was clear about when and how the Second Coming of Jesus would occur. Miller taught that Jesus would return to earth in a physical form, and he also calculated a specific date. Miller gained some followers, calling themselves Adventists, who waited expectantly with him.

When Jesus did not come on March 21, 1844, the last possible date Miller established, he recalculated the date for seven months later. When the Second Coming did not occur as expected for a second time, it was called the **Great Disappointment**, and many of his original followers left Miller. Some Adventists modified their teaching. They said that the Second Coming was preceded by an **investigative judgment** in which God would judge the living and the dead, pronounce the findings, and then execute judgment. Only after the investigative judgment was complete could Jesus return to earth and begin his thousand-year reign. They believed that the investigative judgment began in 1844 and that it would continue until the Second Coming.

The Seventh-day Adventist Church, officially formed in 1863, came from this movement. Ellen G. White (1827–1915), a follower of Miller, was considered a prophetess among the Seventh-day Adventists. She wrote several books and gave lectures throughout much of the nineteenth-century

English-speaking world. Besides looking to the Bible for information about the Second Coming, church members strictly followed the Bible for Sabbath and dietary laws. As the Jewish Sabbath had been Saturday and early Christians also observed it, Saturday, the seventh day, was restored as the Sabbath. Seventh-day Adventists prohibited alcohol, nicotine, and caffeine use because of their harmful effects on the body, the temple of the Holy Spirit.

Ellen G. White

Beliefs and Practices

Seventh-day Adventists believe the Bible is the sole source of authority for their members. However, their interpretation of the Bible deviates in many areas from most other Christians'. For example, Seventh-day Adventists believe that Jesus' act of redemption was potentially for everyone but is effective only for those who genuinely believe. They also hold that the righteous will be resurrected to heaven with the Second Coming of Jesus, whereas the unrighteous will be annihilated in hell. Hence, they do not believe that all souls are immortal.

Seventh-day Adventists are initiated through instruction and baptism by immersion. Saturday, the seventh day, is their day of worship. Concerning creation, Seventh-day Adventists deny the theory of evolution and take a literal approach to understanding the creation stories of the Bible.

In addition to abstaining from alcohol, nicotine, and caffeine, many Seventh-day Adventists are vegetarians. Some also abstain from dancing, going

---

Great Disappointment The occasion when many Adventists left William Miller after Jesus' Second Coming did not occur on March 21, 1844, the second date Miller calculated Jesus would return by.

investigative judgment According to the Adventists, the time prior to the Second Coming when judgment will take place on the living and the dead.

Baptism in the Caribbean Sea in Guadeloupe.

to the theater, and any other activity deemed harmful to the soul. Ironically, though Ellen White played a significant role in the foundation of the Seventh-day Adventists, the church does not sanction the ordination of women.

Catholics Dialogue with Seventh-day Adventists

Seventh-day Adventists agree with many Catholic doctrines and teachings, including belief in the Trinity, the divinity of Christ, the virgin birth, and the resurrection of the dead. Their baptism is considered valid by Catholics and other Christians. Seventh-day Adventists believe in the doctrine of Original Sin and that both faith and good works merit a person's salvation.

However, Seventh-day Adventists also hold teachings contrary to Catholic teachings. For example, Catholics (and other Christians) disagree with Adventists who say that in not keeping Saturday as the Lord's Day, most Christians are breaking the covenant God made with Moses on Mount Sinai. Most Christians celebrate Sunday as the fulfillment of the Sabbath, for Sunday is the day that Christ rose from the dead. St. Justin Martyr wrote:

> We all gather on the day of the sun, for it is the first day [after the Jewish Sabbath, but also the first day] when God, separating matter from darkness, made the world; and on the same day Jesus Christ our Savior rose from the dead. (1 *Apology*, 67)

All Christians believe in the Second Coming of Jesus, and Catholics are no exception. At every Mass, Catholics proclaim that Christ will "come again." As part of Adventists' belief in the Second Coming, they hold that the unrighteous will be destroyed in hell's fires. Catholics believe that every human possesses an immortal soul (see *CCC*, 366), and that each person "receives his eternal recompense in his immortal soul from the moment of his death" (*CCC*, 1051).

SECTION *Assessment*

Reading Comprehension

1. Summarize the origins of the Adventist movement.
2. Why do Seventh-day Adventists worship on Saturday rather than on Sunday?
3. Why does the Catholic Church hold that Sunday is the proper day of worship?

Vocabulary

4. What was the *Great Disappointment*?

For Reflection

5. Why do you think some Christians wish to forecast the exact date of Jesus' Second Coming?
6. Do you think it is important to have a specific day of the week for communal worship of God? Why or why not?

Flash Search

7. What was Harold Camping known for?
8. Research and summarize the effect the Seventh-day Adventist Church had on the work of John Kellogg.

Section 3
WATCH TOWER BIBLE AND TRACT SOCIETY

A Brief History

Charles Russell (1852–1916) officially founded the Jehovah's Witnesses, then known as Zion's Watch Tower Bible and Tract Society, in Pennsylvania in 1884. Raised a Presbyterian, Russell had been studying with other Bible students attempting to pinpoint the Second Coming of Jesus. He calculated that the fall of 1874 was the time when Jesus would establish his invisible reign in heaven and that 1914 was the year Satan would be expelled to earth. He also believed that would be the time for the earthly battle of Armageddon between Satan and Jesus. When nothing occurred in the fall of 1914, other dates were set, but no battle of Armageddon ever took place.

Charles Taze Russell

Russell was succeeded as president of the Watch Tower Society by Joseph Rutherford (1869–1942). Rutherford gave further shape to the Society by centralizing it after the headquarters were moved to Brooklyn and refining the missionary work of the followers. Rutherford believed that the establishment of Jesus' invisible reign was a **theocracy** and that the Society must be ready for Jesus' rule. In 1931, Rutherford adopted the name "Jehovah's Witnesses" to emphasize Jehovah (another name for Yahweh), the God of the Hebrew Scriptures, as the one, true God and those who witnessed to Jehovah as the faithful followers of the one God. Nathan Knorr (1905–1977), the next president, expanded the publication of Jehovah's Witnesses materials, translated a Bible used by all Jehovah's Witnesses known as the *New World Translation of Holy Scriptures*, and established the Watch Tower Bible School of Gilead in New York for the training of leaders.

Presently Jehovah's Witnesses can be found throughout the world. However, they do not always find a welcome, for their allegiance is not to any government but only to God's theocracy. Their various publications are translated into numerous languages for worldwide distribution. In Europe, their affiliated group is known as the International Bible Students Association.

Beliefs and Practices

A Watch Tower cart stand in Munich, Germany.

Many of the beliefs of Jehovah's Witnesses are traditional Christian beliefs. Jehovah's Witnesses believe the Bible is God's Word and the sole source of religious and moral authority. They believe that Jesus is the Son of God, born of a virgin, and the reconciler of humankind to God.

However, Jehovah's Witnesses interpret the Bible in several ways that many traditional Christians do not accept as orthodox. Also, many traditional biblical scholars reject the Jehovah's Witnesses' *New World Translation of the Holy Scriptures*, citing that the translation sources are not the original Hebrew and Greek biblical texts and that the translation is bent to reflect the Society's teachings.

---

theocracy A government that is ruled by God or by one who is divinely inspired.

Jehovah's Witnesses believe that they represent the primitive church and that salvation comes only through the Society's beliefs and works. Jehovah's Witnesses hold that all others who claim to be Christians are false Christians and that all who fail to acknowledge Christ in any way are pagans.

Jehovah's Witnesses do not acknowledge the Holy Trinity. They call Jesus the Son of God; however, they believe that he is not God but instead is subject to God. They believe that Jesus was the Archangel Michael before his earthly birth. Nor do the Jehovah's Witnesses believe that the Holy Spirit is God, believing instead that he is merely a vehicle to explain how Jehovah is present to and connects with creation.

Jehovah's Witnesses explain Jesus' Crucifixion and Resurrection in a spiritual sense. Jehovah's Witnesses do not believe that Jesus was crucified on a cross. Neither do they believe in Jesus' bodily resurrection. They understand the Greek word for *cross* to mean one piece of timber, like a stake or a pole without a crossbeam. Since the cross and crucifix were not used as a symbol by the earliest Christians, Jehovah's Witnesses think of them as pagan symbols.

Jehovah's Witnesses have a strong idea of what will happen at Armageddon. They believe that Jesus will be victorious over Satan, the earth will be purified, and Jesus will set up a theocracy. In the meantime, Satan is on earth using everything at his disposal to win the battle. In particular, secular governments and all the world's religious traditions are instruments of Satan. Hence, Jehovah's Witnesses pledge allegiance to no government but Jehovah's. They do not salute a flag, serve in public office or the military, or vote in open elections. Children of Jehovah's Witnesses who attend public schools are not allowed to celebrate Halloween, Christmas, or any other holiday. In time of war, Jehovah's Witnesses are categorized as conscientious objectors and are dismissed from participation in the armed services.

Regarding the afterlife, Jehovah's Witnesses do not believe in damnation or a hell that is eternal. When a person dies, the soul dies. At the time of the resurrection of the righteous, Jehovah will create a new, perfect body and reinstate the soul of the person.

Bible study is an integral part of the life of a Jehovah's Witness. Besides the Bible, the periodicals *The Watchtower* and *Awake!* are very important to the Society. A common practice is to distribute these and other literature door to door and on street corners.

A Kingdom Hall in Belper, England.

The place of worship for Jehovah's Witnesses is a Kingdom Hall, where the congregation is known as the "company." There is no day of rest, for every day is holy. Rather than times of worship, Jehovah's Witnesses have various kinds of meetings on each day of the week in which there are talks on topics found in a recent *Watchtower* or training for multiple ministries, especially door-to-door witnessing.

The average Jehovah's Witness who attends meetings during the week and solicits door-to-door is known as a *publisher.* Each publisher has a neighborhood for which he or she is responsible, while each Kingdom Hall is responsible for a geographical area containing several neighborhoods.

The only particular day celebrated by Jehovah's Witnesses is the annual Memorial of Christ's Death, because of Christ's command in the Bible to do so. Neither Christmas nor Easter is celebrated because Jehovah did not command it. The first Christians did not observe those days, and since they are marked by other "false" Christians and pagans, Jehovah's Witnesses believe them to be pagan feasts. Jehovah's Witnesses do not celebrate birthdays for the same reasons.

A controversial belief of Jehovah's Witnesses, established in 1945, is the prohibition of medical blood transfusions. Blood transfusions are interpreted as "eating blood," something forbidden by Jehovah in the Old and New Testaments. The controversy often becomes heated when a child requires a blood transfusion—perhaps to save his or her life—and the parents refuse. Governmental child protection agencies sometimes attempt to override the parents' decision through legal means.

All the teachings and practices of Jehovah's Witnesses have one goal: to establish a theocracy on earth. Jehovah's Witnesses hope to purify the world of all evil before Christ sets up his earthly Kingdom.

Catholics Dialogue with Jehovah's Witnesses

As outlined previously, there are many readily apparent differences between the beliefs of Jehovah's Witnesses and Catholic beliefs. One of the most central differences is the Jehovah's Witnesses' understanding of Christ's divinity. Jehovah's Witnesses believe that although Christ is God's Son, he is inferior to God the Father and created by him. They hold that the title of Christ as "firstborn" of God's creation implies that he succeeded from God and is inferior to God. Catholics believe, rather, that there was no time when the Son did not exist (see John 1:1–3). Jesus Christ is begotten, not made. He is equal to the Father. He is both God and man.

Jehovah's Witnesses use the Bible to support their beliefs. There are two problems with their approach. First, like some other Christians, they are apt to quote passages out of context, using only those passages that support their beliefs while ignoring other passages that contradict their beliefs. Second, the Jehovah's Witnesses use their own translation of the Bible, the *New World Translation*, which is regarded by many impartial theologians as a translation made without scholarly care and thus highly inaccurate.

SECTION *Assessment*

Reading Comprehension

1. What is the significance of the name "Jehovah's Witnesses"?
2. What is the goal of Jehovah's Witnesses' teaching and practice?

3. Why do Jehovah's Witnesses not celebrate holidays and birthdays?

For Reflection

4. In your opinion, have Christian holidays become too secularized? Why or why not?

Flash Search

5. Look up a legal case in which a judge ruled against Jehovah's Witness parents and allowed a blood transfusion to take place. What was the reasoning of the court?

Section 4
CHURCH OF CHRIST, SCIENTIST

A Brief History

Mary Baker Eddy (1821–1910) of New Hampshire founded the Church of Christ, Scientist (commonly known as Christian Science) in 1879. Eddy was raised in a strict Protestant Congregationalist home, where she grew to love the Christian Bible. She was ill for much of her childhood and early adulthood. She sought various healing methods, both conventional and unconventional, but never got better. When Eddy was in her forties, she fell on an icy sidewalk and severely injured herself. On reading one of Jesus' miracles from the Bible, she suddenly realized that sickness and suffering are merely illusions and can be overcome by right thinking. Eddy believed that the discovery of this right mind, the mind of God, allowed her to be instantly healed. She spent several years intensely studying the Bible to learn precisely what her discovery meant. Her book, *Science and Health*, which Eddy revised several times, forms the basic Christian Science religious doctrine.

Mary Baker Eddy

Eddy founded the First Church of Christ, Scientist in Boston, where it still exists today. The church expanded rapidly during the first half of the twentieth

Although she first published Science and Health with Key to the Scriptures *in 1875, Mary Baker Eddy continued revising and updating it for the rest of her life.*

century before membership leveled off. Though local churches are self-governing, Eddy's *Manual of the Mother Church* sets guidelines for them. There are Christian Science churches throughout the world, mostly in predominantly Protestant countries.

Beliefs and Practices

Through her vigorous study of the Bible, Mary Baker Eddy came to believe that the teachings of Jesus, especially those concerning healing, had been lost over the centuries. She intended to recapture such teachings for her generation. Eddy considered the Bible and her book *Science and Health* equally authoritative texts.

To Eddy and her followers, God is not a masculine God but a Father-Mother who is reliable and compassionate. Christian Scientists deny the divinity of Jesus, though they do refer to Jesus as the Son of God. What is distinctive about Christian Scientists is their belief that physical healing comes through spiritual means—or God—alone. Though suffering and death—the effects of evil—may seem to exist, they are only illusions that can be removed when a person develops a union with God. Prayer is the treatment for physical ills. Christian Scientists pray to possess the Mind of Christ so that the physical is healed through the healing of the mind and heart.

A Christian Scientist turns to a registered Christian Science practitioner when in need of physical healing. The church authorizes and pays these practitioners to devote themselves full-time to assisting the healing of other church members through prayer. These practitioners are not intercessors; they believe that only God heals through God-given laws. Rather, the practitioner prays with the member for guidance.

Contrary to popular belief, Christian Scientists do not excommunicate members of their church for seeking outside medical advice. They encourage their members to adhere to public health laws, including immunization requirements. They also seek medical help for baby deliveries. They visit dentists and eye doctors as well.

Though Christian Science does not have a creed per se, *Science and Health* outlines six tenets:

1. As adherents of Truth, we take the inspired Word of the Bible as our sufficient guide to eternal Life.

2. We acknowledge and adore one supreme and infinite God. We recognize his Son, one Christ; the Holy Ghost or divine Comforter; and man in God's image and likeness.

3. We acknowledge God's forgiveness of sin in the destruction of sin and the spiritual understanding that casts evil as unreal. But the belief in sin is punished so long as the belief lasts.

4. We acknowledge Jesus' atonement as the evidence of divine, efficacious Love, unfolding man's unity with God through Christ Jesus the Way-shower; and we acknowledge that man is saved through Christ, through Truth, Life, and Love as demonstrated by the Galilean Prophet in healing the sick and overcoming sin and death.

5. We acknowledge that the crucifixion of Jesus and his resurrection served to uplift faith to understand eternal Life, even the allness of Soul and Spirit and the nothingness of matter.

---

6. And we solemnly promise to watch and pray for that Mind to be in us which was also in Christ Jesus; to do unto others as we would have them do unto us; and to be merciful, just, and pure.

The presence of a Christian Science Reading Room near every Christian Science Church highlights the importance placed on study. The public is welcomed into Christian Science Reading Rooms to peruse the church's resources in order to find out more about the religion. Always available in a reading room is the current week's "lesson sermon" from the Mother Church taken from the "pastor of the church"—that is, the combination of the Bible and *Science and Health*. The lessons comprise the sermons that will be read at every Christian Science Church worldwide on the coming Sundays. There are twenty-six rotating subjects.

Sunday service is quite simple. Two readers are chosen from the congregation. The selected readers read from the Bible, *Science and Health*, and the lesson sermon from the Mother Church. There may also be public testimonials on healing.

Catholics Dialogue with Christian Scientists

Christian Science denies most Catholic dogma and doctrine, including the existence of a Creator God, the divinity of Christ, redemption, free will, Original Sin, actual sin, Magisterial teaching, the sacraments, the resurrection of the body, angels, demons, eternal rewards and punishments, and the necessity of faith, grace, and prayer.

As for the healings taught and claimed by Christian Science, they are separate from the gift of miracles that were given to the Apostles (see Mark 16:17–18). The gift of healing is not intended to be a regular part of Christ's gift of priesthood, for physical healing is not essential to a person's salvation. Rather, the Catholic Church believes that God heals physically and spiritually at God's pleasure and often through the Sacrament of the Anointing of the Sick. While Christian Scientists find suffering illusive, Catholics find it redemptive, believing that it is through our own suffering that we share in the suffering of Christ. And as we share in Christ's suffering, we also share in his Resurrection.

SECTION *Assessment*

Reading Comprehension

1. What did Mary Baker Eddy discover about healing?
2. Why is it incorrect to say that Christian Scientists are hostile to the medical profession?
3. What is the role of registered Christian Science practitioners?
4. Name one Christian Science belief that contradicts Catholic doctrine.

For Reflection

5. What do you think is the connection between physical health and spiritual health?
6. What do you think Jesus means when he tells people that it is their faith that has healed them?

Flash Search

7. What is the *Christian Science Monitor*?

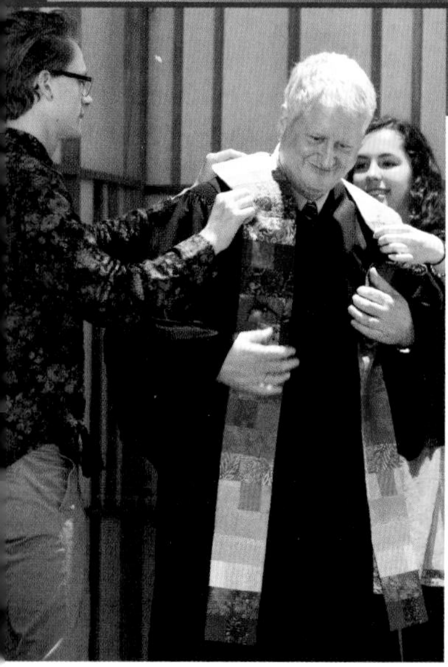

Section 5
UNITARIAN UNIVERSALISTS

A Brief History

The Unitarian Universalist Association was formed in 1961 by a consolidation of the Universalist Church of America and the American Unitarian Association. Congregations associated with this association are commonly called Unitarian.

Although their predecessor organizations began as Christian denominations, Unitarian Universalists (often called Unitarians) today do not consider themselves Christian, as they believe that spiritual wisdom can be found in all the world's religious traditions. In its origins, the Universalist movement advocated a belief that all will be saved and no one will suffer eternal damnation. In its origins, the Unitarian movement held that the Christian God is one entity rather than a Trinity. Some famous Americans have been Unitarians (John Adams, Ralph Waldo Emerson, and Susan B. Anthony) and Universalists (P. T. Barnum and Clara Barton).

Susan B. Anthony, women's rights activist.

Headquarters for the Unitarian Universalist Church in the United States is in Boston, but there is no central control over the many congregations. Each congregation is autonomous in all matters of government, finance, and communal religious practices. On the international level, the Unitarian Universalist Association is connected with religious groups through the International Association for Religious Freedom.

P. T. Barnum, showman, politician, and businessman.

The Unitarian Universalist Association has no formal creed, though it does affirm seven principles. They have no sacred text, for they believe that the various sacred texts of the world contain much wisdom and guidance. Unitarians are encouraged to form their own beliefs and moral judgments based on experience, science, and reason. Ultimate authority comes from within the individual. Unitarians believe that wisdom is found in all the religious traditions of the world.

Beliefs and Practices

Unitarian Universalists follow a covenant of beliefs called the "Unitarian Universalist Statement of Principles and Purposes" that offers guidelines not only on what they should believe but on how they should live their lives. These are the seven principles member congregations covenant to affirm and promote:

1. The inherent worth and dignity of every person.
2. Justice, equity, and compassion in human relations.
3. Acceptance of one another and encouragement to spiritual growth in our congregations.
4. A free and responsible search for truth and meaning.
5. The right of conscience and the use of the democratic process within our congregations and in society at large.
6. The goal of world community with peace, liberty, and justice for all.
7. Respect for the interdependent web of all existence of which we are a part.

These are the six sources of the "living tradition" that member congregations affirm and promote:

1. Direct experience of that transcending mystery and wonder, affirmed in all cultures, which moves us to a renewal of the spirit and an openness to the forces that create and uphold life.
2. Words and deeds of prophetic people which challenge us to confront powers and structures of evil with justice, compassion, and the transforming power of love.

3. Wisdom from the world's religions which inspires us in our ethical and spiritual life.
4. Jewish and Christian teachings which call us to respond to God's love by loving our neighbors as ourselves.
5. Humanist teachings which counsel us to heed the guidance of reason and the results of science and warn us against idolatries of the mind and spirit.
6. Spiritual teachings of Earth-centered traditions which celebrate the sacred circle of life and instruct us to live in harmony with the rhythms of nature.

The religious practices of Unitarian Universalists vary from congregation to congregation, though most have regular weekly worship. Some call themselves a society or fellowship rather than a congregation. Unitarian Universalists draw from various sources for their communal worship: the Judeo-Christian heritage, other major world religious traditions, Earth-centered religions such as Native American religious traditions, humanism, prophetic men and women, and direct experience.

Catholics Dialogue with Unitarian Universalists

Unitarians typically do not believe in the divinity of Christ or the doctrine of the Holy Trinity. Unitarians do put into practice the message of love and service to the poor expressed in their principles and in the purpose of the Gospel, especially in the **Beatitudes**. However, there are few other doctrinal agreements between Unitarians and Catholics. One reason for this is that Unitarians have no formal doctrine of beliefs.

Beatitudes Meaning "surprise happiness"; the eight Beatitudes preached by Jesus in the Sermon on the Mount respond to a person's natural desire for happiness.

SECTION *Assessment*

Reading Comprehension

1. Why is the Unitarian Universalist Church not considered a Christian church?
2. What are some sources Unitarians draw on for worship?

For Reflection

3. What would it be like to participate in a religious community without a formal creed?
4. Create a "Statement of Principles and Purposes" for your own life with at least five items.

Flash Search

5. Besides John Adams, three other US presidents were Unitarian. Who were they?

B

APPENDIX B
Indigenous Religious Traditions

Introduction
WHO ARE INDIGENOUS PEOPLE?

The oldest religious tradition studied thus far in this book is Hinduism, the origins of which date roughly to 1500 BCE. Many indigenous religious traditions began long before then. An *indigenous religious tradition* is one originating in a particular region and among specific people with traditions from the distant past.

Indigenous people reside on every continent but Antarctica. As a small example, there are the Tibetans in Asia, the Basotho in Africa, the Warlpiri in

Hausa animism is practiced in parts of Nigeria. Practitioners believe that there are both good and bad spirits that can be controlled through ritual, dance, and music. This person is possessed by Dogoa, a spirit who brings sickness to humankind.

The Big Horn Medicine Wheel in Wyoming rests within the land originally lived on by the Crow people. The medicine wheel is a sacred site to many people of many nations and was declared a National Historic Landmark in 1970.

Australia, the Sami in Europe, the Yupik in North America, and the Aymara in South America. These various indigenous groups are quite diverse around the world and within continents. Nevertheless, there are a few identifiable common beliefs and practices among indigenous religious traditions around the world:

- An underlying spiritual power or life force animates all things visible and invisible.
- Spirits are alive in a spirit world that permeates heaven and earth and all things in between. Humanity is part of one large living organism.
- Ancestors are venerated.
- Specialized **shamans**, medicine men and women, priests and priestesses, and spirit mediums engage with the spirit world.
- Sacred stories, myths, and legends are passed on orally from one generation to the next.

To illuminate the notion of indigenous religious traditions, we will explore Native American and indigenous African religious traditions.

---

shamans People who can access the spirit world, either good or evil, often through a trance at a ceremony or ritual. They often practice divination and healing.

Section 1
NATIVE AMERICAN RELIGIOUS TRADITIONS

For our purposes, "Native Americans" will refer to those peoples who first began migrating thousands of years ago to present-day Canada, the United States, and Mexico through the Bering Strait. In Canada, they are called First Nations people and Inuit; in Mexico, they are called Native Mexicans. Today, some Native American peoples straddle political boundaries; examples are the Akwesasne Mohawks along the Canada–United States border and the Tohono O'odham along the Mexico–United States border. Like other religious traditions, Native American religious traditions have sacred stories, beliefs and practices, sacred time, and sacred places and spaces.

Sacred Stories and Sacred Scriptures

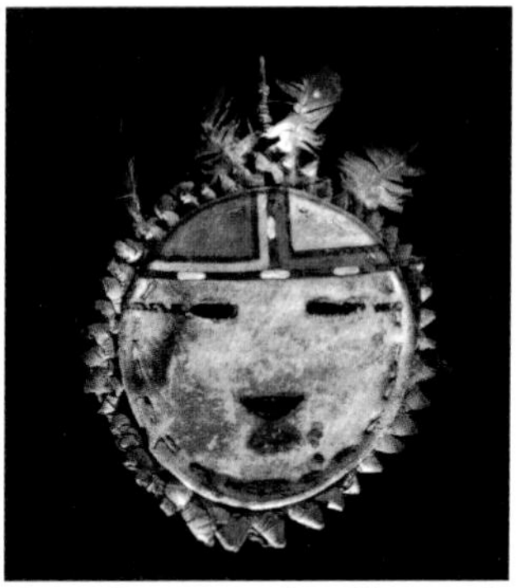

A mask representing Tawa, the Hopi sun god. He was the first being in existence. The Hopi Tribe is a sovereign nation located in northeastern Arizona.

Elders orally pass the sacred stories or myths on to the next generation. However, the stories are not set in stone; each story has several variations. Creation stories are the most prevalent. They are categorized into two major types: **emergence myths** and **earth-diver myths**.

In emergence myths, spirits or mythological creatures begin in a world below the earth's surface. Starting in darkness, they work their way upward through several increasingly brighter worlds until they reach earth. The earth, where full humanity completes the emergence, is often called the Fourth or Fifth World. The Hopi and Pueblo Nations tell emergence myths.

In earth-diver myths, a supreme being sends a spirit into primordial waters to return to the surface with sand or mud through which it creates earth. The Iroquois tell a creation story in which a Sky Woman falls into the hands of water creatures. Land does not yet exist, so the water creatures dive into the waters, bring up mud, and spread it on the back of Big Turtle. Big Turtle grows until it is the size of the earth. Sky Woman has a daughter who becomes Earth Mother.

Beliefs and Practices

The sacred stories and myths of Native Americans and their teachings are enacted through sacred ceremonies throughout the year. Beliefs of Native Americans vary widely, but there are some similarities. Most Native Americans believe in a supreme being or spirit. The more familiar names are the Great Spirit or the Great Mystery. This rather impersonal spirit may create the world, but lesser spirits, **tricksters**, animals, and natural powers such as wind, rain, and sun design the world and, most often, create human beings.

For both religious and practical reasons, Native Americans believe they must balance both the spiritual and the natural worlds. All that is living, both spiritual and material, is holy. The boundary between the two is often ambiguous, for both possess power. Each individual and social group must honor and respect the spirits, ancestors, wind, rain, forest, sun, Mother Earth, and Father Sky. You may have heard of the relationship between the Lakota Nation and the buffalo. Before killing a buffalo, Lakotas asked forgiveness for what they were about to do. After killing the animal, they thanked the buffalo for providing so much to their people.

---

emergence myths Creation stories where spirits, holy people, tricksters, and the like start in a deep world of darkness and emerge into higher worlds until they reach earth fully developed.

earth-diver myths Creation stories in which a spiritual entity (or entities) goes into a primordial body of water, scoops up mud or sand, returns to the surface, and creates land from the sludge.

tricksters In mythology, characters (humans, animals, gods or goddesses, or spirits) who defy conventional behavior and trick people.

In addition to the external world, the inner world of dreams relays messages from the spirit world to the individual. Messages of danger, protection, or need for preparation are common. An example is the vision of Wovoka (1856–1932), a Northern Paiute who claimed he had a vision and message from the Creator. The message said that if the people would turn away from their unrighteous ways of living and follow the narrow path of goodness, they would reunite with their beloved ancestors and halt further westward expansion by white people. The ceremony that was to enact this self-giving became known as the Ghost Dance.

Sacred Time

For Native Americans, the sacred breaks into linear time. In fact, the sacred is neither linear nor a construct but circular and experiential. Time is what happens during a season. For example, there is "snow melting" season and "long shadow" season. Sacred time is further marked by ceremonies where there is storytelling, singing, dancing, and drumming. Ceremonies may focus on petitioning the spirits for a good hunt or for a good harvest; healing; thankfulness; or rites of passage.

A woman in a jingle dress. Traditionally, 365 metal cones are secured on the dress—representing each day of the year—and a prayer is put into each cone. During the honor beats of a song, the jingle dress dancer uses her fan to spread the prayers into the four directions as the prayers are released from the dancing cones.

The Ghost Dance (see the subsection "Beliefs and Practices") began in 1889 with the Northern Paiutes and then quickly spread to other Native American peoples, who adopted and adapted it as their own. It was a five-day event that focused on the purging of old ways and self-sacrifice. One of the goals of the Ghost Dance was to unite the living and the dead so as to form a unified front to defend the people in battle and to limit further westward expansion by white people. The Ghost dancers created "Ghost shirts" made of cotton, believing they protected the wearer from harm.

The drum represents an unbroken circle of connection to the creator at the center and the world and all living things that circle around it. The sound of the drum is the heartbeat of Mother Earth.

Unfortunately, the 1890 massacre of Lakota people at Wounded Knee, South Dakota, proved otherwise.

The Sun Dance is a summer ceremony lasting three or four days. The harrowing experience tests participants physically, mentally, and spiritually. Many participants pierce their bodies and fast from food and water, indicating their willingness to sacrifice their entire selves for a greater good. Through this dance and prayer, they petition the Great Spirit for their community, family, health, and children not yet born.

Life-Cycle Celebrations

Like most other peoples and cultures, Native American religious traditions mark transitional life events.

Birth

In preparation for a child's birth, the mother and father observe certain rituals and taboos. The woman may abstain from certain foods, believing they might affect the baby. Pregnant Cherokee women do not wear anything tied around their necks or stand in doorways. There are certain hand-washing rituals for both the mother and the father. After the baby is born, a common practice is to bury the placenta.

Coming-of-Age

Most Native American peoples have coming-of-age ceremonies for both boys and girls who reach puberty. Generally, the ceremony for the young women is public, while the young men's ceremony is private. The ceremonies usually last several days during which the young adult endures physical, mental, and spiritual testing.

Elder women instruct the young woman on living an adult life, including her familial and social responsibilities. Among the Navajo, or Diné, a young woman learns to grind corn and prepare a special cake that she bakes in a hole in the ground created for the occasion. On the last day, the young woman is the personification of **Changing Woman**, a goddess representing all change in the Diné tradition.

The sweat lodge with coals burning in the center is the location of the coming-of-age ceremony for Diné young men. Before the young man enters the sweat lodge for the first time, his male relatives lash him with a yucca bundle. The elders tell him that the lashes will be far worse if he ever strays from the good. Within the lodge, the elder men instruct the young man about

In a traditional Navajo wedding cornmeal is put in the basket and the bride, accompanied by her parents, presents it to the groom as an offering.

Changing Woman The most respected goddess of the Navajo, or Diné, people. She represents all transitions, such as the changes of life, of the seasons, and between darkness and light.

life. During those four days, the young man fasts from food and drink, and he seeks a message from the spirit world. The goal of the ceremony is for him to prepare to always avoid evil and become instead a spiritual person.

Marriage

Marriage ceremonies differ among the various Native American nations. However, in most marriage ceremonies, the couple stand before someone of authority and commit to each other. The ceremony generally takes place in the evening. Where it takes place, who presides, what guests to invite, and the exchange of vows are widely diverse.

Death

Most Native American peoples believe there is an afterlife, with the person's spirit departing from the body at the time of death. There are various rituals to coax the spirit out of the body, if necessary.

Native American burial rituals can take hours or days. The Chippewa Nation believes the spirit leaves the body after the person's burial and takes four days to reach its destination. Some bury the deceased with food and possessions. Burial grounds are very holy places for Native Americans. The burial sites usually face east and are either in the ground or above ground. The body is placed in chambers or covered with a mound of rock. Some Native American people cremate the deceased and place their remains in an earthenware jar.

Sacred Places and Sacred Spaces

Because their religious traditions are based on sacred places and not on linear time, Native American religious traditions are tied to specific geography. Native American creation stories tell of the creation of a people and their place in the universe. Native Americans cannot transport the land that they hold sacred. For example, the Nez Perce cannot move their holy Tolo Lake, and the Apaches cannot transport Oak Flat, a sacred land in Arizona that has been the subject of ownership disputes with the United States government. Because one cannot carry sacred places and spaces, the migration of Native Americans forced by the United States government was an attempt by the United States government to at once possess their land and destroy their religious traditions. Sacred places for Native Americans are not only sacred for rituals and ceremonies but are also places where their ancestors' spirits dwell.

Members of the the San Carlos Apache Nation attend a protest outside the US Capitol against an attempt to trade part of Oak Flat (in Arizona) to a copper mining company in 2015. The land is sacred to the San Carlos Apache Indian Reservation and many other Arizona tribes.

Arriving to Today

The arrival of Europeans in 1492 and their subsequent Manifest Destiny to possess the land from the Atlantic Ocean to the Pacific Ocean destroyed a way of life that Native Americans lived for thousands of years. There is a movement among many Native American nations to reclaim the cultures, religious traditions, and languages that were stripped from them. It is vital for their survival that their peoples know and pass on their traditional ways of life.

The United States Congress passed the **American Indian Religious Freedom Act** in 1978. Recognizing that the United States government had prohibited Native Americans from practicing their religious traditions, this legislation overturned that policy, allowing Native Americans access to their sacred places and their sacred materials. However, this act made no provisions

---

American Indian Religious Freedom Act A legislative act passed by the United States Congress in 1978 acknowledging that government policy had prohibited Native Americans from practicing their religious traditions. It allowed Native Americans access to their sacred places and use of their holy objects.

for enforcing the religious freedom it intended to grant and put Native American nations in conflict with those who want to use their sacred places for commercial reasons.

There are Native Americans who practice Christianity. There are even more Native Americans who practice a Christianity that unites with Native American spiritual traditions. It has taken a long time, but Native American peoples, their culture, and their traditions have gained great honor and respect in the United States.

SECTION *Assessment*

Reading Comprehension

1. What is the most prevalent type of story in Native American religious traditions?
2. What is the general belief among Native Americans about a supreme being?
3. How do Native Americans understand the relationship between humans and the natural world?
4. Why are sacred places so essential to Native Americans?
5. What is the flaw in the American Indian Religious Freedom Act of 1978?

Vocabulary

6. Explain the difference between *earth-diver myths* and *emergence myths*.

For Reflection

7. "Religion carries culture. If religion dies, culture dies." Write about why you agree or disagree with this statement.

Flash Search

8. What is the Native American Church more commonly known as? Why?

Section 2
AFRICAN RELIGIOUS TRADITIONS

The continent of Africa is almost three times the size of the United States. It contains fifty-four countries, from Algeria, Libya, and Egypt in the north to South Africa and Lesotho in the south. The diversity of this vast continent is staggering. Different ethnic groups, languages, cultures, and religious traditions abound. Indigenous African religious traditions are no marginal group, having the third-largest group of adherents behind Christianity and Islam. We will focus on the general patterns present within the diverse indigenous African religious traditions.

Sacred Stories and Sacred Scriptures

The essential beliefs and moral expectations of African religious traditions are passed from one generation to the next through sacred stories, myths, legends, rituals, dance, and song. There are no written scriptures. Often, a young person is trained specifically in the remembering of the stories. Usually as an adult, the person is responsible for passing on the oral traditions.

The sacred stories of these traditions tell how the earth came to be, how a people came to be, how culture came about, the role of spirits and deities, how to interact with supernatural beings, and what happens when a person dies, among other things. Some myths tell the origin of ethnic groups, different races, and death. Myths also tell stories of the migration of a people and of the purpose of war. Complementing the sacred stories, rituals and ceremonies enact teachings and expected moral behaviors.

Oral tradition is more flexible than written tradition. When passed on to the next generation, a story may be altered a bit in content or emphasis to

Women dancing during a Yoruba religious ceremony in a temple in Benin City, Edo, Nigeria, dedicated to the Orisha (a spirit sent by the Almighty) named Olokun. Olokun is highly praised for their ability to give great wealth, health, and prosperity to their followers.

address the people's present personal and communal needs. For the most part, African creation myths put humans in the center of the universe rather than as just a little cog in a big machine.

Creation myths are the most prevalent of all sacred stories. Not only are there emergence myths (as found in Native American creation stories) in indigenous African religious traditions, but also there are **ex nihilo creation myths**. The Kuba people of Central Africa believe it was the spontaneous nausea of their God, Mbombo, alone in the primordial darkness and water covering the earth, that prompted creation ex nihilo. A great pain came to the stomach of Mbombo from nowhere, causing him to vomit into existence the sun, stars, and moons. The sun evaporated some of the water, forming the clouds and baring the hills. After a short rest period, Mbombo vomited into existence the animals.

---

ex nihilo creation myths From the Latin for "out of nothing"; creation stories in which the universe is formed from a void.

Serer children of Senegal in West Africa.

Creation from chaos myths are another category of creation myths. The Serer people of Senegal tell such a story. The supreme being, Roog, created both the universe and earth. Roog first created the deep seas of the underworld. Then came the air of heaven, including the sun, the moon, and the stars. Primordial trees were next. He then created the animal world with the jackal as the mother of all animals. Lastly, Roog created male and female human beings.

Other myths tell how spirits are to relate to the supreme being. The Yoruba people of West Africa tell the story of the Orisha, spirits sent to earth by the supreme God, Olodumare, as guides for all living creatures. The Orisha explained that after Olodumare completed the creation task, they wanted the power to guide the entire universe for sixteen years. Olodumare would not give up his power to lesser spirits but was willing to give them a trial run for sixteen days. They agreed. Within less than eight days, the entire universe came to a halt due to the incompetence of the Orisha. They dragged

---

creation from chaos myths Creation stories in which the universe is created from unformed matter. These contrast with ex nihilo creation myths.

themselves to Olodumare and asked for forgiveness. Olodumare put the universe back in order, and the Orisha were devoted to him from then on.

Beliefs and Practices

Indigenous African religious traditions have no systematic doctrinal statements. Instead, they have spirits, deities, ancestors, sacred stories, and divinations that reveal what a particular ethnic group believes. The people's beliefs inform every aspect of their personal and communal lives. Indigenous Africans are very pragmatic people; that something works (a wound heals or crops thrive) is more important to them than what they believe about those issues.

Most indigenous African religious traditions believe in a supreme being. Though generally impersonal and difficult to approach, the supreme being is connected to the universe, nature, and eternity. This deity is also omnipotent, omniscient, and omnipresent. God's roles are creator, sustainer, protector, and controller. *Nyame*, the name of the God of the Akan people of Ghana, means "he who knows and sees everything." Ngai, the supreme being of the Kamba people in Kenya, is the creator God of the entire universe and all that is in it. God is usually singular, but there can be dualities of God, like two persons in

The Kikuyu people of Kenya worship Ngai while facing Mount Kirinyaga—also known as Mount Kenya—because he rests there when he comes to earth.

one being. God can be male and female or androgynous. The authority, will, and blessings of God are not doubted.

The cosmos and the natural world are intertwined. Day, night, sun, moon, rain, wind, thunder, stars, and nature provide the people with their daily needs. The spiritual infiltrates all life, animate and inanimate. Humans do not dominate the created world but respect it and strive to live in harmony with it. The spirit world is not holier than the earthly world, for divine action takes place in both. African religious traditions hold that humanity has contact with spirits, which may include ancestors. It is much more common to thank the spirits than the supreme God for a good harvest. Humanity has no desire to offend the spirit world, for it can be dangerous for the entire group.

Nevertheless, humans pray not only to the supreme being but to the intermediaries between humans and God or the deities. Often, God is worshipped through these secondary spirits, deities, and sometimes ancestors. Some secondary spirits have humanlike attributes; some may have masculine or feminine energy, traits, and characteristics; and others may be androgynous. Indigenous African religious traditions believe that these supernatural beings significantly influence the fertility, prosperity, and longevity of a people and their world.

The Makishi masquerade is performed at the end of an annual initiation ritual for Luvale, Chokwe, Luchazi, and Mbunda boys between the ages of eight and twelve who live in the northwestern and western provinces of Zambia. The Makishi represents the spirit of a deceased ancestor who returns to the world of the living to assist the boys.

Ancestor veneration is an essential tradition among indigenous African religious traditions. Death is not the end of life but a transition to another world, where ancestors are an animating power. How one acts in this world affects one's circumstances in the next world. Whatever one's flaws in this world, they are gone in the next. Ancestors need attention from relatives left on earth. People do not want to cross their ancestors, for they can wreak havoc on their lives. Darkness falls not only on an individual but on an entire people if ancestors are ignored.

The deceased do not automatically become revered ancestors upon their death. One only becomes an ancestor by dying a "good death," which is loosely understood as a natural death. A person who dies from an accident or act of violence (not a good death) becomes a ghost or an evil spirit. Those who have died good deaths remain ancestors for as long as the community remembers them, typically for at least four or five generations. For kings and cultural heroes, the duration of remembrance is much longer. An act of remembrance can be as simple as setting a table of food near where the ancestor is buried.

A shopkeeper selling traditional herbal medicines at the Manzini Wholesale Produce and Craft Market in Eswatini, Africa.

Indigenous African religious traditions have various types of spirit mediators. They may be shamans, priests or priestesses, diviners, medicine men, or medicine women. These special practitioners help bring about spiritual and moral balance. Divination and dreams are standard tools for discerning how to keep that balance. These practitioners' functions can be interchangeable. For example, diviners are often knowledgeable in herbal medicines. Their overall role is as preservers and guardians of the tradition of their particular community. They reveal the will of the spirits, deities, or supreme being.

They heal physical, mental, emotional, and spiritual maladies using traditional herbal medicines. One spirit mediator may be called upon to bring rain, while another may be called at another time to bring an end to flooding.

Spirit mediators engage with both good and bad spirits through divination, rituals, and ceremonies. Through magic, they communicate with the spirit realm, seeking to thank, coerce, or guide. Evil spirits and wicked or unrighteous people are subjects for the special practitioners. They may use magic to influence the outcome of the situation when a wicked person uses witchcraft or sorcery to gain the upper hand or harm an individual or a community or an unrighteous person neglects his or her obligations to the family, community, elders, or ancestors.

Divination is a widespread practice among indigenous African religious traditions. Many people seek out diviners regarding a child's birth, health issues, marriage prospects, and occupation-related issues. The divination method may be as simple as reading the signs in flowing water or as complex as uncovering the mathematically intricate meanings of where specialized sticks are cast.

Sacred Time

As it is for Native American religious traditions, sacred time for indigenous African religious traditions is generally seasonal. Seasons, day and night, sun and moon, and the rhythmic pattern of agriculture dictate the time for festivals, ceremonies, and rituals. An event's purpose often has to do with the rejuvenation of life and the new turn in the cosmological cycle. The telling of sacred stories renews time in the cosmos and among humans. The events help to re-create order out of chaos, to reorder the world. Sometimes a spirit mediator determines when a sacred event should take place outside of a circular cycle. Celebrating the birthday of a chief would be an example of such an exception.

At most sacred times, spirits and deities are honored. Prayers, sacrifices, offerings, and libations are presented as a means to engender harmony. It is common for a shaman to enter a trance prompted by drumming or singing. In this altered state, the shaman embodies a spirit, deity, or ancestor, performing a sacred dance or specific movement. Once the trance subsides, the shaman relates to the people knowledge gleaned from the experience.

A voodoo devotee performs at the annual Voodoo Festival in Ouidah, Benin.

Voodoo Day is an example of an official public holiday in Benin. **Voodoo** are spirits. On Voodoo Day, sacrifices are made to the deities, and joyous song and dance are shared. Those who practice voodoo today are critical of modern media for exaggerating voodoo practices.

Sacred Places and Sacred Spaces

By definition, indigenous religious traditions are tied locally to particular regions and particular tribes. For the Basotho people of Lesotho, the local caves are sacred. The fig tree is sacred to the Kikuyu people of Kenya. Orimiri, the "great water," commonly known as the Niger River, is sacred to the Igbo (or Ibo) people of Nigeria.

Some indigenous African religious traditions construct shrines for their ancestors. The caretaker for the shrine is usually the eldest son. As the "living dead," ancestors are very fussy. If their shrine exhibits lack of proper care, they may rain down misfortune to not only the caretaker but the entire community.

---

voodoo A word for spirits in present-day Benin in West Africa, where the practice of the voodoo religious tradition first began centuries ago. The spirits could be powerful deities or natural entities such as rivers, trees, rocks, and the like.

Arriving to Today

Indigenous African religious traditions are not static. Through the introduction of Christianity in the second century, the arrival of Muslims in the seventh century, the dawn of colonialism in the fifteenth century, and periodic migrations over the millennia, indigenous Africans and their religious traditions have had to make significant adaptations over the centuries. African scholars speak of the "triple heritage" of Christianity, Islam, and indigenous African religious traditions that are closely connected in several African cultures. In some African societies, this "triple heritage" is almost **syncretistic**.

Nor have indigenous African religious traditions stayed on the continent of Africa. Through the transatlantic trade of enslaved people from the sixteenth to the nineteenth centuries, African-inspired religious traditions found their way to Brazil, Jamaica, Cuba, and Haiti. In these and other places—known as the African Diaspora—these religious traditions have names like Candomblé, Rastafari, Santería, and Vodou, respectively. The United States and Britain have pockets of converts to African religious traditions.

Ethiopian Orthodox Christians pray during the annual Timkat Epiphany Festival in Gondar, Ethiopia.

---

syncretistic Involving a combination or amalgamation of beliefs or practices from different religious traditions.

SECTION *Assessment*

Reading Comprehension

1. What does it mean to say that indigenous African religious traditions are oral traditions?
2. From where do practitioners of indigenous African religious traditions derive their beliefs?
3. Why must practitioners of indigenous African religious traditions care for their ancestors?
4. What are three things that dictate the timing of celebrations for indigenous African religious traditions?
5. Name one sacred place or space found in indigenous African religious traditions.
6. Some African scholars suggest the "triple heritage." To what does this refer?

Vocabulary

7. What is the difference between an *ex nihilo creation myth* and a *creation from chaos myth*?
8. What does it mean to say that some indigenous African religious traditions are *syncretistic*?

For Reflection

9. Most indigenous African religious traditions call their supreme being "God" in the local language; how is this not the same as the Judeo-Christian God?

Flash Search

10. Look up and report on one way indigenous religious traditions are incorporated into the Catholic liturgy in Africa.

C

APPENDIX C
Atheists, Agnostics, and Nones

A sad but increasingly common phenomenon exists today of people ignoring God by claiming no belief in or acknowledgment of him, disaffiliating from religion, or both. There have always been those, known as atheists or agnostics, who claim nonbelief in God. More unique nowadays are people who still hold belief in God but don't want anything to do with a church or religion. Sometimes members of this group call themselves "spiritual but not religious." These people who are unaffiliated with any religion are also known as *nones*. In fact, even atheists and agnostics are also nones.

The Meaning of Atheism and Agnosticism

Secular humanist pins.

Both atheism and agnosticism involve nonbelief in God. An *atheist* is someone who denies God's existence. An *agnostic* does not know whether God exists, saying that it cannot be proved. Most agnostics are in reality practical atheists, acting as if God does not exist or as if his existence does not matter. Agnostics argue that the existence of God cannot be proven or disproven, so there is no place to talk about "belief" in whether God exists.

Modern atheism takes many forms, including the following:

- *secular humanism*, a belief that makes humanity and human potential its god to the exclusion of any belief in or reliance on the one, true God
- *Marxist communism*, which looks to the economic or social order as the sole source of human freedom
- *Freudianism*, which claims that belief in God is mere wishful thinking
- *materialism*, which asserts that the physical, material world is the only reality and denies any spiritual reality

Atheism contradicts the virtue of religion because it rejects or denies God.

How Individualism and Consumerism Have Shaped the Nones

Christians believe that God created each person uniquely in his own divine image. Faith is a gift from God that should be treasured and cultivated. There is nothing wrong with promoting and celebrating individuality. However, those who are nones or who call themselves spiritual but do not wish to participate in religion risk driving themselves away from one another.

When an individual creates his or her own understanding of God, others, and self, the person may not be willing or able to listen to or dialogue with others. This attitude carries over to participation in religion, where the person may retreat from religious community whenever he or she disagrees with an aspect of the religion or even with another person in the community. This level of autonomy is defeating, not life-giving.

Choosing to not participate in a religion is choosing to live alone with one's faith.

Other nones disregard religion based on their view of it as a consumer product. From a modern consumer's perspective, religious experience is a kind of product to be consumed with little thought of its connectedness to its tradition and doctrine or to faith. People compare religion to other products such as a new phone or car, judging their level of satisfaction with what the product provides to them. Religion is different from a consumer product. It demands our participation and gift of self, not consumption.

GLOSSARY

adhan In Islam, the "call to prayer."

ahimsa In Hinduism, Jainism, and Buddhism, the intentional avoidance of violence or injury against another living thing by acts of omission or commission, be it word or deed.

Allah The Arabic word for God. The word's origins are from Semitic writings in which the word for god was *il*, *el*, or *eloah*. *El* and *eloah* were also recorded in the Hebrew Bible.

American Indian Religious Freedom Act A legislative act passed by the United States Congress in 1978 acknowledging that government policy had prohibited Native Americans from practicing their religious traditions. It allowed Native Americans access to their sacred places and use of their holy objects.

anatman The Buddhist doctrine of "no soul" or "no self," stating that a permanent, unchanging, independent self does not exist, though people act as if it does. Ignorance of anatman causes suffering.

ancestor veneration A religious practice referring to various ways of showing respect and reverence for family ancestors after their deaths. It is based on the belief that deceased family members are still living in some fashion.

anti-Semitism Prejudice or hostility toward Jewish people.

apocalypse A prophetic or symbolic revelation of the end of the world. Several Jewish and Christian texts from around the second century BCE to the second century CE include apocalyptic writing.

apostasy The abandonment of one's religion.

Apostles A term meaning "ones who have been sent"; originally, the twelve men whom Jesus chose to help him in his earthly ministry. The successors of the twelve Apostles are the bishops of the Catholic Church.

arhat From the Sanskrit for "worthy one"; a concept of Theravada Buddhism that refers to one who has attained Nirvana in his or her present lifetime and is thus liberated from the cycle of rebirth.

Ark A repository traditionally in or against the wall of a synagogue for the scrolls of the Torah.

ascetic A person who renounces material comforts to live a self-disciplined life, especially in the area of religious devotion.

asceticism The practice of self-denial and self-discipline, particularly for religious or spiritual reasons.

atman In Hinduism, the individual soul or essence.

avatar The incarnation of a Hindu god, especially Vishnu, in human or animal form. According to Hindu belief, Vishnu has been incarnated nine times. The tenth avatar will usher in the end of the world.

Beatitudes Meaning "surprise happiness"; the eight Beatitudes preached by Jesus in the Sermon on the Mount respond to a person's natural desire for happiness.

Bhagavad Gita One of the stories within the *Mahabharata* epic, the most quoted of all Hindu scriptures throughout the centuries. It is a dialogue between Arjuna, a righteous warrior, and his charioteer, Krishna, an avatar of Vishnu, about personal detachment.

bhakti In Hinduism, the devotional way of achieving liberation from the cycle of death and rebirth, emphasizing a devotee's loving faith in the gods.

bimah The elevated platform in a Jewish synagogue where the person reading aloud from the Torah stands during the service.

blasphemy Any word or deed that defames that which is considered sacred by a group of people. In Christianity, blasphemy is any thought, word, or act that expresses hatred for God, Christ, the Church, saints, or other holy things.

bodhisattvas In Mahayana Buddhism, people who compassionately refrain from entering Nirvana in order to help others enter first.

bodhi tree The large, sacred fig tree at the Mahabodhi Temple at Bodh Gaya where Siddhartha the Buddha achieved enlightenment. *Bodhi* means "awakening" or "enlightenment."

Brahman In Hinduism, Ultimate Reality or Absolute Reality; the ultimate ground of all being.

Brahmins Hindu priests; also the highest social class in the Hindu caste system.

Buddha When capitalized, the term refers to Siddhartha Gautama. It is from the Sanskrit word meaning "to awaken," or one who has attained enlightenment.

butsudan In Japanese households, the Buddhist family altar, generally containing memorial tablets for deceased ancestors. Historically, it was maintained in addition to the kamidana.

caliphate A government under a caliph, who is at once a political and religious leader in Islam.

caliphs Islamic temporal and spiritual leaders regarded by Sunni Muslims as successors of Muhammad.

canon An authoritative list of books accepted as Sacred Scripture. For Catholics, this is the twenty-seven New Testament books and forty-six Old Testament books that are accepted as inspired by the Church.

caste One of the hereditary social classes in Hindu India that determine the occupation and social possibilities of its members.

catechumens Unbaptized persons who are preparing for full initiation into the Church through the Sacraments of Christian Initiation by engaging in formal study, prayer, and spiritual reflection.

Ch'an Buddhism A monastic Chinese school of Mahayana Buddhism that teaches that all can reach enlightenment but must be directed by a spiritual master. Meditation is the dominant method of spiritual cultivation.

Changing Woman The most respected goddess of the Navajo, or Diné, people. She represents all transitions, such as the changes of life, of the seasons, and between darkness and light.

Chinese Rites Controversy A dispute within the Catholic Church during the seventeenth and eighteenth centuries over whether Chinese folk religion rites and offerings to ancestors constituted idolatry. The Jesuits believed the rites were compatible with Catholicism; the Dominicans did not. Pope Clement XI decided in 1704 in favor of the Dominicans, but his teaching was relaxed in the twentieth century to allow for some participation in those rites by Chinese Catholics.

chun-tzu According to Confucius, a person who lives by the ideals of li and jen and is not petty, arrogant, mean-spirited, or vengeful.

Church Fathers Church teachers and writers of the early Christian centuries whose teachings are a witness to the Tradition of the Church.

Communion of Saints In Christianity, refers to the unity in Christ of all those living on earth (the pilgrim Church), those being purified in purgatory (the Church suffering), and those enjoying the blessings of heaven (the Church in glory).

council The gathering of all bishops in the world in their exercise of authority over the universal Church. The pope usually calls a council.

covenant A binding and solemn agreement between human beings or between God and his people, holding each to a particular course of action.

creation from chaos myths Creation stories in which the universe is created from unformed matter. These contrast with ex nihilo creation myths.

Crusades A series of military expeditions by Western Christians in the eleventh through thirteenth centuries designed to take the Holy Land back from Muslims.

cult An external religious practice, observance, or devotion surrounding a deity, holy person, or religious object of a particular religious tradition.

Dalai Lama The head lama of Tibetan Buddhism who was the spiritual and political leader of Tibet until the Communist Chinese takeover forced his exile to India.

Dead Sea Scrolls A series of mostly partial manuscripts containing both biblical and nonbiblical material discovered in 1947 by a Bedouin boy in caves near the Dead Sea.

dervish Another name for a Sufi; a Muslim who has taken a vow of poverty and austerity.

deuterocanonical A term meaning "of the second canon"; refers to seven books in a Catholic Bible that are not found in the Hebrew Bible or in most Protestant Bibles.

devas From the Sanskrit for "shining ones"; celestial beings in the Hindu tradition.

dharma From the Sanskrit meaning "uphold." In Hinduism, it is that which is in accordance with the laws of the cosmos and of nature—for example, righteous acts. In Buddhism, it is the teachings of the Buddha.

Diaspora A Greek word meaning "dispersion"; originally referring to the large community of Jews living outside of Palestine, today, the term refers to Jews who live outside of Israel.

divination The attempt to ascertain hidden knowledge or foretell future events by the interpretation of omens or through supernatural means (e.g., the analysis of cloud formations or the casting of bones).

doctrines Principles, beliefs, and teachings of a religion.

earth-diver myths Creation stories in which a spiritual entity (or entities) goes into a primordial body of water, scoops up mud or sand, returns to the surface, and creates land from the sludge.

ecumenism The movement, inspired and led by the Holy Spirit, that seeks the union of all Christian faiths and eventually the unity of all peoples throughout the world.

emergence myths Creation stories where spirits, holy people, tricksters, and the like start in a deep world of darkness and emerge into higher worlds until they reach earth fully developed.

enlightenment The state of being awakened about life's illusions and removed from the cycle of rebirth.

evangelization From the Greek root word translated into English as "Gospel"; the "sharing of the Good News."

ex nihilo creation myths From the Latin for "out of nothing"; creation stories in which the universe is formed from a void.

feast days Periodic commemorative festivals; for Christians, days celebrated with special liturgies to commemorate the sacred mysteries and events tied to Christian redemption or to honor Mary, the Apostles, martyrs, or saints.

feng shui The Chinese practice of positioning objects—especially gravesites, buildings, and furniture—to achieve harmony based on belief in yin and yang and the flow of chi, the vital life force or flow of energy.

Five Classics A collection of five ancient Chinese books used by Confucians for study. They were written or edited by Confucius.

Five Pillars of Islam The foundational principles and practices of Islam that were set forth by Muhammad and are practiced by all Muslims.

Five Precepts The basic moral standard by which all Buddhists are to live. The Five Precepts are (1) do not take the life of any living creature; (2) do not take anything not freely given; (3) abstain from sexual misconduct and sexual overindulgence (for monastics, abstain from any sexual activity); (4) refrain from untrue or deceitful speech; and (5) avoid intoxicants.

Four Books During the Ming and Qing dynasties, the accepted curriculum that needed to be studied and passed in order to hold civil office.

Four Sights The four encounters that Siddhartha had on an unannounced journey outside of his father's palace that each taught him something about the world: an old, crippled man (old age); a diseased man (illness); a decaying corpse (death); and finally an ascetic (riches do not lead to inner liberation). These were the inspiration for Siddhartha to become a monk.

frieze A wide decorative band on a wall, often near a ceiling.

Gentile A person who is not of Jewish origin.

Gnosticism From the Greek word for knowledge; it is one of the earliest Christian heresies. It stressed the importance of secret knowledge passed on to a select few. It denied the goodness of creation and the material world.

Great Disappointment The occasion when many Adventists left William Miller after Jesus' Second Coming did not occur on March 21, 1844, the second date Miller calculated Jesus would return by.

guru From the Sanskrit for "teacher"; a Hindu teacher and guide in philosophical and spiritual matters.

Hadith A word meaning "tradition"; the sayings and stories of Muhammad that are meant to form guidance for living out Islam.

hafiz A Muslim who has memorized the Qur'an.

Hajj The annual Muslim pilgrimage to Mecca, Saudi Arabia. It is a mandatory religious duty for Muslims at least once in their lifetime providing they are financially and physically able.

halakhah The legal part of the Talmud, an interpretation of the laws of Scripture.

harakiri Ritual suicide by disembowelment by sword formerly practiced by Japanese samurai or decreed by a court in place of the death penalty.

Hasidism An Orthodox Jewish sect founded by the Baal Shem Tov in Poland in the eighteenth century that emphasizes religious experience.

Havdalah A religious ceremony that symbolically ends Shabbat. It is usually recited over kosher wine or kosher grape juice.

Hellenization The adoption of Greek ways and speech, as happened with many Jews living in the Diaspora.

heresy For Christians, an obstinate denial after Baptism to believe a truth that must be believed with divine faith, or an obstinate doubt about such truth.

Hijrah A term meaning "migration"; recalls the establishment of Islam in 622 CE, when Muhammad and his followers escaped from his enemies and left Mecca for Medina. The Hijrah marks the start of the Islamic calendar.

Holy of Holies The sanctuary inside the tabernacle in the Temple of Jerusalem where the Ark of the Covenant was kept.

hsiens Meaning "immortals"; Taoists who have reached their ultimate goal—physical immortality.

huppah A canopy under which the bride and groom stand during a Jewish wedding ceremony.

I Ching Meaning "Book of Changes"; an ancient Chinese book of wisdom and divination manual; one of the Five Classics of Confucianism.

iconoclasm A term meaning "breaking of icons"; the belief that there should be no human depiction of the sacred, for it places the icon rather than what the image represents as the object of worship.

icons Traditional religious images or paintings that are especially popular among many Eastern Christians.

idolatry Giving worship to something or someone other than the one, true God.

imam A leader for prayer at a mosque who is chosen for his knowledge of Islam and his personal holiness; also, a spiritual leader of the line of Ali held by Shi'ah Muslims to be a rightful successor of Muhammad.

Incarnation A term meaning "enfleshment"; for Christians, the taking on of human nature and a human body by God's Son, Jesus.

inculturation Defined by Pope John Paul II as "the incarnation of the Gospel in native cultures and also the introduction of these cultures into the life of the Church" (*Slavorum Apostoli*, 21).

intercession An offering or prayer of petition to God on behalf of another.

investigative judgment According to the Adventists, the time prior to the Second Coming when judgment will take place on the living and the dead.

jen The virtue of altruism. It has to do with one's humanness.

Ka'bah The first Islamic shrine, which Muslims believe Abraham rebuilt on the spot in Mecca where Adam had originally built it. Destroyed by pagans, it was reclaimed and purified by Muhammad when he captured Mecca in the seventh century. The Ka'bah is currently enclosed within the Great Mosque of Mecca.

kami The Japanese name for any kind of spiritual force or power.

kami body An object into which it is believed the kami descends during a Shinto worship service. Often the object is a mirror or sword.

kamidana Japanese for "kami shelf"; a home shrine dedicated to a kami.

karma In Hinduism and Buddhism, the sum of a person's actions in this and previous states of existence, viewed as deciding their fate in future existences (reincarnations).

kimonos Long robes with wide sleeves traditionally with a broad sash as an outer garment typically worn by Japanese women.

koan A paradox used in Zen Buddhism to train the adherent to abandon ultimate dependence on reason, opening the opportunity for enlightenment.

kosher From the Hebrew word *kaser*, meaning "proper"; commonly refers to food permitted by Jewish dietary laws. Jews observe kosher laws to remind themselves that they are to be a holy and separate people.

lamas In Tibetan Buddhism, teachers and often heads of monasteries.

li From the Chinese meaning "proper" or "rites"; the Confucian practice of proper behavior specific to one's relationship to another. It includes the rituals that must be properly performed in order for one to be called a chun-tzu, or "superior one" or "gentleman."

liturgy A definite set of forms for public religious worship; the official public worship of the Church. The Seven Sacraments, especially the Eucharist, are the primary forms of Catholic liturgical celebrations.

Lotus Sutra A Mahayana Buddhist text teaching that enlightenment is available to all Buddhists because of the great compassion of bodhisattvas.

madrasah A school or college of Islamic studies. Muhammad was the teacher of the first madrasah, which was in Mecca.

Magisterium The official teaching authority of the Church. The Magisterium is the bishops in communion with Peter's successor, the bishop of Rome (the pope).

Mahabharata Part of the Hindu smriti scriptures, an epic about the feud between the Pandava and Kaurava families over inheritance. Within the large epic are smaller stories, often philosophical.

Mahayana Buddhism Literally the "Greater Vehicle," a branch of Buddhism that accommodates a greater number of people from all walks of life toward enlightenment. It is strongest in Tibet, China, Taiwan, Japan, Korea, and Mongolia.

mandalas In both Hinduism and Buddhism, geometric figures representing the universe. Their construction may be part of ritual and/or meditation.

Mandate of Heaven The Chinese concept used to morally legitimize the rule of the kings of the Zhou dynasty and the early emperors of China. T'ien (meaning "heaven") would bless the authority of a just ruler but would give the mandate to another if the ruler proved unjust.

mantras Sacred verbal formulas that are repeated in prayer or meditation.

martyrs Witnesses to the truth of faith who endure even death to be faithful to their beliefs.

matsuri Japanese for "festivals"; term refers to Shinto festivals predominantly celebrated at local or regional shrines.

maya Sanskrit for "illusion"; a teaching of the Upanishads that only Brahman is permanent; everything else is only an illusion.

menorah A candelabra found in both Jewish homes and synagogues, usually having nine branches, especially for Hanukkah, but sometimes seven.

mezuzah A Hebrew word meaning "doorpost"; a small parchment containing Hebrew Scripture, usually the Sh'ma, that is placed in a case on or near the right doorframe at the home of an observant Jew. This fulfills the commandment in Deuteronomy 6:9 to "inscribe [God's instructions] on the doorposts of your house and on your gates."

Middle Way The Buddhist teaching that liberation from samsara comes neither through severe ascetical practices nor through wild indulgences but in the middle of the spectrum between those two opposites.

midrash A type of scriptural interpretation found in rabbinic literature, especially the Talmuds. Midrash assumes that the Scriptures provide answers for every situation and every question in life.

minaret A tall, slender tower attached to a mosque from which a muezzin calls Muslims to prayer.

mitzvot Commandments of the Jewish law.

moksha In Hinduism, the transcendent state of ultimate liberation from samsara, the endless cycle of rebirth.

monotheistic Subscribing to the doctrine or belief that there is only one God.

mosques Called *masjids* by many Muslims; buildings for personal and communal Islamic prayer and worship. Mosques can also be used for social, educational, and funerary events.

muezzin The man appointed at the mosque to call Muslims to prayer five times a day.

murti The image of a deity in artistic form. Not an idol to be worshipped, it points to the deity.

myths Traditional or ancient stories that help explain a people's creation, customs, and/or ideals.

neo-Confucianism A movement in China in the eleventh century that promulgated the resurgence of Confucianism while reinterpreting it in the light of Taoist and Buddhist influences.

Nirvana A term meaning "extinction" or "blowing out"; refers to the release from suffering, impermanence, delusion, and all that keeps the cycles of rebirth (samsara) going. Nirvana is the spiritual goal for all Buddhists.

Original Sin Adam and Eve's first sin of disobedience; also, the condition of sinfulness, resulting from Adam and Eve's sin, into which all humans are born.

pagoda An eastern Asian tower, usually built with roofs curving upward at the division of each of several stories and erected as a temple or memorial.

Pali Canon The authoritative Buddhist scripture of Theravada Buddhists, written in the Pali language. It is an important but not definitive scripture for Mahayana Buddhists. The Pali Canon is another name for the Tripitaka.

patriarchates The offices and jurisdictions of high-ranking bishops called patriarchs with authority over the other bishops within their territories. The five ancient patriarchates were Rome (which after 1054 became the only Western see) and Constantinople, Alexandria, Antioch, and Jerusalem (which became Eastern Orthodox sees).

pogroms Organized massacres of communities, particularly of Jewish people.

polygamy The practice or religious custom of having more than one wife or husband at the same time.

puja The ritual worship of a god or goddess in both Hinduism and Buddhism.

Pure Land Buddhism An East Asian school of Mahayana Buddhism with a great devotion to the buddha Amitabha. Pure Land Buddhists believe that chanting "Amitabha" with great sincerity of heart will gain one entrance into the realm of the Pure Land. Pure Land Buddhism holds belief in more than one buddha.

Qur'an In Muslim belief, God's final revelation, superseding the Jewish and Christian Bibles. The word means "recite" or "recitation." It is the holiest book for adherents of Islam.

rabbi A Hebrew word for "my master" or "my teacher"; someone who is authorized to teach and judge in matters of Jewish law.

Ramadan The ninth month of the Islamic calendar, which is a month of prayer and fasting to commemorate the Night of Power, the first revelation to Muhammad by God. Ramadan fasting satisfies the Fourth Pillar of Islam.

Ramayana Part of the Hindu smriti scriptures, an epic about the adventures of Prince Rama, who journeys to rescue his wife, Sita, from the demon-king Ravana.

rebbe A Hasidic rabbi.

relics Items of religious devotion, especially pieces of the body or personal items of an important religious figure.

rishis Hindu holy persons or sages.

samsara In Hinduism, the endless cycle of birth, death, and rebirth or reincarnation until one has achieved oneness with Brahman (Ultimate Reality). Hindus believe that the illusion that a person is an individual rather than being one with Ultimate Reality fuels samsara. Buddhists believe much the same thing, but they believe that life is full of suffering.

samurai From a word meaning "to serve"; a member of a hereditary feudal warrior class that served Japanese rulers. Samurai cultivated such virtues as loyalty, honor, and courage.

sangha Originally the name for the Buddhist monastic community. Later it came to describe the entire community of monks, nuns, and laypersons.

Sanskrit From a word that means "perfected"; an ancient Indo-Aryan language that is the language of Hinduism and the Vedas.

satori The name for sudden enlightenment as advocated by the Rinzai school of Zen Buddhism, as opposed to gradual enlightenment taught by the Soto Zen school.

satyagraha The policy of nonviolent resistance initiated by Mohandas Gandhi in the first half of the twentieth century as a means of pressing for political reform.

sects Religious groups that separate from or distinguish themselves within a larger religious denomination.

Septuagint The earliest Greek version of the Hebrew Bible, completed around the second century BCE.

Shabbat The seventh day of the week; the Jewish Sabbath.

Shahadah The first, and most important, of the Five Pillars of Islam. It is a witness statement or a profession of faith that proclaims that there is no other god than Allah and that Muhammad is the messenger of Allah.

shamans People who can access the spirit world, either good or evil, often through a trance at a ceremony or ritual. They often practice divination and healing.

shari'ah The revealed and canonical law of Islam based on the Qur'an, Sunnah, and Hadith that prescribes religious and temporal duties.

Shi'ah The smaller of the two main branches of Islam that accepts the legitimacy of the successors of Muhammad starting with his cousin and son-in-law, Ali, whom they regard as the first imam.

Shinto The indigenous religious tradition of Japan. It was the state religion of Japan until the end of World War II.

Sh'ma A Hebrew term meaning "hear"; the first word and the name of a prayer observant Jews pray every morning and evening.

Shoah The Hebrew word for "calamity"; the mass murder of Jews by the Nazis during World War II.

shofar A ram's horn used as a musical instrument in Jewish religious rituals, especially on Rosh Hashanah and Yom Kippur.

shogunate A form of military government that ruled Japan while emperors were the nominal leaders from the twelfth until the nineteenth century.

shruti From a word that means "that which is heard"; the most revered body of Hindu sacred scripture.

smriti Meaning "that which is remembered"; Hindu scriptures in the form of epics and stories that shed light on the more abstract and esoteric shruti scriptures. The *Mahabharata* and the *Ramayana* are smriti scriptures.

Soka Gakkai A Japanese Buddhist "new religion" founded in 1930 that emphasizes the power of the Lotus Sutra and advocates nonviolence. Today, it is not only the largest of Japan's new religions but also an international organization.

soma A hallucinogenic beverage that was used in ancient India as an offering to Hindu gods and in Vedic ritual sacrifices.

Spanish Inquisition A bureau or commission that had branches in most of the larger dioceses of Spain that was empowered to call on civil authorities to help weed out heretics. Once the heretics were discovered, the Church authorities conducted a trial with those accused presumed guilty and required to prove their innocence.

spirit tablet A placard placed in a household shrine or temple to honor ancestors.

Sufism A mystical element of Islam. Practitioners seek a direct relationship with Allah through ascetic religious practices beyond those required for a Muslim.

Sunnah The body of traditional customs and practices of Muhammad that are models for observant Muslims and shared through the oral tradition.

Sunni The larger of the two main branches of Islam that accepts the legitimacy of the leadership of all of the first four caliphs of Islam as successors of Muhammad.

surahs Chapters, or sections, in the Qur'an. Each surah is a separate revelation received by Muhammad.

sutras Discourses in Buddhist scriptures that are attributed to Siddhartha Gautama.

syncretistic Involving a combination or amalgamation of beliefs or practices from different religious traditions.

Talmud Two long collections of Jewish religious literature that include and have commentaries on the Mishnah, the Hebrew code of laws that emerged about 200 CE.

tantric A word to describe literature written in Sanskrit that is concerned with ritual acts of body, speech, and mind.

Taoism From the Chinese root word *Tao*, meaning "Way"; a Chinese mystical philosophy founded by Lao-tzu that teaches conformity to the Tao by "action without action" and simplicity. The Tao is considered to be the driving force of the universe.

teshuvah A Hebrew term meaning "return"; the act of repentance in Judaism.

theocracy A government that is ruled by God or by one who is divinely inspired.

Theosophist An adherent of Theosophy, a late nineteenth-century esoteric philosophical movement with roots in Western philosophy, Hinduism, and Buddhism. Theosophy is the belief that one can have profound insight into God and the universe through ecstasy and other phenomena. Helena Blavatsky, a Russian immigrant to the United States, is credited with founding the movement.

Theravada Buddhism The more traditional of the two main branches of Buddhism, claiming their roots in the historical life of Siddhartha Gautama. It is found mainly in Thailand, Laos, Cambodia, Myanmar, and Sri Lanka. Mahayana Buddhists sometimes uncharitably call it Hinayana Buddhism, meaning "Lesser Vehicle."

Three Jewels of Buddhism The ideals at the heart of Buddhism: the Buddha, the dharma, and the sangha.

Torah A term meaning "law" or "instruction"; the first five books (and the first of the three sections) of the Hebrew Bible. It also refers to the parchment scroll of these writings used in Jewish rituals. It can also refer to the body of Jewish Sacred Scripture.

transcendent A term that means "lying beyond the ordinary range of perception."

Transcendental Meditation A trademarked meditation technique derived from Hinduism that promotes deep relaxation through recitation of a mantra.

transubstantiation What happens at the consecration of the bread and wine at Mass when their entire substance is turned into the Body and Blood of Christ, even though the appearances of bread and wine remain.

tricksters In mythology, characters (humans, animals, gods or goddesses, or spirits) who defy conventional behavior and trick people.

Tripitaka From the Sanskrit meaning "Three Baskets"; the compilation of three collections of early Buddhist texts. The Tripitaka is also known as the Pali Canon.

ulama Muslim scholars trained in Islam and shari'ah.

Ultimate Reality In Hinduism, Brahman is the highest reality in the universe.

usury In the Middle Ages, the charging of interest on a loan. Later the definition became charging of an exorbitant, perhaps even illegal, amount of interest on a loan.

Vajrayana Buddhism Literally meaning "Diamond Vehicle," the prominent branch of Buddhism in Tibet.

Vedas Ancient scriptures composed in Sanskrit that are the foundation of Hinduism. The word *Veda* means "knowledge." The most important Veda is the *Rig Veda*, which consists of 1,028 hymns praising the gods of the Aryan tribes who invaded India from the northwest starting around 2000 BCE.

voodoo A word for spirits in present-day Benin in West Africa, where the practice of the voodoo religious tradition first began centuries ago. The spirits could be powerful deities or natural entities such as rivers, trees, rocks, and the like.

witnessing Giving testimony of one's religious faith to another.

wudu The ritual washing of the mouth, nose, ears, face, hands, arms, top of head, and feet that a Muslim must perform before salah, the Second Pillar of Islam.

wu wei Meaning "nonaction," but often interpreted as "action without action"; a Taoist concept that centers on allowing the Tao to unfold without human interference.

yin and yang Meaning "shaded and sunny"; opposite but complementary energies in Chinese religious traditions, philosophy, and culture.

yogas Paths to moksha that endeavor to unite action (body), knowledge (mind), and devotion (soul). The three paths are karma yoga, jnana yoga, and bhakti yoga.

yogi A practitioner of yoga, particularly in its meditative forms.

Zen Buddhism The Japanese version of Ch'an Buddhism.

Zionism From Zion, the name for the historical land of Israel; the movement with origins in the nineteenth century that sought to restore a Jewish homeland in Palestine in response to anti-Semitism.

INDEX

Note: page numbers in *italics* indicate images